Critical Thinking

Andrew LAWLESS

Critical Thinking

Andrew LAWLESS

OXFORD
UNIVERSITY PRESS

OXFORD
UNIVERSITY PRESS

Oxford University Press is a department of the University of Oxford.
It furthers the University's objective of excellence in research, scholarship,
and education by publishing worldwide. Oxford is a registered trade mark of
Oxford University Press in the UK and in certain other countries.

Published in Canada by
Oxford University Press
8 Sampson Mews, Suite 204,
Don Mills, Ontario M3C 0H5 Canada

www.oupcanada.com

Library and Archives Canada Cataloguing in Publication
Lawless, Andrew
Critical thinking / Andrew Lawless.
Includes index.
ISBN 978-0-19-544340-0

1. Critical thinking. I. Title.

BF441.L385 2013   153.4'2   C2013-901056-4

Cover image: iStockphoto/Thinkstock

Oxford University Press is committed to our environment.
This book is printed on Forest Stewardship Council® certified paper
and comes from responsible sources.

Printed and bound in Canada

1 2 3 4 — 17 16 15 14

For Jane

Contents

Preface

Critical thinking texts seem to fall into two broad categories: those which allow the instructor to pick and choose chapters as he or she wishes and those which are more definitely sequential. This text belongs to the latter category. It was conceived as a way of teaching a critical thinking course, of moving from topic to topic in a sequence that allows students to develop the requisite skills. It was also written with the recognition that since the overwhelming majority of critical thinking courses are term courses, it needed to be kept to a manageable length. It is not possible to give students everything in 12 or 14 weeks, but it is possible to provide them with a secure foundation to build on. To this end, the text contains hundreds of exercises to help students develop their skills. Often, more learning takes place in the doing than in the teaching.

The text begins with a succinct description of what a critical thinking course is about: learning to recognize, construct, and evaluate logical arguments. Students need to be able to sort out premises and conclusions and then understand the ways in which the former support or fail to support the latter. The text is consistently directed toward this goal.

One example of how this goal structures the text is the treatment of fallacies. Too often they are taught out of context, enclosed in a chapter isolated from the rest of the text. I have instead distributed them throughout the text, introducing them in the contexts where they will make the most sense. The largest group is in Chapter 3, where fallacies of relevance are introduced as a way of building on a preliminary definition of a "good" argument—one that has relevant and true premises. Other types of informal fallacies— of ambiguity and presumption—as well as two formal fallacies are introduced where they are relevant to the discussion at hand. The number of fallacies is kept to a minimum. The idea behind this approach is that if students understand these fallacies, which are thoroughly explained and accompanied by examples, they will be able to spot others even if they don't have names for them. The goal is to stimulate understanding of the *concept* of a fallacy rather than to enforce rote learning of individual fallacies.

Since arguments are either deductive or inductive (or some combination of the two), four of the nine chapters deal with these modes of reasoning. Should a reader feel that this is too much logic for a critical thinking text, my response is twofold. First, logic is the foundation of critical thinking. Without a secure grasp of its basic principles a student is in the position of occupying the second storey of a house that has no first floor. (Courses that ignore logic often look more like exercises in debating techniques than in critical thinking.) Second, there are admittedly loose but nonetheless important analogies between deduction and literacy, and induction and numeracy. Deduction instils the grammar of critical thought while induction instils the practice of rational estimation. Because literacy and numeracy are, regrettably, issues for many students, instructors may find logic hard to teach—but that is all the more reason to do so. What's more, despite the difficulties I think that it's the most fun to teach and that students get the most reward from being taught it. The final chapter on the scientific method, which shows how logic drives our investigations of the world, is intended in part to demonstrate the indispensability of logic to critical thought.

That said, the text also stresses the importance of judgment. Maybe I have read too much continental philosophy, but it seems to me that many of the definitions we make and distinctions we draw are not as definite as we often pretend they are. For example, I point out that the border between deduction and induction is blurred by the fact that, strictly speaking, inductive arguments are invalid. This can lead to some rather strange conclusions, ones that get even stranger when abduction is added to the mix. I argue that in some cases a reader may have to decide whether an argument is deductive or inductive (or abductive) by making a judgment about the author's intention, and in others she will have to apply the principle of charity, selecting the option that sets the argument in the strongest light. Nor can vague terms always be excised from arguments, and handling them requires judgment. Finally, in the chapter on the scientific method, imagination is added to the mix of qualities that separate critical thinking from mechanical thinking.

In closing, let me offer a few words on the style of the text, which is informal. I speak directly to the reader, who is addressed as "you" or included in the conspiratorial "we." I am also present in the text, referring to myself and sometimes to my experiences. Some readers of drafts of this text have noted—sometimes with approval, sometimes with disapproval—this "unusual" feature. It's the approach I prefer, but also one I think works well and that has the added virtue of honesty. Authors of texts often seem at pains to disguise the fact that somebody actually wrote the thing. Since judgment is important, I think students are better served by a human author (teacher), who sometimes admits that things are not as definite as we might like them to be and who expresses opinions as well as espouses truths. In *On Liberty*, John Stuart Mill argued that we need to protect the individual from the tyranny of the majority, for otherwise critical thought withers and dies. For the same reason, in what follows I am trying, at least a little, to protect my readers from the tyranny of the author.

Acknowledgements

I want to express my gratitude to Tamara Capar, my editor at Oxford University Press, for her wise direction and her generous encouragement and support through a long process. I thank her, as well, for keeping me sane at times when I felt anything but. I wish to thank Valerie Racine for her prompt, careful, and insightful reading of the first draft of this text; my brother, Jerry Lawless, for his patient and lucid explanations of some of the central concepts of probability; and Mariela Libedinsky for providing me with an invaluable student's-eye view of some passages. Finally, my thanks go out to two or three generations of students in my critical thinking class at Vanier College in Montreal who taught me a great deal about what works and what does not. All of you have made this text better than it would otherwise have been.

The author, along with Oxford University Press, would like to acknowledge the reviewers whose thoughtful comments and suggestions have helped shape this text:

BRENDA COLE, *Algonquin College*

ROBERT FAHRNKOPF, *Douglas College*

NORMAN GALL, *Medicine Hat College*

SHEREEN HASSANEIN, *Seneca College*

JONATHAN KATZ, *Kwantlen Polytechnic University*

MARK MERCER, *Saint Mary's University*

DAVID SCULLY, *Algonquin College*

DENISE WALES, *Seneca College*

MARK YOUNG, *Red Deer College*

CHAPTER ONE

Getting into Arguments

1

- Recognizing arguments
- Distinguishing premises and conclusions
- Evaluating premises
- Distinguishing arguments from explanations
- Identifying reports on arguments and counterarguments
- Finding arguments in longer passages of text
- Editing arguments for clarity
- Identifying implicit assumptions
- Applying the principle of charity

I. The Basics of Critical Thinking

This section introduces arguments and shows you how to recognize them.

What Is an Argument?

The term "critical thinking" refers to the activity of recognizing, constructing, and evaluating arguments. In critical thinking, arguments are not simply disagreements. They come in a variety of shapes and sizes, but they all consist of two bits of information: *what* their authors believe is true and the reasons *why* they believe it is true. The "what" is called the **conclusion**; the "whys" (there are usually, though not always, more than one) are called **premises**. This yields the following definition of an argument:

> *Definition:* An **argument** *is a set of premises leading to a conclusion.*

The point of an argument is to convince people that the conclusion is either absolutely or at least very probably true. There are different kinds of arguments and different ways to evaluate them, but they all share this basic structure: "whys" supporting "whats"; premises supporting conclusions. This is the fundamental structure of critical thinking.

The reason why arguments are important is that "whats" without "whys"—conclusions without premises—are uninformative. In fact, without premises there are no conclusions, only unsupported claims. This is worth emphasizing:

> *Definition:* A **conclusion** *is a claim supported by premises.*

If, for example, I tell you that the rise of social media is good for democracy, I have simply made a claim. You know *what* I think, but not *why* I think it. But if I support this claim by adding that social media allows for the free flow of uncensored information, that only this kind of information provides citizens with the knowledge required to understand what their governments are doing, and that this knowledge is essential to a functioning democracy, I have now told you why I think social media is good for democracy. I have given you an argument that looks like this:

> **E1:**
> *Premise: **Because** social media allows for the free flow of uncensored information;*
> *Premise: **Because** only uncensored information provides citizens with the knowledge required to understand what their governments are doing;*
> *Premise: And **because** this understanding is essential to a functioning democracy;*
> *Conclusion: **Therefore**, social media is good for democracy.*

You are now in a position to assess what I have said and respond to it. A fundamental rule of critical thinking is that critical thinkers do not simply offer (or accept) unsupported claims: they make arguments and produce conclusions. Their "whats" are supported by "whys."

Of course, we don't always feel that arguments are necessary because a lot of the time we're talking to people who share our beliefs. If, for example, Bob expresses the opinion that soccer is a boring game to a group of friends who happen to share this view, none of them is likely to ask him why he thinks soccer is boring. They will simply nod their heads in agreement, reflecting only on what a wise person he is. But if Bob voices the same opinion in a sports bar during the World Cup, he may well be asked to defend his position. When an opinion is not universally accepted as true, arguments are necessary. (Even when an opinion is universally accepted by a group of people, arguments are important. Even long-standing "obvious" truths sometimes need to be tested.)

In Bob's case, the moment someone challenges his claim he has to decide whether he wants to be a critical thinker or whether he's content to be an uncritical assertor of opinions. If he opts for the uncritical path, he may simply respond that he just doesn't like soccer and that's all there is to it. This may lead to an argument in the everyday sense of simply disagreeing with someone—"Soccer is just boring." "No, it's not." "Yes it is!" "You're crazy!" "Look who's talking!"—but not to a genuine critical argument. That will occur only if Bob takes the critical thinker's path and attempts to provide premises in support of his claim. He may, for example, insist that there are not enough goals in soccer and that too much of the play consists of aimlessly passing the ball around in mid-field. Those listening to him may disagree; they may dispute his premises, insisting that there are plenty of goals and that the play is more end-to-end than he says it is. Conversely, they may accept his premises but insist that they don't support the conclusion that the game is boring. They may argue that Bob is too fixated on goals and misses most of the subtlety of the play. In either case, they will be constructing their own arguments in opposition to Bob's. Critical thinking is always an option, even in the midst of a World Cup.

It's worth adding that, unlike disagreements, you can construct a critical argument in complete solitude. When you are thinking about your own views you can test them by setting out, for your own assessment, the premises that support them. Critical thinking can and should be directed not only at the claims of others but also at your own claims.

To summarize, in critical thinking arguing is not simply contradicting those who hold different views about a given subject. It is presenting your ideas in a clear and orderly fashion by providing premises in support of a conclusion. The purpose of an argument is to demonstrate that your conclusion is true or at least probable and that it should therefore be accepted or at least given serious consideration.

Two Arguments

Even if we don't always notice them, arguments are all around us. They're embedded in the conversations we have, in the books and magazines we read, and in the social media we follow, including 140 character versions of them on Twitter. Here, for example, is a tweet from US President Barack Obama:

> **E2:** *When we sacrifice our commitment to education, we're sacrificing our future. We can't let that happen. Our kids deserve better.*

This is an argument. *What* President Obama is claiming—his conclusion—is that Americans can't sacrifice their commitment to education. His premises, the reasons *why* he is claiming this, are (1) that sacrificing education means sacrificing the nation's future and (2) that the youth of the nation deserve better than that. So his argument, slightly rewritten, looks like this:

> *Premise: When we sacrifice our commitment to education, we sacrifice our future.*
> *Premise: Our children deserve better than that.*
> *Conclusion: We cannot sacrifice our commitment to education.*

Readers of the tweet can now consider this and respond. Here is what one skeptical reader had to say: "If Barack Obama actually tweeted himself I'd follow him. But it's all highly controlled and filtered. Not worth much." Although it doesn't speak directly to the content of Obama's tweet, this too is an argument. The tweeter concludes that Obama's tweets aren't worth much because they aren't really his thoughts; someone else is tweeting for him. Slightly rewritten, this argument looks like this:

> *Premise: If Barack Obama wrote his own tweets they would be worth following.*
> *Premise: But he does not write his own tweets.*
> *Conclusion: Therefore, his tweets are not worth following.*

Other readers can now think about whether they agree and, if so, whether this lessens the value of the thoughts expressed in the president's tweets. Not everything on Twitter is an argument—not by a long shot—but a surprising amount of it is. People are busy telling the world what they think and why. Like all media, Twitter is a forum for the universal human habit of sharing and discussing ideas.

There are practical reasons for learning to recognize and make arguments. First, when you are in school you write essays, and essays are essentially arguments: you take a position on a topic and then defend it. The more clearly you do so, the better your essay and, by extension, your grade will be. Second, if you are going to share your ideas in the wider world you had better be able to express them clearly, because if you can't people will stop listening. That's why the ability to develop clear arguments is an indispensable requirement for most professions. In the workplace, sloppy or uncritical thinkers who cannot communicate their ideas clearly and efficiently are rarely valued employees. Finally, the ability to think critically is virtually a requirement for life in democratic societies. The Italian author Primo Levi wrote a story about the Nazi concentration camps in which a guard informs a prisoner that

"There is no 'why' here." In short, in the camp there was only the horrific reality of arbitrary power. This is a chilling reminder that to abolish "whys" and leave only "whats" is to extinguish not just arguments, but free speech, independent thought, and even life itself.

Three Skills

If arguments are an essential part of your lives as students, workers, and citizens, there are three basic skills you need to master:

1. You have to be able to recognize arguments when you come across them.
2. You have to be able to sort out the premises and conclusions.
3. You have to be able to assess whether the premises actually support the conclusion.

In practice, the first two of these skills are so closely connected that we can deal with them as a pair.

Recognizing Arguments by Identifying Premises and Conclusions
To spot an argument, it is necessary to be alert to the presence of premises and conclusions. Often this is not too difficult because many arguments include identifying words for premises and conclusions. For example:

> **E3:** *Because we want the team to do well next season and **because** that means being in the best possible shape, we must **therefore** train hard in the off-season.*

This argument is clearly marked. As you have already seen in previous examples, the word "because" indicates a premise, and "therefore" signals a conclusion. This gives us the following structure:

> *Premise: Because we want the team to do well next season;*
> *Premise: And **because** that means being in the best possible shape;*
> *Conclusion: Therefore, we must train hard in the off-season.*

In this case, it is easy to determine *what* the speaker believes is true and *why* he believes it. Being aware of premise and conclusion signals makes it easier to identify and understand arguments. Here is a standard list of indicators, although in practice this list could be greatly expanded:

Premise Indicators

assuming that	**because**	considering that	given that
inasmuch as	seeing as/that	since	when

In this list "because" is the anchor word; the other indicators are essentially synonyms or substitutes for it.

Conclusion Indicators

as a result	ergo	consequently	hence
it follows that	so	thus	**therefore**

In this list "therefore" is the anchor word for which the others are possible substitutes. (People like variety, so they don't always want to use the same word even if it always serves their purpose.) Hence, in its most basic form an argument has a "because . . . therefore" structure.

The problem is that in everyday speech premise or conclusion signals may be omitted. For example:

> **E4:** *If we hurry too much we may have to redo our work, and we don't want to risk that. We need to slow down.*

While this argument contains none of the signals listed above, a little attention will reveal its structure, which looks like this:

> *Premise: **(Because)** if we hurry too much we may have to redo our work;*
> *Premise: And **(because)** we don't want to risk that;*
> *Conclusion: **(Therefore)** we need slow down.*

In addition, arguments are not always set out in this formal premise–conclusion order. For example:

> **E5:** *You should exercise more, **seeing that** you want to lose weight.*

Here, the conclusion precedes the premise. The formal structure is as follows:

> *Premise: **Seeing that** you want to lose weight;*
> *Conclusion: You should **(therefore)** exercise more.*

E5 is a fairly common informal argument order because people have a tendency to begin by telling others *what* they believe is true and then to support this with the premises. While this is a perfectly reasonable approach, it has one effect that you need to be aware of: when an argument begins with the conclusion, it will contain no conclusion signal. There is a very simple reason for this. Since the conclusion is technically the *end* of the argument, a conclusion signal cannot be inserted at the beginning of an argument. Imagine rewriting **E5** as follows:

> **E6:** ***Therefore** you should exercise more, **seeing that** you want to lose weight.*

This is, to say the least, a rather awkward construction. To make it work we would need to put the conclusion phrase at the end, as was done in the rewrite of **E5** above. Even then the "therefore" is slightly clumsy and would often be omitted in everyday speech.

It is also not uncommon for a conclusion to be wedged between premises, as in the following argument:

E7: *Since most of our investment portfolio is in gold we are in danger of going broke. This is* **because** *the price of gold is likely to sink drastically in the near future.*

There are two premise signals here, but nothing that indicates the conclusion, which is tucked into the second part of the opening sentence:

Conclusion: We are in danger of going broke.

In this case, isolating the premises—which the bolded signal words allow you to do—makes the conclusion stand out. Using these premise signals as our guide, we can set the argument out as follows:

Premise: **Because** *most of our investment portfolio is gold;*
Premise: And **because** *the price of gold is likely to sink drastically in the near future;*
Conclusion: We are **therefore** *in danger of going broke.*

Because the order of premises and conclusions can vary in everyday speech, there is no substitute for careful reading. When conclusion and premise signals are present they are reliable guides, but when they are not you have to think carefully about where they should be inserted. In **E7**, for example, there is really only one place a conclusion signal would make sense.

Now that you are aware of indicator words and of the possible absence of them, let's go back and re-examine President Obama's Twitter argument in **E2**:

When we sacrifice our commitment to education, we're sacrificing our future. We can't let that happen. Our kids deserve better.

Notice that his argument has no indicator words. Because of this, its structure may not be immediately apparent to some readers. In fact, they may not recognize it as an argument at all, seeing it instead as a straightforward pronouncement. So let's insert some indicator words and see what happens:

E8: **Because** *sacrificing our commitment to education means sacrificing the future, and* **because** *our kids deserve better than that,* **therefore** *we can't let that [sacrificing our commitment to education] happen.*

The structure of the argument, indeed the fact that this is an argument, is now absolutely clear and, as such, easier to evaluate.

Here's another example:

E9: *It is an exaggeration to call the oil leak in the Gulf of Mexico an unprecedented disaster. The vast majority of off-shore drilling rigs are safely producing oil all over the world, and no doubt they will become even safer after this experience. What's more, the spilled oil eventually disperses and disintegrates with little long-term effect on the environment.*

Because this passage lacks premise and conclusion signals, it too is scarcely recognizable as an argument. But, once again, watch what happens when we insert some indicator words:

> *It is an exaggeration to call the oil leak in the Gulf of Mexico an unprecedented disaster. [It is an exaggeration]* **because** *the vast majority of off-shore drilling rigs are safely producing oil all over the world, and* **because** *they will become even safer after this experience. [And it is also an exaggeration]* **because** *the spilled oil eventually disperses and disintegrates with little long-term effect on the environment.*

Now it is evident that the first sentence is the conclusion, supported by three subsequent premises. The result looks like this:

> *Premise:* **Because** *the vast majority of off-shore drilling rigs are safely producing oil all over the world;*
> *Premise:* **Because** *they will become even safer after this experience;*
> *Premise: And* **because** *the oil eventually disperses and disintegrates with little long-term effect on the environment;*
> *Conclusion: It is* **therefore** *an exaggeration to call the oil leak in the Gulf of Mexico an unprecedented disaster.*

When you come across arguments without indicator words, one good strategy is to ask yourself *what* the writer or speaker wants you to believe. Whatever it is will be the conclusion. In **E9** it is obviously the first sentence. Once you have isolated the conclusion check to see if the rest of the passage makes claims in support of it. If you want to double check, write the argument out as we have done here, inserting indicator words.

It would probably be boring if everyone meticulously signalled every premise and conclusion, but sometimes doing so is a real service to those who are reading or listening to an argument. Premise and conclusion signals are valuable and sometimes indispensable guides for readers or listeners. If you are trying to craft a careful and perhaps difficult argument—in an essay, say, or a class presentation—it is a good idea to include as many indicators as necessary to ensure that your audience can follow you. They need to be able to see that you have an argument rather than just a list of points.

As a final example, consider the following contribution to a discussion:

> **E10:** *The government needs to try to find ways to keep tuition fees down. Students are piling up a lot of debt. They spend years paying it off. They can't get on with their lives, buy houses, and the like.*

While this passage is not unclear, the inclusion of premise and conclusion signals can make it stand out more clearly as an argument:

> **Because** *students are piling up a lot of debt that they will spend years paying off and* **because** *this means that they can't get on with their lives, buy houses, and the like,* **therefore** *the government needs to try to find ways to keep tuition fees down.*

Now the argument looks like an argument and not simply a series of comments. Even in relatively simple cases like this including signals is a good idea, but since people don't always follow this advice, a critical thinker also has to be a critical reader and listener who can recognize where those missing signals ought to go.

Evaluating Arguments

The remaining necessary skill—the ability to distinguish good arguments from bad ones—is by far the most difficult. Because there are different kinds of arguments, there are different ways in which premises can support—or fail to support—conclusions. As a result there are, as you will discover in subsequent chapters, different ways to evaluate arguments. There are, however, two general characteristics that all good arguments possess:

1. Their premises are relevant to the conclusion.
2. Their premises are true (or at least very probably true).

There is a close relationship between relevance and truth. Relevant premises—ones that offer support for a conclusion—must be checked for truth because a false premise provides no support for a conclusion *even if it is relevant to it*. Consider the following argument:

E11:
Premise: Because the sun goes around the Earth;
Premise: And *because* the Earth is at the centre of the universe;
Conclusion: Therefore, the sun must be close to the centre of the universe.

These premises are relevant to the conclusion because if they were also true, then given the small size of our solar system in relation to the universe, they would provide absolute support for it. However, both premises are false and therefore offer no support for the conclusion. (This does not mean that the conclusion is necessarily false; only that these premises do not support it.) Nonetheless, a critical thinker who recognized that the premises were relevant, but knew nothing about the universe, would not know whether **E11** was a good argument until he or she found out whether the premises were also true. So if premises are relevant, make certain they are true. If you are unable to determine whether they are true, you have to accept that they give support to the conclusion only *provisionally*. You cannot count on them, but neither can you discount them.

While it is usually possible to assess relevance, it is not always a straightforward matter. Consider this argument:

E12:
Premise: Because I really don't want to fail;
Conclusion: Therefore, you should pass me.

Let's assume the premise is true. Unfortunately, it seems irrelevant to the question of passing or failing, and therefore its truth doesn't matter. Note, however, that an instructor who thought it was relevant would find the argument at least somewhat persuasive. While it is unlikely that many instructors would take this view of the matter, there might be more disagreement about the following:

E13:
*Premise: I failed the test **because** I was so upset over breaking up with my girlfriend;*
*Conclusion: **Therefore**, I think you should give me a rewrite.*

Despite many years of teaching experience, I have to admit that it is not absolutely clear to me whether, *if true*, this is a relevant reason for getting a rewrite. I tend to think not, but like many things in life, the line between what one is allowed to be upset over and what one is not allowed to be upset over is not absolutely clear. Teachers may genuinely disagree; some may argue that this premise is relevant, others that it is irrelevant. This is a judgment call and judgments are part of critical thinking.

Figure 1.1 summarizes this subsection in diagram form. In short, to support to a conclusion a premise has to be relevant and true.

Figure 1.1

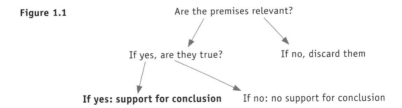

EXERCISE 1.1

Exercises marked by an asterisk (*) have answers included in the Answer Key at the end of the text.

I. Identify and list the premises and conclusions in the following arguments. If a premise or conclusion lacks an indicator word, insert one.

*1. Because your profits depend on unsound environmental practices, and since that actually hurts the economy, your company must therefore change its ways.

2. It's not fair to smoke around non-smokers because second-hand smoke is harmful and when something is harmful, it is not fair to expose non-participants to it.

*3. Since the ban on using electronic devices while driving has reduced accidents, we should therefore extend it to include pedestrians. Half the recent road deaths have been pedestrians, many of whom were distracted by using electronic devices while walking.

4. Inasmuch as we do not get along very well, and inasmuch as life is too short to spend with people I cannot get along with, we should stop seeing one another.

*5. Only when criticism is randomly distributed across the political spectrum is there no reason to suspect bias. But in your blog all criticism is directed at the Conservatives. So your blog is biased.

6. There is no reason to believe atheists because they are completely devoid of faith in a higher power.

*7. The moral rule that tells us we ought to keep our promises is unnatural because people will always break promises when it suits them.

8. All the evidence indicates that the victim was not merely some poor person who was in the wrong place at the wrong time. Ergo, he was murdered.

*9. Three different studies have concluded that undergraduates do worse on open-book exams than they do on regular exams. Given that our mandate is to help students succeed, I think it's reasonable to ban open-book exams.

10. When the explanatory power of one theory is the same as that of another, simplicity is our only guide. Since theory A is simpler than theory B, we should go with theory A.

*11. Sci-fi movies are boring. I've seen dozens of them and they always put me to sleep. Only nerds enjoy them, and nerds only like boring things.

12. Uncritical thinking leads to sloppy reasoning, and sloppy reasoning leads to a multitude of errors. Hence, uncritical thinking leads to a multitude of errors.

*13. Because Tony does everything his girlfriend tells him to without exception, and given that anyone who does this is a drowning man, it follows that Tony is a drowning man.

14. James likes detective novels; Sonia likes detective novels; Arturo likes detective novels; Kulamith likes them, too, as does Ming Wu. They are all intelligent people whose taste I trust. Maybe I should read some detective novels.

*15. Capital punishment is wrong because governments should not be in the business of executing their citizens.

16. Since confession is good for the soul, a lifelong sinner like you should try it sometime.

*17. No one shld have #rspct 4u k, b/c u never rt when u take our stuff.

Continued >

18. 4wiw, he's too nice to twis intentionally. Prbly a dweet.

*19. Assuming that this news network only broadcasts propaganda and lies to viewers, there is no reason to watch it.

20. More test trials of the engine would be useless; we've already run 250 of them. I think we can accept the results.

II. *For each of the following arguments, indicate whether the premises are relevant if true and, where possible, whether they are actually true.*

*1. I think a broken clock is better than one that runs slow because a broken clock is accurate twice a day. (With apologies to Lewis Carroll)

2. Don't sign up for that course because it makes a lot of demands on one's time and you are already too busy.

*3. I don't think I should vote for that party because I never have in the past.

4. The reviews for that movie were terrible, the theatre is too far away, we have other things we need to do today, and Mars is in Orion. So we shouldn't go.

*5. You should stay in school because you have nothing better to do right now.

6. You shouldn't order lobster because you don't like fish.

*7. I wouldn't have that boil lanced because that's a really dangerous procedure.

II. Arguments and Explanations

This section will show you how to distinguish arguments from explanations.

Not everything that looks like an argument actually is one. Sometimes what you are dealing with is an explanation. It is important to be able to distinguish arguments from explanations because in everyday speech people have a tendency to refer to both as explanations. One basic difference between an argument and an explanation is the direction in which they run. An argument *looks forward*: the premises offer reasons why you should accept that a particular conclusion is true. An explanation *looks backward*: it begins with a fact—which by definition is already accepted as true—and then enumerates the reasons that make it true. Hence:

> **Definition:** An **explanation** sets out the reasons why something that is uncontroversially accepted as true is true.

An argument is necessary when its conclusion is not universally or uncontroversially believed to be true—when there is genuine room for doubt. In that sense, its purpose is to convince people of the truth of its conclusion. As the above definition stipulates, an explanation begins with a fact that is already accepted as true and provides, for those who may not be aware of them, the reasons why it is true. For example, compare the following two examples:

E14: *Because Joan has lied to us several times, we shouldn't trust her.*

This is a very simple argument that, set out formally, looks like this:

Premise: Because Joan has lied to us several times;
Conclusion: Therefore, we shouldn't trust her.

It is an argument because the speaker is trying to persuade his audience that Joan should not be trusted. He wants them to accept his conclusion. Now compare **E14** to the following:

E15: *We don't trust Julio because he has lied to us several times.*

Unlike **E14**, this is an explanation. Here it is taken as a fact that "we" don't trust Julio—it's not up for debate—and the reason why "we" don't is then given. So **E14** *argues* that we should not trust Joan, whereas **E15** *explains* why we don't trust Julio.

It is important to pay attention to the wording of these passages. The presence of the word "shouldn't" in **E14** suggests an *argumentative* intention: not trusting Joan is a decision that "we" need to make. The wording of **E15** gives the assertion that "we" don't trust Julio, indicating an explanatory intention: the lack of trust is a fact to be explained. To underwrite this distinction we use different terminology to indicate the parts of the explanation. The fact that is being explained is called the **explanandum** and the explanatory reasons are called **explanans**. The short form is **Em** for explanandum and **Es** for explanans, as follows:

Em: We don't trust Julio;
Es: Because he has lied to us several times.

Note that the formal order of an explanation is the reverse of an argument: the explanandum—which mirrors the conclusion of an argument—comes first and the reasons for the fact—which mirror the premises of an argument—come after. Note also that in **E14** "because" is used to indicate a premise and in **E15** it is used to indicate an explanans. Premise signals in arguments do double service as reason indicators for an explanans in an explanation. As a result, their presence in a passage of text will not tell you whether you are reading an argument or an explanation—only the intention of the passage will do that.

To summarize, an argument is required when the conclusion is open to doubt and its truth needs to be demonstrated; an explanation is required when a particular fact is not in doubt but someone nonetheless requires reasons for its existence. If you are trying to persuade a friend that the economy will be stronger if people reduce their carbon footprints, you are mounting an argument because that is not something everyone believes to be true; it is not uncontroversial. But if someone asks why, for example, the carbon footprint of a specific country is very low, she is asking for an explanation of that particular fact.

Let's put this distinction to work on some more examples.

> **E16:** *(Em) If traffic congestion very slowly increases in a city, it is difficult to recognize that it is in fact getting worse (Es) because our perception of what constitutes normal congestion slowly changes along with the traffic conditions.*

This is clearly an explanation. The fact being explained (Em) is that it is hard to notice very slow incremental increases in traffic congestion. We are then told (Es) why this is so.

> **E17:** *The Internet has completely changed the music industry. Because most songs can now be downloaded for free, musicians have lost one of their major sources of revenue.*

This too is an explanation. The passage accepts as a fact that the Internet has changed the music industry and explains why it has. Set out formally, it looks like this:

> *Em: The Internet has completely changed the music industry;*
> *Es: **Because** [the birth of the Internet] meant that most songs could be downloaded for free;*
> *Es: And **because** this meant that musicians lost one of their major revenue sources.*

> **E18:** *Since the ability to download songs for free on the Internet has destroyed a major source of revenue for musicians, and since most of that downloading is illegal, governments should be doing more to prevent song theft.*

This is an argument. Its author is trying to persuade us that governments ought to be doing more to prevent the illegal exchange of music on the Internet. This is not an uncontroversial opinion—not everyone would agree with it—and controversial opinions require arguments to back them up. So, formally, **E18** looks like this:

> *Premise: **Since** the ability to download songs for free on the Internet has destroyed a major source of revenue for musicians;*
> *Premise: And **since** most of that downloading is illegal;*
> *Conclusion: Governments should **therefore** be doing more to prevent song theft.*

To repeat, the purpose of an argument is to convince you of something that is open to doubt; the purpose of an explanation is to show why an accepted truth (a fact) is true.

How Arguments Become Explanations and Explanations Become Arguments

If you pay close attention to the intention of a passage, it is usually reasonably easy to tell whether it is an argument or an explanation. Just remember that you *explain* what is already accepted as true and *argue* what is open to doubt. One difficulty, however, is that arguments and explanations are not perfectly stable categories, because one generation's fact often becomes another's fiction. Until the sixteenth or seventeenth century, teachers of astronomy would explain to their students that the sun and the other planets orbited Earth, offering detailed accounts of how and why they did so. But since the sun and the other planets do not orbit Earth, almost every aspect of this explanation was wrong. The Polish astronomer Nicolaus Copernicus (1473–1543) was the first to *argue* that it was wrong; that in fact Earth and the other planets orbited the sun. Once the scientific community accepted his argument, it became the *explanation* teachers offered to their students. This process is part of the development of knowledge. In the course of it, many explanations are called into doubt because the "facts" they explain—the explananda—is no longer accepted uncontroversially as a fact. When that happens, arguments arise and continue until a new "fact"—a new truth—emerges. Not so very long ago, it was uncontroversially accepted (by most men at least) that women should not be allowed to vote. Many men were quite happy to explain why this was so. Today, their great-grandchildren would very likely explain why such a view is an archaic form of stupidity.

EXERCISE 1.2

Designate each of the following as an argument or an explanation. If it is an argument, set it out as a series of premises (P) leading to a conclusion (C). If it is an explanation, set it out as a series of explanans (Es) that proceed from an explanandum (Em).

*1. Natural selection entails an interface between genes and the environment. Genetic mutations are random, but the environment determines whether that mutation is beneficial, harmful, or neutral in terms of the organism's chances of survival.

2. I love you because you have a good soul.

*3. I don't think Ovechkin is a better player than Crosby. If you gave Crosby better wingers he'd be leading the scoring race by 20 points.

4. The best way to write an essay is by writing an outline first. When you do that, you know where your argument is going, which allows you to keep it focused.

*5. You're an idiot because you constantly do stupid things.

6. .02 U shd 4give him b/c, cmiw, u're divine

Continued >

*7. .02 U'll 4give him b/c u're divine.

8. What you have just said is not an argument because an argument has to put forward premises in support of a conclusion and you haven't done that.

*9. Let me explain why you ought to vote for the Green Party. It's the only political party that shows genuine concern for the state of the environment and that is the single most important issue facing the world today.

10. Dogs have four-chambered hearts because they're mammals and all mammals have four-chambered hearts.

*11. There are no absolute moral values. Everyone has different views on what's right and what's wrong and they always will.

12. Given that Ray cheats all the time and gets straight A's in school and given that Bonnie does the same, it's just not true that cheaters never prosper.

*13. The value of mortgage funds tends to go up when interest rates go down because the mortgages in the fund are now yielding a higher rate of interest than new mortgages are.

14. Reality television marks the end of civilization as we know it because it has erased the borders between reality and fantasy and turned people away from the real business of living their lives.

*15. In the past, population growth has led to the collapse of some civilizations. It forced people to expand farming from the prime lands first chosen onto more marginal land to feed the growing number of hungry mouths. It also forced them to adopt unsustainable practices that led to environmental damage, resulting in agriculturally marginal lands having to be abandoned again. This resulted in food shortages, starvation, wars . . . and overthrows of governing elites by disillusioned masses.[1]

16. He got in trouble with the professor because I told him a joke in class that was so funny he lol-ed hcore.

III. Reports on Arguments and Counterarguments

This section will deal with two important members of the argument family: reports on arguments and counterarguments. Understanding how they work will give you a better sense of arguments as a form of discussion.

---

1 Adapted from Jared Diamond, *Collapse* (New York: Viking, 2005).

Reports on Arguments

It is common practice to refer to arguments others have made. These second-hand accounts are called **reports on an argument**. Here's an example:

> **E19:** *My professor has this argument that if you study more than a couple of hours a day you will get lower grades. He has all sorts of data on it. Finally, someone agrees with me.*

"My professor has this argument" indicates that **E19** is a report on an argument. Unlike a straightforward argument, one issue that arises with a reported argument is how complete and accurate an account of the original it is. This one is very incomplete; it really only gives us the conclusion. We are told nothing specific about the professor's supporting data. This is probably not surprising since the second sentence suggests that the reporter's purpose is to put forward what an "expert" has claimed as support for her desire not to study so much. Based on that suspicion, it would be important to try, so far as is possible, to assess the accuracy of the report. The best course of action would, of course, be to ask the professor for her version of the argument, but if that's not an option it would still be necessary to consider whether this is the kind of thing a professor is likely to say to students. Search the Internet for something like "over-studying: reports on." If you can't find similar arguments, you have grounds for suspecting either that the student made it up or that the professor's point of view is not widely shared. Finally, if you are familiar with the source of the argument or the subject matter, think carefully about whether the report is plausible in light of what you already know. Remember that a report on an argument suffers from the weakness of all copies: unless you have the original to compare it to you don't know how complete and accurate the report is, and as a result you have to exercise caution when assessing it.

E19 at least attributes the reported argument to a specific source, but that is not always the case, as in the following example:

> **E20:** *Some people claim* that the government should protect some beliefs from public attack no matter whether they are true or not. *These people allege* that this is *because* those beliefs are fundamental to social well-being.[2]

This is a report on an argument, but should you ask who made it the answer will almost certainly be "no one in particular." It seems to be a summary of arguments that are, so to speak, in the air, which means that the reader must decide whether it is a good summary. Does it sound reasonable? Has he or she come across something

---

2 Adapted from John Stuart Mill, *On Liberty* (Harmondsworth: Penguin Books, 1974), 81–2 (originally published 1859).

similar? An unspecific "some people say" report can be very hard to verify or falsify, but if some research turns up nothing like it that is legitimate grounds for suspicion.

The essential point is that when dealing with reports on arguments it is necessary to be on the lookout for distortions and fabrications. We are all open to the temptation of shading reports on arguments to our advantage. For example, consider the following:

> **E21:** *The National Institute for Studies in Education favours* **coddling** *children. They* **allege** *that children do better if they are kept with their own age group,* **no matter how unready they are for promotion.**

This is a short argument, but nonetheless it will help to set it out formally:

> *Premise:* **Because** *the National Institute for Studies in Education* alleges *that children do better if they are kept with their own age group,* no matter how unready they are for promotion;
> *Conclusion: The Institute* **therefore** *favours* coddling *children.*

This report contains a couple of red flags that should arouse a reader's suspicion. In the conclusion, the use of "coddling," a word that means to take too much care of someone, is a negative term almost certainly inserted by the reporter—it is highly unlikely that the authors of the study would characterize their position in this way. In the premise, the use of "allege" and the phrase "no matter how unready they are for promotion" are also negative characterizations unlikely to be found in the original version of the study. (Studies don't "allege", they "demonstrate".) Anyone interested in the study would therefore be well advised to read it for themselves rather than trusting this report, which looks biased and inaccurate. A reasonable suspicion is that the reporter disagrees with the study's findings and is trying to persuade his audience to reject it.

Sometimes reports are inaccurate even when the original argument belongs to someone in the room. For example:

> **E22:**
> *Student: I think we should have an open-book exam. You've told us all term that the point of this course isn't memory work but careful thought, so I think an open-book exam would be appropriate.*
> *Professor (to class): She wants me to facilitate cheating.*

Let's set the student's argument out in the clearest possible fashion:

> *P:* **Because** *you have told us that the point of this course isn't memory work but careful thought;*
> *C: We should* **therefore** *have an open-book exam.*

The professor then reports (or describes) this argument to the rest of the class as one that advocates cheating. Perhaps he really feels that open-book exams do facilitate cheating and has good reasons for believing this to be so, but the student has not asked for permission to cheat and the professor is wrong to report her argument as one that advocates cheating. This is both inaccurate and unfair.

In summary, when reporting an argument it is important to render it as accurately as possible and in as much detail as is necessary to give your audience a fair sense of it. Avoid inserting descriptive passages such as the ones in **E19** and **E21** unless they are in the original argument. When listening to or reading reports on arguments, be wary of extreme or biased-looking language. When you come across this kind of language try, where possible, to check the report against the original.

Counterarguments

Arguments often occur in the context of debates or discussions in what are called **dialogical situations**. These are situations where one person puts forward an argument and a second person objects, offering a **counterargument**. If an argument is any good its premises will provide genuine support for the conclusion, so the point of a counterargument is to show that at least one of the premises is false or irrelevant. Think of premises as a bunch of poles holding up a platform, which is the conclusion. The more poles you knock down in your counterargument, the more likely the conclusion is to collapse. Consider this example (where "C" stands for conclusion and "P" for premise):

E23:

William: (C) Aisha will never get elected to the student council (P) because she's new at the school and no one knows her and (P) because she doesn't know the issues.

Winston: (C) I think she has a good chance. (P) She has posters everywhere and (P) in her speech at the candidates' meeting she certainly seemed on top of the issues.

The premises of Winston's counterargument meet both of William's premises with *relevant* examples. The effect is to cast doubt on William's conclusion.

Compare **E23** to this example:

E24:

Politician A: (C) The government should not declare war on _____ (P) because it claims to adhere to the Geneva Convention, which sanctions only defensive wars and (P) this would not be a defensive war.

Politician B: (C) We should go to war because I believe in this country.

Notice that Politician B's argument doesn't speak to Politician A's. Rather, it simply ignores it. As a counterargument to A it is therefore irrelevant. A counterargument has to put forward premises that are relevant to the premises of the argument it is intended to counter. For example, if B argued that the war under consideration was in fact a defensive war that would be a counterargument because that premise would be relevant.

Sometimes what looks relevant may not be. For example:

E25:
Paula: (C) We shouldn't go to that movie (P) because it's moronic, a complete waste of time.
Pearl: (P) But we have free passes (C) so why not go?

Since Paula's argument isn't about whether the movie is free but about whether it's worth watching, the premise of Pearl's counterargument is, if not totally irrelevant, then at least somewhat beside the point. It doesn't directly deal with the premise that supports Paula's conclusion. Pearl would need to argue that it is better to use the passes on a terrible movie than not use them at all.

Counterarguments don't always require public dialogical contexts because they can occur as a kind of conversation with oneself. (Remember: you can construct arguments in the privacy of your own room.) Someone may, for instance, report an argument and then produce a counterargument to test it:

E26: *A lot of people want less government **because** they think it's important for people to have maximum control over their lives, **but** it's not a good idea **because** the less government we have the more unequal society becomes and that leads to all sorts of problems such as poverty, crime, and a general breakdown of social services. Then people actually have less control over their lives.*

This passage can be set out as follows:

Report on an Argument
*P: **Because** it's important for people to have maximum control over their lives;*
*C: There should **therefore** be less government.*

Counterargument
*P1: **Because** less government means more inequality;*
*P2: **Because** more inequality means more poverty, crime, and a general breakdown of social services;*
*P3: And **because** that means people have less control over their lives;*
*C: Less government is **therefore** not a good idea.*

P3 contradicts the premise of the reported argument and makes possible a contradictory conclusion as well. A reader needs first to think carefully about her assessment of the accuracy of the report. Is this really what a lot of people think? If she is satisfied that it is accurate, she then needs to assess both the truth and relevance of the counterargument's premises. She cannot, after all, accept both arguments.

Sometimes a counterargument may be directed against a bare claim:

E27: *People say that it is morally permissible to break promises sometimes,* **but if it is** *the very idea of a promise becomes incoherent because the point of a promise is that you will do what you say you are going to do.*

Here, the claim in question is that sometimes it is morally permissible to break promises. If someone has offered premises in support of it, we are not told what they are. But it doesn't matter much, since it is perfectly acceptable to mount a counterargument against a claim—a putative conclusion, in effect—even when it's not supported by premises. A counterargument to the claim that it is morally permissible to break promises sometimes might run as follows:

P: **Because** *to say that sometimes it is morally permissible to break a promise is to say that promises need not always be kept;*
P: *And* **because** *this amounts to the incoherent claim that we can make promises that are not promises;*
C: **Therefore**, *it is not morally permissible to break promises.*

Since this is a complicated issue, it's a good idea is to go one step further and construct, as honestly as possible, an argument *in favour* of the position you oppose and then offer a counterargument against it. For example:

E28: *Someone may object that no one reasonably expects us to keep promises made to hostage-takers or to someone about to commit suicide by jumping off a high building.* **But** *these examples are not really relevant* **because** *a promise made under duress—to a hostage-taker or a potential suicide—is not really a promise at all. A promise must be freely given and therefore must be kept.*

This imagined counterargument to **E27** can be set out as follows:

P: **Because** *no one expects us to keep promises made to hostage-takers;*
P: *And* **because** *no one expects us to keep promises made to potential suicides;*
C: **Therefore**, *it is sometimes permissible to break promises.*

This is followed by a counter-counterargument (signalled by "but") that attempts to demonstrate that the cases cited in these premises are not really examples of promises, because a promise has to be freely given. It runs something like this:

P: **Because** *promises made under duress are not really promises at all;*
P: *And* **because** *promises made to hostage-takers and potential suicides are made under duress;*
C: **Therefore**, *these so-called promises are, in fact, not promises at all.*

By adding the imagined counterargument of **E28** and then providing a counter-counterargument, the author of **E27** has defended his position against what he sees as a possible objection. Note that he has done so by putting forward a particular definition of "promise." Anyone who wishes to argue against him must now either dispute this definition or argue that, even in the case of hostage-takers and potential suicides, one's word is freely given.

Arguments need to be tested, and a good way of doing so is by developing a solid counterargument. This stimulates critical thinking because once you have constructed a counterargument and replied with a counter-counterargument you can then try to knock down the counter-counterargument. You can go on in this manner until you have satisfied yourself either that your original argument is correct or that it is not. Arguments and counterarguments are the conversation of critical thinkers, even when those thinkers are solitary ones alone in their rooms.

EXERCISE 1.3

Designate each of the following as either (1) an argument, (2) a counterargument, (3) an argument and counterargument, (4) a report on an argument, or (5) a report on an argument and a counterargument. In the cases of 3 and 5, consider whether the premises of the counterargument are all relevant. With reports on arguments, note any "extreme" language that may cast doubt on the accuracy of the report.

*1. If reputable tests confirm a connection between a physical condition and a disease then we ought to accept that such a connection exists. Tests do show a connection between cholesterol levels and heart disease, so we ought to assume that heart disease is related to cholesterol levels.

2. Joshua: I think most pop music is vastly overrated because for the most part it's merely a rehash of older, more sophisticated forms of music.

   Jocelyn: You're wrong. The best of it blends older forms of music with absolutely original ideas.

*3. The philosopher David Hume argued that the world does not contain causes. *Cause* is simply an idea we impose on the world to make sense of what we observe.

4. I have heard many people claim that friendship is the most valuable thing in the world, but I don't see how that can be since most of my friends are broke.

*5. Some people think the growing worldwide demand for democratic institutions is an effect of the rapid growth of social media, because social media breaks down social barriers. I disagree, however. I don't think technology can create democratic movements unless other social conditions, such as a sufficient level of education, are already in place.

6. Pro basketball is less fun to watch than college basketball because it's all slam and jam with too little emphasis on finesse and outside shooting.

*7. Mohamed: We have to shovel the snow off the cottage roof this weekend because there has been a serious build-up of snow in the last two weeks and the roof is in danger of collapse.

Beatrice: But the forecast is for mild weather this week, so we might as well let Mother Nature do the work for us.

8. Xui Li wants me to believe that it's important to vote in elections because it's our duty as citizens and if we just blow it off we are effectively resigning from society. I would agree if our votes actually had any effect, but they don't. Once they are in power, all parties act in much the same way.

*9. Smith claims that her cat is temporally non-continuous. She says that it keeps showing up in different parts of the house without warning. She followed it around for a week and it kept disappearing and reappearing somewhere else some time later.

10. I talked to Alice a week ago and she got angry with me. I talked to her a month ago and the same thing happened. I talked to her just now and once again she was angry. I think I irritate her somehow.

*11. Li has claimed that we should treat other people with respect even if they don't deserve it because the result of not doing so increases tension in our own lives, which can lead to health problems. He says that there are a number of reputable studies that confirm this.

12. The idea that we should live to work is preposterous. We should in fact work to live. Given that work is by definition painful we should do only as much of it as is necessary and then get on with the business of enjoying life.

*13. Two outlaws from the American west are trapped on a cliff by a posse. Their only way out is to jump into the river far below.

The Sundance Kid: I shouldn't jump because I can't swim, so I'll probably drown.

Butch Cassidy: Are you kidding? The fall alone will probably kill you.[3]

14. Many of the people who are bashing oil companies for spills don't have a clue that they are really the ones to blame. After all, oil companies are simply meeting consumer demand for cheap oil.

*15. Janine tells me that the best option is to be soft on crime. She thinks thugs can be rehabilitated if we treat them with kid gloves.

---

3 Adapted from *Butch Cassidy and the Sundance Kid*.

IV. Extracting and Editing Arguments

This section will deal with extracting arguments from longer passages of text, deleting unnecessary material, and restating them in your own words where necessary.

Extracting the Argument

Most of the arguments we have looked at so far are not too hard to spot because they have been short, often well-sign-posted with premise and conclusion indicators, and not encumbered by too much excess verbiage. However, arguments are often embedded in passages of text from which they have to be extracted and in some cases restated to make them clearer. This can be tricky work that calls for attentive reading and careful paraphrasing. Let's start with a fairly straightforward example:

> **E29:** *I work on the assumption that people who love dogs too much often don't love people enough and an insufficiency of love for one's fellow humans means, **I am sorry to say**, that a person is not to be trusted. So **it pains me to say that**, given your excessive love for dogs, I shouldn't trust you.*

The conclusion is "I shouldn't trust you." But how did the speaker get there? Well, her first sentence contains the following two premises:

> *Premise 1: (Because) people who love dogs too much often don't love people enough;*
> *Premise 2: (Because) an insufficiency of love for one's fellow humans means a person is not to be trusted;*

The first part of the second sentence provides a third premise that needs to be rewritten:

> *Premise 3: (Because) you love dogs excessively;*

The result is:

> *Premise: **Because** people who love dogs too much often don't love people enough;*
> *Premise: **Because** an insufficiency of love for one's fellow humans means a person is not to be trusted;*
> *Premise: And **because** you love dogs excessively;*
> *Conclusion: **Therefore**, I shouldn't trust you.*

This is a simple, direct version of **E29**. It hasn't required much rewriting, but the bolded passages of the original version have been edited out to get at the meat of the argument. As well, premise and conclusion signals have been inserted.

Now let's turn to a longer and more complex passage written by the famous astrophysicist Stephen Hawking (for convenience, the sentences have been numbered):

> **E30:** *(S1) The . . . goal of science is to provide a single theory that describes the whole universe. (S2) **However**, the approach most scientists actually follow*

*is to separate the problem into two parts. **(S3)** First, there are the laws that tell us how the universe changes with time . . . **(S4) Second**, there is the question of the initial state of the universe. **(S5) Some people feel** that science should be concerned with only the first part; they regard the question of the initial situation as a matter for metaphysics or religion. **(S6)** They would say that God, being omnipotent, could have started the universe off any way he wanted. **(S7) That may be so, but** in that case he could also have made it develop in a completely arbitrary way. **(S8)** Yet it appears that he chose to make it evolve according to certain laws. **(S9)** It **therefore** seems equally reasonable to suppose that there are also laws governing the initial state.*[4]

S2, **S3**, and **S4** inform the reader that there are two broad research interests that scientists have:

1. How the universe changes over time
2. What its "initial state" was

S5 and **S6** then provide a *report on an argument* about those interests, which is attributed to that amorphous group, "some people." Finally, **S7**, **S8**, and **S9** contain a counterargument to the report, signalled by the phrase "that may be so" that opens **S7**.

Let's look first at the reported argument in **S5** and **S6**. **S5** contains its conclusion, which is that "some people" think the following:

C: Scientists should only investigate how the universe changes (number 1 above). (What its initial state was [number 2 above] is not a matter for science but for religion or metaphysics.)

For the time being, we will leave the sentence in parentheses aside.

S6 supplies two premises for this argument. However, as the sentence stands they are condensed into what looks like one premise, so they need to be identified and stated explicitly. When this is done, the result is the following report on an argument:

*P1: **Because** God is omnipotent;*
*P2: And **because** an omnipotent God could have started off the universe in any way he wanted;*
*C: **(From S5) Therefore**, Scientists should only investigate how the universe changes.*

Conclusion **C** can be rewritten in the negative to make it flow more directly from the premises and from the number 2 claim:

C: The initial state of the universe is not a matter for scientific investigation.

---

4 Stephen Hawking, *A Brief History of Time* (Toronto: Bantam Books, 1988), 10–11.

S7, **S8**, and **S9** constitute a counterargument to this report:

> **P1:** *(S7) **Because** an omnipotent God could have made the universe develop in a completely arbitrary way;*
>
> **P2:** *(S8) And **because** God appears instead to have made it develop in a law-abiding way;*
>
> **C:** *(S9) **Therefore**, it seems reasonable to suppose that God also began the universe in a law-abiding way.*

S8 has been expanded and **S9** has been paraphrased in an effort to make the counterargument stand out more clearly. When you are trying to make sense of argumentative passages, this kind of editing can be very helpful. When it's done properly, the different argument structures (arguments, reports, counterarguments) and the relationship between them are much easier to grasp. But always remember that when you edit you must take care to retain the original meaning of the passage.

You will notice that **S1** has been ignored. If we put it together with **S2**, we derive the claim that scientists profess to do one thing but actually do another. While that is interesting in its own right, it is not particularly relevant to the argument and counterargument in the rest of the passage, so it is best left out of our consideration. But think for a moment about the conclusion of the counterargument: "It is reasonable to assume that God also began the universe in a law-abiding way." It doesn't really counter the reported argument, whose conclusion is "The initial state of the universe is not a matter for scientific investigation." How can we have a counterargument that doesn't counter?

I shall leave you to ponder this problem until Section V below, but for now consider this example:

> **E31:** *(S1) It's always something: oil, natural gas, water, lumber; but no matter what the motivation we should not invade Fredonia **for the simple reason that** we have no quarrel with it. (S2) I understand perfectly well that they are rich in natural resources and we aren't, but so what? (S3) The mere fact of need does not justify naked aggression against someone who is not your enemy, perhaps not even against someone who is your enemy. (S4) **There are those who might want to argue** raison d'état and dress it up as enlightened self-interest, **but if so** they are wrong. (S5) No enlightened democracy can ever go down that road and remain true to its founding principles—that is, remain enlightened. (S6) I call on you with every fibre of my being to step aside from the path of war.*

Unlike Hawking's argument, this passage reads like a speech, complete with impassioned language and exhortations to action. It contains only a single informal premise indicator ("for the simple reason that"), although the bolded phrase "there are those who might want to argue" signals an imagined counterargument. Finally, the phrase "but if so" signals a counter-counterargument. So there is definitely a dialogical structure to this passage. It's just a matter of sorting out exactly what it is.

The best way to proceed is by identifying the author's original argument, which is found in the second half of the first sentence:

E31.1
P: *Because* we have no quarrel with Fredonia;
C: *Therefore*, we should not invade Fredonia.

The first half of **S1** and the entirety of **S2** constitute a possible counterargument to **E31.1**. It looks like this:

E31.2
P: *Because* our country needs access to Fredonia's natural resources;
C: *Therefore*, we should invade it.

So now we have **E31.1** as an argument for which **E31.2** is a possible counterargument. The author of the passage then puts forward a principle in **S3**—need does not justify naked aggression—which acts as the basis of a counterargument to the counterargument of **E31.2**. It goes like this:

E31.3
P: *Because* to invade a country with which we have no quarrel is an act of naked aggression;
P: And *because* naked aggression cannot be justified on the basis of our need for natural resources;
C: *Therefore*, the fact that we need Fredonia's natural resources is not a justification for invading it.

E31.3 represents a sharpening of the author's original argument in **E31.1** by taking into account the imagined counterargument of **E31.2**.

S4 then offers up a possible counterargument to **E31.3**. It speaks to the (possible) claim that *raison d'état*—national self-interest—justifies doing things a country would not otherwise do. It is a condensed argument, which can be expanded as follows:

E31.4:
P: *Because* important national interests can justify aggression against another country;
P: And *because* important national interests are at stake in this case;
C: *Therefore*, invading Fredonia is justified.

In **S5**, the author seeks to refute this counterargument by putting forward an argument based on the claim that his country considers itself an enlightened democracy. Restated somewhat, it looks like this:

E31.5:
P1: *Because* a country that engages in naked aggression is not an enlightened democracy;
P2: And *because* we are and want to remain an enlightened democracy;
C: *Therefore*, naked aggression against another country is not possible.

The author's point is that his country can't have it both ways: it cannot invade Fredonia *and* remain an enlightened democracy. Hence, if it is to be true to its enlightened principles, his country must not make war on Fredonia. Anyone who disagrees must either reject **P1** of **E31.5** by constructing an argument against it—not an easy argument to make, though not an impossible one either—or reject **P2**, though that entails a concession most people would be absolutely unwilling to make. In any case, **E31.5** brings the choices out in the open.

What we see in this passage is the way in which someone can work through an issue by presenting a series of arguments and counterarguments. On the one side you have **E31.1**, **E31.3**, and **E31.5**, which present the author's view, and on the other side you have **E31.2** and **E31.4**, which present imagined or possible counterarguments to his view.

Dealing with Extraneous Material

Like **E31**, arguments are often condensed and devoid of premise and conclusion signals. Clarifying them requires expanding premises and conclusions and inserting indicator words. When this is done the dialogical structure of the passage and the arguments it contains stand out more clearly. But, again like **E31**, it is also necessary to edit out extraneous remarks that are intended to make the argument more persuasive but which are, strictly speaking, irrelevant. **S6** in **E31** is a case in point: it is a slightly overwrought restatement of the conclusion of the opening argument. Since the author is trying to be as persuasive as possible he has good reasons for including it, but it contributes nothing to the content of the argument.

It is worthwhile to take another look at these embellishments. Consider the following argument:

> **E32:** *(P1)* **Since** *you tell me that you have respect for all people—**and who will ever argue that that is not a good thing?**—(C) you will naturally be in favour of a form of government that provides everyone with basic religious, political, and economic liberties,* **because** *(P2) without them "respect" is an empty word.*

The bolded phrase inserted between the dashes exists as a kind of declaration of support for the first premise (P1), but it is irrelevant to the argument. Therefore, it can be omitted when setting **E32** out formally:

> P1: *Because* *you tell me that you have respect for all people;*
> P2: *And* *because* *without a form of government that provides everyone with basic political, religious, and economic liberties "respect" is an empty word;*
> C: *Therefore, you will naturally be in favour of a government that provides these liberties.*

Notice the way in which the wording of **P2** and **C** has been changed. The pronoun "them" in the original premise has been replaced by a full statement of the idea it stands for, and in the conclusion the full statement has been replaced by "these." That's because the premise now precedes the conclusion and it is necessary to state the full idea before condensing it to the pronoun "these."

Sometimes editing calls for extensive rewriting, as in this argument:

E33: *(S1)* ***For goodness' sake***, *we don't need to vet every single airline traveller. (S2)* ***I know that's what my colleague here wants to do, but let's not listen to the ramblings of a paranoid person.*** *(S3) Sure, an 80-year-old Scottish lady could be carrying a bomb, but the chances that she is are so small that they are not worth contemplating. (S4) And anyway, if she is a threat our excellent intelligence service will undoubtedly know that and check her out.*

First, some deletions are advisable, which have been bolded. Stripped of its opening phrase, the rest of **S1** is the conclusion of an argument:

C: We don't need to vet every airline passenger.

S2 contributes nothing toward this conclusion; it merely tells us, by way of insult, that this is a counterargument against a colleague's position. We can therefore edit it out of the passage. This leaves **S3** and **S4** as the premises of the argument. **S3** will become clearer if we restate it as follows:

S3: The chances that an 80-year-old Scottish lady is carrying a bomb are very small.

S4 can be left as it is:

S4: If she is a threat our excellent intelligence service will undoubtedly know that and check her out.

Thus, the edited argument looks like this:

E33.1:
P: ***Because*** *the chances that an 80-year-old Scottish lady is carrying a bomb are very small;*
P: And ***because*** *our excellent intelligence service will know if she is a threat and check her out;*
C: ***Therefore***, *we don't need to vet every airline passenger.*

While this is clear enough, notice that the conclusion is general, referring to "every airline passenger," while the premises are very specific, referring only to an 80-year-old Scottish lady. Obviously, she is intended as an example of the kind of person the speaker feels need not be subjected to strenuous security checks. As a result, the premises can reasonably be restated in more general terms:

E33.2:
P: ***Because*** *the chance that some people are a threat to airline security is very small;*

> P: And **because** our intelligence service will distinguish them from those who are genuine threats;
> C: **Therefore**, we don't need to vet every airline passenger.

Now the argument is in a form that allows a reader to give it full consideration. Editing arguments to present them in their clearest light can take some work, but when you want to give an argument careful consideration you are well advised to undertake it. Sections V and VI below will develop this idea.

EXERCISE 1.4

Edit each of the following arguments, deleting passages that are not part of the argument and, where necessary, restating premises and conclusions to make them clearer. If reports on arguments or counterarguments are present, set them out clearly.

*1. Systems of education, which are cumbersome beasts at the best of times, rarely work in the best interests of students if this government report is to be believed, and since given the sagacity of this particular government I am sure it ought to be, I think we can conclude that systems of education are indeed cumbersome beasts that rarely work in the best interests of students.

2. Ballet is a high art form. The dancers are lithe and elegant, the choreography is intricate yet subtle, and the music is absolutely beautiful. What can anyone say against it?

*3. I have no idea how you can say that. You must be nuts, because when someone claims—as you just have—that there are extraterrestrials on the moon waiting to invade Earth, they are really and truly nuts.

4. OMG! U'r tgtbt. U did that 4 me?

*5. You really must listen closely: there is no way—no way at all—that Smythe could be the murderer. In the first place, he is possibly the least-violent person I have ever met—and I have met a lot of people. But there's more, much more: there is no physical evidence linking Smythe to the crime scene nor is there any motive that I can think of. If you really need something more, I can add that Jones is a much more likely suspect for reasons of motive and opportunity. So please spare me your insane theories about Smythe.

6. I'm certain all patriotic citizens will agree that we need to tighten our border security, because if we do not there is sure to be a terrorist attack in the near future, and no one wants that, do they?

*7. Despite what my colleague has said, there is no absolute justification for the values of any culture. Certainly, I have never seen an irrefutable argument that there is. But if there is no absolute justification, then we are caught between the Scylla of relativism and the Charybdis of ethnocentrism. So, when it comes to cultural values, you have to be either a relativist or an ethnocentrist.

8. My mother goes on these long two-week hikes. She goes all over the place: Europe, Asia, South America. She says hiking is a wonderful experience because it takes you to places you can only get to by walking and because it gets you away from the busyness of everyday life. Fine. But given how boring walking even three blocks is, she has to be insane to want to walk 300 kilometres. It's crazy. And who wants to go to places you can only get to by walking? There must be nothing there.

*9. The government's unwillingness to fund abortions to improve the health of mothers in poor countries indicates contempt for the women it says it wants to help. When will the government do the right thing for women instead of playing politics with their lives?

It's not for us to decide whether a woman should choose to have an abortion. That decision belongs to her. Our role should be to ensure that she has reproductive rights and access to real options for her health and that of her children. We have the means and opportunity to make a difference; unfortunately, we have neither the will nor the leadership.

10. Experience teaches us that when someone controls things other people really want, he or she also has control over them, if you see what I mean. And of course, the more things a person controls the more control he or she has over others. It's a sad conclusion, I know, but a true one. Given that the top 1 per cent of the population controls 40 per cent of the goods in North America, this is basically a dictatorship of the super-rich.

*11. Every time I see people celebrating the Olympics I want to cry. I am very upset about where this country is headed. How can so many people enjoy something that has devoured billions of dollars that could otherwise have been spent on helping the poor in Vancouver?

A nation is judged by the way it treats its most vulnerable citizens, and it is a disheartening statement about our priorities when the speed of a luger going down a hill generates greater public reaction than human suffering does.

V. Identifying Implicit Assumptions

Section IV showed you how to delete extraneous material from arguments and how to expand condensed premises and conclusions. This section deals with cases where it is necessary to insert implicit assumptions into arguments.

*Definition: An **implicit assumption** is a premise or conclusion that has been left unstated but which is necessary if an argument is to be presented in its complete form.*

Two Basic Examples

An assumption may be left implicit for a number of reasons—some good and some bad. The best reason is that it is sufficiently obvious that it can be taken for granted. It may be so obvious to the person making the argument that she doesn't even realize she has left it unsaid. Since this is also true of explanations, I'll mention one of them before moving on to arguments. Should someone ask me to explain why Socrates was mortal, I would respond "because he was human," omitting to add the all-too-obvious additional explanans that humans are mortal. I would not omit that explanans consciously; it just would not occur to me to state it. (But if I were talking to an extraterrestrial with no knowledge of Earth I would be well advised to include it.) Simple arguments work the same way:

> **E34:** *You need to stay in and study tonight because you have an exam tomorrow morning.*

This argument actually relies on two implicit premises:

> *IP1:* **Because** *you want to pass*
> *IP2:* **Because** *you need to study to pass*

Like the explanation of Socrates's mortality, these premises seem to go without saying and have therefore been omitted. But they are nonetheless part of the complete argument, which looks like this:

> *P1:* **Because** *you have an exam tomorrow morning;*
> *IP1:* **Because** *you want to pass it;*
> *IP2: And* **because** *you need to study to pass;*
> *C:* **Therefore**, *you need to stay in and study tonight.*

Conclusions can also be left implicit because sometimes we let people draw their own conclusions. For example:

> **E35:** *You've been invited to a party tonight but you have an exam tomorrow morning that you really need to pass.*

This looks like a straightforward assertion, but in fact it's an argument with an implicit conclusion:

> *C:* **Therefore**, *you can't go to the party.*

E35 also has an implicit premise:

> *IP: If you go to the party you can't study.*

So the full argument looks like this:

> *P:* **Because** *you have an exam tomorrow that you really need to pass;*
> *IP: And* **because** *if you go to the party you can't study;*
> *C:* **Therefore**, *you can't go to the party.*

Finally, consider this example:

E36: *If you skip work tomorrow you will be fired, and you don't want that to happen.*

The full argument, with the implicit conclusion inserted, is as follows:

P: **Because** *if you skip work tomorrow you will be fired;*
P: And **because** *you don't want to be fired;*
IC: **Therefore**, *you will go to work tomorrow.*

Some More Difficult Examples

While leaving assumptions implicit causes no problems in simple cases like **E34**, **E35**, and **E36**, with unfamiliar or complicated arguments difficulties may arise. For example, let's go back to Stephen Hawking's argument in **E30**. It included the following report on an argument about why the origin of the universe was not a matter for science, but rather for theology or metaphysics:

E37:
P: *(S6)* **Because** *God is omnipotent;*
P: *(S6)* And **because** *an omnipotent God could have started the universe in any way he wanted;*
C: *(S5)* **Therefore**, *how the universe began is not a concern for scientists.*

There are gaps in this argument that need to be filled in with implicit premises. To be precise, Hawking seems to be relying on two implicit premises:

E37.1:
P: *(S6)* **Because** *God is omnipotent;*
P: *(S7)* **Because** *an omnipotent God could have started the universe off in any way he wanted;*
IP: **Because** *this means that there are no natural or necessary laws governing the start of the universe;*
IP: And **because** *the absence of such laws means that there is nothing for scientists to investigate;*
C: *(S5)* **Therefore**, *how the universe began is not a concern for scientists.*

Inserting the implicit premises allows us to see more clearly how the conclusion that the origin of the universe is not a matter for scientific investigation has been derived. In fact, without them, Hawking's reported argument seems to be leaping to a conclusion.

Now let's look at **S5** of **E30**, because it contains a second claim that also requires closer attention. It is that those who think the origin of the universe is not a matter for science regard the question of the initial situation as a matter for metaphysics or religion. This conclusion seems to be based on the following implicit premise:

IP: *What is not a matter for science is a matter for metaphysics or religion.*

So now we have a second argument that runs like this:

E37.2:
P: *Because* how the universe began is not a matter for scientists to investigate;
IP: And *because* what is not a matter for scientific investigation is a matter for metaphysics and religion;
C: *Therefore*, how the universe began is a question for metaphysics and religion.

Note that the first premise of **E37.2** is the conclusion of **E37.1**. Once it is supplemented with an implicit premise, we arrive at the conclusion of **E37.2**. When the argument is set out like this, you can perhaps see that the implicit premise in **E37.2** is in fact a rather curious one. It asserts that there are only two kinds of investigations: scientific and metaphysical or religious. That may be so, but it surely can't be obvious to everyone that it is. Inserting the implicit assumption has made the argument clearer but also more debatable. Many readers may not be quite so ready to accept it when they read it in its fullest form.

Now let's turn to the counterargument, which is signalled by the phrase "That may be so, but . . ." that introduces **S7** in **E30**. This phrase shows that in the counterargument contained in **S7**, **S8**, and **S9**, Hawking is not arguing about whether an omnipotent God created the universe. He is neither accepting nor rejecting that claim; he is simply ignoring it. His point is that *even if* the universe was created by an omnipotent God, it doesn't change the fact that scientists are well within their rights to ask questions about the initial state of the universe. His argument runs as follows:

E38:
P1: (S7) *Because* an omnipotent God could have made the universe develop in a completely arbitrary way;
P2: (S8) And *because* God did not do so (he made it develop in a law-abiding way);
C: (S9) It is *therefore* reasonable to suppose that God made the universe begin in a law-abiding way.

This argument also relies on an implicit premise:

IP: *God will act consistently.*

Since this implicit premise actually cancels **P1** in **E38**, we can therefore insert it in place of **P1** to get:

E38.1:
IP: *Because* it is reasonable to assume that God's actions are consistent;
P2: And *because* God made the universe develop in a law-abiding manner;
C: *Therefore*, it is equally reasonable to assume that God also made the universe begin in a law-abiding manner.

One possible response to this counterargument is, who knows? After all, an omnipotent God can do what he likes without being restrained by the demand for consistency.

So here, too, inserting the implicit assumptions makes the argument look more debatable than it may have appeared in its condensed form.

And finally, we need to clear up the issue I left you with at the end of Section IV, where I pointed out that the conclusion of Hawking's counterargument—see **C** immediately above—doesn't really counter the conclusion of the reported argument: that the initial state of the universe is not a matter for scientific investigation. To get all the way there Hawking relies on an unstated argument that follows from conclusion **C** above, and to which he appends an implied premise and conclusion:

> **P: Because** it seems reasonable to assume that the universe began in a law-abiding way;
>
> **IP: And because** what is law-abiding is a matter for scientific study;
>
> **IC: Therefore**, the initial state of the universe is a matter for scientific study.

So **E30** reports an argument to the effect that the initial state of the universe is not a matter for scientific investigation and then develops a counterargument. While it looks detailed, the arguments are in fact quite condensed, to the point of being simply implied in one case. Anyone who is really interested in the whole argument and wants to think about it carefully would be well advised to set it out in the explicit way we have done in this and the previous section.

In closing, remember that implicit assumptions sometimes occur for devious reasons. For example, here's an argument every teacher has fielded:

> **E39:** I worked hard on this essay so I deserve a good mark.

The implicit premise is easy enough to spot here:

> **IP:** If you work hard on something you should be rewarded.

Unfortunately, that is not necessarily so: an essay has to be judged on its merits rather than on the labour time invested by its author. That's why a student will generally omit the implicit premise—stating it will draw attention to the weakness in the argument.

EXERCISE 1.5

For each of the following, insert the implicit assumptions (premises or conclusions) necessary to complete the argument.

*1. Basketball is a better game than golf because it is more athletic.

2. Employees can take early retirement, but their pensions will be reduced if they do and nobody wants that.

*3. Becoming a professional athlete requires a high level of natural talent, which is not measurably increased by hard work.

Continued >

4. War is always wrong, and invading Afghanistan was an act of war.

*5. Children should not be subject to corporal punishment. Like adults, they have the protection of civil rights legislation.

6. Cats are better pets than dogs because they cost less to look after.

*7. Religious people are not the only ones who can appreciate religious works of art. There is no reason why atheists and agnostics cannot also enjoy them. After all, their appeal comes not from any transcendent quality, but from their aesthetic and emotional appeal.

8. Because studies show that many university graduates are not as literate as they need to be to succeed in their chosen fields, universities are failing to do what they are required to do.

*9. "An individualistic account of knowledge [has serious flaws]. An isolated 'rational' individual who monitors experience without bias or preconceptions is not a scientist but a person who remembers everything and knows nothing."[5]

10. In the course of the game, Jones attacked Ingerman from behind, injuring him seriously. But Jones was only doing what the coach told him to do.

*11. If existing scientific theories bind the scientist too tightly, then there can be no surprises, anomalies, or crises in science. But without surprises, anomalies, and crises, science will not continue to develop.[6]

VI. The Principle of Charity

When you are extracting arguments from passages of text, editing them, and inserting implicit assumptions, always obey the **principle of charity**. It tells you to cast the argument in its strongest possible form. In other words, if there is more than one way to restate an argument, choose the strongest possible version of it. This is especially important if you are going to attempt a counterargument. There is not much use rejecting a weak, unpersuasive, or confused form of an argument when a stronger, more persuasive or clearer one is available. Make the opposition as credible as possible. In **E33**, for example, a flippant statement about aged Scottish ladies was replaced by a general argument about unthreatening airline passengers. That was a charitable but defensible bit of editing because it presented the argument in the strongest light without distorting it.

---

5 Adapted from Barry Barnes, "Thomas Kuhn," in *The Return of Grand Theory in the Human Sciences,* ed. Quentin Skinner (Cambridge: Cambridge University Press, 1985), 97.

6 Adapted from T.S. Kuhn, *The Structure of Scientific Revolutions*, 2nd ed. (Chicago: University of Chicago Press, 1973), 100–1.

But consider this example:

E40: *The New England Patriots are the worst team I have ever seen. Sure they went 14–2 in the regular season, but they choked in the first round of the playoffs.*

Since it's a good bet that a team that won 14 of 16 games in the regular season is not the worst one the speaker has ever seen, it is probably not very useful to argue that point. In other words, experience suggests that, taken literally, this is an inane argument. The principle of charity therefore advises us to treat this assertion as an exaggeration and assume that what the speaker means is that a really good team would not perform so poorly in the playoffs. Since the Patriots did perform poorly, they are not a really good team, or at least not as good as they appeared to be. The result is a very charitable (perhaps too charitable) version of the argument:

P: *Because* *a team that goes 14–2 in the regular season and loses in the first round of the playoffs is not really as good as their regular season record suggests;*
P: And *because* *this is what the Patriots did;*
C: *Therefore*, *the Patriots are not as good as their regular season record suggests.*

A counterargument would aim at demonstrating that the Patriots are, despite the playoff loss, a good team and that losing was not the result of bad play.

Now consider this argument:

E41: *After William Jones, Lamar Smith, and Arthur Robertson were executed, evidence came to light that proved their innocence. Capital punishment should be abolished.*

This is a condensed argument that moves—perhaps leaps—from three specific cases to a very general conclusion, and a reader might want to raise objections. But before doing so it is a good idea to think charitably about some implicit premises the person making this argument might have had in mind. Two obvious candidates are:

IP1: *Because* *the state cannot absolutely guarantee that innocent people are not executed;*
IP2: And *because* *a society ought to avoid absolutely executing innocent persons;*

IP1 can actually be appended to the comment about Jones, Smith, and Robertson to yield the following:

IP1a: *Because* *the cases of Jones, Smith, and Robertson make it clear that the state cannot absolutely guarantee that innocent people are not executed;*
IP2: And *because* *a society ought to avoid absolutely executing innocent persons;*
C: *Therefore*, *capital punishment should be abolished.*

This is a charitable, and defensible, version of the original argument. Note the use of "absolutely" inserted into **IP1a** and **IP2**. It defends the argument against someone who would be willing to accept a few mistakes.

Finally, consider this argument:

E42: *Free speech should never be restricted in any way because it's a core value I deeply believe in.*

The problem here is that the premise asserts a subjective preference, and subjective preferences generally weaken an argument. The fact that I like or approve of something is not a strong reason why everyone else should. As such, it is hard to tell what implicit premise might strengthen **E42**. There is also a problem with vagueness: is the point that a core value should never be restricted or that a core value the speaker deeply believes in should never be restricted? Perhaps the most charitable interpretation is this:

E42.1:
*P: **Because** free speech is a core value of this society;*
*IP: And **because** core values should never be restricted in any way;*
*C: Free speech should **therefore** never be restricted in any way.*

However, this may be *too* charitable. We have to be careful not to "read in" ideas that are not plausibly there and to "read out" ones that are. The speaker's statement of personal belief has been edited out, and this may well be a change she would reject. When editing, accuracy takes precedence over charity. The point of the principle of charity is to present an argument in its strongest form, but not to distort it by making it stronger than it really is. That is what **E42.1** seems to do.

EXERCISE 1.6

Use the principle of charity to insert or restate a premise or a conclusion such that each of the following is then presented in its strongest possible form.

*1. We need to do something about concussions in contact sports.

2. Novels are so irrelevant. No one wants to read them anymore.

*3. Given that virtually everyone has a cellphone these days, there should be a law against using them while driving.

4. Perhaps Brown is guilty, but he acted with the best of intentions.

*5. We shouldn't go there because it's too crowded and, really, nobody goes there anymore.

6. Since critical thinking skills allow those who possess them to understand arguments more clearly, everyone should try to acquire these skills.

*7. Students who plagiarize should be shot because they completely undermine the point of education.

8. Because voting is mandatory in Australia, people are more politically aware than they are here, so voting should be mandatory here.

*9. Given that cleanliness is next to godliness, there's no point in being clean.

10. Since money doesn't grow on trees, we can therefore spend freely.

*11. Canada should become a republic like the United States because it is the twenty-first century, after all.

12. You shouldn't accuse people of plagiarizing. I was accused of it, but I didn't do it.

VII. Summary

This chapter has introduced you to *arguments,* the pathways of critical thinking. Since an argument consists of a conclusion (*what* its author thinks is true or at least very probable) supported by premises (the reasons *why* it is true or reasonable or probable), the best way to be able to recognize one is by being able to identify *premises* and *conclusions*. It is also important to be able to distinguish between arguments and *explanations* and to recognize the subspecies of arguments: *reports on arguments* and *counterarguments*.

Since arguments can be embedded in longer passages of text, it is necessary to be able to extract them. In doing so, it helps to set the argument out as clearly as possible, an exercise that may involve restating parts of it. Since arguments or parts of arguments may be condensed, you also have to look for any *implicit assumptions* (either premises or a conclusion) that are necessary to complete the argument. Finally, be mindful of the *principle of charity,* which tells you that when you restate someone else's argument, put it in the strongest *possible* form. Be charitable, but not too charitable.

Something to Think About

Try to apply the principle of charity to the following "argument" allegedly from a student essay.[7] I have changed (and deleted) some of the terminology while keeping the structure intact. Can you make sense of it? My unsuccessful effort is included with the Answer Key, on page 297. In fairness, this looks much like the work of some famous philosophers I could mention but won't:

"Being is being unique. Being, reality, essence, or truth is uniqueness. The geometric point in the centre of the circle is nature's symbol of the immeasurable uniqueness within its measurable effect. A centre is always unique; otherwise it would not be a centre. Because uniqueness is being, or that which makes being what it is, everything that is real is based on a centre."

---

7 Adapted from http://instruct.westvalley.edu/lafave/writsamp0.htm.

CHAPTER TWO

Diagramming Arguments

- Independent and codependent premises
- Diagramming arguments
- Recognizing premises that act as sub-conclusions
- Recognizing and inserting implicit assumptions into diagrams
- Diagramming longer and more difficult arguments
- Dealing with wordy arguments

This chapter is about diagramming arguments—literally about drawing connections between premises and conclusions. Learning to diagram arguments is an excellent way of developing your grasp of how they are put together and, therefore, of how they can be evaluated, attacked, or defended.

I. Independent and Codependent Premises

This section will introduce the two kinds of premises used in arguments and show you how to diagram them.

Independent Premises

Let's begin with a definition:

> *Definition: An **independent premise** is one that does not rely on any other premise for its contribution to the argument.*

Independent premises stand completely on their own. For example:

E1: *(C) You should allow me to write a make-up test **because** (P1) my bus was late. (P2) Plus, I got A's on the first two tests.*

Using the skills developed in Chapter 1, we can write the argument as follows:

*P1: **Because** my bus was late;*
*P2: And **because** I got A's on the first two tests;*
*C: **Therefore**, you should allow me to write a make-up test.*

In this example, neither premise relies on the other. Each one offers a distinct reason for accepting the conclusion, which means that each one offers *independent* support for it. If one of the premises were removed the other would not be affected (although the argument would not be as strong, insofar as two relevant and true premises are better than one). To indicate independence, we use the following diagram that connects the premises to the conclusion but not to one another:

Here is another example:

E2: *(P1) That club is really far away (P2) and it never has live music. (C) It isn't worth going to.*

Once again, we list the premises and the conclusion:

*P1: **Because** that club is really far away;*
*P2: And **because** it never has live music;*
*C: **Therefore**, it isn't worth going to.*

Like **E1**, each of **E2**'s premises is a distinct reason for accepting the conclusion. Hence, they too are independent and a diagram of **E2** would be identical to **E1**.

An argument can have more than two independent premises. In theory, it can have any number. For example:

E3: *My game console, my email, my Facebook page, and my cellphone have all been hacked. I am not being paranoid about being pursued.*

Strictly speaking, there are four premises here:

P1: Because *my game console has been hacked;*
P2: Because *my email has been hacked;*
P3: Because *my Facebook page has been hacked;*
P4: *And* **because** *my cellphone has been hacked;*
C: Therefore, *I am not being paranoid about being pursued.*

Each of these premises is an independent piece of evidence for the conclusion that the speaker is not being paranoid: someone really is out to get him. The diagram for **E3** is simply an extension of **E1**:

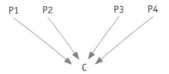

So to recap, independent premises offer distinct reasons for accepting a conclusion and as such they are not connected to other premises. They are, in effect, a list of premises in support of the conclusion. It's worth adding that there is safety in numbers: the more relevant and true premises in support of a conclusion, the stronger the argument.

Codependent Premises

In contrast to independent premises, codependent premises rely on one another.

Definition: Codependent premises support the conclusion as a pair or a set.

For example, consider another version of **E2**:

E4: *(P1) That club is really expensive (P2) and expensive clubs are never worth the money, (C) so it isn't worth going to.*

In this argument, **P1** and **P2** are codependent premises because they offer support for the conclusion only when they are taken together. On its own, **P1** might seem to offer some support for **C**, but only if we assume **P2** as an implicit premise. Otherwise, **P1** would be open to the objection that lots of clubs are worth going to even if they are expensive. So **P1** supports **C** only when paired with **P2** and is therefore codependent with it. If **P2** were changed to read "Expensive clubs are always worth the money," **P1** would then offer a reason for going to the club as opposed to not going. So the very intention of **P1** is determined by **P2**, which means that given **C**, **P2** is *implicit* in **P1**. In other words, it has to be stated (or at least be assumed) as a premise to get to **C**. Conversely, **P2** would not support **C** without the information supplied by **P1**. If the club was inexpensive **P2** would be completely irrelevant. So it is only as a linked pair of premises that they provide support for the conclusion. To indicate the codependence of these premises, we use the following diagram:

Like independent premises, any number of codependent premises can be strung together. For example:

E5: *(P1) It's possible to purchase books on the Internet, (P2) and Internet shopping is easier than going to a store. (P3) What's more, people always follow the path of least resistance. (C)* **So** *bookstores as we know them are doomed.*

In this argument it takes the combination of all three premises to support the conclusion. **P1** offers support for the conclusion only if **P2** and **P3** are true. If Internet shopping was not easier or if people did not always follow the path of least resistance, **P1** would be irrelevant. Similarly, **P2** is relevant only if **P1** and **P3** are true, and **P3** is relevant only if **P1** and **P2** are true. The relevance of each premise depends on the truth of the other two, which means that they are a codependent set. Hence, the diagram of **E5** looks like this:

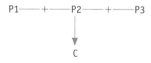

So while independent premises are a list of distinct reasons for accepting a conclusion, codependent premises stand or fall as a single set of reasons. That means that an attack on one of them is an attack on all of them. If one of the premises in **E3** is false there is still support for the conclusion because the other premises are relevant. But if any one of the premises in **E5** is false the argument collapses because that makes the other premises irrelevant—there is no compelling reason to conclude that bookstores are doomed.

Distinguishing between Independent and Codependent Premises

Distinguishing between independent and codependent premises can sometimes call for careful reading, but with a little practice it is not too difficult to manage. Compare the following two arguments:

E6:
(A1) (C) Goldfish aren't pets (P1) **because** *a pet has to be capable of interacting with its owner (P2) and goldfish can't interact with their owners.*
(A2) (C) Goldfish aren't pets (P1) **because** *they don't interact with their owners (P2) and they are always distracted by thoughts of world domination.*

A1 offers a pair of codependent premises in support of the conclusion that goldfish aren't pets. By contrast, the premises in **A2** constitute two independent reasons for accepting that conclusion. Like all codependent premises, the premises of **A1** *share information*. To be specific, these premises share information about animals interacting with their owners. We are informed in **P1** that pets have to be able to interact with their owners and in **P2** that goldfish cannot do that. This sharing, or transferring, of information between premises is what makes them codependent. By contrast, in **A2** a goldfish's interaction with its owner and its being distracted by thoughts of world domination are discrete reasons for accepting the conclusion. No information is shared between these premises.

With this in mind, let's return to **E5**. First consider **P1** and **P2**:

P1: **Because** *it's possible to buy books on the Internet*
P2: **Because** *Internet shopping is easier than going to a store*

As you can see, information about Internet shopping is shared between **P1** and **P2**, making these premises codependent. Now look at **P2** and **P3**:

P2: **Because** *Internet shopping is easier than going to a store*
P3: **Because** *people always follow the path of least resistance (i.e., do what is easiest)*

Here, information about the easiest course of action is shared between **P2** and **P3**. As a result, **P2** is codependent with **P3**. Since **P1** is codependent with **P2**, **P2** is in effect the linchpin connecting **P1** to **P3**, thereby uniting all three premises into a codependent set. Note, however, that with three premises there are two items of shared information: the first is about Internet shopping and the second is about doing what is easiest. **P1** informs us that Internet shopping is now possible; **P2** connects this claim to the claim that Internet shopping is easier than going to a store; and **P3** connects this to the claim that people always do what is easiest. Information flows through the three premises, connecting them. That's why a false or irrelevant codependent premise is like a virus that affects all the other premises in the set.

Sometimes independent premises may look as if they share information and therefore be taken for codependent premises. In **E3**, for example, the premises all refer to electronic devices being hacked. Nonetheless, each of those premises is a separate and discrete bit of evidence in support of the conclusion: a list of things that have been hacked. While the assertion that a particular electronic device has been hacked is common to all the premises, *no information is shared or transferred* from one premise to the next; delete one and the rest remain in place.

Now compare the following two arguments:

E7: *(P1)* **Because** *all humans are mortal (P2) and* **because** *all students are human, (C)* **therefore** *all students are mortal.*

P1 and **P2** are clearly a pair of codependent premises that share information about humans, and so they stand or fall as a pair.

E8: **Because** *all humans are mortal,* **because** *all gerbils are mortal,* **because** *all giraffes are mortal, and* **because** *all beavers are mortal,* **therefore** *all mammals are mortal.*

While **E8** may look like **E7**, it is actually like **E3**. All it amounts to is a list of mammals that are mortal. Like **E3**, it enumerates some "things" that share a characteristic, but there is no sharing of information between the premises. Like **E3** or **E6(A2)**, you can delete any one of the premises—strike it off the list, in effect—and the others will remain in force. That is not the case with **E7**. If **P2** were omitted from that argument it would still have to be assumed—treated as an implicit premise—to make **P1** relevant.

In summary, the first thing to consider when looking at an argument is whether you are dealing with an unconnected *list* of premises—a collection of evidence, so to speak. If so, you have an argument with independent premises. If, on the other hand, the premises share information and therefore stand or fall as a set, you have an argument with codependent premises.

EXERCISE 2.1

Exercises marked by an asterisk (*) have answers included in the Answer Key at the end of the text.

Diagram each of the following basic arguments.

*1. The murder was not premeditated because if it were the murderer would have brought a weapon. But he did not bring a weapon.

Continued >

2. Property rights are guaranteed in our constitution and yet the government has not respected the property rights of Aboriginal peoples. So the government cannot justify its actions in this regard.

*3. She should leave you because you're always working, you're self-absorbed, and you're having an affair with someone else.

4. The government should scrap the long gun registry because it is way too expensive and, moreover, it's unconstitutional.

*5. On average, women live several years longer than men, so women should expect to be widowed because they tend to marry men who are older than they are.

6. Long distance runners need a diet rich in carbohydrates and since you are a long distance runner you need to eat lots of carbohydrates.

*7. The senator should not have to resign because the money she took from Mega-Corp was not for work that was related to any of her governmental duties. Besides, she gave most of the money to charity, has otherwise led an exemplary life, and has served her country honourably for many years.

8. You should ask her out now because she hasn't been in town long enough to hear about your reputation. In addition, I heard that she's lonely.

*9. Democracy is the only viable system of government because the only alternatives are dictatorship or anarchy. Both of these are terrible systems of government, and terrible systems are not viable.

10. Global warming is a myth created by scientists. Scientists are simply self-interested academics who need people to pay attention to their research, and no one is going to pay attention to research that says everything is okay.

*11. If you have talent it's easier to be motivated, and if you are motivated you are more likely to succeed, and that means you will likely have more control over your life, which in turn means that you will be happier. So talent does contribute to happiness.

12. URSKTM, UR2GTBT, 143.

II. Arguments with Both Independent and Codependent Premises

Independent and codependent premises are not mutually exclusive; an argument may contain both. This section will examine some examples of this.

Some Basic Combinations

Let's begin with a fairly basic combination of independent and codependent premises:

> **E9:** *(C) I don't think we should go on holiday there (P1)* **because** *it's hot in the summer (P2) and neither of us reacts well to heat. (P3) It's also too expensive.*

P1 and **P2** are codependent premises that share information about hot places; the support each gives to the conclusion requires the presence of the other premise. **P3**, however, is a separate claim that lends support to the conclusion independently of **P1** and **P2**. Hence, a diagram of **E9** looks like this:

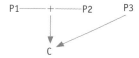

Now consider a longer argument:

> **E10:** *(P1) He was seen leaving the scene of the crime; (P2) he and the deceased had been arguing earlier in the day; (P3) he has a history of violence; (P4) he was the only person with access to a Glock .45, (P5) and that was the murder weapon. (C) I think* **we can conclude that** *he is our prime suspect.*

This may look like a long list of independent premises, but it's not. **P1**, **P2**, and **P3** are independent premises supporting the conclusion, but **P4** and **P5** are codependent. Without **P5**, **P4** is not necessarily evidence of guilt. Nor would **P5** be evidence without **P4**. The relevance comes from the fact that they share information about the murder weapon. The diagram for **E10** therefore looks like this:

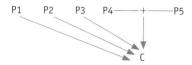

There are many, many possible arrangements of premises, and therefore a great, almost infinite, variety of possible diagrams. Obviously, it's not possible to demonstrate them all, but one argument structure you need to be aware of is that of premises supporting other premises. For example, **E9** might have been expanded to read as follows:

> **E11:** *(C) I don't want to go on holiday there (P1)* **because** *it's hot in the summer—(P4)* ***the average daytime high is 34 degrees Celsius****—(P2) and neither of us reacts well to heat. (P3) It's also too expensive.*

The new premise, **P4**, is independent evidence for the truth of **P1**. It could, of course, be hot even if the average temperature was not 34 degrees Celsius, but if **P4** is true then so is **P1**. So it fits into the diagram as follows:

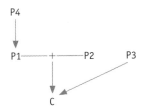

Now here's a more complex example of how premises support other premises:

E12: *(C) Human rights are not universal. (P1)* ***Because*** *rights are the result of agreements among people (P2) and* ***because*** *such agreements are contractual, (P3) rights are contractual. (P4) What is contractual is not universal (P5)* ***because*** *contracts vary from society to society (P6) and* ***because*** *they are liable to change even within a society.*

Let's see how the conclusion has been derived. First, **P1** and **P2** support **P3** as follows:

P1: ***Because*** *rights are the result of agreements among people;*
P2: And ***because*** *such agreements are contractual;*
P3: (Therefore), rights are contractual.

Since **P1** and **P2** are codependent premises that share information about agreements among people, a diagram of this part of the argument will look like this:

In the second half of the argument, the premise signal words introducing **P5** and **P6** indicate that they offer support for **P4**:

P5: ***Because*** *contracts vary from society to society;*
P6: And ***because*** *they are liable to change even within a society;*
P4: (Therefore), what is contractual is not universal.

P5 and **P6** are, however, independent premises. **P5** talks about contracts varying *among* societies and **P6** talks about them varying *within* societies—the information they contain is not shared. Take either one away and the other will retain its relevance. Hence, the diagram for this part of the argument is as follows:

We can now place the two parts of the argument side by side and get on with the next task, which is to work out how to connect them:

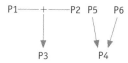

To do so, it is necessary to think about the relation between **P3** and **P4**, so let's set them out along with the conclusion:

*P3: **Because** rights are contractual;*
*P4: And **because** what is contractual is not universal;*
*C: **Therefore**, human rights are not universal.*

It's evident that **P3** and **P4** are codependent premises because they share information about contracts. So the complete diagram of **E12** looks like this:

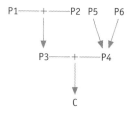

Since **P3** and **P4** are supported by other premises, this is a layered structure that makes for a persuasive argument *if* the premises are true and relevant.

Sub-Conclusions

In **E12**, you may have noticed that **P3** and **P4** look like conclusions to arguments within a larger argument, and indeed they are. To indicate this, "therefore" was inserted in parentheses along the way. What this demonstrates is that an argument is often a group of smaller arguments, and therefore contains sub-conclusions.

*Definition: A **sub-conclusion** is the conclusion of an argument within a larger argument, in which it has the role of a premise.*

E12 is a composite of three smaller arguments, and in it **P3** and **P4** are sub-conclusions. Even very simple arguments may be composed of two or more smaller arguments and may therefore contain sub-conclusions. For example:

> **E13:** *(P1)* ***Because*** *there is a recession (P2) people will lose their jobs (C)* ***and as a*** *result there will be a lot of houses on the market.*

P1 leads to **P2**, which leads to **C**, so the diagram looks like this:

P1

P2/SC

C

Like **P3** and **P4** in **E12**, **P2** in **E13** can quite reasonably be treated as a sub-conclusion (**SC**) because it is derived from **P1**. Like **P3** and **P4** in **E13**, it would sound quite natural with a conclusion signal:

> *P2/SC: People will* ***therefore*** *lose their jobs.*

However, it is also quite clearly a premise leading to the main conclusion **C**.

When a premise is a sub-conclusion, it is sometimes introduced with conclusion signals. For example:

> **E14:** *(P1)* ***We can conclude that*** *teachers are overly particular* ***because*** *(P2) they never stop splitting hairs, (P3) and splitting hairs is a real sign of being overly particular. (P4) And* ***since*** *overly particular people tend to talk a lot, (C)* ***it follows that*** *teachers tend to be talkative. (P5) Certainly my critical thinking teacher was.*

E14 contains two connected arguments. First, there is one to show that teachers are overly particular and then, based on that argument, a second one to show that they are talkative. In the first argument, **P2** and **P3** are codependent premises (they share information about splitting hairs) in support of **P1**, which is why it's introduced with a conclusion signal. This part of the argument runs as follows:

> *P2:* ***Since*** *teachers never stop splitting hairs;*
> *P3: And* ***(since)*** *splitting hairs is a real sign of being overly particular;*
> *P1/SC:* ***We can conclude that*** *teachers are overly particular.*

P1/SC is then linked codependently to **P4** (they share information about being overly particular) as follows:

> *P1/SC:* ***Since*** *teachers are overly particular;*

*P4: And **since** overly particular people tend to be talkative;*
*C: **It follows that** teachers tend to be talkative.*

The diagram of the argument looks like this:

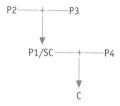

Just to keep you on your toes, an independent premise (**P5**) has been included and has to be added to the diagram of **E14**:

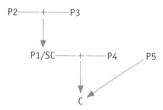

There are three reasons for introducing sub-conclusions. First, since they may not be obvious to some readers it is necessary to be explicit about their presence in arguments. Second, they underline the "group" structure of many arguments. Third, as in **E14**, there may be premises that bear conclusion signals just because they are sub-conclusions. In practice it is not essential to designate sub-conclusions in a diagram, but if you are not aware of them you can be fooled by these signals. To emphasise this point, here is one last example:

> **E15:** *(P1) **Because** gymnasts are pound for pound stronger than football players, (P2) and **because** they are also more flexible and better coordinated, (P3) they are **therefore** better athletes than football players. (C) **So we have to conclude** that gymnastics is more demanding than football (P4) **because** the athleticism required by a sport is an indication of how demanding it is.*

Like **E14**, **E15** has two conclusion signals: one in **P3** as well as **C** itself. This tells the reader that she is dealing with an argument within an argument. **P1** and **P2** are independent premises in support of **SC/P3**, which is codependent with **P4**, which as a pair lead to **C**. This yields the following diagram:

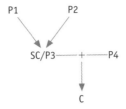

In summary, because arguments may actually be groups of arguments, some premises function as sub-conclusions on the way to the main conclusion. Even though it isn't necessary to designate them as such (but go ahead if you want to), you need to be aware of them. Sometimes you will run across more than one conclusion signal, and this clearly tells you that the argument contains a sub-conclusion and therefore that it is a group of arguments. But even when this is not the case, be alert to situations where a premise can bear both a premise and a conclusion signal.

EXERCISE 2.2

I. Diagram the following arguments. Indicate any premises that you think could reasonably be designated as sub-conclusions.

*1. Money can't necessarily buy happiness because some things that make people happy—such as a child's smile—can't be bought.

2. Romantic movies are wonderful because they speak to the heart, and when our hearts are spoken to we become more alive. What's more, romantic movies take us away from our boring lives, and anything that can do that is wonderful.

*3. Judged sports should be excluded from the Olympics because there is too much subjectivity in them, and subjectivity undermines the appearance of fairness. It is crucial that Olympic sports be seen as fair. So because boxing is a judged sport, it should be excluded from the Olympics.

4. There's no point in going back to school. I have a well-paid job, I have good employee benefits, and I have good prospects for promotion. I also really like what I'm doing and when that's the case you should keep doing what you're doing.

*5. Because space travel over huge distances will not be possible for a very long time, if ever, and because you and I will not live that long, we will never get to other solar systems. Nor are we likely to receive messages from outer space. So it is likely that we'll never know for certain whether there is other intelligent life out there.

6. Given that long passes make the game a more wide-open affair, and given that wide-open games can be dangerous on the smaller NHL ice surfaces, they should cut out long passes by putting the red line back into the game. There have been too many injuries since they took it out.

*7. Since if we adopt your standard we'd never wear any makeup, and since we like wearing makeup, and since we also like doing what we like, we shouldn't listen to people like you. And anyway, you're never in favour of anything that's any fun.

8. Because I lost my job I had to borrow money for school, and because of that I had to carry a higher debt load, which led to my nervous breakdown.

*9. Since the cost of holding the Olympics is prohibitive—just look at what the last Games cost—and since they pose real security risks, we should not bid on them. We also have more urgent priorities that the bid money could be spent on.

10. Skiing is overrated. It's too cold, there are long lineups for the lifts, and it's all downhill. So we shouldn't go skiing.

*11. The Olympics are well worth the cost of holding them. Cities that host them benefit from increased tourism, athletes get to compete at the highest level, and for two weeks the world comes together. And if something is worth it, we should go for it.

12. Since when you give your word to someone you should keep it, and since he gave his word to me, he should therefore have done what he said he would. But he didn't, so what he did was wrong.

II. *Make an argument that will fit each of the following diagrams. You can order the premises and conclusion any way you want as long as you retain this structure.*

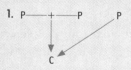   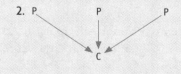   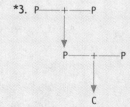

Continued >

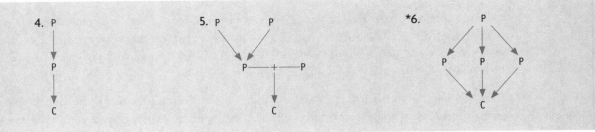

III. Implicit Assumptions

This section will build on Section V of Chapter 1, as well as on an idea introduced in Sections I and II above: it is important to be aware of implicit premises and conclusions. Where they occur, they have to be inserted into diagrams.

So far as premises are concerned, the basic rule is that an **implicit premise** is always going to be codependent with a premise that is already present in the argument. In short, with codependent premises, each premise implies the other, and if one is left out it should be inserted. For instance:

E16: *(P1) Elections cost a lot of money (C)* **so** *they should not be called on a whim.*

Like some of the examples we looked at in Section V of Chapter 1, this is a very simple argument that is not likely to cause any confusion. Still, it is important to be aware of the implicit premise it contains, one that is perhaps sufficiently obvious that we scarcely think about it:

IP: Expensive undertakings require a serious reason.

It's even possible to add a second implicit premise—a whim is not a serious reason—but we can let commonsense assume it. So the diagram of the argument looks like this:

An independent premise cannot be implicit for the simple reason that since it is independent of every other premise in an argument, none of them can imply it. For example:

E17: *(P1)* **Because** *Fitzroy had motive to steal from Chesterton (P2) and* **because** *he had opportunity as well, (C) he is* **therefore** *probably the thief.*

P1 and **P2** are independent premises. Take either one away and the other will still stand. It's possible that the speaker has other reasons for suspecting Fitzroy. Maybe he had previously been cheated by Chesterton and wanted revenge, but since neither of the premises implies this we cannot insert it. With independent premises, you play the hand you are dealt—you cannot arbitrarily add a new card.

One very good reason for paying attention to implicit premises is that sometimes you run across one that is debatable or even outright false. When it is brought to light its codependent premise will look much less relevant than it did when its accompanying premise was merely implicit. After all, an implicit premise may be overlooked. Since diagrams of codependent premises require the insertion of implicit premises, they can shine a revealing light on arguments. For example:

E18: *(C) Abortion should be against the law **because** (P1) it is wrong to kill people.*

The implicit premise here—codependent with **P1**—is:

IP: Fetuses are people.

The problem is that this is not, strictly speaking, true. In most jurisdictions in North America we become legal "persons"—beings with civil liberties protected by law—only at birth. From the point of view of the person making this argument, the implicit premise may well be better left unsaid because stating it will probably invite disagreement.

Conclusions can also be left implicit. Imagine that someone ruminating on the frailty of the human species were to say the following:

E19: *Well, (P1) humans are mortal and (P2) mortals make mistakes.*

Any competent English speaker will easily fill in the implicit conclusion:

IC: Therefore, humans make mistakes.

So the diagram will look like this:

As in this example, implicit conclusions follow most naturally, but not exclusively, from codependent premises. Compare the following argument with **E19**:

E20: *(P1) Chess is boring, (P2) checkers is boring, (P3) and backgammon is boring, so . . .*

The most *probable* implicit conclusion to this string of independent premises is:

IC: Strategic board games are boring.

Hence, the principle of charity would suggest reading it in and diagramming the argument as follows:

But "reading in" requires care. Consider this example:

E21: *(P1) I'm really interested in him, (P2) the term is almost over, (P3) and I won't see him until next fall, so . . .*

What follows? Is it "I should speak to him," "I should ask him out," or "I should give him my cell number"? There is no way to tell exactly what the speaker has in mind even though the idea of making contact is certainly implied. Unlike conclusions that follow from codependent premises, ones that follow from independent premises cannot always be pinned down with any degree of certainty. Respect the principle of charity and enter conclusions where they seem evident, but be careful not to leap to too specific a conclusion, one that takes you beyond what the evidence allows.

EXERCISE 2.3

Find the implicit premise or conclusion in each of the following and insert it into a diagram of the argument with the premises numbered. One of these examples contains no implicit assumptions.

*1. Rocks do not make good pets because they have no emotional lives, they're heavy to carry, and they can hurt you if you drop them on your foot. Besides, a pet should have a heartbeat.

2. They say only about 25 per cent of eligible voters under the age of 25 bother to vote in any given election. Well, why should they? None of the political parties understand their concerns and none of them listen to what they have to say. Parties tailor their messages almost exclusively to older voters.

*3. According to quantum physics, a subatomic particle can take two different paths at the same time. Since we can't really comprehend that sort of idea, there is no point in even thinking about quantum physics.

4. Theft is defined as taking what you do not have title to. In the treaties the First Nations peoples signed with the European settlers, they ceded only a small portion of the land that is North America. Yet Europeans have taken almost all the land.

*5. Physics is difficult; chemistry is difficult; biology is difficult; physiology is difficult.

6. Since students need to be prepared for the working world, universities need to teach more practical things.

*7. Studying philosophy, literature, and art are important aspects of higher education. Such disciplines make us more rounded people by opening us up to ideas and experiences we would otherwise know nothing about.

8. Since illiterate and semi-literate adults earn much less than those who are literate—all the studies confirm that—and since no one wants to be consigned to a low-income ghetto, schools really need to focus on literacy.

*9. People who don't like baseball are barbarians. Unlike football, which is a warlike game played by gladiators in stadiums, baseball is a peaceful game played in parks. What's more, baseball is a relaxed game where no clock is ticking; it just goes on until it's over.

10. Judged sports should not be in the Olympics because the essence of the Olympic ideal is fairness. Yet look at boxing, gymnastics, and ice skating: these are judged sports where the scoring is notoriously open to abuse.

*11. If you go to a professional basketball game you will pay several hundred dollars for a decent ticket for the privilege of being bombarded by extremely loud music even when the play is on. It's not worth going.

12. U std him up. He shd h8 u.

*13. She has texted me every day, she has asked me for help with her essay, she has offered me rides home, and she has asked me out for coffee.

14. Control freaks are always neurotic, and Arturo is a control freak.

IV. More Difficult Arguments

This section will deal with diagramming more complex arguments.

The Benefits of a Clear Picture

By providing a clear picture of an argument's structure, diagrams help you to understand it and to work out whether (and how) it can be defended or refuted. In Chapter 1 you learned that a false or irrelevant premise weakens an argument, but if the premise is independent this is not necessarily fatal if other supporting premises remain. For example:

E22: (C) The Raptors aren't worth watching. (P1) They play a boring style, (P2) they have no real stars, (P3) they lose far too many games, and (P4) besides, I just don't like them.

P4 is, strictly speaking, irrelevant. The fact that the speaker doesn't like the Raptors is not really evidence that they aren't worth watching. However, if we delete that premise we are still left with three reasons which, if true, give support to the conclusion. By contrast, showing that a codependent premise is false or irrelevant may destroy an argument because it has a domino effect, taking its codependent premise down with it along with any independent premises that support either of the pair. For instance, consider this diagram:

E23:

If you wanted to refute this argument, discrediting **P4** or **IP**—showing that at least one of them was false or irrelevant—would do the job because as one goes down so does the other. That means that if you refute either **P4** or **IP**, **P1**, **P2**, and **P3** no longer have anything to support. On the other hand, successfully attacking any or all of **P1**, **P2**, and **P3** will weaken the argument but not destroy it.

To get a clearer sense of this, consider a word version of **E23**. The implicit premise will be omitted below and then added in once we figure out what it should be.

> **E24:** *(P1) Since Twitter is like an ongoing conversation, (P2) since Facebook allows you to share photos and keep track of people, (P3) and since smartphones allow you to contact people no matter where you are, (P4) social media allows you to keep in touch with people really well. (C) Therefore, everyone should get more involved with social media.*

As we saw in **E23**, if **P1**, **P2**, and **P3** are false it weakens **P4** (we no longer have evidence that it is true) and, by extension, the whole argument. **P4** is a sub-conclusion, but without its supporting premises it would only be an unsupported premise. We would, accordingly, have less reason to accept it, though we might still do so. But experience shows that **P1**, **P2**, and **P3** are true, so attacking them is not a good strategy, which leaves **P4** in place. However, **P4** is linked to an implicit codependent premise, and we now need to see what it is:

> **IP:** *Everyone should want to keep in close contact with other people.*

It is not clear that **IP** is true. A lot of people may have no good reason for being in close contact with others. If so, the argument is a lot weaker because **P4** and **IP** are codependent premises. So if you wanted to attack **E24**, showing that **IP** is false would be a good strategy because **P4** would become irrelevant.

Or would it? We have a strange situation here. Suppose **IP** is shown to be false but someone insists on retaining **P4** as an independent premise supported by **P1**, **P2**, and **P3**. This would alter the structure of the argument as follows:

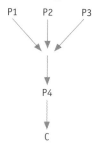

On a generous application of the principle of charity, the premises still give *some* support for **C**, but not nearly as much as the **E23** structure does. In fact, the conclusion the premises now support is closer to something like this:

C': *Therefore, those who* want *to be in close contact with people should be involved with social media.*

As always happens with codependent premises, refuting **IP** has had the effect of destroying the relevance of **P4** as a premise for **C**. It may retain relevance as an independent premise for **C'**, but that is a different argument. The rule holds: as one codependent premise goes, so goes the other.

As arguments grow in complexity, understanding their architecture—how they are constructed and where their vulnerable points are—becomes more and more important. With this in mind, let's examine an argument that is slightly longer and more difficult than the ones we have already seen:

E25: *(P1) Voters are alienated from the political process (P2) **because** they have become apathetic and lazy. (P3) **This is because** no one takes the time to understand the issues. (P4) Most voters prefer style over substance in the news they read, watch, or listen to (P5) **because** they want information to be simple and superficial, (P6) **because** frankly they can't follow more complicated discussions. (P7) Dictatorial leaders thrive when voters are alienated, (C) and when that happens democracy shrinks away to almost nothing.*

While **E25** may seem harder to follow than **E24**, it's actually pretty easy to put everything in order. To begin, **P2** is signalled by the word "because," which tells us that it supports **P1**. (Think of this structure: "believe x because y.") In turn, **P3** supports **P2**: not taking time to understand the issues is put forward as evidence of being apathetic and lazy. The result is this:

*(P3) **Because** voters don't take the time to understand the issues, (P2) voters have become apathetic and lazy and (P1) **therefore** voters are alienated from the political process.*

So the diagram for the first three premises is as follows:

Next, turn your attention to **P4**, **P5**, and **P6**. The latter two independent premises, both introduced by "because," indicate the same straightforward structure as above: **P6** supports **P5**, while **P5** supports **P4**. This yields the following:

> *(P6) Because voters can't follow complicated discussions (P5) they want informa-*
> *tion to be simple and superficial, (P4) and **so** they prefer style over substance in*
> *the news they consume.*

Now the two strings have to be put together. A little attention will show that the argument runs backward from **P6** to **P1**, which is one of the principal points the author is arguing. Hence, what we have is a string of independent premises in reverse order:

Let's put this into words:

> *P6: **Because** voters can't follow complicated discussions;*
> *P5: **Because** they **therefore** want information to be simple and superficial;*
> *P4: They **therefore** prefer style over substance in the news;*

*P3: **Because** voters **therefore** don't take the time to understand issues;*
*P2: And **because** they **therefore** have become apathetic and lazy;*
*P1: They are **therefore** alienated from the political process.*

Note that there are conclusion signals in every premise after the opening **P6**. That's the sub-conclusion effect: a chain of independent premises is like a series of short arguments, each premise being a conclusion of the previous one. Since readers intuitively understand this, conclusion signals sound appropriate, although they are a bit awkward.

From **P1** the author derives:

P7: When voters are alienated, dictatorial leaders thrive;

And from there proceeds to:

C: When that happens (i.e., when dictatorial leaders thrive), democracy shrinks away to nothing.

So **P7** follows from **P1**, and **C** follows from **P7**. The argument is a straight line of independent premises:

P6

P5

P4

P3

P2

P1

P7

C

Once diagrammed, it's easy to restate the argument clearly:

(P6) Because voters can't follow complicated discussions (P5) they want information to be simple and superficial, (P4) which means they prefer style over substance in the news (P3) and therefore don't take time to understand political issues. (P2) This makes them apathetic and lazy (P1) and as a result they become alienated from the political process. (P7) When that happens dictatorial leaders thrive and (C) as a result democracy shrinks away to nothing.

You are now in a position to evaluate the argument. Take it step by step and decide whether you agree or disagree with what is being said. Does each premise reasonably lead to the next one? Are there implicit premises that may need to be inserted?

An important lesson to be drawn from **E25** is that the *order of exposition*—the order in which the premises and conclusion appear—is seldom the same as the *formal order* of the argument, which is what a diagram captures. Some rearranging of premises is usually necessary (and the conclusion has to go to the end). Diagramming an argument makes it a lot easier to keep track of the premises and put them in formal order. When doing so, it isn't unusual to have to make decisions about implicit premises. If you think one really does go without saying you can omit it, but it is important to think about whether your audience will still follow you. If in doubt, put the implicit premise in. Moreover, inserting an implicit premise may, as in **E24**, reveal that an argument is much weaker than it appears when it is left out; that is one reason why people leave some premises implicit. By showing connections clearly, diagrams can expose both connections and disconnections among premises and places where an implicit premise has to be inserted if the argument is to be complete. This is a valuable aid to making, understanding, and evaluating arguments.

EXERCISE 2.4

Write out the premises and conclusions for each of the following arguments, restating them where necessary and inserting any implicit assumptions. Number the premises and produce diagrams.

*1. All the studies done on this topic clearly state that there is absolutely no evidence that prayer has any observable effect. Maybe prayer has an effect on God, but in that case God doesn't seem inclined to do anything about it. The war in Libya is a serious matter but, on the evidence available, it is not going to be changed in any way by appeals to God.

2. I just read a study that argues partying reduces the number of colds you get. The study says that students who regularly went to parties got 25 per cent fewer colds, mainly because they are more active and energetic than non-partygoers to begin with, and because of this they have better immune systems. The study also suggested that partygoers are more sociable than non-partygoers and so have probably been exposed to more germs over the years and have therefore developed better immune systems.

*3. Far from helping the economy, the stimulus package may actually undermine it because a stimulus package makes people believe that they are always entitled to government aid, and this will sap their initiative. In addition, because those who were most responsible for the recession are the most likely to be rewarded by bank bailouts and forgiveness of bad mortgages, bad habits will be encouraged, which will further undermine the economy. Finally, the government will have to run a deficit, because there is no way it can meet these obligations and balance its budget.

4. The government wants to cut support for postsecondary education, but that's horribly wrong because then the number of students able to afford higher education will shrink drastically—everything in our experience suggests as much—and if that happens, a lot of people will be unable to get ahead in life. When governments start to pursue policies that are horribly wrong they undercut the very fabric of the community, so that's what will happen here.

*5. The skeptic can doubt everything except that he doubts, because to doubt he doubts is also to doubt. And since to doubt is to think, neither can the skeptic doubt that he thinks. This means that the skeptic cannot doubt that he exists.

6. A perfect being must exist, otherwise I would not be here.

*7. People say that if evolution is true then our lives have no meaning, but that's not so because all evolution suggests is that there is no preordained purpose to our lives, and a lack of preordained purpose does not indicate a lack of meaning because, even without preordained meaning, we can decide what makes our lives meaningful. So people should stop going on about how evolution destroys meaning.

8. "No social order ever disappears before all the productive forces for which there is room in it have been developed, and new, higher relations of production never appear before the material conditions of their existence have matured in the womb of the old society. Therefore since mankind only takes up such problems as it can solve, we will always find that the problem itself arises only when the material conditions necessary for its solution already exist or are at least in the process of formation."[1]

*9. If there really are magical powers then our trust in the laws of nature is misplaced, and since experience shows us that misplaced trust is foolhardy, if there are magical powers our trust

---

1 Karl Marx, "Critique of Political Economy," in *Marx & Engels: Basic Writings in Politics and Philosophy* (New York: Anchor Books, 1959), 44.

Continued >

in science is foolhardy. But since there are no magical powers—because every claim that someone possesses them has been discredited by reputable tests—there is no reason to mistrust science.

10. The proper approach to resolving various constitutional issues is to find a way for different views to coexist, not to cling to one and reject the other, because this approach focuses on minimal impairment of cultures and proportionality in judgment. Neither of these things exists when a *niqab*-wearing woman is banned from working for government agencies or having access to services she has paid for in her taxes.

*11. "Evolution is not a theory in crisis. It is not teetering on the verge of collapse. It has not failed as a scientific theory. There is evidence for evolution, gobs and gobs of it. It is not just speculation or a faith choice or an assumption or a religion. It is a productive framework for lots of biological research, and it has amazing explanatory power. There is no conspiracy to hide the truth about the failure of evolution."[2]

12. Because an event is a specific occurrence in time, no one event is necessarily connected to any other. What we call the relation of cause and effect is thus merely the recognition that one event has regularly been followed by another. But regularity is not the same thing as necessity.

*13. The philosopher of science T.S. Kuhn argued as follows: when there are competing scientific theories the question of which is the better theory cannot be settled by reference to the standards of either theory, since it is precisely those standards that are being questioned. Hence, any argument that does refer to one of these sets of standards will necessarily be circular, because it will amount to claiming that the theory is true because it is true.

14. _____ deserved to win the Oscar for best picture. It was a serious film that showed us something important about the human condition while managing not to be preachy. At the same time it worked as a taut thriller. This combination of art and entertainment is hard to achieve. The film's main competitor, _____, was wonderful to look at but it had a hackneyed storyline and was almost completely devoid of intellectual content. Technical innovation alone should not be enough to win an Oscar.

*15. My English teacher argues that going to see Shakespeare performed on the stage is a far better use of my time than playing video games, but she's wrong. After all, pleasure is a legitimate pursuit, and since I get much more pleasure out of video games than I do out of Shakespeare, I should go with the games. Moreover, times change and standards change with it. Since I'm a child of my times and the teacher is a child of her times, her standards are different than mine, but I don't think they are necessarily better.

---

2 Todd C. Wood, "The Truth about Evolution." *Todd's Blog*, September 30, 2009.

V. Wordy Arguments

This section deals with passages of text that require editing to get them into a straight-forward argumentative form.

As you saw in Chapter 1, some arguments contain sections that are beside the point, verbose, or overly emotional, and a critical thinker needs to strip them away to get at the core argument. For example, consider the following:

E26: *Desperate for funding, our universities seem to have become culpably blind to the extremely important issue of women's rights (or lack thereof), a fact that seems to account for their joyful acceptance of petrodollars from _____. Is it the case that we are so desperate for funds that we congratulate ourselves on doing something we should condemn—the government's insistence that women must have a male chaperone to attend school? This is absolutely shameful by Canadian standards. Our universities are implicitly serving to oppress women by supporting gender apartheid.*

This passage is emotionally charged, containing a number of turns of phrase—"culpably blind," "joyful acceptance," "gender apartheid"—that call for caution. While the choice of words is appropriate insofar as it expresses the author's feelings, the critical reader needs to be wary of them when evaluating the argument. It's a good idea, therefore, to restate the argument in more neutral language:

Because (P1) universities want the money that _____ students bring, (P2) they are willing to accept that government's insistence that women students from _____ have male chaperones while attending school. (P3) This violates Canada's commitment to gender equality. (C) Hence, our universities are implicitly contributing to the oppression of women.

The diagram of this argument is quite straightforward:

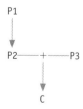

To make this argument as clear as possible, we could insert a codependent implicit premise alongside **P2** and **P3**:

IP: To violate our commitment to gender equality is to oppress women.

Just as you need to calm down emotionally charged arguments, you also need to distinguish the relevant parts of wordy arguments—that is, the parts that actually belong to the argument—from the irrelevant bits. Consider the following argument:

E27: *(P1) What specific part of human nature so miraculously frees pedestrians of the debilitating distraction of electronic devices, yet inflicts drivers with a mental and physical impairment that is apparently worse than driving drunk? (C) If drivers in motion are subject to fines for playing with their electronic toys behind the wheel, then pedestrians should also be penalized for their tinkering with electronic toys while afoot. (P2) Let me offer an example: the other day I witnessed no fewer than three pedestrians completely absorbed in text messaging crossing six lanes of two-way traffic downtown during rush hour.*

This argument opens with a **rhetorical question**, that is, a question whose answer is deemed to be obvious (**E26** also contained one). In an argument, take the implied answer to this question as a premise which makes that claim. (That does not mean that you necessarily accept the claim! Even though the author of the rhetorical question takes the answer to be true, you may disagree. Go back to **E26**: not everyone would agree with the answer [no] the author has in mind there.) In this case, the letter writer is obviously assuming that drivers and pedestrians are equally susceptible to being distracted by electronic devices. His sarcastic use of "miraculously" underlines this fact. So let's call the rhetorical question **P1** and rewrite it as a simple claim:

P1: Pedestrians are as susceptible as drivers to being distracted by electronic devices.

P2 offers independent support for this contention in the form of the author's observations. But it is very wordy and can be simplified for the purpose of bringing out the argument:

P2: I have seen three pedestrians commit dangerous acts while using electronic devices.

(The acts could be listed separately to provide three premises.) The conclusion, which is also needlessly wordy, can be stated more directly as follows:

C: If drivers are fined for using electronic devices when driving, pedestrians should also be fined for using them in traffic.

So the argument can be restated as follows:

*P2: **Because** I have seen (three) pedestrians commit dangerous acts while being distracted by electronic devices;*

*P1: And **because** that indicates that they are equally as susceptible as drivers to being distracted by electronic devices;*

*C: **Therefore**, if drivers are fined for using electronic devices while driving, pedestrians should be fined for using them in traffic.*

Behind all the verbiage is a very straightforward argument:

It's easy to get lost in a tangle of words and emotional phrases and to give up on the argument. It takes discipline to try to untangle things, but diagrams can make the task easier because it engages you in the exercise of making everything fit. No one is going to diagram every argument she comes across, but doing so with intricate, emotional, wordy, or important ones is never a bad idea.

EXERCISE 2.5

Edit the extraneous material and produce a clear and concise version of each argument, then diagram it. Once again, be alert for implicit assumptions.

*1. Look, here's what I think. Tell me if you disagree. What I think is that when people really want something they will try to get it, no matter what. So when people don't really go after something it's because they don't really want it. But since people sometimes say they want something and yet don't go after it, they don't really want it. That's irrefutable.

2. Women athletes should not be paid as much as men because professional sport is a business and in business what someone is paid is a function of demand, and men are in more demand than women. Now you can disagree with me if you want—lots of feminists do— but how many people come out to see women play hockey or soccer? They have to pay the spectators to go watch that stuff.

*3. Rebecca is using scare tactics to defend the legislation that protects the Canadian music industry. She claims that without this protection we would be deprived of the current rich choice of Canadian artists. I don't understand that at all. How would more competition in

Continued >

the music business reduce our choice? Wouldn't it increase it? Besides, under the legislation Canadians currently pay more than Americans for albums by Canadian musicians. Just compare the prices in New York to those in Toronto.

4. Let's get serious. Stop the propaganda. The Earth has been warming and cooling in natural cycles for thousands of years; long before man had a chance to leave a "carbon footprint." To think that we poor creatures are powerful enough to affect the global climate, particularly the temperature, is ludicrous, silly, and inane. Stopping a hurricane or a volcanic eruption would be easier than trying to raise or lower the temperature of the Earth.

5. I cannot believe you think hockey is a less interesting sport than soccer. In the first place, hockey is faster—after all it's played on skates—and in the second place it's more physical—there is a lot of body contact. With your antiviolence attitude you may think that's irrelevant, but it's not. It makes the game more of a challenge and is a greater test of the player's courage. I think you are just taking an anti-Canadian stance to get under my skin. How can you say that with a straight face?

6. Giving up smoking is the easiest thing in the world. I know because I've done it thousands of times. (Mark Twain)

*7. "After a lifetime, or what seems like two, of listening to the big government/small government 'debate,' it may be time to redefine the issue. As much as anything, that is because neither party produces a smaller government. One side supports a stronger national safety net. The other supports a bigger military. Either way, the results in terms of budget size and government employees remain about the same. Both sides want reductions in the other side's agenda. And both sides are reluctant to tell voters they have to pay for what they want."[3]

8. All marriages should be arranged. As Mark Twain said, youth is wasted on the young. They're idiots who don't know what the hell they're doing most of the time. Let young people choose their mates and two-thirds of the time divorce or at least a breakup follows. In societies where marriage is arranged this rarely happens. Since marriage is supposed to be forever, arranged marriages work better than when young people decide on mates for themselves.

*9. "[O]ne of the things that makes politics hard for . . . voters in the United States is just how impossibly large this nation is . . . [N]o matter what you do, it's often going to feel like it's

---

3 Gary Hart, "Restore the Republic." *The Huffington Post*, 22 March, 2010.

a meaningless drop in the ocean. And given the legislative process, time passes between campaigning and enacting bills into law, and by then many people have moved on to other parts of their lives. But individuals, and especially small groups of people, really can make a difference. This battle over health care reform is one time when it wasn't just the lobbyists, or the interest groups, or the politicians [who had an effect]. [W]hole bunches of small groups of people, in states and Congressional districts across the nation, turned a handful of Senate races and a dozen or two House races around and, sixteen or so months later, their work is . . . most likely going to change the country. If you're one of them, it's a day to be proud of what you've done."[4]

10. You know, it's really a lot harder for young people to get established in today's world. It's as if the older generation is out to get us. Full-time jobs are becoming more and more scarce; baby boomers are refusing to retire and are hogging the jobs that still exist; employers offer fewer and fewer job benefits. It's an awful mess—just sickening.

*11. Universities have an obligation to protect the free exchange of ideas on campus, no matter how offended some people may be by the expression of these ideas. Yesterday, it was Ann Coulter who was silenced. Who will it be tomorrow? Unpopular ideas will necessarily offend many people, but their expression is essential to the process of democracy.

12. According to a recent poll, if voters under the age of 25 voted in substantial numbers the Green Party would win the election. More's the pity, then, that this age group doesn't vote. Only 20 per cent of them did in the last election. This means, unfortunately, that Parliament is made in the image of older voters. Dementia rules!

*13. Every year during the NCAA basketball tournament we get a generalized debate about what to do with the ungainly beast we call intercollegiate athletics. Everyone seems to be looking desperately for the perfect model. But I'm here to tell you that there is no such thing, for it is its imperfections and problems that constitute its beauty. Anyone who loves diversity has to love this tournament and even look forward to the day when it expands to 128 teams. For three glorious weeks in March and early April, the NCAA's anarchistic family comes together around basketball. Everyone involved is able to dream, both universities with undergraduate enrolments of 60,000 and private colleges with enrolments of 1500. Whether the dreams are great or small—win a round or win it all—the tournament is the ultimate meritocracy. The best players play, and the best teams advance. No one gets a free pass; everything is earned.

---

4 Jonathan Bernstein, "Elections Matter." *The Daily Dish* blog, 22 March, 2010.

Continued >

14. I'm fed up with all these award show for films and music and literature. What's the point? It's all about art, and one's view of art is largely subjective. So what we are getting with these award shows is a reward system for the most popular products, not the best. In fact, since our view of art is subjective, there is no "best" at all. It's all a myth.

VI. Summary

Diagrams are a valuable aid to critical thinking because they provide a kind of road map for setting out and evaluating arguments. Here is a short checklist of questions that will help you develop diagrams and evaluate the results:

1. How do the premises combine to form the argument (i.e., what is its structure)? Remember that the order of exposition—the author's order—may not be the same as the formal order of the argument.
2. Is it one argument or a group of arguments? (i.e., are there sub-conclusions?)
3. Do implicit assumptions have to be inserted?
4. Are there gaps or leaps in the argument that can't be fixed with implicit premises?
5. Are there irrelevant premises?
6. Are there false premises?
7. Do parts of the argument need to be simplified or rewritten to remove emotionally charged language or wordy passages?
8. Once the argument has been edited and diagrammed, where are its most vulnerable points? How can it be attacked or defended?

Something to Think About

I have always found that the best way to take lecture notes is by constructing some sort of diagram; not an argument diagram necessarily, but something that gives me a picture of what I am listening to. If I simply take pages of notes, I need to sort it all out later—do the work over, in effect. What was the topic? What were the main subtopics? What examples were used and what did they relate to? Not long ago I participated in a team-taught course where five of us took turns lecturing in the first meeting of the week. Then each of us took our own group of students for a seminar later in the week. Even though we used PowerPoint presentations, when colleagues were lecturing I wanted a good summary to work from in the seminar. My strategy was to note the topic of the lecture in the centre of the page and then draw arrows out to subtopics and yet more arrows to indicate elaborations of those topics. I almost always kept this diagram to a single page. Then I could glance at it and bring back the lecture. Moreover, since the process of making the diagram was a listening aid, it served a double purpose. Had I lost a diagram after a class (with me, that's always a possibility) my retention of the lecture would be the better for having made it. Here's a partial sample of a page:

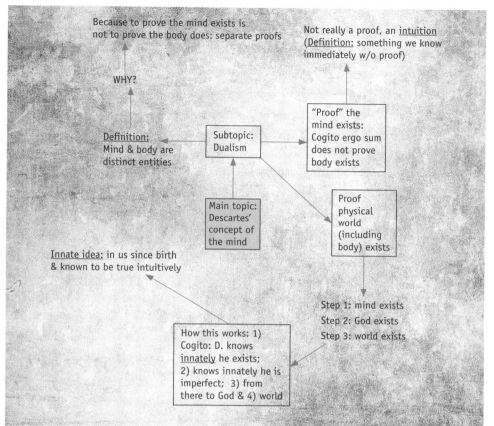

Because to prove the mind exists is
not to prove the body does: separate proofs

WHY?

Not really a proof, an <u>intuition</u>
(<u>Definition:</u> something we know
immediately w/o proof)

<u>Definition:</u>
Mind & body are
distinct entities

Subtopic:
Dualism

"Proof" the
mind exists:
Cogito ergo sum
does not prove
body exists

Main topic:
Descartes'
concept of
the mind

Proof
physical
world
(including
body) exists

<u>Innate idea:</u> in us since birth
& known to be true intuitively

Step 1: mind exists
Step 2: God exists
Step 3: world exists

How this works: 1)
Cogito: D. knows
<u>innately</u> he exists;
2) knows innately he is
imperfect; 3) from
there to God & 4) world

The point is not whether you understand the details of this diagram—after all you weren't at the lecture. The point is that if you are the one doing the diagramming your understanding and your recall will be much better for having done it. You can also do this with reading: work from marginal notes and underlining in the text to produce a diagram of what you have read. (You can do this on a computer, of course.) As a colleague of mine used to say, you have to work the material. At first it may feel awkward, but after a while you will find it comes almost naturally. And once it does you will be a more efficient student, which means that you will learn more in less time.

3

Where Arguments Go Wrong

- Rhetoric as the art of persuasion
- Informal fallacies: irrelevant premises
- Informal fallacies: exaggerated premises
- Rhetorical strategies: loaded terms, code words, euphemisms
- Biases: social and cognitive

In this chapter we will examine some of the ways in which arguments go wrong. First we will look at problems caused by inserting premises that may sound relevant but are in fact irrelevant. Second, we will consider the ways in which biased thinking subverts arguments.

I. Rhetoric and Informal Fallacies of Relevance

This section will introduce the concept of rhetoric and examine one pernicious form of it: fallacies of relevance.

The term **rhetoric** comes from the ancient Greek word for "speaker." A speaker's goal is, unsurprisingly, to get people to believe what he says. The philosopher Aristotle (384–322 BCE) thus defined rhetoric as "the faculty of observing in any given case the available means of persuasion."[1] He distinguished two such means: one involves stirring up an audience's emotions or otherwise distracting their attention while the other comes "from the speech itself, when we have proved a truth . . . by means of the persuasive arguments suitable to the case in question."[2] In other words, the speaker may make the audience *feel* that what he is saying is true or he may, through rational argumentation, *demonstrate* that it is true. Aristotle's teacher, Plato (427–347 BCE), was suspicious of the professional rhetoricians (or orators) of his day because he thought they practised only the first kind of persuasion, ignoring rational arguments and swaying audiences with emotional and otherwise irrelevant appeals. In short, they subverted critical thought. As a result, Plato huffed, the orator has "no need to know the truth about things but merely to discover a technique of persuasion . . ."[3]

Plato's view of the matter is not completely fair. As Aristotle recognized, persuasion relies on a variety of techniques and the fact that some are non-rational does not automatically make them bad. In fact, insofar as rhetoric entails paying attention to language (searching for *le mot juste*) it is a good thing. It is perfectly acceptable to dress an argument up a little by appealing to the audience's emotions, imagination, and aesthetic sensibilities so long as it still has a rational, truth-seeking core. But sometimes, as Plato said, less honourable motives are at work. A good comparison is the house selling process, when vendors paint over cracks in walls, put out flowers, and generally do things to make the place look better than it really is. The warning that applies to house sales—*caveat emptor* (buyer beware)—also applies to the marketplace of ideas. A critical thinker has to be able to recognize when rhetorical tricks have been used to disguise the lack of a rational argument. Bad arguments—ones with premises that are emotionally powerful but untrue or irrelevant—can succeed in convincing an audience every bit as well as (and sometimes better than) ones that

---

1 Aristotle, "Rhetoric," 1355^{b}1, 27-8, in *The Complete Works of Aristotle*, Volume Two, ed. Jonathan Barnes (Princeton: Princeton University Press, 1984), 1255.

2 *Ibid.*, 1356^{a}1, 13-21.

3 Plato, "Gorgias," 459bc in *Collected Dialogues*, eds. Edith Hamilton and Huntington Cairns (Princeton: Princeton University Press, 1964), 242.

have true and relevant premises. The point of critical thinking is to be able to distinguish between these types of arguments and to be persuaded only by the latter.

Fallacies are among the most common deceptive rhetorical devices.

*Definition: A **fallacy** occurs when, for one reason or another, the premises do not support the conclusion.*

Fallacies fall into two broad categories: formal and informal. In this chapter, we will be concerned with **informal fallacies**, which are ones where the problem lies in the content of the premises. Informal fallacies have been categorized in a number of ways and literally hundreds, if not thousands, of them have been identified. The ones you will meet in this section and the next are examples of **fallacies of relevance**. As you know, a good argument must have premises that are true and relevant to the conclusion. While in many cases it's difficult to assess the truth of a premise without doing some fact checking, it is generally possible to assess its relevance, which is the first line of defence against being persuaded by a bad argument. This point was discussed in Chapter 1 but it will be useful to review it here:

E1(A1):
P1: Sir Thomas Crapper invented the flush toilet;
P2: Almost all of Crapper's working life was in the nineteenth century;
C: Therefore, the flush toilet was probably invented in the nineteenth century.

A2:
P1: The flush toilet was invented in the sixteenth century;
P2: The Protestant Reformation took place in the sixteenth century;
C: Therefore, Shakespeare wrote plays in the sixteenth century.

In **A1** the facts are not well known. Some readers will think the premises of **A1** are true, some will think one or both are false, and others simply won't know. Nonetheless, everyone can agree that the premises are relevant to the conclusion because, if they are true, they give it very strong support. Unfortunately, the premises are false, which means that, based on them, we don't know whether the conclusion is true. (It's not.) By comparison, in **A2** the premises and the conclusion are all true but the premises are irrelevant to the conclusion. They give us no reason to accept the claim that Shakespeare wrote plays in the sixteenth century. Once again, not every reader will know whether the individual statements are true or false, but because its premises are clearly irrelevant **A2** can be rejected without checking to see whether they are. That's not the case with **A1**, where the premises are relevant and so truth has to be checked.

Bear in mind that even though **A2**'s premises are irrelevant they don't contain fallacies. Fallacies are much more subtle, which is why it's important to examine them in detail. What follows is a sampling of informal fallacies that supply irrelevant premises in support of a conclusion. If you understand them you will be able to recognize other fallacies of relevance when you come across them.

Appeal to Pity

The **appeal to pity** fallacy occurs when a person tries to distract her audience by making them feel sorry for her. The appeal is irrelevant *if* it does not speak to the actual issue under discussion. Here's an example:

> **E2:** *You should let me rewrite this test because I can't afford to flunk this course. If I do my parents will throw me out of the house.*

All sorts of consequences follow from failing a test, but the teacher is not responsible for them and cannot accept them as relevant reasons for rescinding the failure.

This is not to say that pity—sorrow for someone's suffering—is never a relevant concern. For example:

> **E3:** *You should let me rewrite the test because I wrote it right after my father died. I know I shouldn't have, but I did and I failed.*

This is not a fallacious argument. A teacher will almost certainly make exceptions for a student who has just lost a parent. In fact, this is a very different kind of consideration from **E2**: the death of a parent is a *relevant* reason why someone should be allowed to rewrite a test. It is not an appeal to pity at all, but rather a reasonable argument in favour of compassion. By comparison, in **E2** the appeal is directed solely to *avoiding the consequences of the failure*, which is clearly irrelevant because it does not speak to *why* the student failed. In that example, an appeal to pity is substituted for relevant reasons for being allowed to rewrite.

The point is that to avoid making an appeal to pity you have to offer an *exculpatory* reason—one that frees you from blame—rather than simply trying to avoid the consequence of an action. However, when a reason is offered it needs to be assessed and, as was pointed out in Chapter 1, this can be tricky work. Because arguments occur within social and cultural frameworks that do much to determine what is and what is not an exculpatory reason, there are few universal rules. There could, for example, be cultures in which the death of a parent is not considered a good reason for failing a test. Students sometimes feel that a lovers' quarrel is a good reason for not doing work, but teachers seldom do. To be relevant, appeals must speak to the reasons for the action and not simply to avoiding the consequences of the action, but those reasons must also be ones all parties can accept as exculpatory. The first distinction is one any critical thinker can make; the second depends on a shifting social standard open to negotiation, and in multicultural societies it can cause confusion. In summary, an appeal to pity is essentially a way of saying, "I know there is no good excuse for what I did, but please don't punish me."

Appeal to Flattery

One effective way to persuade people is to tell them how wonderful they are—an **appeal to flattery**. Here is a slightly edited version of an email I received a few years ago:

> **E4:** Hi Sir, I was sorry to see you have left _____ . You were the best prof I had last year. I recommended your class to a bunch of my friends. Anyway, my final grade was 70, which was really fair, but I want to major in philosophy and my average is just slightly low to get into honours. If I had a 72 in your course I'd just get over the edge. Like I said, 70 is fair but I'd really appreciate it if you could give me 72. Anyway, thanks again for a great course.

This is an absolutely blatant attempt to flatter (in this case, a successful one; as the philosopher and politician Edmund Burke said, "Flattery corrupts both the giver and the receiver") and most of us can see through it.

Sometimes, however, the process is subtler:

> **E5:** I think any intelligent person will agree with me.

Here, the speaker is attempting to cajole the audience into agreeing with her on the basis that if they do so they are intelligent. There is an implied argument in **E5**, but it is not absolutely clear what it is. The statement acts as a premise to which a second and flattering *implied* premise needs to be added to generate a conclusion. The result could look like this:

A1:
P: Because any intelligent person will agree me;
IP: And because you are intelligent;
IC: You will therefore agree with me.

But it could also look like this:

A2:
P: Because any intelligent person will agree with me;
IP: And because you do not agree with me;
IC: You are therefore not an intelligent person.

A1 flatters the audience by insinuating that they are intelligent, while **A2** contains the flip side insult that if you do not agree with the speaker you are unintelligent. So **E5** is a double-edged sword.

The basic rule is that flattery is never relevant to an argument but, like appeals to pity, there are nuances. Consider this case:

> **E6:** I think you will work out the answer on your own because you have strong math skills.

This is not flattery, simply an observation, because it constitutes a relevant reason for thinking that the person in question will get the answer. Notice too that in **E6** the speaker is not being self-serving; he is not trying to get some benefit from the person he is speaking to.

Compare this to **E4** where the author of the email was definitely trying to extract something beneficial from me. If there is a relevant reason why a person should do something beneficial for another person, it needs to be stated directly. Flattery is no substitute.

Ad Hominem Argument

As **E5(A1)** demonstrates the flip side of flattery is an attack, and this strategy gives rise to a number of fallacies, such as the ***ad hominem*** argument. The term *ad hominem* means "against the person," which is what an *ad hominem* argument is: a personal attack directed against the arguer in place of a genuine counterargument. The *ad hominem* fallacy is the flagship of attack arguments. For example:

> **E7:** *Joan: I think we need to raise both corporate and personal tax rates if we are going to get out of the recession. After all, we're running a deficit and the country is already deep in debt.*
> *Ai-Li: Of course you favour raising taxes; you're one of those tax-and-spend liberals.*

Ai-Li's response is not a counterargument to Joan's; it is simply an irrelevant attack on Joan characterizing her as a fiscally irresponsible liberal. When an argument is given, you have to speak to it and not the person who has made it. Joan may be a tax-and-spend liberal, but that's beside the point. She has made a coherent argument and it has to be addressed.

Sometimes an "attack" may be relevant and therefore not *ad hominem*. For example:

> **E8:** *Joan: I think we need to raise both corporate and personal tax rates if we are going to get out of the recession. After all, we're running a deficit and the country is already deep in debt.*
> *Ai-Li: The problem is that you're a tax-and-spend liberal who favours raising taxes in every situation. When the economy was booming and there was no deficit you still spoke in favour of tax increases.*

Here, Ai-Li has addressed Joan's argument and her characterization of Joan as a tax-and-spend liberal—that is, someone who always wants to raise taxes—is relevant and has been incorporated into her counterargument. So it's not fallacious.

Appeal to Ridicule

The **appeal to ridicule** is a cousin of the *ad hominem* fallacy where, instead of mounting a counterargument when one is called for, you simply heap scorn on your opponent's argument:

> **E9:** *Pierre: We need to take the blindside head hits out of hockey. It's unfair to target someone's head, especially if he can't see you, and even more to the point it's dangerous. Players have had their careers ended by blindside hits.*
> *Mike: You want to take the violence out of hockey. It's a man's game and I don't want to see it turned into figure skating.*

There's no counterargument here. Mike is simply inviting people to laugh at Pierre's position by characterizing it as unmanly, probably to an audience who thinks this kind of "manly" behaviour is an essential quality of hockey. Some arguments may deserve ridicule (though ridicule is never an argument, but rather a refusal to argue), but not Pierre's. He has taken a reasoned position and Mike's response fails to address it. Mike is simply playing to the audience.

Suppose Mike had answered this way:

> **E10:** *You simply want to take the violence out of hockey. It's a man's game and manly games are violent. It's not figure skating, eh?*

The last sentence would still be ridicule and irrelevant to Mike's argument, but the rest of this response does constitute a counterargument composed of two codependent premises:

> **P1:** *Because hockey is a manly game;*
> **P2:** *And because manly games are violent;*
> **C:** *Hockey has to be violent.*

This certainly isn't the strongest argument ever made—"manly" is a pretty vague term—but at least it's an argument.

Poisoning the Well

When someone uses the **poisoning the well** fallacy, he or she is making a pre-emptive strike. The strategy is to attack the person *in advance* to discredit her, and by association her argument, before she even makes it:

> **E11:** *The honourable member is going to argue, in the manner of all heartless reactionaries, that crime is a major social problem and that we need to put more poor people in prison.*

Like the previous two fallacies, poisoning the well relies on insult. Here, the speaker has attempted to characterize negatively the "honourable member" before she has had a chance to make her argument. Notice the implied premise:

> **IP:** *Heartless reactionaries are wrong about crime.*

If we remove the rhetoric and ignore the comment about putting more poor people in prison, this implied premise can be restated as:

> **IP:** *The honourable member is wrong to say that crime is a major social problem.*

Now we have an argument that runs as follows:

> **P:** *The honourable member is going to argue that crime is a major social problem;*
> **IP:** *Crime is not a major social problem;*
> **C:** *Therefore, the honourable member is going to make a wrong argument.*

From this it follows that we don't need to put more people in prison. Although it's risky to predict what someone will say, these are nonetheless relevant premises. The problem is the speaker has not explicitly made this argument, but has instead relied on the "heartless reactionary" insult (and the pitying description "poor"), which suggests that, given the source of the argument, the argument itself will be beneath contempt. If the fallacy does its work, people will pay less attention to the "honourable member's" up-coming argument.

A subtler way of poisoning the well might run something like this:

E12: *I think you all understand that I have spent 20 years working to ensure that this company is both productive and profitable, even if it often meant making sacrifices in my family life. The proposal I have set before you is not only a sound one, it is the product of two decades of hard work and experience. Our CEO loves it. But my good friend Valerie, drawing on her three long years of experience in the field, disagrees. I am fascinated to hear what this young woman has to say.*

The speaker (who is also guilty of an appeal to pity) has done his best to cut the ground from under his colleague's feet before ceding the floor to her. Even if his listeners are not swayed by the irrelevant appeal to how hard he has worked for the company, his characterization of the "inexperienced" and "young" Valerie disagreeing with a person of his long experience is intended to result in her having a much harder time convincing those in attendance that her position is correct. Will they give her a fair hearing?

Finally, consider this variation on the theme:

E13: *Are we going to hear that lame old chestnut about the need to respect other cultures, no matter how silly their traditions are?*

In this case, the person has been spared but the argument itself has been pre-emptively ridiculed.

Tu Quoque

Closely allied to the strategies of flattery, ridicule, and poisoning the well is the ***tu quoque*** fallacy, which in Latin means "you too." Often referred to as the "look who's talking fallacy," it consists of trying to turn the tables on an opponent who has accused you of wrongdoing by claiming that he is as guilty as you are. Politicians seem particularly attached this fallacy:

E14: *Sure the sponsorship scandal is messy and we're not proud of it, but you have to remember that the Conservatives had plenty of scandals when they were in office. So they have no right to accuse us of wrongdoing.*

Sometimes there is a certain merit in pointing out that the other side is no better than you are—it can make your relative moral statuses clear—but when you have to defend your actions this is not a relevant response. A person's failure to act in a certain way is not necessarily evidence that the action she recommends or the advice she gives is bad. For example:

> **E15:** *You tell me I should quit smoking but you smoke like a chimney, so why should I quit?*

"Quit smoking" is good advice even if it comes from a smoker. Plenty of relevant reasons can be offered in support of it. The speaker's inability to quit is irrelevant; it may in fact be relevant because part of the problem here is addiction.

However, as always, there are nuances. Consider this example:

> **E16:** *You tell me I shouldn't cheat on exams but you cheat all the time, so I don't think I need to listen to you.*

In this case the other person's insistence on cheating would certainly seem to make her advice less compelling. *Moral* advice that you do not follow yourself generally carries little weight, nor should it. In such cases, actions speak louder than words.

Red Herring

"Red herring" is a fox-hunting term referring to the practice of using the strong scent of red herrings to lure dogs away from the trail they are following. The idea is to train the dogs to ignore the scent of the fish and concentrate on the scent of the fox. Hence, the fallacy consists of raising an irrelevant issue and presenting it as a relevant consideration that settles the argument in one's favour. Here is an example:

> **E17:** *How can people say that the police overstepped their bounds during the demonstration? Police are the backbone of civil order. They are fine men and women doing a difficult job.*

Even if what the speaker says about the police is true it does not address the question whether the police overstepped their bounds in a particular instance.

In a sense, all fallacies of relevance are red herrings since a **red herring** is just an irrelevant consideration. Hence, the red herring is a kind of catch-all for arguments that don't fit neatly into one of the above types. In its most blatant form, it raises an issue that is so irrelevant it is nonsensical. Consider this hypothetical legal defence:

> **E18:** *My client cannot be guilty of this crime. He has served his country honourably for years.*

The lawyer is insinuating that a long-serving public servant would not commit a crime, but since his client has been accused of doing just that this is a red herring. No one is innocent simply because of who they are.

EXERCISE 3.1

Exercises marked by an asterisk (*) have answers included in the Answer Key at the end of the text.

For each of the following, decide which fallacy is being used. Some examples contain no fallacies.

*1. What right have you to punish me? Haven't you ever done anything wrong?

2. My opponent will surely trot out that lame idea about how an ounce of prevention is worth a pound of cure. Consider it if you will, but I think we need to take a stronger stance.

*3. I think we should all give a respectful hearing to this fine young woman. The experience will do her good.

4. As an economist I'm sure you understand that all credible economists agree with me.

*5. The university's decision to stop offering language courses, including Latin, reminds one of the American politician who famously expressed his disdain for the teaching of foreign languages by saying "If English is good enough for Jesus, it's good enough for me."

6. The Liberals are attacking the prime minister for proroguing Parliament without cause, but all parties do that.

*7. I'm sure you have thought long and hard about this issue, as have I. In my experience, two thoughtful people can always find an acceptable compromise.

8. When you, the jury, contemplate the terrible fact that this child has lost her parents because of this dreadful accident, I am confident you will see the need to find in her favour and grant her the sum of money we have requested as damages.

*9. I just don't see how you can fail me. I mean, I've come to every class and I really like your course.

10. Maybe we should give Sophie's argument some thought; after all, it's not the worst one I've ever heard. Only last week I heard one that made less sense.

*11. The argument that hip hop is a degenerate form of music is just what you'd expect to hear from an old fart like you.

12. Look, you may think I should stay in tonight and study for that test tomorrow, but come on—you're a man of the world.

*13. My client should not be tried on these corruption charges. As a well-known public figure she has been subject to abuse and ridicule. Surely she has suffered enough.

14. You really think we should increase immigration? Only an overeducated, unworldly, inexperienced dweeb would make that argument.

Continued >

*15. I think you ought to give me another chance to write the test. It wasn't my fault I missed it—the bus was late—and anyway you don't seem like the kind of teacher who is going to fail someone for a stupid, bureaucratic reason.

16. What do you mean I haven't studied enough? Do you think I want to fail?

*17. I respect your position, I really do. It's very thoughtful, but I think you'll agree it's not perfect.

18. I don't see how the Church of England can tell me I can't get a divorce when it let Prince Charles get one. After all, when he's king he'll be the official head of the church.

II. Fallacies of Exaggerated Relevance

The seven fallacies in Section I substituted irrelevant appeals for reasoned arguments. A related group of fallacies have premises that raise what seem to be relevant points—ones you might actually want to consider—but greatly exaggerate their significance. A minor consideration is presented as an irrefutable premise. Let's call them fallacies of exaggerated relevance.

Misleading Vividness

Misleading vividness is a common fallacy of exaggerated relevance. This fallacy occurs when a single event or anecdote is described in vivid detail and then presented, without the support of statistical evidence, as a relevant justification for a particular course of action:

> **E19:** *My girlfriend wanted me to drive to Florida this winter, but I refused because one of my friends got into a terrible accident on the interstate just north of Jacksonville last winter—bodies were everywhere. He spent a month in the hospital. It's just not safe.*

The speaker has concentrated on the details of his friend's accident, blowing one incident up into a reason to refuse to drive on a particular highway. He is right to take note of the accident, but if it moves him to do anything it should be to look for data about that stretch of road. Maybe he will find that it is particularly dangerous and maybe not, but he should not let one anecdote, no matter how graphically described, substitute for hard evidence.

Here's another example:

> **E20:** *Don't take that route to the store. I took it last week and got mugged by these really scary guys.*

Once again, without more supporting evidence this fallacy fails to distinguish between what is possible and what is probable. Had the speaker added "It's dark at night and there aren't many people around," the result would have been a persuasive argument in which being mugged was a relevant piece of information.

As you can see, misleading vividness is a fallacy that tends to crop up when events are dangerous or dramatic in some way. Single incidents of floods, airplane crashes, fires, and the like are often cited as reasons for arriving at a particular decision. This is not completely irrational—an airplane crash is extremely dangerous even if it is also extremely rare—but it doesn't make for a good argument.

Appeal to Popularity

The **appeal to popularity** fallacy resides at the opposite end of the spectrum from misleading vividness. It occurs when someone either cites popularity as proof or exaggerates the importance of popularity as proof. For example:

> **E21:** _____ is a great movie. It has set box office records all over the world. Everybody loves it. A half billion fans can't be wrong!

We have to be a bit careful with this example. One simple response to it is "Maybe they can be." Box office records *may* be worth considering when discussing whether a movie is "great," but it does not automatically follow that just because many people like something that what they like is any good. The difficulty with **E21** is that when it comes to taste in film or literature or any type of art, standards can vary quite a bit. There seems to be no objective truth in such matters. So maybe popularity is relevant in some cases—politicians often consider it, wisely or unwisely, a valid reason to pursue certain policies—but it is nonetheless a good idea to be suspicious of it as an argument in favour of a given view. North Americans seem, for example, to have a love affair with certain fast foods that are demonstrably dangerous to their health.

Similarly, the fact that many people believe something is not, in and of itself, proof that what they believe is true. For thousands of years almost everyone believed that the sun orbited Earth, but they were wrong. In many parts of the world most people once believed that slavery was a perfectly acceptable institution or that burning witches was a good idea, but who would agree today? If there is reliable evidence for a belief most people will accept it, but the fact that most people believe something does not constitute proof.

Yet, as always, we have to be careful because there are cases where popularity is definitely a relevant consideration. Consider this example:

> **E22:** *Ronald Reagan was a successful politician. He was extremely popular.*

This is not an example of the appeal to popularity fallacy because popularity is a relevant consideration when it comes to assessing whether someone is a successful politician. After all, it got Reagan elected president twice, and in politics that is a hallmark of success.

Bandwagon Fallacy

The **bandwagon** fallacy is closely related to the appeal to popularity. The difference is that while the appeal to popularity takes the fact that something *is* popular as proof of its goodness or truth, the bandwagon fallacy cites the fact that something is *growing* in popularity:

> **E23:** *There is absolutely nothing wrong with tweeting. Every day a million more people take it up.*

Think of the implied premise in this argument:

> **IP:** *Trends that are increasing in popularity are good trends.*

If so, there was a time when there would have been good reason to take up smoking or to join in the persecution of various groups of people.

The bandwagon also has a reverse effect:

> **E24:** *That television show is beginning to suck. Look at how viewer numbers are declining.*

The show may indeed have, as they say, "jumped the shark" and gone into irreversible decline, but the loss of viewers does not clearly demonstrate that it "sucks." Maybe it got a lot better and a lowbrow audience has moved away from it. The lesson of the appeal to popularity and the bandwagon fallacies is that popularity is proof mainly of popularity. It is evidence that needs to be considered, but it cannot always be accepted as conclusive.

Appeal to Tradition

The **appeal to tradition** fallacy consists of assuming that a belief that has been around for a long time must be true. For example:

> **E25:** *There must be a God because people have believed in one for thousands of years.*

I suspect many readers will see this as a reasonable position to take, but compare it with the following:

> **E26:** *I don't think there's anything wrong with laws the declare homosexuality illegal. After all, they have been in force for centuries.*

Fewer readers will see **E26** as a reasonable position.

The problem is that appeals to tradition rely on the inherent appeal of a longstanding idea, and as such they do have a certain force. A very respectable version of conservative political theory rests on an appeal to the "wisdom of the ages," the view that customs, laws, and beliefs that have stood the test of time must have some merit. But not all beliefs and practices last forever. The appeal to their age may seem appropriate if we still firmly believe them, but not if we are thinking of rejecting them. Therefore, the appeal to tradition has limited relevance when deployed as a defence against criticism of a belief or practice, and its importance should not be exaggerated. Times change, and when they do so does the context within which we consider certain beliefs.

Imagine someone saying the following:

E27: *We have never paid women as much as men. Why should we start now?*

Today this argument would elicit mainly sneers, but 50 or 60 years ago it would have been met with nods of agreement in many quarters. Like **E26**, our views on this matter have changed and an appeal to what we once did is irrelevant. In summary, an appeal to tradition is sometimes relevant, but it is not *necessarily* relevant. Be careful about accepting it.

Appeal to Novelty

Finally, in our ever-changing world beware of tradition's mirror opposite: the **appeal to novelty** fallacy, which are arguments in which the newness of an idea or activity is put forward as a reason for accepting it:

E28: *Look, the latest thing in market-testing techniques is something called "cyber-analysis." I think we ought to try it.*

This argument has some merit. A new technique may be worth investigating, but its newness is not a *sufficient* reason to try it. Imagine someone responding to **E28** this way:

E29: *It's a technique that hasn't been properly tested and that has been developed by Acme Consulting, a company with a record of pitching substandard methods.*

The problem with **E29** is that it exaggerates the importance of a marginally relevant consideration.

However, consider the following:

E30: *Nobody has tried this approach before so at least it has the appeal of novelty, and novelty often works with the public. They're always on the lookout for something new.*

There is no fallacy here. The speaker is aware that the public will be attracted by novelty and puts this forward as a relevant reason for trying a new approach.

To summarize Sections I and II, rhetoric is the art of persuasion but there are good and bad ways to persuade. Where arguments are concerned, a good way necessarily includes giving reasons that are *relevant*. Ones that do not are often examples of rhetoric misused.

EXERCISE 3.2

Identify the fallacy in each of the following. In some cases, there may be more than one fallacy and in others there may be no fallacy at all.

*1. There are a couple of ways you can do this. You can buy the traditional knob-and-dial type of stove, or you can go with this model that's just out: it's completely computerized and programmable. It's new and it's selling like mad; you should try it.

2. The polls show that _____ is going to win the election, so we might as well vote for her.

*3. Anyone who saw the carnage of 9/11—the towers on fire, people leaping to their deaths, the final calamitous collapse—will understand the threat terrorism can pose.

4. The trend lately has been toward longer mortgages—35 or 40 years—with less money down. Why don't we give that a try?

*5. In the long history of the human race, men have been the ones who wage war. Let women stay in support roles where they belong.

6. I think we should continue to make sacrifices to the rain god. Our people have done this since time immemorial and we have never suffered through a long drought.

*7. Just out: 3DTV. You have to have it!

8. Flu shots are a good idea. Without one you are much more likely to get sick, and in some cases very seriously so. There are lots of documented cases of people dying needlessly and painfully from the flu.

*9. We should join a cult. Millions of people belong to one, and besides, they have been around since the time of the ancient Greeks.

10. In elections, people always rush to the frontrunner, and why not? You might as well go with the winner.

*11. I think we should take up wrestling grizzly bears because I hear it's becoming more and more popular every day. Yesterday Igor went three rounds with one.

12. I think wrestling grizzly bears is the worst idea you have ever had. Have you seen Igor? He's a bloody mess; lucky to be alive. He'll never walk again.

*13. Tom: I think gun control is a good idea.
Tina: Are you kidding me? There was something on the news just yesterday about a guy who broke into an elderly couple's home, tied them up, and beat them unconscious before running off with a bunch of cash and jewellery. People need guns to defend themselves.

14. I'm going to vote for the Silly Party because that's what my family has always done—we're as Silly as you can be—and besides, they look like they'll win this time.

*15. I think we should try that new restaurant on Ossington. It's got this chef who does fusions that are completely original.

III. Rhetoric and Loaded Terms

This section will introduce another rhetorical strategy: the use of loaded terms that may carry secondary meanings and therefore convey mixed messages.

Denotation and Connotation

Language is an extremely malleable medium, a lesson Alice learned from Humpty Dumpty in Wonderland:

> "When I use a word," Humpty Dumpty said in a rather scornful tone, "it means just what I choose it to mean—neither more nor less."
>
> "The question is," said Alice, "whether you can make words mean different things."
>
> "The question is," said Humpty Dumpty, "which is to be master—that's all."[4]

We have long since learned Humpty Dumpty's trick of making words bear whatever meaning we want them to have. We can do this because many words have both **denotation** and **connotation**. There are at least a couple of definitions of these terms, but in this text denotation refers to the *literal* meaning of a word. For example, the words "dog" and "horse" denote certain kinds of animals. However, words can also have *associative* meanings that evoke images and feelings or carry messages that exceed their literal meaning; this is their connotation. For instance, in baseball "horse" connotes a big strong pitcher who can be counted on to throw a lot of innings; it's a compliment. By contrast, someone who is a bit of a "dog" is a player who tends to be lazy; it expresses disapproval. As Humpty Dumpty knew, it's possible to make a word carry almost any associative meaning and thus make a sentence mean something very different than it would if the word is taken literally.

Sometimes it's obvious that an associative meaning is in play. To say a baseball pitcher is a horse is patently false if we take it literally, so competent speakers of

---

4 Lewis Carroll, "Alice through the Looking Glass," in *Alice in Wonderland & Alice through the Looking Glass* (London: J.M. Dent & Sons, 1929), 159.

English will know that the word connotes something else, though they may not know what it is or whether it is positive or negative. But consider this example:

E31: *Kathleen Battle is a real diva.*

"Diva" is one of those words where the associative meaning has overwhelmed the literal one. It literally denotes a female opera singer, and as such this sentence is literally true because Kathleen Battle is a famous soprano. However, "diva" has come to connote a difficult and demanding woman, which has become the more common understanding of the word. An Internet search for "famous divas" yields a list that includes Queen Elizabeth, Hillary Clinton, Beyoncé, Madonna, Oprah Winfrey, Paris Hilton, Naomi Campbell, and Jennifer Lopez—not a real "diva" among them. In fact, most of them aren't singers at all, and those who are aren't opera singers.

Another example is "discrimination." It literally means the ability to distinguish between items or actions, but it has come to be so strongly associated with unfair distinctions—racial or sexual discrimination, for example—so much so that many people have forgotten its original neutral meaning. Like "diva," web searches for "discrimination" tend to turn up the connotation rather than the denotation of the word. This is the power of doing what Humpty Dumpty suggests: we can twist the meaning of words, and with it the meaning of what we say.

Loaded Language

It is important to be alert to the presence of loaded words.

Definition: Loaded words are ones where the associative meaning involves deception.

Loaded words can make the negative sound positive and the positive sound negative. When the connotation of a word gets entrenched in our vocabulary, we scarcely notice this shift, and so we may think we are getting a neutral and factual denotation when in fact we are being persuaded to think or act in a certain way. Take the word "blonde." It denotes a hair colour, but it has also come to connote (albeit extremely unfairly) certain negative qualities in a woman. Compare these two descriptions of an event:

E32:
1. *So this driver comes around the corner and almost hits me.*
2. *So this blonde in an SUV comes flying around the corner and almost hits me.*

The first description is neutral, basically a recitation of fact. The second description insinuates something more about the speed and the character of the driver. It seeks to persuade us of *her* (would anyone assume the "blonde" was a man?) many faults. It conjures up an image of someone who regularly does irresponsible things like driving gas-guzzling vehicles at dangerously high speeds. It's a rhetorical attempt to persuade listeners to blame the driver, and the connotation of "blonde" plays a central role in this attempt.

Not every reader will recognize the connotation of "blonde," however, and that's an important point. Connotations vary across time and place, from age to age, and from community to community. So as readers and listeners we have to be sensitive to context because terms that look straightforward may be loaded for specific audiences. In short, some terms may be code words.

Definition: Code words evoke ideas that only a specific audience understands.

When Ronald Reagan was running for president of the United States in 1980 he made a number of remarks like the following:

E33: *I believe in states' rights . . . I believe we have distorted the balance of our government today by giving powers that were never intended to be given in the Constitution to the federal establishment.*

This sounds like a straightforward appeal to return some powers of the federal government to state legislatures. But the term "states' rights" was code for opposition to desegregation and this speech was made in the heart of Mississippi, a state that had resisted integration. So the term appealed to those who would have liked to roll back the gains made by the US civil rights movement in the 1950s and 1960s without offending Americans who supported integration but were unfamiliar with the term's connotation. As such, Reagan's remarks conveyed a double message.

It is not uncommon to hide contentious ideas and darker intentions behind gentler terms. In recent years the phrase "family values" has been used by conservative politicians as an identifying tag for their political views, which include opposition to homosexuality, same-sex marriage, and a general concern for what they see as the moral decline brought on by "secularism." Few people are opposed to families, but that does not mean everyone shares the set of beliefs espoused by social conservatives. They are using a positive term to stand for a set of contentious ideas.

This brings us to a cousin of the code word: the euphemism.

Definition: Euphemisms are terms used to soften blunt hard truths or harsh views.

Unlike code words, many euphemisms are understood by pretty much everyone. When someone says that he has to "wash his hands," most of us know that he has to go to the toilet, and when we hear that someone has "passed away" we know that she has died.

Nonetheless, euphemisms may carry ambiguous connotations and thus operate much like code words. For example:

E34: *Teacher's comment on a report card: Johnny works hard and always participates in class.*

While this may well be literally true, there is a good chance the teacher also means, "He tries, but he's not the brightest bulb in the room." In the sexist days of my youth, girls dreaded being described as having a "great personality" because it was essentially a negative evaluation of how they looked. And when British journalists refer to a politician as being "tired and emotional," they generally mean that he was drunk. As these examples show, euphemisms often operate much like code words—conveying messages that are not stated literally. However, they are not meant to hide the truth, more to soften it.

The decision whether to employ a euphemism is often an important one. For example, imagine a professional sports scout evaluating a prospect's running ability. Here are three possible descriptions he could write down:

E35:
1. *He is not the fastest player in the world.*
2. *He is slow.*
3. *He is lead-footed.*

If the athlete had a choice, he would almost certainly prefer description 1 to 2, and 2 to 3, though it is a case of the least of three evils. "Slow" has the merit of being literal: someone reading the description will understand what it *denotes* in an athlete relative to other athletes. On the other hand, "not the fastest" and the blunt "lead-footed" are loaded terms and you need to think about what they *connote*. The difference between them is that "not the fastest" is a euphemism that softens the blow of the scout's judgment. So while the athlete may benefit from the euphemistic ambiguity of "not the fastest," there is no escape from the harsh "lead-footed," which conjures up an image of someone who can barely move at all. It's an absolute condemnation of the player's speed, far worse than "slow." When the scout sees a slow player who nonetheless has good skills he may choose to use the euphemism "not the fastest," but when the player has few skills he may condemn him with the blunt "lead-footed." Or he may opt for the direct denotation of "slow."

The Politics of Loaded Words

Using loaded words, coded words, and euphemisms are common rhetorical tactics. They obscure harsh ideas and take the edge off blunt truths or unpleasant views. They can also be used to give us a good name and our opponents a bad one. Those who support a woman's right to an abortion are "pro-choice," and those who oppose abortion are "pro-life." Both camps have loaded their self-descriptions positively. When I was a university undergraduate, people of conservative political leanings were routinely described by those on the political left as "reactionary"—hardly a term of endearment—while the left referred to themselves with the self-congratulatory term "progressive." It works. Today, "progressive" has become an almost neutral label for someone on the left side of the political spectrum, just as "family values" has morphed into a label for a certain set of conservative political and moral beliefs.

In this context, consider the following comment from an American conservative political commentator:

> **E36:** *Abortion is simply taking an event in someone's life and being the people that make the decision for a woman. It is sick, and the people that are on that side are just liberals.*[5]

For most of the past three centuries, the term "liberal" (with a small "l") has referred to a person who holds a particular set of political principles, ones that promote individual freedom and civil rights. In recent decades, conservative commentators and politicians in the United States have succeeded in making it connote someone who is seriously misguided or, as in this case, outright evil.

In the end, we all follow Humpty Dumpty's advice, bending words to our purposes: I am annoyed but you are grumpy; I am careful about taking an important step but you are afraid to act; I have rethought my position but you have abandoned yours. Rhetorical tactics such as these can drive us crazy, but we are never going to get rid of them. And they are a risk worth taking, because language would be much poorer without them. A good listener or reader needs to be sensitive to their presence, which means that she needs to be sensitive to the wonderfully plastic and persuasive medium that is language. Playing with the emotional content of words, adjusting and fine-tuning them and creating new connotations, are activities embedded in literature—novels, poetry, song lyrics—and they represent some of our highest cultural achievements. The American philosopher Martha Nussbaum writes that "Literature is in league with the emotions. Readers of novels, spectators of dramas, find themselves led by these works to fear, to grief, to pity, to anger, to joy and delight, even to passionate love."[6] From this perspective, rhetoric is not reason's enemy so much as its playful and sly companion. Both passion and dispassion have a place in thought and we need to be able to call on both. However, we also need to know how to distinguish one from the other. And so, for the most part, a critical thinker has to be a dispassionate thinker.

---

5 Transcript of a radio show posted on rushlimbaugh.com, 27 January, 2010.

6 Martha Nussbaum, *Poetic Justice* (Boston: Beacon Press, 1995), 53.

EXERCISE 3.3

I. For each of the following, identify the terms with connotations and explain what those connotations are. Also indicate whether they are loaded words, coded words, or euphemisms. Where possible, select a more neutral term that could be used instead and explain the difference in effect. Some examples may contain no associative meanings at all.

*1. When will those people ever rise above their tribal disputes?

2. Jenkins strode into the room.

*3. I don't see any reason to pay attention to what Malinowski says. He's hardly an expert in the field. In fact, he's a relative non-entity.

4. The police have a lot to answer for. They grilled my client for over two hours before deciding he was not the person they were after.

*5. I agree that your friend was probably not the most willing accomplice in all this, but why shouldn't she be punished as well as me?

6. You have gone way over the line here. You have no moral or legal right to continue these terrorist attacks on my reputation.

*7. Manchester United's Rooney raced down the field with Cole lumbering along in his wake, unable to close the gap. His cross sailed over the rest of Chelsea's earthbound defenders onto the head of a soaring Fernandez, from which it rocketed into the net leaving the hapless Chech rooted to his line.

8. I think I deserve some credit for my essay. I really sweated over it.

*9. As you may know, we have been struggling with a sizable budget shortfall.

10. "For months, talking heads have been barraging the public with endless statistics and reports which supposedly indicate that economic conditions are improving (or at least getting worse at a slower rate). All these reports are dubbed 'green shoots' and are being touted as a sign that the American economy is now back on track and headed down the path to prosperity."[7]

*11. I don't know why everyone is so worried about a downturn in the economy.

12. "A mob of child-protestors has successfully shut down a speech by Ann Coulter at the University of Ottawa."[8]

---

7 Briggs Armstrong, "A Real Green Shoot." *Mises Economic Blog*, 8 April, 2010.

8 Terrance Watson, in *Western Standard.ca* (blog), 23 March, 2010.

*13. "The Internet was something organic, an interconnected world of communities built from the ground-up by individuals acting of their own volition."[9]

14. _____, ex-member of Parliament and self-described peddler of government grants, was in fine form, chatting up prospective clients.

*15. Moviegoers everywhere will love hearing about the actress's latest exploit.

16. Contrary to the opinion of the braying politicians sitting across the aisle, the prime minister is a statesman who has worked diligently on behalf of his country. We should congratulate him for his efforts on our behalf.

II. *For each of the following, explain how the bracketed words affect the meaning of the sentence differently. Where possible, choose the one you think is better suited to convey the meaning that the rest of the sentence seems to carry.*

*1. Lawyer: My client is (young/immature) and this is the act of a(n) (young/immature) person.

2. Well, yes, my friend got the facts wrong: she (misspoke/lied).

*3. He (walked/ambled) into the room, looking very calm.

4. He (walked/ambled) into the meeting room, 10 minutes late.

*5. Wilma is a (woman of faith/Baptist).

6. Myra is firm in her resolve, and you are (obstinate/unbending).

*7. My parents refuse to raise my allowance. They are a pair of (frugal people/misers).

8. He (bumped/rammed) into me, causing me to fall and hurt myself.

*9. I admit I did (speak forcefully to/shout at) him.

10. Jane doesn't like to cross the park alone after dark. She's a (cautious/timid) person.

*11. Sure, Wilson is (very short/undersized) for a shooting guard, but he's deadly accurate.

III. *Replace the euphemism with a more direct term.*

*1. My opponent tends to be economical with the truth.

2. Right now I'm between jobs.

*3. The action was a success but there was some collateral damage.

4. He was killed by friendly fire.

---

9 Jesse Kline, "The Death of Internet Freedom." *Western Standard.ca* (blog), 7 April, 2010.

Continued >

*5. She's not the swiftest boat in the ocean.

6. He's in the arms of the Lord.

*7. There is a lot of job flexibility in the economy right now.

8. The company is downsizing right now, so there will be some significant restructuring.

*9. We moved quickly to neutralize the terrorist.

10. They pursued a policy of ethnic cleansing.

*11. I do admit that some people in our fair city live in reduced circumstances.

12. My grandfather has a lot of character lines on his face.

IV. Social Biases

In what follows, we will be working with the following definition of "bias":

> *Definition: A **bias** is a predisposition to adopt a particular point of view to the exclusion of other equally good or even better points of view.*

Since we are defining bias as "not being objective," it is important to point out that no perspective is absolutely objective. We all inhabit historical and cultural contexts that shape our points of view. However, some points of view seem so obviously skewed that we can reasonably refer to them as biases.

This section will examine social biases:

> *Definition: **Social biases** are preconceptions that favour one group and penalize others.*

Here are some of the principal kinds of social biases:

Cultural Bias

Cultural bias is a bias in which knowledge, points of view, and social practices that are specific to a given culture or social group are treated as universal bits of information that everyone should possess. For example, IQ tests are supposed to be objective measurements of a person's intelligence, but it is notoriously difficult to eradicate all traces of cultural bias from them. I once wrote an IQ test in which I was asked to explain the meaning of some idioms. One was, "People who live in glass houses shouldn't throw stones." For me, that was a very easy question since I had grown up hearing it in my home. For my friend beside me, who was born in Croatia and had learned different idioms in a different language, it was a more difficult question. The test was slanted in my direction.

Cultural biases can also have a socioeconomic character. In the early grades of school, children from relatively affluent families often (although not always!) have larger vocabularies and more general knowledge than those from low-income families. A teacher must therefore exercise care in deciding what a student ought to know. Consider the following question:

E37: *Which of the following does not belong with the other three: violin, viola, cello, oboe?*

Is this knowledge we can reasonably expect all children to have at the same age? Probably not—a child may not know what a cello and an oboe are, perhaps not even what a viola is. "Violin" may be the only word on the list he recognizes. Lacking that information he cannot be expected to demonstrate the skill the question is supposed to be testing: the ability to sort things into categories.

Even when people share knowledge they may arrange it differently. Give North Americans, especially urban North Americans, a mixture of fruits, vegetables, and implements and ask them to sort them into categories and they will usually distribute them as I have listed them: fruits, vegetables, tools. However, in some rural cultures the distribution will be different. Each implement will be set beside the fruit or vegetable it is used to cut or dig up. To see either of these distributions as objectively the "correct" one would be a form of cultural bias.

Something to Think About

Here are some culturally specific questions. In each case, see if you can select the person who doesn't belong. Think about whether you should know all the answers and what it means if you do not. The answers are in the Answer Key at the end of the book.

1. *Kafka, Kundera, Havel, Dvorak*
2. *Dickens, Eliot, Austen, Bronte*
3. *50 Cent, Lil Wayne, Lady Gaga, Jay-Z*
4. *Pelé, Maradona, Messi, Batistuta*
5. *Goodfellas, Psycho, Gangs of New York, Raging Bull*

In-Group Bias

In-group bias is the tendency to give preferential treatment to members of a group to which you belong. The group could be anything from an entity as large as a religion, ethnicity, or nationality to one as small as a sports team, a chess club, or an informal clique of friends. Not surprisingly, in-group bias creates a mirror out-group bias, which is the tendency to view those who are not part of the group less favourably. In-group biases can look very much like cultural biases, and in some cases there may be little difference. The difference is that with an in-group bias it is not a question of what you know but of who you are. For example:

E38: *She certainly has the qualifications for the position and she interviewed quite well, but I don't know—I'm just more comfortable with Mr. Smith. I feel like he would be a better fit in the office, with all the guys.*

Here, the woman candidate for a job seems to have known everything she was expected to know, to have the proper qualifications, and to have done well in the interview, but is being rejected in favour of a man whom the interviewer thinks would fit in better in what is probably an all-male or predominantly male office. The in-group is men and the out-group is women.

An interesting example of in-group bias concerns musicians auditioning for symphony orchestras. Traditionally, there have been fewer women than men in orchestras; moreover some instruments were traditionally designated as "men's instruments." However, once orchestras began to institute blind auditions—ones where the musicians played behind screens so that the auditioners could not see them—the number of women selected rose. The writer Malcolm Gladwell recounts the story of a woman trombone player who auditioned for the Munich Philharmonic Orchestra in 1980.[10] The audition was blind, and when the music director of the orchestra heard her play he was certain she was the one he wanted . . . until she came out from behind the screen. When the director saw he had selected a woman he changed his mind. In his opinion, a woman ought not to play what he saw as a man's instrument. The musical director almost certainly believed he was making unbiased choices until he ran into the blind audition. Interestingly, when the bias surfaced he did not change his mind. Despite the evidence to the contrary, he simply denied that he was biased.

An in-group bias can be wrong even when it seems right. During times of economic recession, there is often pressure to "buy Canadian" or "buy American." The result is an "us versus them" mentality based on the assumption that we need to look after ourselves first. The problem is that in an integrated world market, "us" and "them" are really not distinct groups. Exclusively buying Canadian or American can hurt both Canadians and Americans.

Stereotypes

A **stereotype** is an oversimplified view of a group or culture. It consists of taking a few characteristics, positive or negative, that some members of the group are *alleged* to have and attributing them to everybody in the group. A view of Canadians as people who wear toques and say "eh" a lot is a stereotype, even though it does describe some of us. Often stereotypes are used as reasons for preferring members of one group over another: group A is hard-working and honest, group B is lazy and dishonest; women are weaker and unable to play the trombone as well as men; everybody who plays chess is a hopeless geek, so let's avoid them; jocks are all dim-witted and prone to violence, so let's cut funding for sport and spend the money on the band. One effect of stereotypes is to give unwarranted support to in-group biases:

> **E39:** *There is no reason to worry about hiring _____s; they're all rich. It's us who needs the jobs.*

---

10 Malcolm Gladwell, *Blink* (New York: Back Bay Books, 2005), 245–8.

Like viruses, stereotypes infect not only those who propagate them but also those who are on the receiving end of them. When I was in high school it was virtually taken as holy writ by students and teachers alike, often in the face of evidence to the contrary, that girls could not do math as well as boys. The truly unfortunate aspect of this stereotype was that many girls believed it and turned away from math; they accepted the stereotype of themselves as true. To be good at math was to be unfeminine, and even if they were good at it now their abilities would decline as they got older. Sadly, this effect is not uncommon.

It is important to note that a stereotype can look positive. Imagine someone saying the following:

E40: *I really like Australians. They are so easygoing and polite.*

This is a stereotype, because not all Australians are going to fit the description any more than they will fit the negative stereotype of people who drink oceans of beer, love cricket, and say "crikey" a lot. Even when it's positive, a stereotype is a form of uncritical thinking and a poor substitute for getting to know individuals.

Cultural biases, in-group biases, and stereotypes are overlapping forms of distorted, uncritical thinking. For those caught in their snares, the opinions they give rise to seem like obvious truths, but they are not. A critical thinker cannot let them take the place of real evidence about particular cases. The relevant question is not, for example, whether members of Religion X are trustworthy. That's a red herring because there is no answer to the question since new members keep showing up. The relevant question is whether the particular person (or persons) you happen to be dealing with, and who happens to be a member of Religion X, is trustworthy. His religious affiliation is irrelevant unless there are specific reasons for bringing it into consideration. For example, Religion X may entail a certain belief—say, pacifism—that makes it difficult for a member of that religion to carry out a particular action—like being a soldier—even if he says he will. But then the question is not even "Is he trustworthy?" but "Can I trust him to do *this*?" One way to avoid stereotypes is by restricting your considerations to the particular case in front of you.

EXERCISE 3.4

For each of the following, indicate which social bias is on display. In some cases there is no bias.

*1. "Let them eat cake." (French Queen Marie Antoinette's alleged response, in 1789, when told that many French peasants had no bread to eat.)

2. I want to go live in the United States. They have it so good over there.

Continued >

*3. "The Indians were savages . . . they were nomads scalping people . . . We don't eat people . . . We don't engage in human sacrifice."[11]

4. I know Jack; we belong to the same golf club. He's a fine fellow and a good worker. I think we should hire him.

*5. The punishment you suggest is excessive. Ms. Hawkins comes from a good family. Her parents have been neighbours of mine for years. I watched her grow up. She's an exceptional young woman.

6. In February 2009, the mayor of a California town sent out an email with a photograph of the Obama White House lawn planted with watermelons. The caption read: "No Easter egg hunt this year."

*7. Our testing shows that James is dyslexic, so he is going to have some trouble learning to read.

8. Liverpool football fans: "We are the champions of the world!"

*9. We should be careful about handing out so many research grants to faculty at second-tier universities. We don't want the quality of research to suffer.

10. What do you mean you've never heard of Abraham Lincoln? Where did you grow up, on the moon?

*11. "I didn't even know [Canada] was in the war. I thought that's where you go when you don't want to fight. Go chill in Canada."[12]

12. What do you mean Columbus didn't discover America? Of course he did.

*13. Everyone hates us!

14. You know how men are!

*15. The Spanish conquistador Pizarro reads his "requirement" to the Incas in the early sixteenth century: "I, Francisco Pizarro, servant of the high and mighty kings of Castile and León, conquerors of barbarian peoples, and being their messenger and Captain, hereby notify and inform you . . . that God our Lord, One and Eternal, created Heaven and Earth and a man and a woman from whom you and I and all people are descended . . . Because of the great multitude begotten over the past five thousand and some years since the world was made . . . God placed one called Saint Peter in charge over all these peoples . . ."[13]

---

11 Ann Coulter at Oregon State University, 19 November, 2001.

12 Doug Benson, panelist on *Red Eye with Greg Gutfeld*, Fox News, 17 March, 2009.

13 Quoted in Ronald Wright, *Stolen Continents* (Toronto: Penguin Canada, 2009), 65.

V. Cognitive Biases

"Cognition" is the process of coming to know something, but sometimes the process is distorted by a cognitive bias.

> **Definition:** A **cognitive bias** is a faulty judgment caused by a failure to evaluate evidence properly.

In this section we will discuss some examples of cognitive biases. The first two below you have already seen in Section II, but it is worth repeating them here to show how fallacies and biases interact.

The Bandwagon Fallacy

As set out in **E23** and **E24** above, the bandwagon fallacy is the tendency to let the fact that others believe some claim is true or some practice is good induce us to believe it as well. This is also a cognitive bias because it substitutes lemming-like behaviour of following the crowd for careful evaluation of evidence. For example:

> **E41:** *Member of a jury: I really thought the accused was innocent, but everyone else thought he was guilty, so I guess they were right. I voted their way in the end.*

The jury member has not cited good reasons for voting guilty; he has simply been swayed by the fact that everyone else thinks the accused is guilty. While a critical thinker should not be stubborn, neither should he abandon his view without a good reason. The certainty of the other jurors seems to have interfered with his ability to think critically.

Misleading Vividness

The misleading vividness fallacy is a cognitive bias because it distorts thinking by inducing people to overvalue or undervalue an experience. For example:

> **E42:** *Did you see the videos of that horrific plane crash yesterday? I have to get on a plane next week. Let me tell you, I am going to buy more life insurance before I do.*

The odds of the speaker's plane going down are no greater now than they were before the crash; nothing has changed except the speaker's subjective perception of the dangers of flying. Sometimes this process can work in reverse. A study has shown that when dams or levees are built to protect flood plains people feel safer because they feel the vivid threat has been removed.[14] As a result, they often take reduced

---

14 E. Yudkowski, "Cognitive Biases Potentially Affecting Judgements of Global Risks." Draft, 31 August, 2006, 2–3. Available at http://singularity.org/files/CognitiveBiases.pdf.

precautions against flooding. But the threat has not been eradicated; there may still be floods. They are now going to be rarer occurrences, but they are also going to be more disastrous because they will be much bigger. The frequency of floods decreases but the damage per flood increases, as does the average yearly damage in some cases.

The Gambler's Fallacy

The **gambler's fallacy** is a fallacy that stems from not understanding how fixed probabilities work. **Fixed probabilities** refer to situations where the odds of an action having a given result remain constant no matter how often the action is carried out. The most commonly cited example is the case of two people flipping a coin and betting whether it will come up heads or tails. Most people are aware that when a fair coin is flipped there is a 50-50 chance of either result. Sometimes, however, there is a run of, say, tails, perhaps four or five in a row. Then people have a tendency to start betting heads, reasoning that it must be "due." Yet the odds on any particular flip of the coin never change: they remain fixed at 50-50. Each flip occurs in isolation, as if the previous ones had never happened. The same thing is true of a roulette wheel, where there are two colours: red and black. A player may feel one of them is due but, like a coin, the odds of the ball landing on red or black do not change.

The point is not to be misled by the **law of large numbers**, which assures us that, when repeated often enough, events such as tossing a coin will tend to even out. Flip a coin five times and you could get four heads and one tails, but flip it 200 times and it will almost certainly be very close to 100 heads and 100 tails. If a coin has come up tails four times in a row, you can be quite certain that if it is a fair coin this will not go on forever. But that doesn't alter the fact that on the fifth flip the odds remain 50–50. What the law of large numbers tells you is that if tails comes up 25 or 50 times in a row, you can be pretty certain that it is not a fair coin, so keep betting tails.

People sometimes fall into the gambler's fallacy when they buy lottery tickets:

E43: *I've got to play my lottery numbers every week. I've been playing for years and they've never come up, so I feel they're due.*

Not so. Even the set of numbers that came up in the previous draw has the same chance as any other set of numbers of coming up this week. People who try to sell the non-existent secrets of winning big lottery prizes will sometimes run the gambler's fallacy in reverse, claiming that when a number has come up a few times it is "hot" and should be incorporated into one's choices. But lottery numbers are never hot or cold because with fixed probabilities the odds do not change.

Not every situation involves fixed probabilities: the more often you cross the street the greater your chances are of being hit by a car. However, in a situation that does involve fixed probabilities no result is ever "due."

The Confirmation Bias

Sometimes it isn't our understanding of the odds that trips us up—it's that we don't sift through the evidence carefully enough. The **confirmation bias** is the disposition to act according to preconceived ideas and to notice only the evidence that confirms these ideas. Someone who has stereotyped a given group of people as dangerous will probably have a tendency to be on the lookout for threatening behaviour in members of that group and to be less aware of friendly signals. Should a member of that group actually attack him he will say, "See? I told you so!" Conversely, a teacher who thinks a given group of students are particularly intelligent may tend to give members of that group higher grades than they may sometimes deserve. The teacher may focus *selectively* on the strong elements of their work and overlook the weaker ones.

The reverse can also hold true. Here's an example from a conversation I once had with a relative about an experience he had in rural Quebec:

E44: *Our car broke down outside Rivière-du-Loup and, do you know, the mechanic at the garage refused to speak English to us?*

What my relative ignored was the likelihood that the mechanic was a unilingual francophone. His reading of the situation was based on his assumption that Quebecers don't much like anglophones. He took the man's failure to address him in English as confirmation of this belief.

The Self-Serving Bias

Now turn the spotlight on yourself. When we evaluate ourselves, we risk falling into the **self-serving bias**, which occurs when people attribute success to their own efforts and talents and failure to external factors such as bad luck or other people's interference. In short, we may *internalize* success and *externalize* failure. For example:

E45: *As CEO of this company I have been responsible for some of the most profitable years in its history. Unfortunately, in the past year market fluctuations have worked against us.*

The speaker is willing to take credit for the good years, but not the bad. While it is possible that her claim is true, it should raise a "bias alert" flag. Her audience should therefore evaluate the evidence carefully.

The self-serving bias is often induced by high pressure situations in which people risk public failure. An athlete will dismiss a loss with, "I guess it just wasn't meant to be"; a politician will attribute upturns in the economy to the wisdom of his party's policies and downturns to uncontrollable forces such as the global market; when things go well a student will say, "I passed the course," but when they go badly he will say, "The teacher failed me."

Sometimes people employ a negative version of the self-serving bias by internalizing failure and assuming they are always at fault even when they are not:

E46: *My boyfriend is always cheating on me. I don't know why I can't make him happier.*

It's possible that the boyfriend's wandering ways have nothing to do with any failure on his partner's part.

The Anchoring Bias

The first five biases in this section have to do with the way individuals frame situations for themselves: they narrow their frame of reference to the point where their perception of a situation is distorted. The **anchoring bias**, which refers to cases where we are misled by inadequate bits of information, is also like this. However, it is often an effect of the way in which other people frame the world for us. Many examples come from the work of psychologists Amos Tversky and Daniel Kahneman,[15] who have studied the effects that different ways of asking a question have on the response. For example, compare these two questions:

E47:
(1) When Wayne Gretzky retired, how many NHL records did he hold alone or share with someone else?
(2) Do you think that when he retired from the NHL Wayne Gretzky held—jointly or shared with someone—more than or fewer than 15 records? Specifically, how many do you think he held?

Question 1 leaves the answer up to you; either you have a sense of what it is or you do not. Question 2 anchors the query by offering a "more or fewer" figure. Research suggests that in this case, whether a person's estimate is over or under 15, it will not deviate very far from that number. But in fact the answer is 61. Lacking other information, people tend to anchor their estimates by keeping them close to the figure supplied to them.

This particular wound to critical thinking can be self-inflicted. Lacking a good sense of what the best decision is, we may let our reasoning be anchored by some bit of information that is too narrow to provide a solid basis for a decision. For example:

E48: *I didn't know which brand of running shoes to buy, and the salesperson didn't know any more than I did, so I went with these. They seem to fit well.*

---

15 For example, see Amos Tversky and Daniel Kahneman, "Judgment Under Uncertainty." *Science*, 185 (September 1974): 1124–31.

Lacking detailed knowledge of running shoes, this person has picked out one characteristic she could evaluate and used it to anchor her decision. She ignored other considerations—how well-ventilated are the shoes? Does she need arch support? Will the soles wear well?—that are equally important. We all do this sometimes because we don't always have access to all the relevant information. It is, however, important to recognize the tendency because it will put a brake on uncritical thinking by reminding us of the need for research.

Loss Aversion Bias

The **loss aversion bias** stems from miscalculating or ignoring what is probable because people often prefer to avoid losses rather than take even moderate risks that will lead to gains. I used to give students a puzzle in which they had to choose between two options. An easy calculation showed that the choices worked out as follows:

> **E49:**
>
> *Option 1:* You have a 99.9 per cent chance of winning $1,000,000 versus a 0.1 per cent chance of getting $0.
>
> *Option 2:* You have a 0.1% chance of winning $1,010,000 versus a guarantee of winning $10,000.

To choose option 2 is virtually to guarantee that you will exchange a million dollars for 10,000 dollars. Yet year after year, that is what about half the students chose. When asked why, the most common response was that they wanted to be sure of getting something.

There are a number of experiments, many of them carried out by Tversky and Kahneman, that demonstrate the loss aversion bias works in much the same way as the anchoring bias. When a situation is given two descriptions—one positive and one negative—people tend to view the positive description as the better of the two even if it is not. For example, consider this scenario:

> **E50:** *One hundred people have been taken hostage. There are two strategies for securing their release. Strategy A has a 50 per cent chance of saving two-thirds of the hostages, whereas Strategy B offers a 50 per cent chance that one-third of the hostages will die. Which strategy is better?*

Something to Think About

The anchoring bias works in other ways as well. Tversky and Kahneman found that when test subjects were asked to multiply $1 \times 2 \times 3 \times 4 \times 5 \times 6 \times 7 \times 8$ in five seconds—that is, so fast they had to estimate the answer—the median estimate was 512. When asked to do the multiplication in reverse order, the median estimate was 2250.[16] Can you explain the discrepancy? The answer is in the Answer Key at the end of the book.

---

16 *Ibid.*

In terms of the number of hostages one can expect to save, the strategies are identical. The only difference is that A has been expressed in terms of lives saved whereas B has been expressed in terms of lives lost. Even when the equivalence is as blatantly obvious as it is here, most people will opt for Strategy A. A critical thinker, however, will recognize that, as described, A and B are identical and ask if there are other things that might differentiate them.

The loss aversion bias often distorts everyday thinking. For example, when gas prices rise by a cent or two people will cut back on their driving even though the loss they suffer from the higher price is minimal. They may also drive halfway across a city to buy cheaper gas even though the fuel they burn by doing so comes close to negating the savings they get at the pump. They have taken a lot of time, which might have been spent in more productive ways, to achieve a very small saving. Like all cognitive biases, the loss aversion bias represents a failure to give situations the careful consideration necessary to make a rational decision. Like all biases, it is a species of lazy and uncritical thinking.

EXERCISE 3.5

For each of the following, identify the cognitive bias. In some cases there may be more than one bias and in others there may be no bias at all.

*1. I think I'm going to buy another Mazda. The last one I owned was pretty much trouble free.

2. I know these blue-chip stocks have been averaging good yearly returns for 20 years now—they seem recession proof—but I am just not comfortable with them. I don't want to take a chance on losing money right now.

*3. I didn't deserve to fail the test. I prepared really well but it was too hard.

4. Did you see the videos of the volcanic eruption in Iceland? If a plane got caught in that it would stall and everyone would die. It's going to be a long while before I fly to Europe again.

*5. I have decided that my neighbour is a terrible person—absolutely horrible! I was in the yard with my daughter yesterday and we heard him swear. He used an absolutely filthy word. There is no excuse for such disgusting behaviour.

6. The Leafs have lost their last six games, which puts them at 26 wins and 32 losses for the season. They tend to win about half their games, and seldom lose more than four or five in a row, so I think we can expect them to go on a winning streak.

*7. I'm going to buy a pair of those minimal running shoes that everybody has. They look so cool.

8. When people have their homes broken into they feel violated. Such crimes call for stiff penalties.

*9. Three seconds to go in the football game: the Lions, who are trailing by three points, have the ball on the Bears' one-yard line. If they can score a touchdown they win the game, but if they kick a field goal they can tie the game and go to overtime. The coach elects to kick the field goal.

10. We know that if she had intended to embezzle the money she would have set up an off-shore account. And she did set up an offshore account, so obviously she did embezzle the money.

*11. Each cigarette you smoke is potentially another nail in your coffin. You should stop.

12. Canadian hockey fan: So what if the American women's hockey team beat Canada in the tournament final? It means nothing. They were just lucky.

*13. We know that the bear population is 25 per cent larger than it was 10 years ago, so we can expect bear–human incidents to have risen by about the same amount.

14. You really ought to get into the housing market—it's so easy to get a mortgage for very little money down.

*15. I think the Conservatives are going to win the next election. Look at the polls: more and more people say they are going to vote for them.

16. This is the most commonly used brand of toothpaste. There must be a reason. Perhaps we ought to try it.

*17. There is no use buying a ticket on tonight's charity draw because I won a raffle last week and lightning doesn't strike twice.

VI. Summary

In this chapter we have looked at some of the ways in which thinkers can be led down the path of uncritical thinking. Rhetoric—the art of speaking persuasively— has a legitimate place in language, but it can be abused. An argument has to per-suade people for the right reasons. One that contains fallacies of relevance is never a good argument since by definition these fallacies lend no relevant support to the conclusion. It's also important to be alert to the presence of loaded language, to the possibly misleading connotations of common words, and to the effects of code words and euphemisms. Finally, biases distort critical thinking in a number of ways. Like fallacies they may insert irrelevant considerations into our thinking, but in addition they may insert ideas that are too narrow or simply untrue. Biases may also induce us to overestimate the importance of certain bits of evidence while excluding others, or they may stem, as in the gambler's fallacy, from a failure to understand what the evidence means.

There are many more fallacies and biases that could have been included in this chapter had space allowed. What is important, therefore, is that you take from this chapter a sense of what fallacies and biases are and of the effects they have on our thinking.

4

Constructing Arguments

- Two guides to critical thinking: save the phenomena and Occam's razor
- The three laws of reason: identity, excluded middle, and non-contradiction
- Deductive arguments
- Valid and invalid arguments
- Sound and unsound arguments

Chapter 3 dealt with some ways in which arguments can go wrong. This chapter will introduce guides to critical thinking and laws of reasoning that will help you keep your arguments on the right track. It will also introduce a formal method of reasoning called deduction, which we will examine in detail in Chapters 5 and 6.

I. Two Guides to Good Reasoning

This section will introduce two general guides to critical thinking. They are meant to focus your attention on two central characteristics of critical thought: thoroughness and simplicity.

Guide 1: Save the Phenomena

This guide comes to us from Plato. A phenomenon is any event or object of experience. Plato is pointing out that our powers of reason are generally applied to solving problems posed by the world around us. These could be practical problems, such as understanding why droughts occur or how to get the girl dancing with your friend to notice you instead. Alternatively, they could be abstract ones of the sort encountered in mathematics or logic. In either case, the basic point is that we don't think until we have something to think about—until some issue captures our attention. Moreover, we seldom think critically until we have something interesting or unusual or important to think about. Then we have to argue our way to a conclusion, and the argument needs to be as *thorough* as possible. This is what **save the phenomena** means: the more thorough an argument (or explanation), the better. Remember, when you are trying to convince others, or even yourself, that a given conclusion is true or at least probably true, you need to develop a thorough argument; an incomplete one will not do, even if its premises are true and relevant.

Consider the following:

E1: *I don't think there is any point in continuing in school because I can get a job right now.*

Even accepting that the premise is true and relevant, this is a weak argument for leaving school. There are a lot of questions the speaker needs to consider: How badly does she need a job? Is the job permanent? How well does it pay? Is it one she would enjoy or at least be reasonably satisfied doing for a while? Is it a real opportunity or just a stopgap? Those are some "pull" questions, ones that ask why she is attracted to the job. Then there are the "push" questions, ones that ask why she wants to leave school. Is she doing well? Does her program interest her? When she finishes, what are the employment prospects and how do they compare to the job she is presently thinking of taking? The questions go on and on, and each answer supplies the speaker with a new premise either for an argument in favour of leaving school or for one in favour of staying in school.

Diagrammatically, an argument that looks like this (which **E1** does) is probably incomplete:

P

C

By contrast, a thorough one looks something like this:

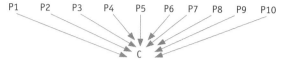

In fact, the speaker in **E1** would do well to have two arguments like this: one in favour of leaving school and one against, which she can then compare. When someone tells you to draw up a list for and against a given decision he is in effect telling you to develop two thorough arguments composed of independent premises.

Now consider the following case, which is taken from a television interview with a juror after a murder trial in the United States:

> **E2:** *I think he's guilty. I didn't trust him. He wouldn't look us in the eye.*

You may recognize this as an example of the anchoring bias, in which a person clings to one scrap of information rather than going in search of more—and possibly more relevant—evidence. Not only does the juror appear to have ignored days or even weeks of testimony, he has failed to consider various plausible reasons why the accused did not look directly at the jury members: nervousness, shyness, politeness, instructions from his lawyer, and so on. Compare **E2** with the following argument:

> **E3:** *I think he's guilty. We have no reason to believe the police are lying about him trying to sell drugs to an undercover officer. He has a record of dealing drugs, he was carrying drugs when he was arrested, and there is an independent witness who saw him approach the officer in the coffee shop.*

This juror has put together an argument for why she thinks the accused is guilty. It consists of three *relevant* (and presumably true) premises in support of her conclusion, whereas **E2** contains only one premise of dubious relevance.

Finally, here's what President George W. Bush famously said after meeting Russian President Vladimir Putin:

> **E4:** *"I looked the man in the eye. I found him to be very straightforward and trustworthy and we had a very good dialogue. . . . I was able to get a sense of his soul."*[1]

This is also a case of the anchoring bias. Considering all that is at stake when two superpowers negotiate, one hopes that President Bush's assessment of President Putin did not begin and end with the fact that Putin looked him in the eye. To save the phenomena you have to think beyond a scrap of information, especially if it isn't even relevant information.

---

1 BBC News Online, 16 June, 2001.

Guide 2: Occam's Razor

The second guide, called **Occam's razor**, is named after the medieval English philosopher William of Occam (ca. 1287–ca. 1349). He is supposed to have offered the following advice: *Entia non sunt multiplicanda praeter necessitatem,* which translates into English as "Entities are not to be multiplied unnecessarily." This is sometimes paraphrased as "keep it simple," but more accurately it is "keep it as simple *as possible*," which means as simple as possible while still saving the phenomena.

As well as being a guide to *efficient* reasoning, this adage also sets an *aesthetic* standard by defining elegance in reasoning. In short, the "razor" stipulates that in reasoning, simplicity (and therefore efficiency) is beauty. If two arguments (or explanations) save the phenomena *equally well*—if they are equally thorough and if their assertions are relevant and true—Occam's razor instructs us to adopt the one that is simpler because it is both more efficient and more beautiful. There is another Latin saying—*pulchritudo splendor varitatis,* meaning "beauty is the splendour of truth"—and Occam seems to be echoing it. This may not always be true: beautiful arguments can be wrong. But it nonetheless is a great advantage to be able to set arguments out in as clear and straightforward a manner as possible.

In fact, let's take writing as an example of how Occam's razor works. Section V of Chapter 2 introduced the problem of wordy arguments. When those arguments were simplified they became clearer—easier to follow. In that Occamite spirit, consider the following sentence (it is not an argument):

E5: *In this essay which I'm going to write, I shall be considering what I believe are the various ideas and theories that a number of important thinkers and writers have had about the issue of democracy.*

This is not an atypical student sentence. In its defence, it saves the phenomena because it tells us what its author is going to do: write an essay in which she will consider what several thinkers have had to say about democracy. Unfortunately, it takes much longer than necessary to communicate this.

Compare **E5** with this sentence:

E6: *This essay will examine some important theories of democracy.*

E6 is one-fourth the length of **E5** and conveys the author's intention equally well, so Occam's razor counsels us to prefer it. If **E6** is not exactly beautiful it is definitely better-looking than the distinctly unbeautiful **E5**. Here, then, is an Occam-like bit of advice about writing: *omne verbum pro vectura eius rem solvate*: every word must pay its way. In arguments, excess verbiage is a form of irrelevance because the extra words do nothing that fewer words will not do.

Think of Occam's razor as encouraging you to avoid the Rube Goldberg sentence or argument. Goldberg (1883–1970) was an American cartoonist, engineer, and artist famous for his elaborate drawings of incredibly roundabout ways to accomplish simple tasks. Figure 4.1 shows his depiction of how the government might collect taxes. Goldberg's cartoons are funny, powerful, and critical reminders of just how inefficient—how addicted to the needlessly complex—people can be.

Figure 4.1
The Local Government Efficiency Machine

By permission of Gary Varvel and Creators Syndicate, Inc.

Critical Thought in the Balance

The razor should also be applied to practical problem solving because inefficiency is a waste of valuable time. For example, consider the following relatively simple puzzle:

> **E7:** *On a table are seven coins and a balance scale. Six of the coins are the same weight while the seventh is heavier. The goal is to use the scale to isolate the heavy coin in the most efficient manner.*

Let's consider three ways of going about this:

1. The one-one rule of procedure: Weigh the coins in pairs, one on each side. Eventually you will isolate the heavier coin, perhaps in the first weighing but perhaps not until the third. Luck aside, only after three weighings are you *guaranteed* to isolate the coin. (If you haven't got it by then it's the one not yet weighed.)

2. The two-two rule of procedure: Place two coins on each side of the scale. One of two things will occur in the first weighing: either the coins will balance or they will not. If they balance, the heavy coin is among the three not yet weighed and the next weighing will isolate it—just put one coin on each side. If they balance it's the excluded one and if they don't balance it's the heavier one. If the first two pairs don't balance, it is one of the coins on the heavier side and all you do is weigh them against each other. This rule guarantees that the coin is isolated after a maximum of two weighings.

3. The three-three rule of procedure: Place three coins on each side of the scale. Again, one of two things will occur: the sides will either balance or not balance. If they balance, then the heavy coin is the excluded one and you have got it in one weighing. If they don't balance, it's one of the heavy side coins and the next weighing will isolate it. Just weigh any two of those three coins and see what happens. Again, a maximum of two weighings is required to isolate the heavy coin.

William of Occam would prefer rules two and three to rule one because they are more efficient procedures. Luck aside, they require a maximum of two as opposed to three weighings to get the job done. However, these methods are not equal. Whereas rule three leaves open the possibility of isolating the heavy coin in one weighing, rule two does not. Therefore, Occam would opt for rule three over rule two. This may seem like a small issue but it is not: if you focus on the question, "What is the most efficient way to a solution?" you will find that you look at problems more carefully. For those who listen to it, Occam's razor instils a critical attitude.[2]

The Order of Precedence

Taken together, the two guides encapsulate the aim of critical thinking, which is to be as thorough and as efficient as possible. Take the "as possible" part of that sentence seriously. The first imperative of critical thinking is to get things right—to save the phenomena by providing a complete argument with true premises. A brief argument may be simpler than a longer one, but it may also be *too* brief to do the job properly, making it neither efficient nor thorough. **E1** and **E2** are examples of simple but un-thorough arguments. Now consider the following definitions of quantum physics that a quick Internet search turned up. Like arguments, definitions have to save the phenomena if they are to be useful:

E8:
D1: The branch of physics based on quantum theory.
D2: The scientific study of subatomic reality.
D3: [A] set of principles describing the physical reality at the atomic level of matter (molecules and atoms) and the subatomic (electrons, protons, and even smaller particles).

D1 is simplest, but says very little. In fact, it is virtually circular. **D2** is margin-ally less simple but more informative, so in terms of saving the phenomena it's an

---

2 Note, however, that if the goal were to adopt the procedure that gave you the best chance of isolating the heavy coin in one weighing, you would select the one-one method. It gives you a 2/7 chance of doing so, whereas the three-three method gives you only a 1/7 chance and the two-two method gives you no chance at all.

improvement. **D3** adds still more information and is therefore even more informative, though definitely more complex. A really thorough definition (which these are not intended to be) might be so complex that the average reader would have trouble understanding it, and that's not very useful. The point is that thoroughness is a fluid standard and so, therefore, is simplicity. Depending on the audience—for example, elementary, high school, or postsecondary students—any of these definitions may be adequate or inadequate. The job of a critical thinker is first to determine the necessary standard of thoroughness and then to present his argument, explanation, or definition *as simply as that standard will allow.*

In passing, that is why word limits are important in essays. The limit is your budget. If you have a thousand words to spend, spend them wisely by saving as many phenomena as you can while staying within your budget. To do so you have to make every word pay its way. Were the limit cut to 750 words or raised to 1250, your standard of thoroughness would change, but not your adherence to the two guides.

EXERCISE 4.1

Exercises marked by an asterisk (*) have answers included in the Answer Key at the end of the text.

In the following passages, either one of the two guides to critical thinking has been ignored or else the author is complaining about someone else ignoring one of them. In either case, identify the guide and explain the problem the passage raises. Be warned: one of the following is actually a justification for ignoring a guide, and in another it is not clear whether there is any problem at all.

*1. It's easy to get to my house from where you are. Just go two blocks north, three blocks east, one block south, and one block west.

2. David Letterman: Why did the terrorists attack us?
   Dan Rather: Because they're evil.

*3. Scientists who are trying to model the origins of the universe have so much data and so many complicated issues to deal with that they have to leave some data out of the model to make it manageable.

4. In the area of height, he's a little short.

*5. If you are ever asked to obtain the sum of a consecutive series of positive integers beginning with 1, the easiest way to go about it is simply to add them up.

6. We should put an end to welfare. Those people just don't want to work.

Continued >

*7. Proponents of "intelligent design" argue as follows: "irreducibly complex" organs like the eye could not be the result of evolution because all the various parts need to be present for the organ to function. Therefore, the organ needs to be created all at once, which means that the slow and gradual development of the evolutionary model is wrong.

8. Tanya: "Look at the strange pattern cut into the field; what do you think it is?"
Toni: "I think it's some sort of message from extraterrestrials. I mean, I have never seen anything like it before, so what else could it be?"

*9. "In *The Blank Slate: The Modern Denial of Human Nature*, Stephen Pinker debunks belief in the human soul, that is, the Ghost in the Machine, as well as the Noble Savage and, in his view the most persistent of the erroneous conceptions of the self, the Blank Slate. He takes all these terms to be simple and naive in a degree that is hardly consistent with the seriousness of the philosophic traditions from which they emerged."[3]

10. "Unfortunately, the . . . economist can only cram a complex and exciting world into simplistic equations by doing violence to the data. First, the . . . economist must assume away most of the complexities of the world. Economic actors are assumed to be 100 percent self-interested, have perfect information about the market, are perfect calculators, and are perfectly rational. Their competitors are assumed to sell products that are perfectly homogenous (that is, exactly the same as everyone else's). There are zero transaction costs, zero negotiation costs, zero barriers to market entry and bankruptcy. If an economist wants to study the costs of market entry, his model will include these costs, but all the other factors will be assumed away or held to be perfect."[4]

*11. Pensions are obsolete because companies can't afford to finance them, private savings plans are a reliable substitute, and anyway, I don't like them.

II. The Three Laws of Reason

Save the phenomena and Occam's razor are good bits of advice, but they are only a first step. The more specific direction of the **three laws of reason** is also necessary. These laws are, in particular, the foundation of the deductive reasoning that will be introduced in Section III of this chapter, but they are also indispensable rules for all critical thought in general. An argument that violates any of them will not work.

---

3 Marilynne Robinson, *Absence of Mind* (New Haven: Yale University Press, 2010), 16.

4 Steve Kangas, "The Methodology of the Chicago School." *The Long FAQ on Liberalism*, Liberalism Resurgent website, www.huppi.com/kangaroo/tenets.htm.

The Law of Identity I: The Need for Clear Definitions

The first law of reason is the law of identity, which is split into two parts for this discussion: the need for clear definitions and the need for consistent definitions. Let's begin with a general definition of the law of identity:

*Definition: The **law of identity** stipulates that every existing thing has a specific nature such that it can be distinguished from all other things.*

A thing that can't be distinguished from other things can't be clearly identified and is, therefore, not really a thing at all. Take yourself: you are you and nobody else. As a result, it is possible to identify you—to distinguish you from other people. Otherwise you wouldn't be a specific person. (This holds true even if you are an identical twin; because twins occupy distinct spatial coordinates, they are distinct beings.) The law of identity is basic to critical thinking because, to avoid confusion, it is essential to know what the terms in an argument mean.

Put differently, critical thinking requires precision. Previous chapters have stressed the importance of relevance and truth in arguments, but these qualities can be difficult if not impossible to assess if you are uncertain what the key terms in an argument mean. In practice, this often entails knowing what their definitions are. To be sure, when terms refer to familiar objects like chairs or cars there is little need for definitions, and even if the need does arise, an ostensive definition will usually do.

*Definition: An **ostensive definition** consists of pointing out an example of the object in question.*

All you do is say, "There, that's a widget" and rely on a person's ability to recognize other widgets when he sees them.

However, a lot of words are abstract—that is, they don't refer to objects—and abstract words have to be defined non-ostensively. However, trouble can arise with non-ostensive definitions. For example:

E9: *Aisha: I don't think that painting is any good.*
   Min Ho: What are you talking about? It sold for millions of dollars.

Aisha and Min Ho are pretty clearly operating with different definitions of "good." She is referring to an aesthetic standard and he is referring to an economic one. This happens with words that cannot be defined ostensively. Pointing to a "good painting," a "good car," and a "good person" will not generate a definition of "good." So until Aisha and Min Ho clarify their definitions, the discussion is likely to go nowhere.

Now consider this exchange:

E10: *Eunice: That movie was awful, no good at all.*
   Stephanie: I disagree; I really liked it.

This may or may not develop into a useful argument. Right now, the only implicit definition of "good" is Stephanie's equation of it with the subjective "what I like," and that's not a very useful definition. If the argument is to go anywhere, Eunice and Stephanie will have to clarify their conception of what makes a movie "good." Only if they agree on a definition can the discussion proceed.

So when it comes to abstract terms like "good" (ones that can't be defined ostensively), things don't always go smoothly. If an extraterrestrial friend from the Galaxy Andromeda were to ask you what "good" means, you might well struggle with the definition. Yet the law of identity still holds: if you can't define "good" in some *clear* way that others can understand, it's dangerous to use it in an argument because the definition may change from person to person. Abstract words are therefore always in danger of becoming what in Chapter 3 I called Humpty Dumpty words—ones where the meaning is so fluid that there is virtually no meaning at all. If goodness is simply subjective—in the eye of the beholder—there can never be an argument about whether some thing or some person is good, because if Arnold calls a movie "good" and Rashida calls it "bad," neither can be wrong. So, when abstract words are introduced into arguments it is necessary to develop workable, non-ostensive definitions for them.

What precisely is a non-ostensive definition? In practice it is many things because people employ a lot of strategies to make their meanings clear, but essentially it is this:

> **Definition:** A **non-ostensive definition** assigns a term to a class and then distinguishes it from other members of that class.

When we don't have access to examples, non-ostensive definitions can be applied even to concrete objects. For example, when the extraterrestrial asks what a chair is and there isn't one around, you might tell her that a chair is a piece of furniture. To put this more formally (because Ms. ET understands logic), you might say, "a chair is an object that belongs to the class of objects called 'furniture'." (Let's assume she knows what furniture is.) Of course, this definition is not specific enough because a lot of things that are furniture are not chairs. So you make distinctions within the class of things that are furniture by adding what are called (in Latin) **differentiae**. Differentiae distinguish between objects within the same class:

> **Non-ostensive definition example:** A chair (object) is a piece of furniture (class) intended for sitting on by one person (differentia, which is the singular of differentiae).

While this definition distinguishes a chair from a sofa, it is still not precise enough because it doesn't distinguish chairs from stools. So for Ms. ET's benefit, you might add that chairs have backs and perhaps some stipulation about the length of its legs. The process can be set out in a diagram like that shown in Figure 4.2. Just follow the arrows to get the definition: a chair is a piece of furniture designed to be sat on by one person and that has a back. This is the law of identity at work. Each step specifies the object by excluding other things—by differentiating chairs from other objects. More differentiae might be necessary to fully distinguish chairs from stools—and therefore to give "chair" an identity—but this should give you the idea.

Figure 4.2
Building a Definition

Now let's try to develop a non-ostensive definition for the abstract word "good." The first problem is that, unlike "chair," it is not absolutely clear where to begin. Given the many possible uses of the word, we could take a number of different approaches, but let's try this:

Provisional definition 1: *"Good" belongs to the class of words that express approval.*

That's a start—we all use "good" to express approval—but now we have to distinguish between different kinds of approval. For instance, "good" may express *moral* approval, as in "that's a good thing to have done" or "he is a good person," or it may express *technical* approval, as in "she is a good dancer" or "that is a good essay." Before we can deal with this distinction, however, we have to step back and ask whether "approval" identifies a subjective (i.e., a purely personal) feeling or an objective (or at least a widespread) standard. But remember, if the word is merely subjective, it has no definition—no specific identity—since it just means, Humpty Dumpty style, "whatever I like." So if "good" has a specific identity, there must be an objective, or at least common, standard that distinguishes it from other qualities. That produces the following:

PD2: *"Good" is an approval word based on a standard of judgment that is not purely subjective.*

A diagram would look like that shown in Figure 4.3.

Figure 4.3
Seeking the Good

While this may help a little, we really haven't got very far with our definition, and many people might argue that this is all wrong. They might insist that approval words are always subjective and therefore can't be defined with any accuracy. (In short, there is nothing that "good" identifies.) Others might argue that *moral* approval words are subjective whereas *technical* ones aren't—that it's possible to identify clearly a good dancer or a good essay but not a good person or a good action. Still others might take issue with this view, arguing that it's clear who good people are or what actions are good but insisting that the technical use of the word is subjective (and so not really technical at all). A good dancer is, for example, anybody you think is a good dancer. Since none of these positions is entirely indefensible, the lesson is that, more often than not, we can't make abstract words obey the law of identity as strictly as concrete words do. There is often, perhaps always, room for disagreement about what they mean.

Be that as it may, critical thinking depends upon the capacity to provide a clear, or at least workable, **standard** definition; that is, a commonly accepted definition of a term. Even if precise definitions elude us, we have to beware of letting words float too freely. For example:

E11: *Akemi: You lied when you told me you were studying because you were out with Janine. She was sitting beside you when you were talking to me on the phone.*
Sam: I didn't lie, I just misspoke.

Sorry Sam, but by the standard definition of "lie" that's what you were doing. A standard definition of lie would be "a statement (class) that is intentionally factually incorrect (differentia) and is intended to mislead (differentia)." This is a reasonably precise definition. Lying and misspeaking belong to the class of false statements, but "intentionally" and "intended to mislead" differentiate lying from misspeaking, and what Sam said certainly seems to fall within the definition of a lie. Since it is sometimes difficult to prove "intention," on a scale of precision "lie" sits somewhere between a word like "chair" and a word like "good." It's not as concrete as the former but not as abstract as the latter; it can be pinned down with a reasonable degree of accuracy. But the fact remains that the farther we move away from an ostensive definition the harder it is to apply the law of identity. While this is a facet of language we have to recognize and respect, we still have to try to apply the law as well as we can.

The Law of Identity II: The Need for Consistent Definitions

Along with clear definitions, the law of identity also calls for *consistent usage*. In fact, clarity can't exist without consistency. If you do not stick to definitions once they have been given, a lack of clarity creeps in through the back door of inconsistent usage. Consider the following rather silly and sexist argument, one I think you will see through pretty easily:[5]

> **E12:** *(P1) Because only man is rational, (P2) and because no woman is a man, (C) therefore no woman is rational.*

It seems evident that "man" has been used to identify two overlapping but not identical sets of people: humankind and male humans. If so, this argument commits an informal fallacy called equivocation.

> *Definition: **Equivocation** occurs when a term carries different but unspecified definitions in the same argument.*

This is a fallacy not of relevance but of ambiguity:

> *Definition: A **fallacy of ambiguity** occurs when it is unclear which of two or more possible meanings a term bears.*

Fallacies of ambiguity trade on the fact that words often have more than one definition. "Bank," for example, can refer to a financial institution, the side of a river, a pile of snow, or a movement by an airplane. It's the same with "man." In its first appearance in **E12** it almost certainly identifies "humankind"—the lack of the indefinite article should alert you to that—while in the second the presence of the indefinite article strongly suggests that it means "male." So the use of "man" is inconsistent: it bears, or certainly seems to bear, two meanings. Only by ignoring this inconsistency in use can the conclusion that no woman is rational be reached. Here is a revised version of the argument in which the definition of "man" is made consistent by substituting what seem to be the proper identities in each usage:

> **E13:** *(P1) Because only* humankind *is rational, (P2) and because no woman is a* male, *(C) therefore no woman is rational.*

But now the premises are irrelevant to the conclusion and the argument has simply fallen apart. So if the original argument looked at all persuasive it was only because of the equivocal use of "man." And indeed, that is often the point of equivocation: it's a rhetorical device employed to cover up distinct meanings that make premises untrue or irrelevant. (On the other hand, it is sometimes just the result of sloppy thinking.)

It is important to note, however, that the demand for consistent usage doesn't force anyone to read **E12** in the **E13** way. There are other readings that get rid of the equivocation. Identify "man" as "male" both times and the equivocation disappears:

> **E14:** *(P1) Because only males are rational, (P2) and because no woman is a male, (C) therefore, no woman is rational.*

---

5 The example was treated in detail in my book *Plato's Sun* (Toronto: University of Toronto Press, 2005), 142–3.

But in this case right-thinking humans with any experience of the world will recognize that **P1** is false, and since **P1** and **P2** are codependent premises, **P2** is irrelevant. Should anyone wish to substitute "humankind" for "male" the same result will occur, except in that case **P2** is false and **P1** irrelevant. The lesson to take from this is that you cannot assess an argument until you know clearly what it says.

Here is a somewhat subtler example of equivocation:

E15: *(P1) Because we should be told everything that it is in the public interest to know, (P2) and because public interest in the prince's sex life is undeniable, (C) therefore we should be told about it.*

The equivocation here is on the term "public interest." In **P1** it refers to "what the public *should* know" while in **P2** it refers to "what the public *wants* to know." These are not the same thing, and if we substituted them for the ambiguous "public interest" we would no longer have relevant codependent premises but rather irrelevant independent ones.

Finally, here is a more serious example of equivocation (this is similar to an argument set out in Chapter 2):

E16: *(C) Abortion should be against the law because (P1) it is wrong to kill innocent people.*

Let's restate this, adding in a little more detail:[6]

P1: Because it is wrong to kill innocent persons;
P2: Because fetuses are innocent persons;
C: It is therefore wrong to kill fetuses.

Leaving aside the point made in Chapter 2—that in most jurisdictions in the West fetuses are not legal persons—and the further question of whether it is even right to kill the guilty, we still have to ask what the term "innocent persons" means in **P1**. Is it someone who has never done anything morally wrong? That doesn't seem right, because in that case the implication is that it *might* not be wrong to kill virtually all of us since most of us have done *something* morally wrong at some point in time. A more reasonable view would be to understand the term as referring to rational beings who have not committed crimes for which they should pay with their lives. We can reasonably add that to be able to commit a crime one has to be able to form the *intention* to commit it. If that seems a better reading, turn to **P2**. The problem that now arises is that this definition of "innocent persons" can't be applied to fetuses because fetuses

---

6 I dredged this argument out of my own head, but it has been pointed out to me that this, or something very like it, is an argument that was developed at length by the late American philosopher Mary Anne Warren.

aren't rational beings who can form the intention to do something. So the definition of "innocent" in **P2** must differ at least somewhat from its definition in **P1**. If so, the argument is equivocating on the term "innocent persons."

A caveat: I don't claim this is an airtight argument against the expanded version of **E16**. There are probably good critical responses to it. (One response might be to insist that "intention" is a red herring; an "innocent" being is simply one who has done nothing that would justify killing it. Whether that is an adequate response, I leave to the reader.) But the fact remains that the meanings of the term "innocent persons" in **P1** and **P2** are not self-evidently identical, and therefore the assumption that they are has to be defended. If it cannot be, **P2** is an irrelevant premise and **C** does not follow.

A Note on Vagueness

Any word with more than one meaning can be used equivocally, but some words are inherently *vague* and therefore particularly open to twists of meaning. Consider the following famous puzzle called the paradox of the heap. It goes like this:

> **E17:** *There is no such thing as a heap of sand because if you look at some sand and decide that it is not a heap then adding something as small as a grain of sand will never make it a heap. Conversely, if you think something is a heap of sand then taking away a grain of sand will never change your view. Therefore, it is impossible either to make or unmake a heap of sand. This means that the idea of a heap of sand is incoherent and there is no use claiming to know what it is.*

You probably disagree with this argument: obviously heaps exist. The difficulty is to explain why you do.

To unravel the confusion, let's apply a non-ostensive definition of a heap as a kind of word:

> **NOD1:** *"Heap" is a quantity word.*

"Heap" has now been assigned to a class of words, but we still need a differentia to distinguish it from other quantity words. So let's add the following:

> **NOD2:** *"Heap" is an unspecific quantity word (unlike "litre", for example, which is specific).*

This means, of course, that an actual heap is an unspecific quantity. By definition then, a heap of sand will not contain a specific number of grains of sand, so talk of adding or subtracting grains of sand is irrelevant—a bit of a red herring.

Suppose for a moment that a heap of sand was a specific quantity—for example, that it consisted of exactly a million grains of sand (with the added stipulation that they are not simply spread around but piled up). If that were true, then when someone added a grain of sand to a collection of 999,999 grains, a heap would be created. And when a grain was added to or subtracted from a million grains, a heap would be destroyed. So if a heap were a specific quantity, the premises in **E17** would be wrong.

But since it is not a specific quantity they are irrelevant. The argument therefore fails both the truth and the relevance test. It has used "heap" equivocally, relying on the fact that readers will know it is an unspecific word but, through reference to grains of sand, slyly giving it a specific definition.

That said, there is another side to this puzzle. It makes the interesting claim that since adding or subtracting a particle as small as a grain of sand will not change our *perception* of whether something is a heap, our perception can never change, no matter how many grains are added or subtracted. This is incorrect, but to see why we have to return to the fact that sometimes it isn't possible to eradicate all subjectivity (and by extension all vagueness) from a term. To a certain extent, heaps of sand exist just so long as people perceive them. Add enough grains of sand (a vague quantity) and most people will identify what they see as a heap; subtract enough and they will not. People will see heaps appear or disappear, *but not at exactly the same time*. There is no fixed border, no precise moment when everyone will perceive or cease to perceive a heap. So here too the puzzle relies on the equivocal use of "heap." It seduces us into trying to pinpoint a specific moment in a vague, unspecific process—the moment when everyone's perception changes. But because unspecific processes do not have specific borders, there is no single moment when this will happen, so there is no use trying to pinpoint one. And the fact that one cannot be pinpointed does not mean that heaps don't exist; it only means that they don't have an absolutely specific identity.

We can look at the technical use of "good," discussed above, in a similar way. Everyone who knows anything about hockey will agree that Sidney Crosby is a "good" player, and I am pretty certain that anyone who has ever seen me play will agree that I am not. But in between Sid and me are all sorts of players with varying degrees of ability, and there will be no universal agreement about where the threshold of "good" lies. At the extremes—Crosby and me—there will be widespread agreement, but not in the middle. In fact, we tend in such matters to employ a whole range of terms— bad, poor, fair, average, above average, and so on—which shade into one another without any precise degree of specificity. That is just how we talk about vague things.

Remember: the point is not that vague terms should never occur in arguments, but that when they do it is necessary to recognize their limitations and not try to make them do work they cannot do. Sometimes legislators will intentionally include vague words in laws and leave it up to the discretion of the courts to interpret them. In Canadian law, an "unlawful assembly" is defined as a group of three or more people who gather for a common purpose and pose a danger of disturbing the peace *tumultuously*.[7] "Tumultuously" is a wonderfully vague word:

---

7 Section 63 of the Criminal Code.

who can say exactly what it means? (So too is "common purpose," but I shall leave that to the side.) For example, an older person's tumult is often an adolescent's quiet evening. The point of inserting the term into a law would seem to be to place responsibility on judges (and juries) to decide whether individual cases pose this sort of danger. It makes them responsible for identifying what "tumultuous" means in a given instance. The reason for this would seem to be that legislators have recognized that "unlawful assembly" is itself a vague term because in one context an action may be tumultuous and in another it may not be. Therefore, judgment about what is tumultuous has to rest in the hands of judges (and juries) rather than legislators. And that's the point: vague words call for judgment in a way that specific words do not.

The Law of the Excluded Middle: Dividing Up the Universe

The second law of reason is the law of the excluded middle:

> *Definition:* The **law of the excluded middle** stipulates that for any identified object X, everything either is X or it is not X.

This *specifies* the law of identity as follows: to identify a term means to be able to distinguish it from everything else in the universe. This entails dividing the universe into two. Take chairs: everything you encounter in the universe is either a chair (X) or it is not a chair (not X). It may seem strange to think of the universe as composed only of chairs and non-chairs, but we all work that way when necessary. If you are looking for a friend in a crowd, you proceed on a "friend–not friend" basis. You apply the law of the excluded middle, just as you do when you are defining a word. Recall Figure 4.2: you learned there that a definition is a chain of division. Let's rearrange the figure to that shown in Figure 4.4.

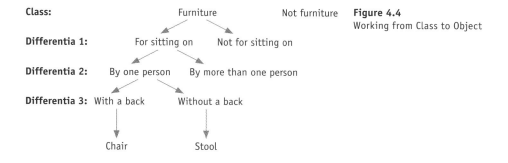

Figure 4.4
Working from Class to Object

At each stage of the definition, there is a choice between two—and only two—options. It's a whole series of "this-or-not-this," "either-or" choices. Everything in the universe is either a piece of furniture or it is not a piece of furniture, and everything in the universe that is furniture is either meant for sitting on or it is not meant for sitting on, and so on. For the purposes of the definition, any third or middle option is excluded. These sorts of "either-or" statements are called **logical tautologies** because they are necessarily or self-evidently true. Put differently, you know **a priori** (in advance of any evidence) that everything you see today will either be a chair or it won't be. You also know a priori that the following statement is true:

> **S1:** *Everyone you meet today will either be named "George" or will not be named "George."*

You do not have to wait to see if this statement is true. By contrast, consider this statement:

> **S2:** *The first person you meet tomorrow will be named "George."*

You will know whether **S2** is true only after you have met someone tomorrow. Hence, its truth or falseness is known **a posteriori**, which means that it is not self-evidently true.

The tautological process of division that constitutes the law of the excluded middle is a useful tool for focusing thought and testing definitions. To see how it works, let's do a little medieval philosophy:[8]

> **E18:** *The great theologian St. Thomas Aquinas (ca. 1225–74) queried another theologian's definition of God's "omnipotence" as meaning that God can do whatever is possible. Applying the law of the excluded middle, Aquinas argued that "possible" could only mean either "naturally possible" or "supernaturally possible." There was no third option. If "possible" meant "naturally possible" then God's power did not exceed that of nature, and that is not particularly impressive for a divine being. But if it meant "supernaturally possible" then it merely meant that God can do what God—a supernatural being—can do, and that is completely uninformative.*

Aquinas's argument is that the use of the word "possible" yields a choice between a definition of God's omnipotence that fails to do justice to a divine being and one that says nothing. Since there is no third or middle option, the word "possible" cannot usefully be part of a definition of God's omnipotence. Aquinas has thus used the law of the excluded middle to demolish what had sounded like a good definition of divine omnipotence. Figure 4.5 shows the argument in diagram form.

---

8 Adapted from Anthony Kenny, *The God of the Philosophers* (Oxford: The Clarendon Press, 1986), 92.

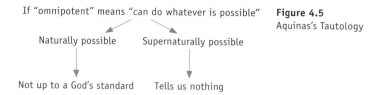

Figure 4.5
Aquinas's Tautology

Go back to the coin-weighing puzzle in **E7** above and you will see that it too is an example of applying the law of the excluded middle to problem solving. That's the point of the phrase, "one of two things will occur." As these examples show, used properly the excluded middle is a useful method of focusing thought.

Not every pair of options is a tautology, though. Sometimes there really is a "middle" option and so, if you are not careful, you may fall victim to a fallacy of presumption called a false dichotomy.

*Definition: A **fallacy of presumption** occurs when a premise of an argument contains an unwarranted assumption; that is, it assumes what would need to be demonstrated.*

A **false dichotomy** is a version of this type of fallacy. It consists of presenting a choice between two options as a tautology when in fact it is not. For example:

E19: *You are either for us or against us.*

This is not necessarily true because neutrality is often an option. Therefore, the speaker cannot assume that it is true without evidence.

Now consider the following:

E20: *If you don't take that job you will have wasted your whole education.*

Here too the speaker is assuming that there are only two options: either take the job or accept that your education has been wasted. Maybe this is true, but it is not *self-evident* that it is. The speaker needs to demonstrate this. So **E20** is also a false dichotomy. Like all fallacies, the fallacy of false dichotomy may simply represent a mistake on the speaker's part, but it may also be used as a rhetorical device to make options that are not exhaustive look exhaustive.

The Law of Non-Contradiction: Making Certain the Universe Stays Divided

The final law of reason is the law of non-contradiction.

*Definition: The **law of non-contradiction** stipulates that for any identified object, X, nothing can simultaneously be X and not X.*

There are two interconnected versions of the law of non-contradiction, both of which come from Aristotle.

Non-Contradiction: Version 1

Version 1: *Contradictory states cannot simultaneously exist.*

This version concerns existence; to be precise, it speaks to what can logically exist. When the existence of a given state or condition is *logically impossible*, it is quite literally unimaginable. It may be *physically impossible* for humans to fly like birds or for objects to move faster than the speed of light, but it is not logically impossible. These states are imaginable. But can you visualize someone simultaneously being taller and shorter (i.e., not taller) than someone else? Can you visualize a round square or a four-sided triangle—that is, a square that is simultaneously not a square and a triangle that is simultaneously not a triangle? Can you *identify* what these contradictory states would look like? To recognize certain states as contradictory and therefore as logically impossible is to recognize that there are aspects of them that cannot simultaneously exist.

The problem is that the contradictory nature of two states is not always readily apparent. Consider the following philosophical nugget:

E21: *What happens when the irresistible force meets the immovable object?*

The answer is nothing, because they can never meet. To see why, consult the law of identity. The definitions of these terms make them *mutually contradictory*: an irresistible force is a force that can move any object, and an immovable object is an object that can resist any force. Given these definitions, the "force" and the "object" cannot, without contradiction, simultaneously inhabit the same universe. One or the other may exist or neither may exist but not both, because if an irresistible force could encounter an immovable object the object would simultaneously move and not move and the force would simultaneously be resisted and not resisted.

Non-Contradiction: Version 2

Version 2: *Contradictory claims cannot both be true.*

This version concerns truth. If, as version 1 stipulates, contradictory states cannot simultaneously exist, then claims that they can are necessarily false. If I say that my brother is simultaneously my height and yet taller than me, there is no way for the statement to be true. The problem is, once again, that there are cases that can be terribly confusing. A particularly bewildering type of contradictory claim is the logical paradox.

Definition: *A **logical paradox** consists of a statement or set of statements that contains a contradiction.*

Here is an example:

E22: *It is a general rule that all general rules are false.*

Let's construct an argument based on the assumption that **E22** is true:

*P1: If **E22** is true, then all general rules are false;*
*P2: But **E22** is a general rule;*
*C: Therefore, if **E22** is true it is false.*

Therefore, **E22** cannot be true because the assumption that it is makes it false, and if by the law of the excluded middle all claims are either true or false, then by the law of non-contradiction no statement can simultaneously be true and false. But if it can't be true, it must be false, which means that we know a priori (i.e., in advance of the evidence) that not all general rules are false—some of them have to be true. This is an interesting discovery. How can it be possible to know *in advance* (a priori) that some general rules are true? Isn't such knowledge a posteriori? That is, isn't it necessary to check the evidence by examining all general rules (which are potentially infinite in number) to see whether any of them are true? If so, it is possible that all general rules will turn out to be false, in which case **E22** would be true . . . and therefore false? It's all very confusing.

The confusion arises from the fact that **E22** is *self-referential*. It presents itself as a general rule that negates all general rules, which creates a contradiction because **E22**'s rule now applies to itself. Compare **E22** to the following version of the famous Liar's Paradox:

E23: *Speaking as a Canadian, I can assure you that all Canadians are consistent liars (i.e., they never tell the truth).*

Once again, if this statement is true then it is false, because it is made by a Canadian and the truth of **E23** would entail that all Canadians, including the speaker, are liars. As with **E22**, the contradiction arises from self-reference. A member of a group cannot claim that everything members of that group say is false because the claim then applies to the speaker.

Not all self-referential statements are paradoxical. If you make the above statements "positive" by substituting "true" for "false" in **E22** and "truth-tellers" for "liars" in **E23**, the contradiction disappears. That is not to say that these "positive" *self-referential* statements are necessarily true; only that they could be without contradiction. To know which they are you would have to check the evidence. For example, if there is at least one Canadian who lies, the "positive" version of **E23** ("All Canadians tell the truth") is false; if not, it is true. Such knowledge is a posteriori.

The Reductio ad Absurdum: The Argument That Erases Itself
The law of non-contradiction gives rise to a powerful argumentative tool called the *reductio ad absurdum*.

Definition: *A **reductio ad absurdum** is an argument that demonstrates a claim is false because it leads to a contradiction (ad absurdum means "to a contradiction").*

For example, consider the view that killing is always wrong and imagine someone wanted to argue against it. To do so, he might construct the following *reductio*:

E24:
(P1) Since killing is always wrong and (P2) and since war involves killing, (P3) this means that no one ought to have declared war on Hitler's Germany. (P4) But Hitler was evil and (P5) evil has to be resisted by any means possible, including war. (C) Therefore, killing is not always wrong.

Let's go through this argument carefully. **P1** and **P2** are codependent premises that lead to sub-conclusion **P3**:

P1: Because killing is wrong;
P2: And because war involves killing;
P3: Therefore, no one ought to have declared war on Hitler's Germany.

P4 and **P5** are codependent premises of a separate argument leading to an implied conclusion:

P4: Because Hitler was evil;
P5: And because evil has to be resisted by any means possible, including war;
IC: Hitler had to be resisted by any means possible, including war.

From **IC** and **P2** we can derive:

IC: Because Hitler had to be resisted by any means possible, including war;
P2: And because war involves killing;
C: Therefore killing is not always wrong.

C contradicts **P1**: the argument begins with one assertion and leads to its opposite. (As well, the sub-conclusion represented by **P3** is contradicted by **IC**.) This is because the principle stated in **P1**—killing is wrong—contradicts **P5**'s principle that evil has to be resisted by any means possible. The attempt to uphold both principles leads to the paradoxical claim that killing both is and is not wrong.

The argument forces readers to choose between two principles: **P1** and **P5**. It is based on the assumption that most people will accept **P5** and reject **P1**. But, as always, it is vitally important to pay close attention to what is being said because there is a rhetorical flourish here that should not be overlooked. **P5** says that evil has to be resisted *by any means possible*. Do you agree, or are there limits to resistance? Is it, for example, acceptable to resist evil with evil, or a "lesser evil" with a "greater evil"? (For example, was it evil to use the atomic bomb on Japan in World War II, and if so was it justified?) Do these questions lead us into another paradox? Maybe it isn't obvious after all that **P5** has to be preferred to **P1**. In any case, the point of a *reductio ad absurdum* is to demonstrate that a given claim leads to its opposite because it conflicts with a basic principle or idea we accept as true. As such, a *reductio* forces us to think carefully about whether a given pair of ideas can coexist—whether they can both be true. And that forces you to think about your priorities.

Combining the Three Laws

There is one further issue to examine. In normal speech, we generally don't pay much attention to these laws. We seldom go around stipulating that everything is either a chair or not a chair. Moreover, we are probably happy to accept that there might be hybrid cases of half-chairs. For the most part this does not cause trouble, but when careful reasoning is called for it can. Imagine the following situation:

> **E25:** *A group of 10 people are invited to an advertising promotion. They are all told to come to a certain conference room in a hotel and also that they must be there by 2:00 p.m. sharp. When the invitees arrive they note that the room has a large digital clock and cameras pointing at the door to the room. The host informs them that everyone who is in the room by 2:00 p.m. will be eligible for a draw for a Caribbean vacation home. Just as the clock reaches 2:00, Tony, the tenth guest, enters the room. Has he made it in time? Video replay shows that at precisely 2:00 p.m. Tony was striding through the door, apparently half in and half out of the room. An argument erupts: is Tony eligible for the draw?*

The question is, where was Tony at 2:00 p.m.? Apparently he was half in and half out of the room and in that sense neither "in it" nor "not in it."

But the promoters can't leave it at that because they have to decide whether Tony is eligible for the draw; he can't be simultaneously eligible and ineligible. So how do they decide where Tony was at precisely 2:00 p.m.? The answer is that they have to resort to the law of identity and specify the definition of "in the room." To do so, they draw a line under the door frame and stipulate that to be "in the room" one must be entirely inside that line. The laws of the excluded middle and non-contradiction then apply as follows: everything in the universe either is entirely inside that line or it is not. This works because we know from the law of non-contradiction that nothing can simultaneously be "entirely inside the line" and "not entirely inside the line." Now the promoters go to the video. If it shows that at 2:00 p.m. sharp Tony was completely inside the line he is eligible for the draw and if not he is disqualified. Until the problem arose, the concept of "in the room" could be left vague, but when an argument broke out it had to be specified, which means that it was necessary to apply the laws of the excluded middle and non-contradiction to *identify* where Tony was. (The definition should, of course, exist in advance. Tony may sue the promoters, claiming that since they could have chosen to define "in the room" as simply touching the line their "after the fact" definition is arbitrary and discriminatory.)

Something to Think About

Here are two puzzles and a question that will help underscore the importance of the three laws of reason. I have provided part of the answer for the first one—enough to get you started. Full answers for both are found in the Answer Key at the end of the book.

1. *You are ushered into a room where there is a very long table with 10,000 slips of paper laid out in a line. You are informed that on the underside of each slip is written a sum of money. No two slips have the same sum written on them and the amounts are distributed in random order. You are not told what the lowest or highest amount is; the sums could start and finish anywhere and the gaps between sums are also random. You are ordered to start turning the slips of papers over, beginning at the left and working your way along. The challenge is to stop at what you think is the highest sum of money. (You cannot turn over all the slips and then choose; you have to decide where to stop.) The question is, what are your chances of managing to stop at the highest sum of money? You know that they are somewhere between 0.0001 per cent (1/10,000) and 100 per cent, but you have to be more precise. That is, you have to identify the odds.*

   Part of the answer: *Apply the law of the excluded middle. It will remind you of something simple—seemingly trivial, in fact—but very important: the highest sum is either in the first 5000 slips of paper or it is in the second 5000. That alone will not give you the answer, but it may get you thinking. Ask yourself this question: if you could have one bit of information other than what the highest sum is, what would it be? The answer is the second highest sum, because then you would simply turn over the papers until a sum higher than the second highest turned up. You don't have that information, but you do know, by the law of the excluded middle, that it is either in the first 5000 slips of paper or in the second 5000. Armed with these two tautologies, you can solve the puzzle and identify the odds of stopping at the highest sum.[9]*

2. *I have a theory (not shared by many people) that when someone has a headache he or she is the only person in the whole universe who cannot know that he does. In short, Tina can know that Timothy has a headache, but Timothy cannot. How can this be?*

In reality, this sort of specification goes on all the time. In hockey, for example, a goal is scored only if the whole of the puck crosses the goal line. And a good thing, too, otherwise we'd have a referee saying something like, "Well, it's kind of a goal; oh what the heck, let's call it 63.6 per cent of a goal," and everything would dissolve into chaos. In football, by contrast, the ball merely has to touch the goal line for a touchdown to occur. So the point is not that there must be any particular definition of what a goal or a touchdown is, only that there must be a *precise* definition. The laws of the excluded middle and non-contradiction tell us what "precise" means.

---

9 This is an example I used in *Plato's Sun*, pp. 147–9.

These laws have to be applied to many parts of our lives. Legislators must often (but, as we have seen, not always) take great care in specifying what certain legal terms mean, and lawyers routinely offer long and careful definitions of the central terms in contracts. I once read a transcript of a trial in which one drug company was suing another for breach of patent (i.e., for copying its product without permission). A question that arose was whether company B's product was *identical* to company A's or merely *similar*. Lawyers for company B argued that their product was merely similar to Company A's and therefore not a copy; a copy had to be identical. The proceedings were then given over to arguments about the definitions of "identical" and "similar." Once again, the lesson is that you can't argue until you know what you are arguing about—until the terms are clearly identified.

To summarize, the three laws of reason impose precision on critical thinking. The law of identity stipulates that, where necessary, terms must have precise borders, and the laws of the excluded middle and non-contradiction show how to draw those borders. Anyone who wants to use a vague term in an argument must either recognize its limitations or make it more precise for the purposes of that argument. Put the laws together and you get a simple but powerful command: *in arguments be sure to define your terms clearly and use them consistently.*

EXERCISE 4.2

I. For each of the following, decide whether one or more of the three laws of reason have been broken. There may be cases where none have been broken. Look, as well, for instances of the fallacies of equivocation and false dichotomy and the use of the reductio ad absurdum.

*1. I'm opposed to giving aid to countries in which people are starving. We will never be able to eradicate starvation, so it is a waste of time even to try.

2. The prime minister said we should declare war on poverty, so I threw a hand grenade at a beggar.

*3. i. Sentence ii is true.
   ii. Sentence i is false.

4. I have this friend who can be a real pain at times. I've found that Advil works really well on pain, so the next time he's bothering me I'll just take an Advil.

*5. As a Canadian, I can assure you categorically that no Canadian ever lies.

6. Every day of the year comes either before Thanksgiving or after it.

Continued >

*7. A tuna sandwich is better than nothing, and nothing is better than sex, so a tuna sandwich is better than sex.

8. People say we ought not to practise discrimination, but every time we make a choice we discriminate.

*9. A proper theory of ethics will explain how people should live their lives. It will show that such knowledge comes only from experience and that where experience is the teacher, there are no theories.

10. If there are laws of nature then there must be a lawgiver, a divine legislator in effect.

*11. Baseball player Yogi Berra: Nobody goes there anymore; it's too crowded.

12. I hear someone screaming in agony. Fortunately, I speak the language.

*13. Scientists tell us that energy neither comes into nor goes out of existence, so how can there be an energy crisis?

14. Knowledge of the world is based on experience, and experience is never absolutely certain. But we can only claim to know things about which we are absolutely certain.

*15. On the first day of class there are two kinds of students in the room: those who will pass and those who will fail the course. We just don't know yet who the members of the two groups are.

16. We have a right to express our opinions, and since we ought to do what is right we ought to express this opinion.

*17. All apples are either red or not red.

II. *You were introduced to the concepts of "a priori" and "a posteriori" knowledge. Let's make sure you understand them. Which of the following are known a priori and which a posteriori?*

*1. If you throw a ball into the air and nothing interferes with it, it will come back down.

2. A sequence has more than one member.

*3. There is an infinite number of real numbers.

4. There are black holes in space.

*5. $(2 + 3) = (12 - 7)$

6. I think, therefore I am.

*7. In a group of 60 randomly chosen people there will be at least one case of shared birthdays.

8. The only two things that will always be with us are death and taxes.

*9. Every even number can be expressed as the sum of two prime numbers.

10. In most courses most students pass.

*11. My sons are older than I am.

12. Every book in every library in the world either has the word "biology" in it or it does not.

*13. Nothing can move faster than the speed of light.

14. If you do not buy a lottery ticket you cannot win.

*15. My wife is either older or younger than I am.

III. Introducing Deduction

This section introduces the method of reasoning called deduction.

What Is Deduction?

> **Definition: Deduction** is a form of reasoning in which one attempts to demonstrate that the conclusion of an argument follows necessarily from the premises.

For example:

> **E26:** *(P1) Since Mariela never texts me before noon (P2) and since it is only 10:00 a.m., (C) that's not her texting now.*

If both premises of **E26** are true then *necessarily* so is the conclusion. You may not know whether they actually are true, but *if* they are the conclusion follows—no one can rationally claim that the premises are true and then argue that the conclusion is false. To do so amounts to claiming, in violation of the law of non-contradiction, that **C** is simultaneously true and false.

Now consider this argument:

> **E27:** *(P1) If the accused is innocent we will have to justify our conduct before a judge. (P2) If we have to face a judge, our jobs will be in jeopardy.*

Here the conclusion has been left implicit. However, a little critical thought reveals that if **P1** and **P2** are true, then what follows necessarily is this:

> *IC: If the accused is innocent our jobs are in jeopardy.*

Not all deductive arguments succeed in establishing the desired relation of necessity between the premises and the conclusion. Compare the following two arguments:

E28:
A1: (P1) Because reptiles lay eggs (P2) and snakes are reptiles, (C) snakes lay eggs.
A2: (P1) Because reptiles lay eggs (P2) and chickens lay eggs, (C) chickens are reptiles.

In **A1**, if the premises are true then so necessarily is the conclusion. It follows *logically*, which is to say *necessarily,* from the premises. But in **A2**, the premises are both true while **C** is false, so obviously the conclusion does not follow necessarily from the premises. Note, however, that if Ms. ET, our logical extraterrestrial, discovered that **P1** and **P2** of **A2** were true she would still not know whether **C** was true or false. All she would know is that it does not follow necessarily from the premises and, based on them, it could therefore be either true or false. To underline this, let's modify **A2**:

E29:
A3: (P1) Because reptiles lay eggs (P2) and snakes lay eggs, (C) snakes are reptiles.

All three statements (**P1**, **P2**, and **C**) are true, but even so **C** does not follow necessarily from **P1** and **P2**. True premises do not guarantee that a true conclusion follows. Once again, consult our logical extraterrestrial friend. Even if you assure her that **P1** and **P2** are true, this will not be enough to convince her that **C** is also true. To achieve that, **P1** would have to be amended to read:

P1a: Only reptiles lay eggs.

Unfortunately, that is false and it may be dangerous to mislead an extraterrestrial in this way.

As this is an important point, here is another example (we examined a version of it in Chapter 2):

E30:
A4: (P1) Since all humans are mortal (P2) and since Socrates is human, (C) Socrates is mortal.
A5: (P1) Since all humans are mortal (P2) and since Socrates is mortal, (C) Socrates is human.

Let's assume that in **A4** and **A5** all statements are true. Even so, there is an important difference between them. In **A4**, **C** follows necessarily from the premises, but in **A5** it does not. In **A5** the premises could be true while the conclusion is false. This is because we cannot identify what "Socrates" refers to in **A5**. The name could, for example, refer to a cat. Hence, it doesn't follow necessarily from the truth of the premises that the conclusion is also true.

Validity and Soundness

When the conclusion of a deductive argument follows necessarily from the premises—as in **A1** and **A4** above—it is said to be **valid**. When the conclusion does not follow necessarily from the premises—as in **A2**, **A3**, and **A5**—it is **invalid**. Hence, the rule of validity:

> *Definition: The **rule of validity** states that in a valid argument the truth of the conclusion follows necessarily from the truth of the premises.*

Be clear that this does not mean the premises and conclusion actually are true. Consider the following argument:

> **E31:** *(P1) Because all gerbils are from Iowa (P2) and because all Iowans are Canadian, (C) therefore all gerbils are Canadian.*

All three statements are false, but because **C** follows necessarily from **P1** and **P2** the argument is valid. Conversely, in **E29:A3** all three statements are true but the argument is invalid because the conclusion does not follow necessarily from the premises.

The point is that validity is a judgment not on the truth of statements but on the *form* of the argument. The relevant question is not "Are the premises and the conclusion true?" but "Does the conclusion follow necessarily from the premises?" That is why you have been introduced to Ms. ET, our logical extraterrestrial. Since she understands deduction but doesn't know whether any statements earthlings make are true or false, all she can assess is the validity of deductive arguments. In doing so she is not, for example, weeding out ones with true premises and a false conclusion but rather looking for ones where *it is possible for this to be so* because she knows that such arguments are invalid.

So far as truth goes, we humans are often in the same boat as Ms. ET. For example:

> **E32:** *(P1) Because Plato was younger than Democritus, (P2) and because Democritus was younger than Cicero, (C) Plato was younger than Cicero.*

While you may recognize this as a valid argument, you may not know whether any or all of these statements are true.[10] Now consider the following:

> **E33:** *(P1) Because there are intelligent beings elsewhere in the universe (P2) and because intelligent beings will always have a sense of morality, (C) therefore there are beings elsewhere in the universe who have a sense of morality.*

While a little research would have revealed that the statements in **E32** are false, there is at present no way of knowing whether the individual premises of **E33** are true or false. All we know is that the argument is valid. **E33** is an example of total ignorance

---

10 They are all false.

Something to Think About

Here's a deductive puzzle. Suppose you run across someone who is apparently human but who turns out to be immortal—or at least unkillable. What do you conclude? My answer is in the Answer Key at the end of the book.

on our part, but we can also suffer from partial ignorance. In **E30:A5** we know **P1** is true but we don't know whether **P2** is true. What we do know is that **A5** is invalid because it is *possible* for both **P1** and **P2** to be true while **C** is false.

What this means is that deduction is a formal method of reasoning:

*Definition: A **formal method of reasoning** is one where there is a precise procedure for determining an outcome.*

In deductive arguments the outcome is validity, not truth. It is always possible to decide whether a deductive argument is valid even if it is not always possible to know whether its statements are true. To express this in terms that have been used throughout the text, in a valid argument the premises are relevant to the conclusion but not necessarily true.

Nonetheless, truth is obviously important since an argument with false statements is not a terribly useful guide to the world, even if it is valid. This means that in addition to wanting a deductive argument to be valid we also want it to be sound.

*Definition: A **sound argument** is a valid argument with true premises (and necessarily, therefore, a true conclusion).*

An argument that lacks either or both of these characteristics is **unsound**. Because they have false premises, **E31** and **E32** are unsound whereas **E28:A1** is sound. But with **E33** we find ourselves back in the same boat as Ms. ET. We know it's valid, but there is no way of determining whether it is sound or unsound. Such arguments are said to be indeterminate.

*Definition: An **indeterminate argument** is one where soundness cannot be determined because the truth or falsity of the premises cannot be determined.*

Figure 4.6 sets out the various judgments one makes in the assessment of deductive arguments.

Figure 4.6
Assessing Deductive Arguments

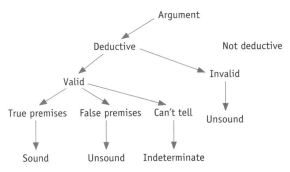

To summarize, deductive *arguments* are valid or invalid but individual *statements*—the premises and conclusion—are true or false. Validity is a judgment on the *form* of the argument (the relation of necessity between the premises and conclusion), and truth is based on the *content* of the statements. Soundness is a two-step judgment, first on the form and then on the content of an argument. When the truth of the premises cannot be determined one way or the other, the argument is indeterminate.

EXERCISE 4.3

I. Decide whether each of the following arguments is valid or invalid. There may be implicit assumptions in some arguments.

   *1. Since she is always calm and because trustworthy people are always calm, she is trustworthy.

   2. Because Eisenhower's decision meant that the Allied forces lost World War II and because that loss meant the end of democracy in the West, Eisenhower's decision meant the end of democracy in the West.

   *3. Because tests show that IQs go up when the tide is coming in and go down when it is ebbing, and because we can trust these tests, we can conclude that intelligence is affected by the tides.

   4. Ken says that he doesn't have a logical mind, but I disagree. Anyone who can pass physics courses must be reasonably intelligent, and any intelligent person has a logical mind. Since Ken has passed all his physics courses he must have a logical mind.

   *5. Disciplines that are abstract and mathematically demanding require a high degree of intelligence. Since astrophysics requires a high degree of intelligence, it is abstract and mathematically demanding.

   6. We don't need to worry about Tina's plane being late because they always announce lateness a half hour before the arrival time and it is now only 15 minutes before the plane is due.

   *7. Things that are boring always put me to sleep, and romantic films put me to sleep so they must be boring.

   8. The Earth cannot be 20 billion years old because the universe is only about 14 billion years old.

   *9. Because you just said that a bad policy is one that has the opposite of its intended effect, and since you have agreed that violence in this school has increased since we implemented a zero tolerance policy, you would have to agree that zero tolerance is a bad policy.

Continued >

10. If you look at all the evidence from every source, you will have to conclude that smoking does contribute to cancer and heart disease. And I know you have looked at all the evidence, so you must think smoking contributes to lung cancer.

II. *Indicate whether each of the following arguments is sound, unsound, or indeterminate.*

*1. Since humans are mortal and mortals don't live forever, humans don't live forever.

2. Since humans are mortal and since they are also mammals, mammals are mortal.

*3. Given that George W. Bush beat Al Gore in the 2000 presidential election and that the candidate with the most votes won, Bush had more votes than Gore.

4. Gerbils are larger than horses and horses are larger than whales, so gerbils are larger than whales.

*5. Since the sun has always risen in the east, it will rise in the east tomorrow.

6. Since the universe has a divine creator and since divine creations have plans, the universe must have a plan.

*7. Because logic is an abstract subject and because some people have difficulty understanding abstract subjects, some people have difficulty understanding logic.

8. Since the universe has a divine creator and since divine creations occur randomly, the universe occurred randomly.

*9. Because humans will be around for the next million years, Earth will survive at least that long.

IV. Summary

This chapter sharpened the focus of critical thinking by introducing the general guidelines of *save the phenomena* and *Occam's razor* before moving on to the more specific *three laws of reason* and finally to the method of reasoning called *deduction*. Occam's razor and save the phenomena are really bits of advice meant to keep reasoning on track. The laws of reason are more restrictive than those guides: violate them and you will have a faulty argument. Finally, deduction is a *formal method of reasoning* because there are precise rules for determining whether an argument is *valid*. Validity is a judgment on the *form* of the argument, which is to say on whether the conclusion follows necessarily from the premises. If an argument is valid, you can then check to see whether its premises are *true*, in which case it is also *sound*. Invalid arguments are always unsound; valid ones can be sound or unsound depending on whether the premises are true. Some arguments are, however, *indeterminate* because it is not possible to assess the truth of the premises and therefore to know whether they are sound or unsound.

CHAPTER FIVE

Sentential Logic

- Sentences as the foundation of deductive arguments
- Sentences and truth values
- Simple and compound sentences
- Logical constants and variables
- Symbolizing sentences
- Symbolizing basic syllogisms
- Symbolizing longer and more complex arguments

This chapter will introduce you to the fundamentals of a form of deductive reasoning called sentential logic. You will learn how to construct arguments, symbolize them, and begin to evaluate whether they are valid.

I. Identifying Sentences

Defining Sentences

Sentential logic is the kind of deductive logic you were introduced to in Chapter 4. As the name implies, sentences—premises and conclusions—are the basic units of this logic. The essential characteristic of these sentences is that they are, by the law of the excluded middle, either true or false. Put differently, every sentence in an argument has one of these two **truth values**.

In Chapter 4 you learned that it is not always possible to know whether a sentence is true or false but, for our purposes here, that is not as important as knowing *what* would make it so. Consider the following three sentences:

> **E1:**
> *S1: Janelle's car is red.*
> *S2: Human life is sacred.*
> *S3: Sentence S3 is false.*

S1 is a straightforward statement of fact. It makes an empirical claim about the world.

> *Definition: An **empirical claim** is one that can be verified by sensory experience.*

If you know which car is Janelle's, you can simply look to see whether it is red. If it is, the sentence is true; if it is another colour, the sentence is false. Of course, empirical claims don't have to be as self-evident as this one is. If I say that Juan-Victor is heavier than Filipe, it may not be clear from looking at them whether this is true, but we can weigh them to see whether it is. In the same manner, scientists often measure effects they cannot perceive without the help of sophisticated instruments. Nonetheless, statements about those effects are empirical because it is clear to the scientists what empirical results will make them true or false.

But what about **S2**? Is it an empirical claim? Note that in **S1** both "Janelle" and "red car" are concrete terms with definite denotations, so they can be defined ostensively. In **S2**, we can ostensively define "human life" by pointing out examples of human beings, but the predicate "sacred" is an abstract term. We may feel we know more or less what it means, but since no one can point to "sacred" in the same way he can point to cars or humans or red objects, there is no ostensive definition for it. Therefore, while it's possible to run a simple empirical test to see if **S1** is true, there is no simple or uncontroversial test that will verify or falsify **S2**. How, therefore, do we determine a truth value for it?

In contrast to **S2**, consider the following:

> **E2:** *Most Canadians believe that human life is sacred.*

This is definitely an empirical claim because it's clear what fact would make it true. A majority of Canadians would have to believe that human life is sacred. Someone could conduct a public opinion poll to see if this is so. Nor would there be any need to worry about how the respondents defined "sacred" because the pollster would only be interested in how many Canadians agreed with the statement, "Human life is sacred." But what if the pollster also wanted to see whether the following claim is true?

E3: *Most Canadians define "sacred" in the same way.*

She could run another poll, so **E3** is also is an empirical claim.

The point is that we can gather evidence that will support or refute **E2** and **E3** because we know what evidence would be decisive. But even if **E2** and **E3** turned out to be true, that would still not constitute proof that **S2** is true. It would show that most Canadians *believe* it is true but, as you learned in Chapter 3, to believe a sentence is true is not to demonstrate that it is true—beware the fallacy of the appeal to popularity. So **S2** isn't an empirical claim, but rather a normative statement.

*Definition: A sentence that makes a **normative statement** expresses an opinion about how things ought to be, or sets a standard of behaviour or achievement that people are supposed to meet.*

In other words, normative sentences like **S2** are "ought sentences" that *express values* rather than state facts. Someone who accepts **S2** is placing a certain value on human life and indicating how humans ought to be treated. But since normative sentences cannot be verified or falsified by evidence (if they can be they are no longer normative but empirical) then strictly speaking they have no truth value. This would seem to disqualify them as sentences that can be used in arguments.

But let's not be too hasty. Normative statements are important. It is very likely that many people believe the sentence "Human life is sacred" to be true or false and are willing to support their beliefs with arguments. After all, statements that express a moral principle or belief are an important part of our conversations. They are often about the foundation of our lives, integral to some of the most fundamental arguments we have, and so they have to be treated seriously. People take reasoned positions for and against normative statements about the morality of capital punishment, abortion, genetic engineering, large carbon footprints, inciting war, the conduct of war, and so on, and it would be counterproductive (nonsense really) to disqualify them from arguments simply because they are not empirical. Moreover, normative statements do not necessarily lack clarity. **S2** means something like "human life is created and protected by a higher being," and surely almost everyone understands what that means. So, for the most part, we need to invoke the principle of charity (and commonsense) and allow clear normative sentences and the values they express into arguments. In other words, we need to treat normative sentences *as if* they have truth values.

For example, consider the following argument:

E4: *(P1) Since human life is sacred (P2) and since what is sacred should never be destroyed by humankind, (C) we should never take another person's life.*

E4 moves from the normative statement that human life is sacred to the conclusion that we should never take a human life. Since it's a valid argument, anyone who accepts the premises must also accept the conclusion. This has radical implications for activities such as the conduct of war and the practice of capital punishment. Depending upon how one defines a fetus, it may also have implications for the practice of abortion. Someone who is unwilling to accept these implications will either have to argue that one of the premises in **E4** is false or he will have to insist that since the premises are unverifiable (not empirical) they are meaningless. In the latter case, he is rejecting arguments with normative statements. A person who takes this view will simply walk away from **E4**, and while that is not totally unreasonable it does curtail a discussion that most people consider important. A better strategy is to accept that sentences in an argument can make normative statements so long as it is sufficiently clear what it would mean for them to be true.

In some cases, the normative and the empirical are intertwined. For example:

E5: *It is always wrong to harm animals.*

This sentence makes a normative statement that is worth discussing because the empirical claim that humans harm and even kill animals is certainly true. Given this truth, it is hard to see how it is reasonable to ignore the normative **E5** on the grounds that it cannot be empirically verified.

A better approach would be to try to clarify what "wrong" means in this sentence and then to discuss whether harming animals falls under that definition of "wrong." Like the words "good" and "heap," which we examined in Chapter 4, "wrong" is one of those vague, ambiguous words that remind us that the border between fact and value is not always immediately and indisputably clear. Compare these statements:

E6:
S4: To say that 2 + 2 = 5 is wrong.
S5: It's wrong to force students to take critical thinking courses.

S4 is certainly verifiable and to that extent seems to be an empirical claim. However, many philosophers and mathematicians argue that mathematical statements are not empirical because they are part of an abstract system and so don't really refer to the world at all, but without getting into that argument what we can say is that for ordinary purposes **S4** operates like an empirical claim. A teacher could quite clearly show a young student why the claim that $2 + 2 = 5$ is wrong. In fact, she could do so by setting out two blocks and then two more blocks and counting to four. In effect, she would be showing the child ostensively what the words "two," "four," "plus," and "equals" mean. As long as the student could identify the blocks as distinct objects, he could follow the explanation.

S5 needs some clarification, however. Here we need to define "wrong" because its meaning is less clear than in **S4**. If it means something like "morally wrong"—we should not force students to do something against their wills—it would seem to be a normative statement. But if it means something like "it's not helpful" then perhaps there is empirical data to support this claim. The lesson is, as it always is, that we need to start with the law of identity, define our terms, and then decide whether we are dealing with a normative statement or an empirical claim. Clearly defined, both can be deployed in arguments even though it is important to understand that normative statements cannot be demonstrated to be true in the absolute way empirical claims can.

Now let's turn to **S3** in **E1**: "Sentence S3 is false". You may recognize this as a version of the Liar's Paradox. If **S3** is true then it is false, because that is what it says. But if it is false then it is true, because what it claims is that it is false. So **S3** is simultaneously true and false. But by the laws of reason this cannot be; we cannot imagine how to assign it a truth value. Let's review our three laws of reason from Chapter 4 in this context:

1. The law of identity entails that *every sentence in an argument has to be identified by its truth value.*
2. The law of the excluded middle requires that *all sentences in an argument are either true or false.*
3. Finally, the law of non-contradiction stipulates that *no sentence in an argument can be simultaneously true and false.*

Given these laws, a paradoxical sentence cannot be part of an argument. We can imagine how the normative **S2** could be true or false—we know what it would mean for it to be one or the other—but not the paradoxical **S3**. So, comparing **S1** and **S2** to **S3**, we arrive at the following rule:

> *Sentence rule: An argument can contain* any empirical claim or normative sentence that is not paradoxical.

S1 and **S2** both obey this rule, but **S3** does not. However, while empirical and normative sentences both meet the criterion set out by the sentence rule, there is an important reason for keeping the distinction between them clearly in mind: only arguments with empirical sentences can be sound because normative sentences don't have truth values.

In Chapter 4 we saw that validity is a judgment on the *form* of an argument. In short, a valid deductive argument shows that a conclusion follows necessarily from the premises. For example, consider the following two arguments:

E7:
> *A1: (P1) Because all swans are white (P2) and because the birds in that river are swans, (C) therefore the birds in that river are white.*
> *A2: (P1) Because human life is sacred (P2) and because Boris is human, (C) therefore Boris's life is sacred.*

A1 and **A2** are valid arguments because their conclusions follow necessarily from their premises. However, in **A1**, **P1** makes an empirical claim that is false: not all swans are white. So **A1** is *unsound*. But what about **A2**? We can verify **P2**, but the truth of the normative **P1** is up for debate. Since there is no commonly accepted procedure for determining its truth, we can't decide whether **A2** is sound or unsound. As a result, **A2** is *indeterminate*.

But, as was pointed out in Chapter 4, arguments that make only empirical claims can also be indeterminate. For example:

> **E8:** *(P1) Because there are intelligent beings elsewhere in the universe (P2) and because intelligent beings will be able to communicate with us, (C) therefore, there are beings elsewhere in the universe who will be able to communicate with us.*

P1 and **P2** are empirical sentences insofar as they are definitely either true or false. The problem is that, at present, we have no way of knowing which they are. So **E8** is also indeterminate.

That's why validity is so important: while the claims that constitute arguments such as **E8** may one day be verified,[1] arguments that contain normative statements can only show us what is implied if those norms are *accepted as true*. **E7:A2** shows us that we cannot simultaneously accept **P1** and then claim that Boris's life is not sacred. While there is no way to demonstrate to everyone's satisfaction that **P1** is true, we know what follows *necessarily* from believing that it is. The same holds for **E4**.

Understanding what follows necessarily from value statements is an extremely important part of critical thinking. For one thing, it brings contradictions among beliefs

---

1 They can be verified because we may at some point come into contact with intelligent life elsewhere in the universe. But they will almost certainly never be falsified because the universe is far too vast for us to explore. So, even if we never find intelligent life, the possibility that it exists will remain.

to light. Imagine a person professing **E4** (that all human life is sacred) and then supporting her country going to war. It is reasonable to ask how she reconciles those positions. It would seem that she will either have to modify **E4** in some way—build in some exception for "just wars" perhaps—or drop her adherence to one of the positions. We looked at this issue when we considered *reductio ad absurdum* arguments in Chapter 4, and it is one you should always bear in mind. While there is no law that forces a person to be consistent in her beliefs, once inconsistency is detected it is awfully hard to defend.

Other Kinds of Sentences

It is important to recognize that lots of non-contradictory sentences are neither empirical nor normative. Greetings ("Hello there") are one example; questions ("What day is it?") are another. While these are clearly not claims, a line of poetry, such as, "She walks in beauty, like the night / Of cloudless climes and starry skies,"[2] does look like a sentence with a truth value. Strictly speaking, Lord Byron is making a non-paradoxical claim about how a woman walks and as such it could be inserted into an argument. However, someone reading the poem is probably not very concerned with its literal truth value, and with good reason. In the first place, poetry is generally judged by other standards: aesthetic and emotional ones, for example. Second, the line is a metaphor—a bit of rhetoric—and it is notoriously difficult, if not impossible, to translate metaphors into straightforward empirical claims. What does "walk in beauty, like the night / Of cloudless climes and starry skies" denote? An argument that relies on metaphors is likely to fall some distance short of clarity.

There are other bits of language such as commands ("Go away!"), pleas ("Help!"), oaths ("I swear"), and so on that may seem to carry truth values. But when considering them, it is useful to distinguish, as we just did with poetry, between the act of judging sentences to be true or false and judging them according to other standards such as sincere/insincere, or honest/dishonest. Imagine someone greeting you with the following sentence:

E9: *Nice to see you.*

If you take **E9** to mean, "I am pleased to see you," you could ask whether it is true or false, because the speaker may be lying; she may not be the least bit pleased to see you. But it is probably more appropriate to think of her as being sincere or insincere,

---

2 Lord Byron, "She Walks in Beauty," 1814.

because just by uttering the greeting she has been polite, and what you want to know is what emotion lies behind the politeness. Your question is not so much, "Is what she said true?" but rather, "Does she really mean it?" and that is a slightly different question.

In a similar vein, when someone says, "I promise," the statement cannot be false (or true) because to say "I promise" is to promise. Perhaps the speaker does not intend to keep his promise, in which case the sentence "He intends to keep his promise" is false. But that is a different issue because the question of intention can arise only because someone has actually made a promise.

These points are subtle and require careful thought, but if you do think about them carefully they can sharpen your sense of what kinds of claims are suitable for arguments. It is possible to make virtually any non-paradoxical sentence fit into an argument, but you would be well advised to consider how meaningful a sentence is in that context.

EXERCISE 5.1

Exercises marked by an asterisk (*) have answers included in the Answer Key at the end of the text.

I. *Mark each of the following statements as suitable (S) or unsuitable (U) for an argument. If it is suitable, designate it as a normative statement (NS) or an empirical statement (ES). If the sentence requires clarification before being designated S or U, indicate that by RC and explain your reasons.*

   *1. Love hurts.

   2. Rembrandt's paintings are more aesthetically satisfying than Van Gogh's.

   *3. You ought to do unto others as you would have them do unto you.

   4. Earth is the fifth planet from the sun.

   *5. As a general rule, general rules are true.

   6. Gerbils make good pets.

   *7. I am telling the truth.

8. Every day of the week is either Saturday or it's not.

*9. It's an absolute rule that there is an exception to every rule.

10. What's the difference?

*11. 'Twas brillig, and the slithy toves / Did gyre and gimble in the wabe.

12. The law of non-contradiction cannot be contradicted.

*13. No one should exceed the speed limit.

14. How lovely you are!

*15. I wandered aimlessly through the darkening streets.

16. I want you to leave me alone.

II. *Drawing on this section and Section III of Chapter 4, designate each the following arguments as sound (S), unsound (U), or indeterminate (I).*

*1. Because all humans make mistakes and because beings that make mistakes are imperfect, all humans are imperfect.

2. Because no humans ever make mistakes and because Todd is human, Todd never makes a mistake.

*3. I'm perfect because okapis can fly, and if okapis can fly I'm perfect.

4. Quarks are subatomic particles, and since subatomic particles have indeterminate velocities, quarks have indeterminate velocities.

*5. Since it is best to enjoy life as much as you can, and since partying is the best way to enjoy life, it is best to party a lot.

6. Because an elephant is larger than a goat and because goats are larger than cats, elephants are larger than cats.

*7. Since humans do not appear to live forever and since I'm human, it does not appear as if I will live forever.

8. Because capital punishment is wrong and because that country practises capital punishment, that country is doing something wrong.

*9. Because capital punishment is wrong and because Canada practises capital punishment, Canada is doing something wrong.

10. Because idle hands are the devil's tools and because your hands are idle, you are being used by the devil.

*11. Basketball is a sport since any athletic contest with precise methods for determining a winner is a sport, and basketball does have a precise method for doing that.

II. Connecting Sentences: Logical Constants

Sentences supply the content of arguments, but they can't just sit there ignoring one another. To get a valid argument they have to be properly connected so that the conclusion follows necessarily from the premises. In this section we will go through that process in detail.

Definitions

In what follows, we will ignore the distinction between normative and empirical sentences, putting both into one pot called "logically acceptable sentences" and treating them alike. In this pot of logically acceptable sentences there are *simple* sentences and *compound* sentences. Thus far we have dealt primarily with simple sentences.

> *Definition: A **simple sentence** is an empirical or normative sentence composed of a single subject and a single predicate.*

Here are some examples:

E10:
S1: Gerbils are mammals.
S2: Humans are morally imperfect.
S3: Chess is difficult.
S4: Hang-gliding can be dangerous.
S5: Politics is a necessary evil.

These sentences (**S2** and **S5** are normative, the others are empirical) all deal with a single idea and so have one subject and one predicate.

Along with simple sentences, arguments also contain compound sentences.

> *Definition: A **compound sentence** consists of two simple sentences connected by a logical constant.*

Now I have introduced a new term:

> *Definition: A **logical constant** is a term that links simple sentences together to make compound sentences.*

Take the simple sentence "It is Thursday" and link it to the simple sentence "I got paid" by means of the logical constant "and." The result is the compound sentence "It is Thursday *and* I got paid." Since compound sentences are an indispensable part of sentential logic, we need to go through the logical constants one by one. But before we do, it is necessary to introduce another concept: symbolizing arguments.

We are going to be examining the *form* rather than the *content* of deductive arguments and to do so we will symbolize the arguments. In other words, since our interest lies in whether arguments are *valid* rather than whether they are *sound*, we will delete the content of the premises and the conclusion and replace them with variables.

> *Definition:* A **variable** *is a letter that signifies a simple sentence.*

Variables serve the same function in logic as they do in mathematics, where X and Y can stand for any number. By tradition, in sentential logic the variables begin with P and carry on from there. As well, we will insert symbols for the logical constants, so a fully symbolized argument will have no words at all.

> *Definition:* To **symbolize** *an argument is to substitute variables for the individual simple sentences and symbols for the logical constants.*

The Logical Constants

Below are the standard logical constants.

Conjunction = and = &
As you have just seen, a conjunction reads "It is Thursday *and* I got paid." If we substitute the variable P for the simple sentence "It is Thursday," Q for the simple sentence "I got paid," and the symbol & for the logical constant "and," this compound sentence is rendered *symbolically* as:

> *(P & Q)*

A conjunction claims that both its simple sentences are true.

Disjunction = either…or = ∨ or ∨̲
There are two symbols for a **disjunction** because there are two ways of disjoining sentences: *inclusively* and *exclusively*. An **inclusive disjunction** is symbolized as:

> *(P ∨ Q)*

An **exclusive disjunction** is symbolized as:

> *(P ∨̲ Q)*

Using our standard compound sentence for this section, both read "*Either* it is Thursday *or* I got paid." But we have to distinguish between inclusive and exclusive uses. First, the *inclusive* disjunction claims that *at least one* of its component simple sentences is true. It therefore allows for *three true options*, which we can express by using the conjunction:

1. It is Thursday and I did not get paid (P is true and Q is false)
2. It is not Thursday and I got paid (P is false and Q is true)
3. It is Thursday and I got paid (P and Q are both true)

The inclusive disjunction excludes, therefore, only one possibility: that it is not Thursday and I did not get paid, which is to say that P and Q are both false. By contrast, the *exclusive* disjunction allows only for options 1 and 2. These are (1) that P is true and Q is false or (2) that P is false and Q is true. So it claims that *exactly one of the component simple sentences is true.*

Often it is difficult to tell which of the disjunctions a speaker or writer intends. Some authorities get around this difficulty by claiming that there is no such thing as an exclusive disjunction in logic, but in fact people often understand it to be implied. After all, we understand tautologies as exclusive disjunctions. Or consider the following:

E11: *Either there is an irresistible force or there is an immovable object.*

Given that the definitions of these terms are mutually exclusive, this compound sentence can only be understood exclusively. That is, the speaker must be claiming that *exactly* one of these options is true.

Even when the law of non-contradiction is not involved, the context may strongly suggest the exclusive is intended. For example:

E12: *Either we get the car repaired or we cancel our holiday.*

Here, the speaker certainly seems to be saying that exactly one of these alternatives will come to pass. However, unlike **E11**, in **E12** both options could turn out to be true without there being any violation of the law of non-contradiction. Therefore, the inclusive disjunction cannot be absolutely ruled out in this case.

Now consider this:

E13: *Either Emmanuel failed his calculus test or Robin did.*

It really isn't possible to be absolutely certain whether this compound sentence is to be understood exclusively or inclusively. Unlike **E12**, the context of **E13** doesn't provide any clues. Even if Emmanuel discovers that Robin has failed, he still can't be certain he is in the clear. In real life, it is important to be sensitive to a speaker or writer's intention. Does he intend the inclusive or exclusive disjunction? If you are unsure, ask (if that is possible). But since logic is driven by the law of identity, logicians generally choose to be deaf to this nuance and invoke the disjunction rule:

Disjunction rule: Treat all disjunctions as inclusive unless doing so entails a violation of the law of non-contradiction.

Based on this rule, both **E12** and **E13** are read as inclusive disjunctions. If you want to create an exclusive disjunction, one option is to invoke the law of non-contradiction explicitly by introducing the sentence as follows: "Exactly one of these claims is true."

Hypothetical = if...then = →

A hypothetical sentence reads, "If it is Thursday *then* I got paid." The compound sentence is symbolized as follows:

$(P → Q)$

An important point is that the hypothetical *is the only compound sentence where the order of the variables matters*. The rule of commutation applies to all the others:

> **Definition:** Where the **rule of commutation** applies, the order of the variables can be reversed without affecting the meaning of the compound sentence.

By this rule, "It is Thursday and I got paid" means exactly the same as "I got paid and it is Thursday." Symbolically,

> *(P & Q) = (Q & P)*

Similarly:

> *(P ∨ Q) = (Q ∨ P)*

But, for the hypothetical:

> *(P → Q) ≠ (Q → P)*

For example:

E14:
S1: If it's a cocker spaniel then necessarily it's a dog.
S2: If it's a dog then necessarily it's a cocker spaniel.

These sentences obviously do not mean the same thing. Given what we know about dogs, **S1** is true but **S2** is false. However, since we aren't concerned with content that is not really the point.

Consider this example:

E15:
S3: If it's a turtle then necessarily it's a mammal.
S4: If it's a mammal then necessarily it's a turtle.

Here, both sentences are false, but even if **S3** were true it would not *entail* the truth of **S4**. ("Entail" means that something is a consequence of something else.) The reason why the rule of commutation does not apply to hypothetical sentences has to do with what a hypothetical is, not with the truth value of the simple sentences it connects. A hypothetical sentence is a *conditional* statement. It claims that the truth of Q follows from the truth of P. In other words, the hypothetical sentence **(P → Q)** claims that P *entails* Q. It does not, however, claim the reverse, that Q entails P.

The point is that if Q is going to *follow from* P, it has to come after P. That is why you cannot apply the rule of commutation and reverse the order of hypotheticals. Because the principle of commutation does not apply to a hypothetical, it is the one compound sentence where it is necessary to name, or *identify,* the places on either side of the logical constant to keep them distinct. The variable on the left of the arrow (note the obvious: an arrow goes in one direction only) is called the **antecedent** while the one on the right is called the **consequent**. Like this:

   (antecedent → consequent)

"If" signals the antecedent and "then" signals the consequent.

Biconditional = if and only if = ↔

A biconditional sentence reads, "It is Thursday *if and only if* I got paid." A longer way to express this is by conjoining two hypotheticals: "*If* it is Thursday *then* I got paid *and if* I got paid *then* it is Thursday" (i.e., "I get paid every Thursday and only on Thursday.") In contrast to hypothetical sentences, biconditional **entailment** runs in both directions, so the rule of commutation applies. Written symbolically, a biconditional compound sentence looks like this:

   (P ↔ Q)

When indicating the biconditional in a written sentence you can use the abbreviation "*iff*," as in "It's Thursday *iff* I get paid." (William of Occam approves of this.)

Negation = not = ~

A negated simple sentence is symbolized as follows:

   ~P

This is stated as "not P," as in "It is *not* Thursday." However, compound sentences may also be negated:

   ~(P & Q)

Here, brackets are required to indicate that it is the compound sentence that is being negated. Stating a negated compound can seem a little awkward. It reads "It is not true that the simple sentences P and Q are both true." In short, the claim is that at least one of them is false.

   Negation is unlike the other logical constants in that it cannot be used to combine simple sentences into compound ones. It is, nonetheless, a necessary logical operator since all sentences have opposites, or **denials**. For example:

E16:
S1: It is Thursday
S2: It is not Thursday.

The *affirmative* **S1** and the *negative* **S2** are denials of one another. That means that by the laws of the excluded middle and non-contradiction, the exclusive disjunction applies to them: *exactly one of them is true*. Without negation, we could not express these two possibilities.

   It is important to understand, however, that **negation** *is not the same thing as falsehood* and **affirmation** *is not the same thing as truth*. For example, the denial of the affirmative sentence "It is Thursday" is the negative sentence "It is not Thursday," and the denial of the negative sentence "It is not Thursday" is the affirmative sentence "It is Thursday." Either sentence can be true or false depending on what day of the week it is when you express it. As I am writing this on a Tuesday, right now the negative sentence, "It is not Thursday," is true, and the affirmative sentence, "It is Thursday," is false. Lacking precise information, all you know is that *a sentence and its denial must have opposite truth values*. We will return to this point below.

When negation is used in a conjunctive sentence, "but" is generally substituted for "and," as in: "It is Thursday *but* I did *not* get paid" (P & ~Q), or "It is *not* Thursday *but* I got paid" (~P & Q). When both simple sentences are affirmative or negative use "and."

As these distinctions can make one's head spin, Tables 5.1 and 5.2 list negation meanings and the logical constants used in sentential logic, respectively.

Table 5.1 What Negations Mean

SENTENCE	CLAIM
(~P & Q)	Not P is true and Q is true.
~(P & Q)	P & Q are not both true.
(~P ∨ Q)	At least one and possibly both of not P and Q is true.
~(P ∨ Q)	Both P and Q are false.
(~P ⊻ Q)	Either not P is true and Q is false, or not P is false and Q is true.
~(P ⊻ Q)	Either both P and Q are true or both are false.
(~P → Q)	If not P is true then Q is true.
~(P → Q)	It is not true that if P is true then Q is true (i.e., P does not entail Q).
(~P ↔ Q)	Not P is true iff Q is true.
~(P ↔ Q)	It is not true that P is true iff Q is true.

Table 5.2 The Logical Constants

CONSTANT	MEANING	SYMBOL	COMPOUND
1. Conjunction	And/but	&	(P & Q)
2. Disjunction	Either . . .or		
a) Inclusive		∨	(P ∨ Q)
b) Exclusive		⊻	(P ⊻ Q)
3. Hypothetical	If . . . then	→	(P → Q)
4. Biconditional	If and only if (iff)	↔	(P ↔)
5. Negation	Not	~	~P
			~(P & Q)

Sentences with More than Two Variables: Order of Precedence

Sometimes a compound sentence will contain more than two variables. For example:

E17: If *(P) we are going to go to the movie* then *(Q)* either *we need to go to an ATM or (R) carry a credit card.*

This sentence contains three variables and two logical constants—a hypothetical and an inclusive disjunction. Without parentheses it reads: P → Q ∨ R. This yields two possible meanings:

1. **P → (Q ∨ R):** If P *then* at least one of Q or R.
2. **(P → Q) ∨ R:** Either if P then Q *or* R

The far more natural reading is the first, P → (Q ∨ R). And in fact it's the correct one insofar as the **order of precedence** gives the hypothetical logical constant precedence over the disjunctive. This means that the hypothetical sign stands on its own while the disjunctive sentence acts as its consequent. Therefore, **E17** is a hypothetical sentence.

Now consider the following sentence:

E18: *(P)* Either *we go to Rome* or *(Q) we go to Bangkok* and *(R) enjoy ourselves.*

In this example, it is not absolutely clear whether this sentence should read (1) (P ∨ Q) & R or (2) P ∨ (Q & R). Once again, we need an order of precedence, and in this case a conjunction has precedence over a disjunction. Therefore, lacking more explicit information about the speaker's intention, option (1) is the correct *logical* reading, even though it may not seem self-evident that it is contextually the right one.

But be alert: a too-mechanical application of the order of precedence of the logical constants can produce an incorrect reading. For example:

E19: Either *(P) we go to dinner and (Q) go to a movie or (R) we stay home.*

Here, the natural reading is (P & Q) ∨ R rather than P & (Q ∨ R,) which the conjunction's precedence over the disjunction might seem to dictate. But since the disjunction envelops the conjunction of P and Q, the natural reading is in fact the only possible one.

Table 5.3 Order of Precedence of Logical Constants	
1.	Hypothetical, →
2.	Conjunction, &
3.	Disjunction, ∨ or ⊻
4.	Biconditional, ↔

Variables connected by the logical constant that is lower on the order precedence are put in parentheses while the one that is higher stands on its own, and the sentence takes the higher one's name. If you want to make it clear that all three variables are part of a single compound sentence, simply add a second set of parentheses, enclosing the whole sentence as follows:

$$((P \lor Q) \& R)$$

This indicates that the sentence is a *conjunction* but that one part of it—one of the *conjuncts*—is an exclusive disjunction.

EXERCISE 5.2

For the following compound sentences, assign each of the simple sentences a variable and then write the compound sentence symbolically. If there are more than two variables insert parentheses to create the correct reading according to the order of precedence.

*1. Either it is too cold to play golf or it is too expensive to play golf.

2. If it is impossible to exceed the speed of light then space travel is virtually impossible.

*3. Either it is Monday or it is not Monday.

4. If there are mistakes, corrections will be required.

*5. If it rains tomorrow then I won't go shopping and I will get some work done at home.

6. It is not true that I will pass the test iff I study for it.

*7. I can't both go home and stay away.

8. He is either older than me or younger than me.

*9. I am going home right now and if I don't return within the hour then I will text you.

10. I can't go home and I can't stay away.

*11. This procedure will work if and only if we begin right away and we don't stop until it is absolutely finished.

12. It is not possible to read this story and not be moved by it.

*13. It is not true that if you read this story you will be moved by it.

14. If love is a two-way street then either we are going forward or we are going backward.

Continued >

*15. It is not true that I am not sympathetic to your cause and emotionally distant from all your concerns.

16. We will go to the movie if and only if you don't work late and are not too tired.

*17. If it's Thursday then if I get paid then I will go to the movies.

III. Syllogisms

This section will introduce a basic kind of deductive argument called a syllogism.

> **Definition:** A **syllogism** is a deductive argument that has two premises and a conclusion.

We will examine the two basic kinds of syllogisms—mixed and pure—and look at some standard forms of each.

The Form of an Argument

Before getting started on syllogisms, let's go over how to symbolize a *deductive argument*. The first step is, of course, to distinguish the premises and the conclusion. You have seen that this is done by putting the individual sentences that make them up in parentheses, as follows:

(P1) (P2) (C)

Next, separate the premises from the conclusion by bracketing the premise side of the argument and then linking it to the conclusion by means of the hypothetical logical constant:

[(P1) (P2)] → (C)

Now the premises have to be *conjoined* as follows:

[(P1) & (P2)] → (C)

The conjunction is important because it asserts that both premises are true. Finally, encase the whole argument in parentheses as follows:

{[(P1) & (P2)] → (C)}

This structure is actually a symbolic rendering of the rule of validity:

> **Rule of validity:** If P1 and P2 are both true then necessarily so is C.

Mixed Syllogisms

Since syllogisms are the foundation of all longer and more complicated deductive arguments, it is important to have a solid grasp of them. In all syllogisms, at least one of the premises has to be a compound sentence. Sometimes this sentence is referred to as a "rule," which is to say that it sets out the conditions of the argument. A sentence like "It is Thursday" is only a statement of fact. The same goes for "I got paid." But link the two by means of a logical constant to form the compound sentence "If it is Thursday then I got paid" and you have a statement that can be linked *codependently* to a simple sentence. Without at least one compound sentence a syllogism would not be a syllogism, only a string of unrelated sentences. For instance, consider this example:

E20: *It's Thursday. I got paid.*

Nothing follows necessarily from these simple sentences. But compare **E20** to the following:

E21: *(P1) If it's Thursday then I got paid (P2) and today is Thursday, (C) therefore I got paid.*

Here, the compound sentence **P1** establishes a condition that is then applied to the codependent simple sentence **P2**. From these premises **C** follows necessarily. This is a mixed syllogism:

Definition: *A **mixed syllogism** consists of two premises, one of which is a compound sentence and one of which is a simple sentence. The conclusion is also a simple sentence.*

Note that in **E21**, **P1** could have been written informally as the apparently simple sentence "I get paid on Thursdays." But when it is translated into formal sentential logic, it is necessary to create a compound sentence by dividing it into two simple sentences and linking them with a logical constant. In practice, that means that simple sentences such as "I get paid on Thursdays" become hypotheticals that tell us that if condition P (the antecedent: "It is Thursday") is met, Q (the consequent: "I get paid") will follow.

With this in mind, consider the following argument:

E22: *(P1) Because elephants are bigger than mice (P2) and because the animal in the bushes is an elephant, (C) therefore the animal in the bushes is bigger than a mouse.*

This is a syllogism with codependent premises **P1** and **P2**, and from them **C** follows necessarily. Rewritten in the style of formal sentential logic it becomes the following:

E23: *(P1) If an animal is an elephant then it is bigger than a mouse (P2) and the animal in the bushes is an elephant, (C) therefore the animal in the bushes is bigger than a mouse.*

In Chapter 6, you will see how this precise form of statement facilitates testing arguments for validity.

Mixed Hypothetical Syllogisms

There are a number of basic forms of mixed syllogisms. Let's turn first to mixed hypothetical syllogisms; **E21** and **E23** are examples of this kind of syllogism:

> **Definition:** A **mixed hypothetical syllogism** is a mixed syllogism in which the compound premise is a hypothetical sentence.

There are two standard types of mixed hypothetical syllogisms. First, there is the *modus ponens* (**MP**), which is Latin for "mood of agreement." In an **MP**, the compound hypothetical premise is followed by a simple premise that *affirms the antecedent* of the hypothetical premise and a simple conclusion that *affirms the consequent* of the hypothetical premise. For example, let's rewrite **E21** assigning each simple sentence a variable:

E24:
P1: If (P) it is Thursday then (Q) I got paid;
P2: And (P) it is Thursday;
C: Therefore, (Q) I got paid.

Symbolically, the syllogism looks like this:

MP:
P1: P → Q
P2: P
C: Q

Translated into the linear style introduced earlier, we get:

MP: {[(P → Q) & (P)] → (Q)}

The short way to describe an **MP** is just to say that it *affirms the antecedent*, which, to repeat, means that the simple premise (P2 above) is the same as the antecedent of the hypothetical compound premise. So the compound sentence (P1) asserts that *if* P is true then so is Q; the simple premise (P2) then affirms that P is indeed true, from which the conclusion that Q is true follows necessarily.

The opposite of the **MP** is the *modus tollens* (**MT**), which is Latin for "mood of disagreement." An **MT** is a mixed hypothetical syllogism in which the simple premise denies the consequent of the compound hypothetical premise while the conclusion denies the antecedent. For example:

E25:
P1: If (P) it is Thursday then (Q) I got paid;
P2: But (~Q) I did not get paid;
C: Therefore, (~P) it is not Thursday.

Symbolically, this reads as:

MT:
P1: $P \rightarrow Q$
P2: $\sim Q$
C: $\sim P$

In linear style:

MT: $\{[(P \rightarrow Q) \& (\sim Q)] \rightarrow (\sim P)\}$

The short description of the **MT** is that it *denies the consequent*. As with the **MP**, in the **MT** the compound premise (P1) asserts that if the antecedent is true then so is consequent. But here the simple premise (P2) *denies* that the consequent is true and from this denial it follows necessarily that the antecedent is false.

Some Invalid Look-alikes

It is important not to confuse the **MP** and **MT** with the following invalid forms, which closely resemble them:

A1: $\{[(P \rightarrow Q) \& (Q)] \rightarrow (P)\}$
A2: $\{[(P \rightarrow Q) \& (\sim P)] \rightarrow (\sim Q)\}$

A1 and **A2** commit formal fallacies. The informal fallacies you have encountered in earlier chapters weaken an argument through the use of irrelevant, ambiguous, or presumptuous premises, but they do not necessarily make them invalid—formal fallacies do.

*Definition: A **formal fallacy** is a flaw in the structure of an argument that renders it invalid.*

A1 is the formal fallacy known as **affirming the consequent**. For example:

E26:
P1: If (P) it is Thursday then (Q) I got paid;
P2: And (Q) I got paid;
C: Therefore, (P) it is Thursday.

From Q ("I got paid") in **P2**, the conclusion P ("It is Thursday") does not follow necessarily because the fact that I get paid on Thursdays does not mean that I cannot be paid on other days as well. Recall that the hypothetical premise establishes an entailment that runs from P to Q but not from Q to P. Asserting Q in the second premise provides no necessary grounds for asserting P in the conclusion.

A2 is the formal fallacy of **denying the antecedent**. For example:

E27:
P1: If (P) it is Thursday then (Q) I got paid;
P2: But (~P) it is not Thursday;
C: Therefore (~Q) I did not get paid.

This syllogism also ignores the possibility that I could be paid on days other than Thursdays, and so the conclusion does not follow necessarily from the premises. In mixed hypothetical syllogisms one can affirm the antecedent or deny the consequent, but one cannot deny the antecedent or affirm the consequent.

A Reminder about Negation

It is important to keep in mind how affirmations and denials relate to negation because there is a potential source of confusion that you need to avoid. P represents an *affirmative* sentence and ~P a *negative* one. But to affirm a sentence means to maintain the negation or lack of negation from one occurrence of a variable to the next, and to *deny* a sentence means to add or delete the negation sign in the second occurrence. Take the following hypothetical sentence:

$(P \rightarrow \sim Q)$

To create an **MT** from it, it is necessary to *deny* the consequent ~Q in the simple premise. That means that the premise will read Q. The conclusion will then deny the antecedent, so it will read ~P. This yields the following:

MT: $\{[(P \rightarrow \sim Q) \& (Q)] \rightarrow (\sim P)\}$

Negation has to be handled with care, but all will go smoothly if you remember the difference between these pairs of rules:

Rule 1: Sentences are affirmative *(P)* or negative *(~P)*.
Rule 2: Sentences, whether affirmative or negative, can be affirmed *or* denied.

With respect to rule 2, the denial of P is ~P and the denial of ~P is P. Understanding how denials and affirmations work can be very useful. Where hypotheticals are concerned they provide equivalent ways of saying things. Every hypothetical sentence has a transposed version, which is its equivalent.

Rule of transposition: To write the **transposition** of a hypothetical sentence, switch the antecedent and the consequent and then deny each of them.

Table 5.4 contains a list of transpositions.

Table 5.4 Transpositions	
$P \rightarrow Q$	$\sim Q \rightarrow \sim P$
$P \rightarrow \sim Q$	$Q \rightarrow \sim P$
$\sim P \rightarrow Q$	$\sim Q \rightarrow P$
$\sim P \rightarrow \sim Q$	$Q \rightarrow P$

One thing transposition reveals is that the **MP** and the **MT** are simply different ways of saying the same thing. Take an **MP**:

{[(P → Q) & (P)] → (Q)}

Rewrite it with the transposition of the opening premise and the result is:

{[(~Q → ~P) & (P)] → (Q)}

This is an **MT**.

The Disjunctive Syllogism
Now let's consider the **disjunctive syllogism (DS)**, which runs as follows:

E28:
P1: Either (P) it is Thursday or (Q) I will get paid;
P2: And (~P) it is not Thursday;
C: Therefore, (Q) I will not get paid.

Symbolically, this reads as follows:

DS:
P1: P ∨ Q
P2: ~P
C: Q

In linear style:

DS: {[(P ∨ Q) & (~P)] → (Q)}

A **DS** consists of a compound premise that is an *inclusive disjunction* that sets out a pair of alternatives. It is conjoined to a simple premise that *denies* one of the alternatives and a conclusion that *affirms* the other one. Along with the **MP** and **MT**, the **DS** is a basic form of mixed syllogism. But note that, unlike mixed hypothetical syllogisms, there is only one valid form of **DS** because affirmation is not possible, only denial. If you affirmed P in the second premise of **E28** nothing would follow necessarily because in an inclusive disjunction both sentences could be true. Consider the following pair of premises:

{[(P ∨ Q) & (P)] → (?)}

Based on the premises, Q and ~Q are equally possible conclusions. This means that neither follows necessarily, and so either conclusion would make the argument invalid.

Pure Syllogisms

We turn now to pure syllogisms.

Definition: A **pure syllogism** is a two-premise argument in which the premises and conclusion are all compound sentences.

The most basic form of pure syllogism is the **chain syllogism (CS)**, which consists of three *hypothetical* sentences, set out as follows:

E29:
P1: If (P) it is Thursday then (Q) I got paid;
P2: And (Q) if I got paid then (R) I'm going to the movies;
C: Therefore, (P) if it is Thursday then (R) I'm going to the movies.

Symbolically, this yields:

P1: $P \to Q$
P2: $Q \to R$
C: $P \to R$

In linear form:

CS: $\{[(P \to Q) \mathbin{\&} (Q \to R)] \to (P \to R)\}$

The first thing to notice is that a pure syllogism has to have at least three variables—three simple sentences—whereas a mixed syllogism can get by with only two. In the **CS**, the consequent of the first premise and the antecedent of the second are the same simple sentence: in this case, Q. In effect, they cancel one another out, leaving as the conclusion the antecedent of the first premise and the consequent of the second. (It really is a chain: P is linked to Q and Q is linked to R, so P is linked to R.) Think of it as a dating issue: Petra wants to meet Ramon, and since Quan knows them both he can make the introductions and then disappear, leaving Petra and Ramon happily together.

However—and this is true of all deductive arguments—the order of the premises is not significant. Let's rewrite **E29** as follows:

$\{[(Q \to R) \mathbin{\&} (P \to Q)] \to (P \to R)\}$

The common variable (Q) is still the antecedent in one premise and the consequent in the other, so it links the other two variables together, each of which retains its location as an antecedent and a consequent. Like the **MP**, the **MT**, and the **DS**, the **CS** is always valid. But also like them, it is important to take care with negations because a variable and its denial make diametrically opposed claims.

Consider the following argument:

E30:
P1: If (P) it's Thursday then (Q) I got paid;
P2: And (~Q) if I did not *get paid then (R) I will go to the movies;*
C: Therefore, if (P) it's Thursday then (R) I will go to the movies.

Symbolically, this reads as:

$\{[(P \to Q) \mathbin{\&} (\sim Q \to R)] \to (P \to R)\}$

Since Q and ~Q are contradictory claims—denials of one another—there is no common variable and this is not a chain argument. **E30** is therefore invalid.

However, consider this syllogism:

E31: *{[(P → Q) & (~R → ~Q)] → (P → R)}*

The transposition of the second premise is (Q → R). So **E31** is equivalent to:

{[(P → Q) & (Q → R)] → (P → R)}

This is obviously a chain syllogism.

Other Kinds of Syllogisms

A lot of deductive reasoning takes the basic syllogistic forms of the **DS**, **MT**, **MP**, and **CS**. However, syllogisms can be constructed using the other logical constants as well. What's more, logical constants can be mixed and matched in a whole variety of ways. For example:

E32:
P1: (P) It is Thursday if and only if (Q) I got paid;
P2: And (R) I shall go to a movie if and only if (Q) I got paid;
C: Hence, it is not possible that (P) it's Thursday and (~R) I do not go to the movies.

This pure syllogism is symbolized as follows:

P1: P ↔ Q
P2: R ↔ Q
C: ~(P & ~R)

In linear form:

{[(P ↔ Q) & (R ↔ Q)] → ~(P & ~R)}

Remember, a phrase such as "It is not possible that" acts like "It's not true that." It negates the whole of the conclusion, which means that the negation sign is placed outside the bracket.

Here's another example, this time of a mixed syllogism:

E33:
P1: It's not possible that (P) we study and (Q) go out tonight;
P2: And (Q) we really have to go out tonight;
C: Therefore, (~P) we can't study.

This is symbolized as:

P1: ~(P & Q)
P2: Q
C: ~P

Something to Think About

There are other kinds of deductive logic, ones that make use of different symbols. One such kind, which goes back to Aristotle, is called categorical logic. It divides sentences into terms—two to a sentence—and uses quantifiers ("all," "some are," "some are not," "none") to give the argument its formal structure. Here is a basic syllogism, where ∀ stands for "all":

P1: ∀ A are B
P2: ∀ B are C
C: ∀ A are C

Translate this into a syllogism in sentential logic. The answer is in the Answer Key at the end of the book.

In linear form:

$\{[\sim(P \ \& \ Q) \ \& \ (Q)] \rightarrow (\sim P)\}$

This argument is also valid.

EXERCISE 5.3

I. For each of the following, assign variables to the simple sentences and then symbolize the syllogism. Indicate whether it is a disjunctive syllogism (DS), a chain syllogism (CS), a modus ponens (MP), a modus tollens (MT), the fallacy of affirming the consequent (AC), or the fallacy of denying the antecedent (DA). If it is none of these, write (N).

*1. Either unemployment rates decline or we will enter a recession, but unemployment rates will go up so we will enter a recession.

2. If I have a headache I do not go out of the house, and I have a headache, so I will not go out today.

*3. If I get paid then I am going out to celebrate, and if it is Thursday then I get paid, so if it is Thursday then I am going out to celebrate.

4. If what we are feeling is not an earthquake then it is not life threatening. But it is life threatening, so what we are feeling is an earthquake.

*5. If I had passed this exam I would have graduated, but I failed, so I didn't graduate.

6. If life expectancy continues to rise we will have to make spending cuts in other areas, because if life expectancy continues to rise we will have to spend more on elder care and we can do that iff we cut spending elsewhere.

*7. If we want to revise the manuscript we can't wait until Monday. But we have to wait until then, so we can't revise the manuscript.

8. If people stop reading novels society will begin to decline, because if people don't read novels then they do not develop sufficient insight into the human condition, and if they don't do that society will begin to decline.

*9. Math is difficult because it's abstract, and if something is difficult then it's abstract.

10. Love is a strong emotion, and if something is a strong emotion then it is bad for you, so love is bad for you.

*11. If someone is arrogant they are self-absorbed, and if someone is self-absorbed they tend to megalomania, which is in turn a kind of psychosis. So arrogant people are psychotic.

12. If I were more musical then I would be able to dance better, and if I could dance better I would have a better social life, so if I were more musical then I'd have a better social life.

*13. If wishes came true I'd be rich, and since I am rich then wishes do come true.

14. Rock 'n' roll is dead because if a music genre is alive then it's relevant to people under 30, which rock 'n' roll is not.

*15. Either I stay home and work tomorrow or I get way behind, and I can't afford to get behind, so I can't go out tomorrow.

16. Hippopotami do not make good pets because they are too big to sit on the couch, and if you are too big to sit on the couch then you do not make a good pet.

*17. Jazz is free form, and if something is free form it is hard to understand. Therefore, jazz is hard to understand.

II. *Designate each of the following as either an MP, an MT, or as one of two formal fallacies of denying the antecedent (DA) or affirming the consequent (AC).*

*1. {[(Q → P) & (Q) → (P)}   4. {[(~Q → ~P) & (Q)] → (P)}   *7. {[(# → *) & (~*)] → (~#)}

2. {[(~P → Q) & (~Q)] → (P)}   *5. {[(P → ~Q) & (~Q)] → (P)}

*3. {[(~P → ~Q) & (P)] → (~Q)}   6. {[(~Q → P) & (~Q)] → (P)}

III. *For each of the following, assign variables to the simple sentences and then symbolize the argument.*

*1. Exactly one of these options is true. Either we cancel the game or we play in these conditions, and since we certainly don't want to play in these conditions we have to cancel the game.

2. Cancer can be cured iff research is adequately funded. But since cancer research is not adequately funded, cancer will not be cured.

*3. It's not true that if people go on tweeting obsessively then civilization will come to an end, and if civilization doesn't come to an end then all is well with the world. So, if people go on tweeting obsessively then all is well with the world.

4. It's not possible that Bob and Rita are both telling the truth. But I know that Bob is, so Rita is lying.

*5. Either Jamal will present that material or Ai Li will. But if Jamal presents the material then he can't chair the meeting. So, either Ai Li presents that material or Jamal can't chair the meeting.

Continued >

6. We can reduce our carbon footprints iff we consume less energy, and we can consume less energy iff we drive less. We can, therefore, reduce our carbon footprints iff we drive less.

*7. James is unhappy and Anna isn't unhappy, but it's not possible that Sonia is happy and James is not happy. Therefore, if Sonia is happy then Anna is unhappy.

8. If I can't earn more money next summer then I will have to drop out of school, and I can earn more money iff the economy improves. Therefore, I can continue in school iff the economy improves.

*9. I'll pass this course iff hell freezes over, and hell will freeze over iff global warming slows down, so it's not possible that global warming will continue at the same pace and I'll pass this course.

IV. Some Tricky Readings

This section contains advice on how to read sentences where the meaning or the order of the variables may not be absolutely clear. In other words, it shows you how to translate some normal ways of saying things into formal logical sentences.

1. *Pay attention to the location of "if" in a hypothetical sentence.* Since "if" signals the antecedent of a hypothetical sentence, wherever it is located is where the sentence begins. For example:

   E34: *(~P) You should* not *sell your stocks* if *(Q) the market is depressed.*

   When "if" sits in the middle of the sentence, as it does here, that is where you begin the hypothetical sentence: the second part comes first and the first part comes second. **E34** therefore reads formally as "*If the market is depressed then* you should *not sell your stocks*," or **(Q → ~P)**. Compare this with the incorrect reading of **(~P → Q)**. You can see that these sentences do not say the same thing; one is not the transposition of the other.

2. *"When" sometimes stands in for the hypothetical.* Changing **E34** to read "You should not sell your stocks **when** the market is depressed" does not affect the meaning of the sentence. Like "if," "when" is the beginning of the hypothetical proposition: "*When the market is depressed you should not to sell your stocks.*" If you insert the hypothetical, the sentence reads "*If the market is depressed, then you should not sell your stocks.*"

3. *Logical constants may be wholly or partly suppressed.* To take one example, the "then" of a hypothetical sentence is often omitted, as in "If it's sunny tomorrow we'll play tennis." Sometimes a comma is inserted in its place, but not always. Still, where there is an "if" there must be a "then," so look for where it should go. Similarly,

arguments often omit the "either" in "either. . .or." If none of the premises seem to have a logical constant, either it's not an argument or a logical constant has been suppressed somewhere. As was the case with "when" above, most of the time you will be able to reconstruct a compound premise by inserting a hypothetical sentence. For example:

E35: *Efficient employees need reasonable holidays and since you want efficient employees, give them reasonable holidays.*

"Efficient workers need reasonable holidays" is really a compound sentence that should be rewritten as "If you want your employees to be efficient, then you must give them reasonable holidays." Now it's obvious that the argument is an **MP**.

4. *Do not confuse "if and only if" (iff) with "only if."* They may seem to mean the same thing but they do not. The *biconditional* "iff" means "if P then Q and if Q then P." Entailment runs both ways, so the two variables stand or fall together. Not only does "only if" mean something different, its meaning can vary with its location in a sentence. For example:

E36: *(P1) "Only if (P) you join Facebook (Q) will you be able to keep up with all your friends. (P2) But because (~P) you won't join, (C) (~Q) you won't able to keep up with them.*

P1 reads: "Only if P, Q." This formulation is translated as follows:

Only if P, Q = Q → P

So slightly rewritten, **P1** reads "If you are able to keep up with your friends, then you have joined Facebook," **P2** reads "You have not joined Facebook," and **C** is "You will not be able to keep up with your friends." So symbolically the argument reads:

{[(Q → P) & (~P)] → (~Q)}

E36 is an **MT**.

Now compare **E36** to the following argument:

E37: *(P1) (P) You would be able to keep up with your friends only if (Q) you joined Facebook. (P2) But because (~P) you are not able to keep up with your friends, (C) (~Q) you did not join Facebook.*

The formulation is as follows:

P only if Q = P → Q

So **P1** is a straightforward hypothetical sentence. Symbolically **E37** reads:

{[(P → Q) & (~P)] → (~Q)}

As you can see, **E37** commits the formal fallacy of denying the antecedent and is invalid. Table 5.5 presents a chart of meanings for "iff" and "only if" to help you keep them straight. Note that sentences 2 and 3 in the table are equivalent.

| Table 5.5 What Conditionals and Biconditionals Mean |||
	SENTENCE	SYMBOLS
1.	P iff Q	P ↔ Q
2.	P if Q	Q → P
3.	Only if P, Q	Q → P
4.	P only if Q	P → Q

5. *Sentences may be condensed.* Just as people condense arguments, so too do they condense sentences, especially when they are repeated in an argument. For example:

E38: *(P1)* If *we allow inflation to continue unchecked* then *unemployment will rise* and *(P2) we don't want* that *to happen,* so *(C)* we have to bring inflation under control.

In **P2** it is important to understand what it is *that* "we" don't want to happen. "That" refers to the consequent of **P1**: we don't want unemployment to rise. In this and virtually all instances, "that" refers to the phrase that comes immediately before it in the sentence.

There can, however, be subtle twists. For example, consider the following argument:

E39: *(C) We need to cut down on our spending* because *(P1) we will go broke if we don't,* and *(P2) we certainly don't want that to happen.*

Here, the phrase "if we don't" in **P1** refers to **C**: "We need to cut down on our spending." This is because "if" signifies an antecedent, and its formal place is before the phrase "we will go broke," which means that its actual predecessor is **C**. That in turn means that **P2**'s "that" refers to P1's consequent, "we will go broke." In other words, it's necessary to reorder **P1** to read "If we don't cut down on our spending, then we will go broke." Once the hypothetical sentence is in its proper logical order, it is apparent that the argument runs as follows:

P1: If (P) we don't cut down on our spending, then (Q) we will go broke.
P2: And (~Q) we certainly do not want to go broke.
C: Therefore, (~P) we will cut down on our spending.

This is an **MT**:

{[(~P → Q) & (~Q)] → (P)}

When writing an argument out formally, always uncondense any condensed sentences. It may seem overly fussy to take the time to do so, but in the end it helps to avoid errors and saves time. Doing so therefore obeys both of Chapter 4's guides to good reasoning.

EXERCISE 5.4

I. *Write each of the following syllogisms out fully and formally, placing the conclusion at the end, then symbolize each argument. Watch out for implicit assumptions. Also indicate the name of the argument—disjunctive syllogism (DS), chain syllogism (CS), modus ponens (MP), modus tollens (MT)—or the fallacy it represents—affirming the consequent (AC), denying the antecedent (DA). If it is none of these, write (N).*

*1. We can't consider moving right now because we can move only if there is another apartment available in the neighbourhood, and right now there isn't.

2. Hearing music is essential to life because something is essential to life if it makes the human spirit soar.

*3. Only if I'm healthy can I really enjoy life, and since I'm not healthy I can't enjoy life.

4. Tom gets really grouchy when he's tired, and since this game will tire him out it will make him grouchy.

*5. Breaks between semesters are too long because students forget a lot of what they have learned from one semester to the next, and that means they really are too long.

6. Either we do our presentation now or put it off until next week, but if we do that we will not be able to finish our other project. So we do our presentation now or we don't finish our other project.

*7. We can't fix the flux capacitor if we don't have the right tools, and we can get back to the future only if we have fixed the flux capacitor. So, only if we have the right tools can we get back to the future.

8. When we rely too much on electronic devices we are less than we could be because we become lazy thinkers when we rely too much on electronic devices, and when that happens we are less than we could be.

*9. Love hurts because all good things do, and love is a good thing.

10. Running is one of the purest of human activities because it's in our nature to run, and what's in our nature is pure.

*11. Cyclists in the Tour de France should take drugs if they want to win. They can't win the race if they don't, and everyone wants to win.

12. We can fully explore the galaxy iff we can find some way around the limitation of the speed of light, but since we don't know how to do that we're stuck here on Earth.

Continued >

*13. Because people become angry if they are treated disrespectfully, and because she hasn't been treated disrespectfully she's not angry.

14. I don't like winter if it's cold for long periods of time, but that's not the case in Canada, so I like Canadian winters.

II. Write the equivalent of each of the following.

*1. If it is not too hot then we will have a picnic.

2. $P \rightarrow \sim Q$

*3. $\sim Q \rightarrow \sim P$

4. You will damage your skin only if you don't wear sunblock.

*5. If we lost this game then we came second.

6. $\sim Q \rightarrow \sim P$

*7. Only if we win this game will we make the playoffs.

8. P only if Q

V. Longer and More Complicated Arguments

Once you have mastered basic syllogisms, it is not difficult to deal with longer arguments (ones with more than two premises) or syllogisms with slight twists in them. Nonetheless, it will help to consider a couple of examples. You have already been alerted to the particular complication in the following example:

E40: *(P1) If (P) politics is the art of the possible then either (~Q) dreamers cannot be politicians or (R) dreams can come true. (P2) But ~(~Q ∨ R) since neither of these alternatives is true, (C) (~P) politics is not the art of the possible.*

The opening premise is a hypothetical sentence whose consequent is an inclusive disjunction. First, assign the following variables for the simple sentences:

P = Politics is the art of the possible
Q = Dreamers can be politicians
R = Dreams can come true

Then, remembering the *order of precedence* for logical constants, symbolize **P1** as follows:

P1: (P → (~Q ∨ R))

Since a condensed **P2** asserts that ~Q and R are both false, we symbolize it as:

P2: ~(~Q ∨ R)

Now it's clear that **P2** denies the consequent of **P1**. Following suit, **C** denies the antecedent of **P1**. The result is the following **MT**:

P1: P → (~Q ∨ R)
P2: ~(~Q ∨ R)
C: ~P

In linear form:

{[(P → (~Q ∨ R)) & ~(~Q ∨ R)] → (~P)}

The key here is to apply the order of precedence, which tells you that the disjunction (**~Q ∨ R**) is the consequent of the hypothetical sentence that is **P1**. Then recognize that **P2** denies this consequent. The denial is indicated by placing a negation sign outside the parentheses. Note also that this **MT** has three variables, but two of them are combined in such a way that the compound sentence they form acts exactly like a simple sentence in a basic **MT**.

Now let's examine an argument with more than two premises:

E41: *(P1) Either (P) the economy has to recover on its own or (Q) the government has to provide economic stimulus. (P2) If it has to recover on its own then (R) people have to be persuaded to start spending again. But (P3) (Q) if the government has to provide economic stimulus then (S) it needs to do so right away. (P4) However, (~S) the government is too broke to do that right away, (C) So (R) people have to be persuaded to start spending again.*

All you need to do is identify the variables and obey the logical constants. The result is:

P1: P ∨ Q
P2: P → R
P3: Q → S
P4: ~S
C: R

In linear form:

{[(P ∨ Q) & (P → R) & (Q → S) & (~S)] → (R)}

Since **E41** is longer than a syllogism, let's break it down and examine it more closely. Notice that **P3** and **P4** amount to:

(Q → S) & (~S)

These are the premises of an **MT** whose implicit conclusion would be **(~Q)**. Let's set this out as follows:

A1:
P3: $(Q \rightarrow S)$
P4: $(\sim S)$
IC1: $(\sim Q)$ *MT*

P1 is the disjunction:

$(P \vee Q)$

Since **(Q)** has been denied by the **IC1** in **A1**, from **P1** and **IC1** we get the following:

A2:
P1: $(P \vee Q)$
IC1: $(\sim Q)$
IC2: (P) *DS*

The conclusion **(IC2)** is (P) "The economy has to recover on its own." The remaining premise is **P2**, which says:

$(P \rightarrow R)$

Add **IC2** to it and we have the premises of an **MP**:

$(P \rightarrow R) \mathrel{\&} (P)$

This yields the conclusion **(R)**: "People have to be persuaded to start spending again." So now we have third argument:

A3:
P2: $(P \rightarrow R)$
IC2: (P)
C: (R) *MP*

By supplementing the four premises with two implicit conclusions, we have derived R, which is the conclusion of **E41**. When you insert the implicit conclusions, you can see that longer arguments can generally be broken down into a series of syllogisms where some of the conclusions have been left implicit. In this instance, we have an **MT**, a **DS**, and an **MP**. Once again, this is why recognizing and understanding basic syllogistic forms is so fundamental to deductive reasoning. Of course, when you are symbolizing longer arguments, you do not have to insert the implicit conclusions. Symbolize only what is there. Nonetheless, being aware of implicit conclusions will help you understand these arguments and find your way through them. We will return to this in Chapter 6.

EXERCISE 5.5

Symbolize the following arguments. Some are syllogisms and some are not. If an argument is a DS, an MP, an MT, or a CS, indicate it with the appropriate letters. If an argument commits a formal fallacy (AC or DA), note that as well. If it is none of these, write (N). If a premise or a conclusion has been omitted from an MP or MT, obey the principle of charity and add it in. Warning: think carefully about how to symbolize "unless" in question 5.

1. *I knew I'd be late if I didn't hurry, but I did hurry so I wasn't late.

2. I would be willing to take statistics only if it is offered in the morning when my brain is functioning. But as it isn't, I am not willing to take it.

*3. If the time it takes Mercury to rotate around its axis is the same as the time it takes to revolve around the sun, it will always present the same side to the sun. If that is so, then that will be the only side we can see. Thus, if Mercury's period of rotation equals its period of revolution, we will only ever see one side of it.

4. If Ellen lost her purse she won't be able to write her exams because her ID card was in her purse and she needs it to write her exams.

*5. Current will not flow unless the circuit is broken, and as this circuit is broken the current is flowing.

6. Socrates is human because he is mortal.

*7. Either I am going to have the life I wanted or I am going to be horribly disappointed because either I will succeed as a dancer or I will not. If I succeed I'll have the life I want, and if I don't succeed I will be horribly disappointed.

8. Life is good only if you want it to be, but you don't want it to be.

*9. One cannot both engage in market speculation and pursue a full-time job because market speculation requires enormous attention to detail and if you have a full-time job you cannot pay such attention.

10. Democracy works if and only if the public is well informed and that's the case if and only if the media does its job. For democracy to work, therefore, the media must do its job.

*11. If my theory is correct then Wilson's theory is wrong and so is Petrocelli's, which in turn means that Wong's conjecture has serious flaws. But since I'm certain that Wong's conjecture is faultless, my theory is false.

Continued >

12. Either we enforce the band's contract or we renegotiate it, but if we do that then either we do it in good faith or simply do it pro forma. But in either case, we risk losing them. If we don't want to run that risk, we need to enforce the band's contract.

*13 Either we work overtime tonight or we work tomorrow, and since we don't want to work tomorrow we need to work overtime tonight.

14. I will not break my word once I give it, and I have given you my word.

*15. Only if we negotiate secretly will the treaty be signed, because if we negotiate openly the media will report every detail, and if they do that protesters will take to the streets, and if that happens we will never get a signed treaty.

Something to Think About

The word "necessarily" has been used a lot in these chapters, so let's think about it a bit. Take the following two sentences:

S1: *In a valid argument, if the premises are true then necessarily so is the conclusion.*

S2: *In a valid argument, if the premises are true then the conclusion is necessarily true as well.*

Can you explain the different meanings of "necessarily" here? The answer is found in the Answer Key at the end of the book.

VI. Summary

In this chapter you have been introduced to the basics of *sentential logic*, a standard form of deductive reasoning. This logic employs two kinds of sentences. A *simple sentence* is a basic subject–predicate sentence, while a *compound sentence* consists of two simple sentences linked by a *logical constant*. All simple sentences in an argument make either *normative* or *factual* claims. Both kinds of claims are considered as possessing *truth values*, though in practice only some factual claims can be fully verified or falsified. This means that, while some arguments can be known to be *sound* or *unsound,* others are *indeterminate.*

The basic form of sentential logic is the syllogism, which has two premises (at least one of which is a compound sentence) and a conclusion. The hypothetical logical constant (→) has been used to link the premises to the conclusion to remind you of the force of the big little word "if" and, through it, of the rule of validity: in a valid argument, *if* both (or all) the premises are true, *then* necessarily so is the conclusion. But remember that validity is not the same thing as truth, and a valid argument does not necessarily have true premises. *Finally, you were introduced to the basic kinds of syllogisms: the modus ponens, modus tollens, and disjunctive syllogism—which are mixed syllogisms—and the chain syllogism, which is a pure syllogism.* Once you have mastered syllogisms, it is not difficult to get a handle on longer arguments.

CHAPTER SIX

Testing for Validity

- Truth tables
- Truth conditions for compound sentences
- Rules of equivalence
- Validity tests using truth tables
- The short method of testing for validity
- Natural deduction: rules of inference

In this chapter we turn our attention to some methods of testing sentential arguments for validity. This is important because a secure grasp of validity illuminates the structure of deductive arguments and makes it much easier to distinguish good reasoning from bad.

I. Truth Tables

Understanding Truth

This section introduces truth tables, which are the basis of all validity tests.

> *Definition: Truth tables* establish the conditions under which compound sentences are true or false.

These conditions are called **truth conditions**. An analysis of the truth conditions for the sentences (premises and conclusions) in an argument tells us whether it is possible for that argument to have true premises and a false conclusion. If it is possible, then according to the rule of validity the argument is *invalid*; if it is not possible, the argument is *valid*. As always, the emphasis is on *possibility*: we will not be considering whether the sentences in an argument actually are true but whether the premise sentences can be true while the conclusion sentence is false. In other words, does the conclusion follow necessarily from the premises? Therefore, as was the case with the discussion of validity in Chapter 5, the distinction between empirical and normative sentences need not concern us here.

Let's begin by distinguishing between the truth conditions of simple and compound sentences. The truth conditions of simple sentences are determined by their referent. A simple empirical sentence makes a claim about how something is, and that claim is either true or false. For example:

E1: *I am older than my brother.*

To discover whether this simple empirical sentence is true you would need to have access to my and my brother's birth certificates. If I was born first, the statement is true; if not, it is false. Similarly, if someone says tells you that it is raining, you look outside to see whether in fact it is. And if you are told that two plus two equals four, you can verify this by consulting the rules of addition. In all such cases, you are checking to see if the sentences accurately describe whatever it is they refer to. So the referent tells you whether the sentence is true or false. As you know, normative statements cannot be checked in this way, but nonetheless if someone says "Human life is sacred" you know that the sentence is true iff there is a quality called "sacred" that applies to human life.

By comparison, for compound sentences there is a step prior to this because before we can know whether a compound sentence is true or false we have to know something more than the truth or falsity of the constituent simple sentences. We also have to know what the logical constants that link these sentences mean. To know, for example, whether the compound sentence "It is Thursday and I got paid" is true, we have to know (1) what day it is and (2) whether I got paid, and for this we check the facts. But we also need to know (3) what the logical constant "and" means. After all, "It is Thursday and I got paid" means something different than, for example, "If it's Thursday then I got paid." So the job of truth tables is to stipulate what the different logical constants mean. In doing so, they specify the truth conditions of compound sentences, and only by knowing these conditions can we determine whether an argument is valid or invalid.

Two-Valued Logic and the Truth Values of Compound Sentences

Since a compound sentence is composed of at least two simple sentences, then by the rules of **two-valued** (or *bivalent*) **logic**—that is, logic that obeys the law of the excluded middle—each sentence bears one of two values: true or false. Simple arithmetic tells us, therefore, that for any compound sentence composed of two simple sentences, P and Q, there are four possible arrangements of truth values (see Table 6.1).

Table 6.1 Distribution of Truth Values		
1.	P and Q are both true.	(T T)
2.	P is true and Q is false.	(T F)
3.	P is false and Q is true.	(F T)
4.	P and Q are both false.	(F F)

From the fact that one variable (one simple sentence) has two possible truth values and two variables have four, we can construct a formula that will tell us how many possible truth values any given number of variables will have. That formula is 2^n, where 2 stands for the number of possible truth values of any simple sentence and n for a given number of variables. For example, for four variables—P, Q, R, S—there are 2^4 (or 16) possible distributions of true and false. To see how to write these tables out, consult the appendix at the end of this chapter. Right now, let's construct basic two-variable tables for each of the logical constants. Based on what you learned in Chapter 5, these tables should be almost self-evident, but it is nonetheless important to set them out clearly.

Conjunction

A *conjunction* is true iff both of its constituent simple sentences are true. When simple sentences are conjoined, the claim is that both of them are true. So for the compound sentence (P & Q) to be true, P and Q must both be true. In all other cases, the compound sentence is false. The truth table is shown in Table 6.2. The two columns on the left set out the possible distributions of truth values for the simple sentences P and

Q. The column on the right indicates the truth value of the compound sentence for each distribution.

Table 6.2 Truth Values for a Conjunction			
	P	Q	(P & Q)
1.	T	T	T
2.	T	F	F
3.	F	T	F
4.	F	F	F

This conjunction rule can be extended to infinity. Take, for example, the compound sentence **S**:

Conjunction S: (P & Q & R & S & T)

Assume that only R is false. That means that conjunction S is false. As my grandmother used to say, with conjunctions one rotten apple spoils the whole barrel.

Inclusive Disjunction

An *inclusive disjunction* is true unless both of its constituent simple sentences are false. This rule is the mirror opposite of the conjunction rule because in a disjunction a single true simple sentence is enough to save even a whole string of false ones. Rewrite the compound sentence **S** as follows:

Disjunction S: (P ∨ Q ∨ R ∨ S ∨ T)

Imagine that only sentence R is true. This means that disjunction S is true. As my grandmother also used to say, one good deed saves a whole day. Table 6.3 shows a truth table for a disjunction.

Table 6.3 Truth Values for an Inclusive Disjunction			
	P	Q	(P ∨ Q)
1.	T	T	T
2.	T	F	T
3.	F	T	T
4.	F	F	F

Hypothetical

A **hypothetical** sentence is true unless the antecedent is true and the consequent false. A hypothetical truth table is shown in Table 6.4. (The bottom two values may seem wrong; I will have more to say about them below.)

Table 6.4 Truth Values for a Hypothetical

	P	Q	(P → Q)
1.	T	T	T
2.	T	F	F
3.	F	T	T
4.	F	F	T

Exclusive Disjunction

An *exclusive disjunction* is true when exactly one of its constituent simple sentences is true. The truth table is shown in Table 6.5.

Table 6.5 Truth Values for an Exclusive Disjunction

	P	Q	(P ⊻ Q)
1.	T	T	F
2.	T	F	T
3.	F	T	T
4.	F	F	F

Biconditional

A **biconditional** is true iff its constituent simple sentences have the same truth values—that is, when either both are true or both are false. Table 6.6 depicts the truth table for a biconditional.

Table 6.6 Truth Values for a Biconditional

	P	Q	(P ↔ Q)
1.	T	T	T
2.	T	F	F
3.	F	T	F
4.	F	F	T

A Strategic Look at the Full Truth Table

Collecting everything in the order presented above, the full truth table for all the logical constants is shown in Table 6.7.

Table 6.7	The Full Truth Table						
	P	Q	(P & Q)	(P ∨ Q)	(P → Q)	(P ⊻ Q)	(P ↔ Q)
1.	T	T	T	T	T	F	T
2.	T	F	F	T	F	T	F
3.	F	T	F	T	T	T	F
4.	F	F	F	F	T	F	T

It is worthwhile to take a little time to examine Table 6.7 in detail. A critical thinker always tries to grasp the order (or structure) of whatever she is examining, so let's do that here. To help you do this, the table is set out in a particular order. The conjunction and the inclusive disjunction are side by side as are the exclusive disjunction and the biconditional. These two pairs are separated by the hypothetical. Let's first consider the features of each of these pairs.

As I said above, the conjunction and inclusive disjunction are mirror images of one another. Both have a "three–one" distribution of truth values, the difference being that the conjunction has three false values whereas the inclusive disjunction has three true values. The conjunction's lone T value is at the top of the table while the inclusive disjunction's lone F value is at the bottom. In short, while the conjunction strictly asserts that both simple sentences are true, the inclusive disjunction generously asserts only that they are not both false. In Section III below we will see why it is important to keep this in mind.

On the other side of the table, the exclusive disjunction and the biconditional also mirror one another, sharing a "two–two" split in truth values. The exclusive disjunction is true when the truth values of the simple sentences are *different*; the biconditional is true only when they are the *same*. This tells us that if a biconditional compound sentence is true then *necessarily* an exclusive disjunction composed of the same simple sentences is false, and vice versa. Unlike the conjunction and inclusive disjunction, there is no overlap of truth values.

The Strange World of the Hypothetical
In the middle of the table is the hypothetical, which, like conjunctions and inclusive disjunctions, has a "three–one" split in truth values. What is ruled out is any instance where the antecedent is true and the consequent is false. This distribution is found on the second row of the truth table.

It is worthwhile to dwell for a moment on the last two rows in the hypothetical column because they can seem counterintuitive. These rows indicate that the combined truth value (F → T) and (F → F) both produce a T value on the truth table. This leads, in the second case, to the apparently astounding conclusion that two false simple sentences can add up to a true compound sentence, as if the insertion of the hypothetical constant has magically changed falsehoods into truth. (This is also the case with the biconditional, but there it makes sense because the biconditional expressly stipulates that the two variables stand or fall together.)

Consider this example:

E2: *If Montana is in Canada then I can fly.*

This compound sentence is true *just because the antecedent is false*. My ability to fly is immaterial. But since I cannot fly, this is a case where two false sentences have been combined to make a true one. Surely that can't be right! But it is, more or less, because a hypothetical sentence follows this rule:

Hypothetical rule: *If either the antecedent is false or the consequent is true, the sentence is true.*

Recall that the hypothetical is the only logical constant where the order of the variables cannot be transposed because the consequent is *conditional* on the antecedent. In other words, what the hypothetical sentence asserts is that *if* the antecedent is true *then* so is the consequent. What it therefore explicitly rules out is the arrangement of truth values on the second row of the truth table, where the antecedent is true and the consequent is false. If, however, the antecedent is false, as it is in the bottom two rows of Table 6.7, we are in effect considering a situation that doesn't exist, and that's what's strange about this.

Imagine we are discussing hockey and I say to you:

E3: *If Crosby scores 50 goals this year, his team will win the Stanley Cup.*

Further imagine you think I'm wrong. So we have a friendly wager on it. The truth table in Table 6.8 tells us that at the end of the season there are four possibilities. The first two conditions give us no trouble: if Crosby scores 50 goals and his team wins the cup, you will probably pay me without complaint, and if he scores 50 goals but his team fails to win, I'll pay you. But imagine the situations envisaged in the third and fourth rows. Let's consider the fourth row where, say, Crosby scores only 30 goals and his team fails to win the cup. Now imagine me showing up at your door to collect on the bet. After all what I said was true, so surely I win!

Table 6.8 A Hypothetical Bet

CROSBY SCORES 50 GOALS	→ HIS TEAM WINS THE CUP	TRUTH VALUE
T	T	T
T	F	F
F	T	T
F	F	T

I doubt you would be willing to pay me in this circumstance. You would reject my apparently logical demand for money, and with good reason, because I did not win the bet. But why did I not win? I did not win because the bet was *conditional* on Crosby scoring 50 goals. If he failed to do so, then the bet was off because the condition that would trigger it failed to materialize. So nobody wins. This situation is very close to what is called a counterfactual conditional:

> *Definition:* A **counterfactual conditional** is a hypothetical sentence in which the antecedent refers to something that did not occur or that is known not to be true.

For example, after the season is over I might say:

> **E4:** If Crosby had scored 50 goals then his team would have won the Stanley Cup.

This is a counterfactual conditional because I am talking about an event that did not occur. In real life, we recognize that a counterfactual conditional cannot bear a truth value, and even in the rarefied world of logic we more or less set it to one side, just as you would do with the bet.

However, standard hypothetical sentences like **E2** are not counterfactuals but rather **material implications**, and for them the following symbolic rule applies:

> *Rule of material implications:* $(P \rightarrow Q) = (\sim P \vee Q)$

This tells us two things. First, from a false antecedent ($\sim P$) any consequent follows: in short, a hypothetical sentence with a false antecedent is always true. Second, a hypothetical sentence with a true consequent is always true (a glance at Table 6.4 will confirm these assertions). Hence, if I start a hypothetical sentence with a false antecedent, such as "If my name is George," and add any other sentence as the consequent—for example, the false sentence "I can fly"—the compound sentence will be true. Were I to add instead the true consequent "I am Canadian" the hypothetical sentence would also be true. One reason for this is that if we stipulated that the hypothetical sentences **F → T** and **F → F** were false they would mean the same as the conjunctions **F & T** and **F & F**, and manifestly they do not mean the same thing. The only way to distinguish them from these conjunctive sentences is to stipulate that they are true. It's an interesting little tear in the supposedly seamless fabric of logic, but you can look at it this way: a hypothetical sentence (a material implication) makes the claim that if P is true then so is Q. Therefore, the only condition where it is false is when P is true and Q is false. And by the law of the excluded middle, if it is not false, it's true!

Determining the Truth Values of Compound Sentences

Anyone who mastered truth tables can determine the truth value of any compound sentence for any distribution of truth values of the simple sentences. However, as always, we need to take care with negations. For example:

E5: *It is not true that (P) we can start the project over again and (Q) finish on time.*

This is a negated conjunctive sentence that reads symbolically as follows:

~(P & Q)

Applying the conjunction truth table from Table 6.2, we get:

	P	Q	(P & Q)
1.	T	T	T
2.	T	F	F
3.	F	T	F
4.	F	F	F

The negation sign outside the parentheses—~(P & Q)—reverses each compound truth value on the table. The values for ~(P & Q) are therefore as follows:

	P	Q	(P & Q)	~ (P & Q)
1.	T	T	T	F
2.	T	F	F	T
3.	F	T	F	T
4.	F	F	F	T

Remember that when a negation sign occurs outside the parentheses you have to determine the truth value of the sentence inside the parentheses first and then negate it. In other words, always work from the inside out with truth tables.

Now let's change the sentence to read as follows:

~(~P & Q)

In this case, the values for ~P would be the negation of the values for P on the truth table. Match it up with Q and the result is the following:

	P	Q	(~P)	(~ P & Q)	~(~P & Q)
1.	T	T	F	F	T
2.	T	F	F	F	T
3.	F	T	T	T	F
4.	F	F	T	F	T

In the first row, where P and Q are both assumed to be true, the conjunction (~P & Q) would read (F & T), which comes out to F. Simply, if P is true, ~P is false. But the negation sign outside the parentheses negates that value, so we end up with a truth value of T. And so on, down the rows.

If more than two variables are involved, the truth table expands accordingly. For example:

E6: *If (P) I accept this job then either (Q) I will have to move or (R) I will have to buy a car.*

According to the order of precedence for logical constants, this is rendered symbolically as:

(P → (Q ∨R))

This means that we are dealing with a hypothetical sentence. A truth table for three variables has $2^3 = 8$ rows. Once you write it out (using the method from the appendix at the end of this chapter), you then write the compound sentence alongside it and inscribe the appropriate truth value for the simple sentences in each row:

	P	Q	R	(P → (Q ∨ R))
1.	T	T	T	T → (T ∨ T)
2.	T	T	F	T → (T ∨ F)
3.	T	F	T	T → (F ∨ T)
4.	T	F	F	T → (F ∨ F)
5.	F	T	T	F → (T ∨ T)
6.	F	T	F	F → (T ∨ F)
7.	F	F	T	F → (F ∨ T)
8.	F	F	F	F → (F ∨ F)

Now work out the truth value for each row. In doing so, you first need to work out the truth values for the inclusive disjunction that constitutes the consequent of the compound sentence. A glance at the inclusive disjunction truth table from Table 6.3 will yield the following values:

	P	Q	R	P → (Q ∨ R)
1.	T	T	T	T → (T ∨ T) = T → T (T)
2.	T	T	F	T → (T ∨ F) = T → T (T)
3.	T	F	T	T → (F ∨ T) = T → T (T)
4.	T	F	F	T → (F ∨ F) = T → F (F)
5.	F	T	T	F → (T ∨ T) = F → T (T)
6.	F	T	F	F → (T ∨ F) = F → T (T)
7.	F	F	T	F → (F ∨ T) = F → T (T)
8.	F	F	F	F → (F ∨ F) = F → F (T)

Only in the fourth row is the antecedent true while the consequent is false, so this is the only distribution of truth values where the compound sentence comes out false. In all other distributions, it is true.

Since critical thinkers are supposed to be efficient, here's a quick method of analysis. By the rule of material implication, if the antecedent is false then the compound sentence is true. A corollary of this (see distributions 1 and 3 in the hypothetical truth table, Table 6.4) is that any hypothetical sentence with a *true consequent* is true. If we apply this knowledge to the above, a quick glance reveals that in the bottom four rows the antecedent, P, is false, so they will all yield a T value. That leaves only the top four rows—where the antecedent P is true—to deal with. If you consult the truth table for a inclusive disjunction (Table 6.3), you will see that in rows 1, 2, and 3, the consequents are true, so those hypothetical sentences are true. Only in distribution 4 is the consequent false. Since the antecedent is true in distribution 4, the result is:

$T \rightarrow F = F$

This tells you, once again, that there is one distribution of truth conditions under which **E6** is false and seven under which it is true.

The quick method of analysis is important because if a lot of variables are involved a truth table would become unmanageably long. But if you really understand the truth conditions for each logical constant, you don't need to write everything out in most cases. You now know, for example, that for a hypothetical sentence all distributions with either a false antecedent or a true consequent are automatically true. With a little practice, you can do a surprising amount of the work in your head, and in fact doing so is a good thing because it instils the habit of imposing order on arguments by understanding their structure rather than blindly following mechanical instructions. In Section IV of this chapter you will learn the "short method" for testing for validity that is based on this understanding of basic two-variable truth tables.

EXERCISE 6.1

Exercises marked by an asterisk (*) have answers included in the Answer Key at the end of the text.

I. Assuming P is true, Q is false, R is true, and S is true, what is the truth value for each of the following compound sentences?

*1. (Q → P)	4. ~(P & Q)	*7. ~ (P → Q)
2. (Q ↔ P)	*5. (P ∨ ~Q)	8. (P → ~(Q ∨ R))
*3. (~P ∨ Q)	6. ~ (P ∨ Q)	*9. ((~Q ∨ R) → P)

Continued >

10. (~R → (P ↔ Q))   14. (P → (~Q & R))   18. [(S ∨ Q) & (P & R)]

*11. ~(~R ∨ Q)   *15. [~(~P ∨ Q) → (R → ~S)]   *19. ((P & (~Q & R)) → S)

12. ((P ↔ R) & ~Q)   16. [~(P & ~S) ∨ (~Q & R)]   20. ((Q ∨ ~R) ∨ (~S ∨ ~P))

*13. ~(~S ∨ Q)   *17. [~(S & ~R) ↔ ~Q)]   *21. (~(~P) & ~ (~S → Q))

*II. A quick test: which of the following hypothetical sentences do you know to be true?

1. If gerbils could speak, they would speak Latin.

2. If wishes were horses, none of us would walk.

3. If Al Gore had won Florida in 2000 then he would have been president.

4. If I am correct then it's snowing in Kirkland Lake.

5. If you get 60 per cent on the test, you will pass.

6. If Earth were the fifth rock from the sun, we wouldn't be here.

7. If someone had assassinated Hitler in 1938, World War II would not have happened.

8. If you want the cheapest alternative then this is it.

9. If you are never going to read a book then this is the one to read.

II. Some More on Equivalents

Equivalents were introduced in Chapter 5, Section III, but a more formal definition of the term is now in order:

> **Definition:** Two compound sentences with the same set of variables but which are connected by different logical constants are **equivalent** if they bear the same set of truth values.

In short, equivalents are different ways of saying the same thing, which means that they can be substituted for one another. In fact, it is possible to write all sentences using only conjunction and negation. For example, (P → Q) can be written as ~(P & ~Q) because they have the same truth values on the truth table:

	P	Q	(~Q)	(P → Q)	~(P & ~Q)
1.	T	T	F	T	T
2.	T	F	T	F	F
3.	F	T	F	T	T
4.	F	F	T	T	T

And since, by the rule of material implication, $(P \rightarrow Q) = (\sim P \vee Q)$, therefore $(\sim P \vee Q) = \sim (P \& \sim Q)$. Equivalents can always be worked out or verified by using the truth table, but for the sake of expediency some standard ones are listed in Table 6.9. You have already been introduced to all but the first of them, but it will help to gather them together in one place and give them their standard names. They will be especially useful when you come to Section V below. (You were confronted with double negation in Exercise 6.1; I hope you worked it out.)

Table 6.9 The Rules of Equivalence*	
RULE	**SYMBOLS**
De Morgan's Rules (DM)	$\sim (P \& Q) = (\sim P \vee \sim Q)$ $\sim (P \vee Q) = (\sim P \& \sim Q)$
Material Implication (MI)	$(P \rightarrow Q) = (\sim P \vee Q)$ etc.
Material Equivalence (ME)	$(P \leftrightarrow Q) = ((P \rightarrow Q) \& (Q \rightarrow P))$ $(P \leftrightarrow Q = ((P \& Q) \vee (\sim P \& \sim Q))$ $= \sim (P \veebar Q)$
Double Negation (DN)	$\sim \sim P = P$
Commutation (Comm.)	$(P \& Q) = (Q \& P)$ $(P \vee Q) = (Q \vee P)$ $(P \leftrightarrow Q) = (Q \leftrightarrow P)$ $(P \veebar Q) = (Q \veebar P)$
Transposition	$(P \rightarrow Q) = (\sim Q \rightarrow \sim P)$, etc.

*Augustus De Morgan (1806–71) was a British mathematician who was a key figure in the development of modern logic.

As was pointed out in Chapter 5, equivalents are helpful because they allow you to translate an argument into a more recognizable form. For example:

E7: *Either (P) we don't stay up all night or (Q) we are too tired to work tomorrow, but (P) we won't stay up all night so (~Q) we won't be too tired to work tomorrow.*

Symbolically, this reads as:

{[(~P ∨ Q) & (~P)] → (~Q)}

It looks like a disjunctive syllogism, but there is something wrong. Instead of *denying* one of the disjuncts, the argument

Something to Think About

If it is possible to write any sentence using only negation and conjunction, why do we not do so? Aren't we disobeying Occam's razor? Explain why, despite using six constants rather than two, we are not ignoring Occam. My answer is in the Answer Key at the end of the book.

affirms one. To verify this error, apply **De Morgan's rules** and translate (~P ∨ Q) into (P → Q). Now the argument reads:

$$\{[(P \rightarrow Q) \;\&\; (\sim P)] \rightarrow (\sim Q)\}$$

This is obviously the fallacy of denying the antecedent, and thus **E7** is invalid.

EXERCISE 6.2

I. Work out which of the following pairs of sentences are equivalents. Indicate all instances of the equivalence rules in Table 6.9. In all other cases, use the truth table to demonstrate equivalence or non-equivalence.

*1. (P → (Q ∨ R)) and (~P ∨ (Q & R))

2. (P → ~Q) and ~(P & ~Q)

*3. (P ∨ ~Q) and (P ↔ Q)

4. ~(~P & ~Q) and (P ∨ Q)

*5. (P → (Q ∨ R)) and ((P ∨ Q) → R)

6. (~P ∨ Q) and ~(P & ~Q)

*7. ~ ~(P & Q) and (~P ∨ Q)

8. (P ∨ Q) and ~(~P & ~Q)

*9. (P ∨ ~Q) and (P ↔ Q)

10. (P ↔ Q) and [~(P & ~Q) & ~(~P & Q)]

*11. [~(P & Q) & ~(~P & ~Q)] and (P ∨ Q)

12. (P & (Q & R)) and (~P ∨ (~Q ∨ ~R))

*13. (~(P & Q) → R) and ((~P ∨ ~Q) → R)

14. (P ∨ ~Q) and (~P → ~Q)

*15. (P ∨ ~Q) and ~(P ∨ Q)

16. (P ↔ Q) and [(P → Q) & (~Q ∨ P)]

*17. (P → Q) and (~ ~Q ∨ ~P)

18. ~(P ↔ Q) and (P ∨ Q)

*19. (~P ∨ ~Q) and (~P & Q)

20. [~ ~(P → Q) & (~ ~Q → ~ ~P)] and (Q ↔ P)

*21. (P → (Q ∨ R)) and (~P ∨ (Q ∨ R))

II. For the following sentences translate premises into equivalents to make validity or invalidity obvious.

*1. {[(~P ∨ Q) & (P)] → (Q)}

2. {[~(~P & ~Q) & (~Q)] → (P)}

*3. {[~(P & Q) & (Q)]} → (~P)}

4. {[~(P & Q) & (Q)] → (P)}

*5. {[~(P & Q) & (~R ∨ Q)] → ~(R & P)}

6. {[(~Q → ~P) & (P)] → (Q)}

*7. {[~(P & Q) & ~(~P & ~Q) & (P)] → (Q)}

III. Doing Validity Tests with Truth Tables

This section will demonstrate how to use truth tables to run validity tests on arguments. This is especially useful with non-standard syllogisms and longer arguments.

Pure Syllogisms

Let's begin with the following example:

> **E8:** *(P1) Exactly one of these options is possible: either (P) we call the election now or (Q) we run the risk of losing power (P2) and if (Q) we run that risk, (R) then we also risk destroying the party. (C) So, if (P) we call the election now then (~R) we do not risk destroying the party.*

Note the opening phrase: "exactly one of these options is possible." It signals an exclusive disjunction. Recognizing that, distinguish the premises and the conclusion and assign variables to the simple sentences, as follows:

> *P1:* Either *(P) we call the election now* or *(Q) we run the risk of losing power;*
> *P2:* If *(Q) we run the risk of losing power* then *(R) we risk destroying the party;*
> *C:* If *(P) we call the election now* then *(~R) we do* not *risk destroying the party.*

This yields:

> *P1:* $P \veebar Q$
> *P2:* $Q \rightarrow R$
> *C:* $P \rightarrow \sim R$

In linear form, the argument reads:

> *{[(P $\veebar$ Q) & (Q $\rightarrow$ R)] $\rightarrow$ (P $\rightarrow$ ~R)}*

Since **E8** has three variables, there are (2^3) eight possible distributions of truth values. Using the table-building method from the appendix at the end of this chapter, we can inscribe these distributions and set them alongside the argument, as follows:

	P	Q	R	{[(P $\veebar$ Q)	&	(Q $\rightarrow$ R)]	$\rightarrow$	(P $\rightarrow$ ~R)}
1.	T	T	T	F	[F]	T	{T}	F
2.	T	T	F	F	[F]	F	{T}	T
3.	T	F	T	T	[T]	T	{F}	F
4.	T	F	F	T	[T]	T	{T}	T
5.	F	T	T	T	[T]	T	{T}	T
6.	F	T	F	T	[F]	F	{T}	T
7.	F	F	T	F	[F]	T	{T}	T
8.	F	F	F	F	[F]	T	{T}	T

Look closely at row 1. In it, P, Q, and R all have T values. According to the truth tables, **P1** therefore works out as follows:

> *(P $\veebar$ Q) = (T $\vee$ T) = F*

P2 yields:

(Q → R) = (T → T) = T

Now we turn to **C**, which reads:

(P → ~R) = (T → F) = F

(Remember that if a variable bears a negation sign, the truth value is reversed.) When truth values have been assigned to all the compound sentences in a row, the truth value of the premise side of the argument for that row is easily determined. Since the premises are *conjoined*, the premise side gets a T value *iff* both premises are true. Otherwise, it gets an F value, as in row 1:

[F & T] = F

That value is recorded in square brackets under the & sign (which is called an ampersand). The truth value of the conclusion is recorded under its logical constant—in this case a hypothetical sign. The truth value for the whole row is then enclosed in braces under the hypothetical sign that links the premise side of the argument to the conclusion. In row 1, since the truth value for the premise side is F and the truth value for the conclusion is also F, the formula

{[F] → F} = T

gives you the truth value for that row.

When all the rows are completed, a quick glance will confirm whether the argument is valid or invalid. If any of the rows have a final truth value of F, then the argument is *invalid* because that means that it is possible for the premises to be true while the conclusion is false. Remember, *an argument is valid iff the truth value for all rows is T.* This tells you that the conclusion follows necessarily from the premises. Since this is *not* the case here (see row 3) the argument is invalid.

Now let's go back to the quick method of analysis: apply the rule that an argument is invalid iff it is possible for the premises to be true and the conclusion to be false by scanning the conclusion column for F values. Since only rows 1 and 3 of **E8** have conclusions with F values, they are the only two rows you need to check. In essence, in a quick analysis you are scanning for invalidity rather than validity. Since argument structures like **E8**, where only a quarter of the rows have F values for the conclusion, are pretty common, this is a useful strategy.

Let's look at another example:

> **E9:** *Either (P) we recalculate these coordinates or (Q) we risk getting way off course. If (Q) we do that, then (R) our expedition is doomed. Therefore, (~R) if our expedition is not to be doomed (P) we need to recalculate these coordinates.*

Symbolically, the argument reads:

P1: $P \lor Q$
P2: $Q \to R$
C: $\sim R \to P$

Translated into linear form we get:

$\{[(P \lor Q) \ \& \ (Q \to R)] \to (\sim R \to P)\}$

Now, instead of asking whether **E9** is valid, ask whether it is invalid. Begin by working out the truth value for the conclusion, as follows:

	P	Q	R	{[(P ∨ Q)	&	(Q → R)]	→	(~R → P)}
1.	T	T	T					T
2.	T	T	F					T
3.	T	F	T					T
4.	T	F	F					T
5.	F	T	T					T
6.	F	T	F	T	[F]	F	{T}	F
7.	F	F	T					T
8.	F	F	F	F	[F]	T	{T}	F

Only in rows 6 and 8 is the conclusion false (make certain you understand why it is false in each case). Therefore, these are the only rows you need to test fully. As you can see, in both cases the premise side is also false, and the fourth row of the hypothetical truth table (Table 6.4) will tell you that "F → F" yields a T value. So all rows yield T values, which means that the argument is valid.

Sometimes, however, there may be more F values in the conclusion than T values, as in the following argument:

E10: $\{[(P \ \& \ Q) \ \& \ (Q \ \& \ R)] \to (P \ \& \sim R)\}$

The truth table for this argument is as follows:

	P	Q	R	{[(P & Q)	&	(Q & R)]	→	(P & ~R)}
1.	T	T	T	T	[T]	T	{F}	F
2.	T	T	F	T	[F]	F	{T}	T
3.	T	F	T	F	[F]	F	{T}	F
4.	T	F	F	F	[F]	F	{T}	T
5.	F	T	T	F	[F]	T	{T}	F
6.	F	T	F	F	[F]	F	{T}	F
7.	F	F	T	F	[F]	F	{T}	F
8.	F	F	F	F	[F]	F	{T}	F

In six of the eight rows the conclusion has an F value. However, imagine you have written out the distributions for P, Q, and R but not yet entered truth values for each of the rows. Since the premises are conjunctions, both variables have to be true to make the compound sentence true. That means that, in any row where at least one of the variables has an F value, at least one of the premises will be false—and that will give the premise side of the argument an F value. When that occurs the truth value for that row will necessarily be T, since, by the rule of material implication, (F → F) = T, and (F → T) = T.

Now, since both premises contain *un*negated variables, and since every row of the truth table except row 1 has an F value for at least one of these unnegated variables, you know that every row but row 1 will have a false premise. Therefore, row 1 is the only row you need to test fully. Since all its simple sentences are true, you know that the premise side of row 1 will have a T value. Therefore, the minute you verify that the conclusion is false you know that the argument is *invalid* because it is *possible*, under the distribution of variables in row 1, for it to have true premises and a false conclusion. Knowing the truth table makes you a much more efficient evaluator of validity. **E10** is yet another example of why it is better to think critically than simply mechanically.

Mixed Syllogisms

Thus far we have focused on pure syllogisms, largely because mixed ones are easier to deal with. Insofar as they generally have only two variables, mixed syllogisms require only a basic four-row table. One example will suffice:

E11: {[(P ∨ ~Q) & (~P)] → (~Q)}

Here is a disjunctive syllogism, whose validity can be demonstrated as follows:

	P	Q	{[(P	∨	~Q)	&	(~P)]	→	(~Q)}
1.	T	T	T	T	F	[F]	F	{T}	F
2.	T	F	T	T	T	[F]	F	{T}	T
3.	F	T	F	F	F	[F]	T	{T}	F
4.	F	F	F	T	T	[T]	T	{T}	T

On the two rows where there is a false conclusion (1 and 3), there are also false premises. So **E11** is valid.

To summarize, all it takes to *invalidate* an argument is an F value for just one of the rows—that is, for it to occur under one possible distribution of the variables. That means that the conclusion does not follow necessarily from the premises. Often, the most efficient approach is to look for rows that have false conclusions and then check the premise side of those—and only those—rows. Even when there are a majority of false conclusions, a little critical attention of the sort demonstrated in **E10** can usually shorten the task of determining validity.

Something to Think About

It is one thing to understand truth tables and another to be able to remember them. But since it takes time to consult them every time you do a validity test, memorizing them is not a bad idea. Here's how Occam would advise you to do so.

	P	Q	(P & Q)	(P ∨ Q)	(P → Q)	(P ⊻ Q)	(P ↔ Q)
1.	T	T	T	T	T	F	T
2.	T	F	F	T	F	T	F
3.	F	T	F	T	T	T	F
4.	F	F	F	F	T	F	T

So far as their truth values go, all compound sentences either have a three–one or a two–two split of values. We have already used this to create the following descriptions:

- **Conjunction:** *A conjunction is true iff both (all) of its variable are true.*
- **Inclusive Disjunction:** *An inclusive disjunction is false only if both (all) its variables are false.*
- **Hypothetical:** *A hypothetical is false only if it has a true antecedent and a false consequent.*
- **Exclusive Disjunction:** *An exclusive disjunction is false if its variables have the same truth values.*
- **Biconditional:** *A biconditional is false if its variables have different truth values.*

Since this is bivalent logic, if a variable is not true it is false and vice versa. Hence, there is no need to enter every value: just enter the ones suggested by the descriptions, as follows:

	P	Q	(P & Q)	(P ∨ Q)	(P → Q)	(P ⊻ Q)	(P ↔ Q)
1.	T	T				F	
2.	T	F	F		F		F
3.	F	T	F				F
4.	F	F	F	F		F	

It is not difficult to retain this table in your memory. In fact, if you really understand truth tables you do not have to remember them at all. Understanding either makes memorizing redundant or much, much easier—take your pick.

EXERCISE 6.3

Symbolize the following arguments and then use truth tables to test them for validity.

*1. It is not possible both to fix the flux capacitor and retain the integrity of the vehicle. But if we don't fix the flux capacitor, we will be marooned forever in the past. Hence, if we retain the integrity of the vehicle, we will never get back to the future.

2. Politics is necessarily evil if and only if human nature is prone to error, and since that's just not true politics is not necessarily evil.

*3. We should invest in this stock if it goes up by Wednesday because if it does go up we will know that the takeover is going to happen, and either that will happen or we won't invest.

4. If profits depend on unsound environmental practices, then either the quality of the environment will deteriorate or profits will drop. But jobs will be plentiful if and only if profits do not drop. Therefore, if profits depend on unsound environmental practices, either jobs will not be plentiful or the quality of the environment will deteriorate.

*5. Emily must be very intelligent because she's so articulate, as intelligent people always are.

6. It's not fair to smoke around non-smokers because second-hand smoke is harmful, and if something is harmful it's not fair to expose non-participants to it.

*7. If your grades bother you then you will work harder, but you cannot do that if you spend all your time playing video games. But you do spend all your time playing video games so your grades don't bother you.

8. It is not possible both to take a holiday and pay our taxes. Since we have to pay our taxes, we can't take a holiday.

*9. Either things have improved or the war was a mistake. If it was a mistake then we are going to bring the troops home. So, things have improved if we do not bring the troops home.

10. One cannot both engage in market speculation and pursue a full-time job because market speculation requires enormous attention to detail, and if you have a full-time job you cannot pay such attention.

*11. You can trust someone if and only if she knows logic—which you do not. So I don't trust you.

12. Democracy works if and only if the public is well informed, and that's the case if and only if the media does its job. Thus, for democracy to work, the media must do its job.

*13. Loss is difficult to deal with because it tears at the fabric of the human spirit, and anything that does that is difficult to deal with.

14. Either this is not the unmitigated disaster I think it is or my career is over. But it is not possible that my career is over, and I am still in charge of the whole company. Therefore, if this is the unmitigated disaster I think it is then I am still in charge of the company.

*15. Since we cannot succeed if we don't try, and if we don't try then we ask too little of ourselves, it follows that either we succeed or we ask too little of ourselves.

16. I will not rise early in the morning and stay out late at night, but I will stay out late at night if and only if I have marmalade with my toast. Consequently, either I will not rise early in the morning or I will have marmalade with my toast.

*17. Either I'm dreaming or I'm not dreaming, and I am not dreaming so I am not not-dreaming.

IV. The Short Method

This section will demonstrate a short method for testing validity. It's an application of the method set out in Section III, but one that does not require you to write out the truth table.

The first point to bear in mind is that with this short method you are checking to see whether the argument is *invalid*. In fact, *you are trying to make the argument invalid.* If you cannot do so, then it is valid. Let's apply this method to **E9**, reproduced symbolically as **E12**:

E12: *{[(P ∨ Q) & (Q → R)] → (~R → P)}*

There are three steps to the short method:

STEP 1: *Falsify the conclusion.*

Remember that an argument is invalid iff it is possible for it to have true premises and a false conclusion under at least one distribution of truth values of its constituent variables. So begin by falsifying the conclusion. **E12**'s conclusion is a hypothetical sentence, and since a hypothetical sentence is false only when the antecedent is true and the conclusion is false, ~R will have a T value (R will therefore have an F value) and P will have an F value. Enter these values below the conclusion, as follows:

$$\{[(P \vee Q) \ \& \ (Q \to R)] \ \to \ (\sim R \to P)\}$$
$$\text{T} \boxed{\text{F}} \text{F}$$

STEP 2: *Transfer the values for the variables in the conclusion to the variables in the premises:*

$$\{[(P \vee Q) \ \& \ (Q \to R)] \ \to \ (\sim R \to P)\}$$
$$\text{F} \qquad\qquad \text{F} \qquad \text{T} \boxed{\text{F}} \text{F}$$

Once again, note that since ~R has a T value in the conclusion, R has an F value in the premise.

STEP 3: *Try to make both premises true.*

If you can do so, the argument is *invalid*; if you cannot, it is *valid*. Begin by looking for premises where your hand is forced. For example, in the first premise of **E12** P is false, which means that Q has to be true to make the inclusive disjunction true. Q then has to be true in the second premise as well. This yields the following:

$$\{[(P \vee Q) \ \& \ (Q \rightarrow R)] \ \rightarrow \ (\sim R \rightarrow P)\}$$
$$F \ \boxed{T} \ T \qquad T \ \boxed{F} \ F \qquad T \ \boxed{F} \ F$$

One premise is true and one is false. Since premises are conjoined, that means that the premise side of the argument has an F value:

$[T \ \& \ F] = F$

Since the conclusion is false, you have:

$\{[F] \rightarrow F\} = T$

So **E12** is valid. Had you started with the second premise and assigned an F value to Q to make it true, then the first premise would be false. And that is the point: once the conclusion was falsified, one of the premises had to be false as well. In short, in **E12** it is impossible to have true premises and a false conclusion.

But let's finish the exercise by entering the values for the premise side of the argument and for the argument as a whole:

$$\{[(P \vee Q) \ \& \ (Q \rightarrow R)] \ \rightarrow \ (\sim R \rightarrow P)\}$$
$$F \ \boxed{T} \ T \quad \blacksquare \quad T \ \boxed{F} \ F \quad \blacksquare \quad T \ \boxed{F} \ F$$

The light grey–shaded letters are the truth values for the premise and conclusion sides of the argument. The truth value for the whole argument is shaded in dark grey. (Remember, the dark grey T value does not mean that the individual sentences are true: it means that the argument is valid.)

As **E12** demonstrates, in the short method valid arguments force your hand. Once the conclusion has been falsified, it is impossible to make both premises true. Invalid arguments are, however, a little trickier. Consider **E12** with one small change:

E13: $\{[(P \vee Q) \ \& \ (Q \rightarrow R)] \rightarrow (R \rightarrow P)\}$

Once the negation sign is removed from R in the conclusion, it now has a T value and, accordingly, ~R has an F value. Following step 2, transfer these values to the premises:

$$\{[(P \vee Q) \ \& \ (Q \rightarrow R)] \ \rightarrow \ (\sim R \rightarrow P)\}$$
$$F \qquad\qquad\qquad T \qquad\qquad T \ \boxed{F} \ F$$

Notice that the second premise—a hypothetical with a true consequent—is going to be true no matter what value Q has. This is a pretty good indication that the syllogism is invalid. Q is called an open variable:

> **Definition:** An **open variable** is one where either a T or an F value can be assigned without falsifying the compound sentence in which it occurs.

When you come across an open variable, *do not randomly assign it a truth value*: in a syllogism turn your attention instead to the premise where the truth value of the remaining variable is not open, assign it the appropriate truth value (i.e., the one that makes the premise true), and let this determine which truth value the open variable will bear. That way you won't mistake an invalid argument for a valid one.

In **E13**, therefore, all you have to do is save the first premise by entering a T value for Q, which you then transfer to the second premise. This yields the following:

$$\frac{\{[(P \lor Q) \ \& \ (Q \to R)] \ \to \ (R \to P)\}}{F\boxed{T}T \quad \boxed{T} \quad T\boxed{T}T \quad \boxed{F} \quad T\boxed{F}F}$$

Two true premises make the premise side of the argument true while the conclusion is false, so the argument is *invalid*. But beware: if you are not paying attention, you might assign the open variable Q an F value, in which case the first premise would be false and the argument would look valid! Like every variable, Q can carry one of two values: T or F. Under *one* of these values, the invalid **E13** will have an F value and under the other a T value, whereas in a valid argument it will come out to a T value both times. Remember the rule of validity: in a valid argument, if the premises are true then necessarily so is the conclusion. By contrast, in an invalid argument there is no necessity—if the premises are true the conclusion could be true or false. After all, the opposite of "necessarily true" is not "necessarily false," but rather "not necessarily true."

To repeat, in the short method you are trying to find an F value for the argument by finding a T value for both premises after the conclusion has been falsified. Since **E13** has three variables, there are (2^3) eight possible distributions of T and F values. If you write out the full truth table you will see that the argument has a T value seven times and an F value once. But one F value is enough to invalidate an argument because it means that the truth of the conclusion does not follow necessarily from the truth of the premises. The short method allows you to determine very quickly whether that solitary F value is there.

Of course, unlike **E13**, some conclusions come out false under more than one distribution of their variables. With biconditionals and exclusive disjunctions there are two false distributions, and with a conjunction there are three. In these cases, the short method is extended (it's not so short) because you need to check all possibilities, and this means that you have to fill out two or three rows. For example:

E14: [(P ∨ Q) & (Q ↔ R)] → (P ↔ ~R)}

T	T	F		F		F	F	T		T		T	F	F
F	T	T		F		T	F	F		T		F	F	T

In **E14**, you need to check the two distributions of truth values that will make the biconditional conclusion false. In both instances one of the premises is also false. The two dark grey T values thus indicate that the argument is valid.

One obvious advantage of the shorter method is that it circumvents the tedium of writing out very long truth tables. For example:

E15: {[(P → ~Q) & (Q ∨ R) & (R → S)] → (P → ~S)}

This argument has four variables, and since four variables necessitate a (2^4) 16-row truth table, the shorter method is definitely a time-saving alternative. Since **E15**'s conclusion is a hypothetical sentence, there is only one way that it is false. Assign the appropriate values—T for P and F for ~S—and transfer them to the premises:

{[(P → ~Q) & (Q ∨ R) & (R → S)] → (P → ~S)}

T						T		T F F

Take a moment to contemplate the two premises for which you have truth values. In the first premise your hand is forced—~Q has to be true—but not in the third one, where R is an open variable. So you begin with the first premise, making ~Q true. Q is therefore false in the second premise, yielding:

{[(P → ~Q) & (Q ∨ R) & (R → S)] → (P → ~S)}

T T T		F		T		T F F

Since Q is false, R has to be true to make the inclusively disjunctive second premise true. That completes the assignment of truth values:

{[(P → ~Q) & (Q ∨ R) & (R → S)] → (P → ~S)}

T T T	T	F T T	T	T T T	F	T F F

The two light grey–shaded T values on the premise side indicate that the premises are all true, while the light grey F value in the conclusion indicates that it is false. This of course means that the argument is *invalid*. Once again, the existence of an open variable—R in the third premise—is a strong indication of an invalid argument.

Something to Think About

Now that you have mastered validity, apply your knowledge to the following puzzle, one of many that is the work of the endlessly creative logician Raymond Smullyan.[1]

There was a land of knights and knaves, where knights always tell the truth and knaves always lie. Three of the inhabitants—A, B, and C—were standing together in a garden. A stranger passed by and asked A, "How many knights are there among you?" A answered, but rather indistinctly, so the stranger could not make out what he said. The stranger then asked B, "What did A say?" B replied, "A said that there is only one knight among us." At this point the third man, C, said, "Don't believe B; he is lying." The question is, what are B and C? (i.e., identify each as a knight or a knave and explain your reasoning)

The answer is found in the Answer Key at the end of the book.

EXERCISE 6.4

Using the short method introduced in this section, test the following sentences for validity.

*1. {[(~P → ~Q) & (Q)] → (P)}

 2. {[(P → Q) & (P → R)] → (Q → R)}

*3. {[(~P ∨ Q) & (R → ~Q)] → ~(P & R)}

 4. {[(P ⊻ Q) & (~Q & R)] → (P)}

*5. {[(P ↔ (Q ∨ R)) & (~R)] → (P → Q)}

 6. {[(P → Q) & (~R ∨ Q)] → (P → R)}

*7. {[(R → (S ∨ P)) & (P ↔ Q) & (~S)] → ~(R & ~Q)}

 8. {[(P ∨ R) & ~(P & ~R)] → (R ↔ Q)}

*9. {[(~P ∨ Q) & (~Q ↔ R) & (R ⊻ S) & (~S)] → ~(P ⊻ ~R)}

10. {[~(P & (Q ∨ R)) & (S → ~P) & (~Q)] → (~S ∨ R)}

*11. {[(P ↔ Q) & (Q ∨ R) & (~R ∨ S) & (T → ~S) & (T & U)] → (P → ~U)}

12. {[(P ⊻ Q) & (Q → S)] → (P ⊻ S)}

*13. {[(P & Q) & (P & R)] → (Q & R)}

14. {[(P → Q) & (P & ~R)] → (~Q & R)}

*15. {[(P → Q) & (Q → P) & (P ↔ R)] → (Q ↔ R)}

---

1 Raymond Smullyan, *What Is the Name of This Book?* (New Jersey: Prentice-Hall, 1978). This puzzle is adapted from two puzzles on pages 20–1.

V. Natural Deduction

This section will introduce you to natural deduction. You have already implicitly been asked in Exercise 6.2, section II, to apply the rudiments of natural deduction, but this section will explicitly demonstrate how it works. Unlike the methods introduced in Sections III and IV above, natural deduction is not a method of *testing* for validity but rather of *proving* validity.

> **Definition: Natural deduction** *is a method of demonstrating the validity of an argument working from a set of valid inferences.*

You have already learned many of these inferences in Chapter 5 and in Section III of this chapter. As such, natural deduction nicely sums up the lessons of this and the previous chapter. If you can apply it, you really do understand deduction. Also, though it may not seem so at first sight, natural deduction proofs are actually kind of fun to do—they are like small mazes that you can teach yourself to navigate.

Rules of Inference and Equivalents

Natural deduction employs a set of **rules of inference** to demonstrate the validity of arguments. Four of these inferences are the basic syllogisms you are already familiar with: the **DS**, **MP**, **MT**, and **CS**. Since these syllogisms are always valid, it is possible to use them to demonstrate the validity of arguments they appear in. In addition to the syllogisms, we will use three more inferences: *addition*, *conjunction*, and *simplification*. Let's define them:

> **Addition:** *If any simple sentence is true, then any inclusive disjunction it appears in will also be true.*

In other words, if P (or Q) is true then the disjunction (P ∨ Q) is true as well.

> **Conjunction:** *If two simple sentences are individually true, then a compound sentence in which they are conjoined will also be true.*

If P is true and Q is true then necessarily the conjunction (P & Q) is true.

> **Simplification:** *If a conjunctive sentence is true, then each of its constituent simple sentences is true.*

Thus, if (P & Q) is true then necessarily P is true.

Table 6.10 shows a list of the rules of inference we will be using.

Table 6.10 Rules of Inference

RULE	SYMBOLS
Addition (Add)	$P \rightarrow (P \lor Q)$
Chain Syllogism (CS)	$\{[(P \rightarrow Q) \& (Q \rightarrow R)] \rightarrow (P \rightarrow R)\}$
Conjunction (Conj.)	$P, Q \rightarrow (P \& Q)$
Disjunctive Syllogism (DS)	$\{[(P \lor Q) \& (\sim P)] \rightarrow (Q)\}$
Modus Ponens (MP)	$\{[(P \rightarrow Q) \& (P)] \rightarrow (Q)\}$
Modus Tollens (MT)	$\{[(P \rightarrow Q) \& (\sim Q)] \rightarrow (\sim P)\}$
Simplification (Simp.)	$(P \& Q) \rightarrow P$

As well as inferences, natural deduction makes use of equivalents. Because they allow you to rewrite parts of premises in different ways, equivalents make the rules of inference stand out in clear relief. They have already been set out in Table 6.9, but it will not hurt to repeat them here:

Table 6.11 Equivalents

RULE	SYMBOLS
Commutation (Comm.)	$(P \& Q) = (Q \& P)$ $(P \lor Q) = (Q \lor P)$
De Morgan's Rules (DM)	$\sim(P \& Q) = (\sim P \lor \sim Q)$ $\sim(P \lor Q) = (\sim P \& \sim Q)$
Double Negation (DN)	$\sim \sim P = P$
Material Implication (MI)	$(P \rightarrow Q) = (\sim P \lor R)$
Material Equivalence (ME)	$(P \leftrightarrow Q) = ((P \rightarrow Q) \& (Q \rightarrow R))$
Transposition	$(P \rightarrow Q) = (\sim Q \rightarrow \sim P)$

Proving Validity

Consider the following argument, whose structure may be evident to you by now:

E16: $\{[(P \rightarrow (Q \& R)) \& (P)] \rightarrow (Q \& R)\}$

To prove the validity of this argument using natural deduction, list the premises and conclusion as follows:

1. (P → (Q & R))
2. (P) ⊢ (Q & R)

The line below premise 2 indicates that these are all the premises. The conclusion, which you are going to prove follows necessarily from the premises, is entered to the right of the second premise, introduced by the symbol ⊢, which means "therefore."

The interesting thing about natural deduction is that you have to figure out how to find your way to a proof. In this case, however, it is very simple. Just add a third line, as follows:

3. (Q & R) 1, 2, MP

This indicates that (Q & R) is a valid inference from sentences 1 and 2 by virtue of it completing an **MP**. So the full proof looks like this:

1. (P → (Q & R))
2. (P) ⊢ (Q & R)
3. (Q & R) 1, 2, MP

Now consider this argument, which is from Exercise 6.4, question 13 above:

E17: {[[(P & Q) & (P & R)] → (Q & R)}

Inscribe the premises and the conclusion:

1. (P & Q)
2. (P & R) ⊢ (Q & R)

Commutation asserts that if (P & Q) is true then (Q & P) is true, and from (Q & P) we can, by simplification, infer Q. This yields 3 and 4 below:

1. (P & Q)
2. (P & R) ⊢ (Q & R)
3. (Q & P) 1, Comm.
4. (Q)3, Simp.

From (P & R) in 2, we can, also by commutation and simplification, infer R as follows:

5. (R & P) 2, Comm.
6. (R) 5, Simp.

Now we apply conjunction to get:

7. (Q & R) 4, 6 Conj.

We have now proved that (Q & R) is a valid inference from premises 1 and 2.

Natural deduction works most smoothly when conjunctions, inclusive disjunctions, and hypotheticals are involved, but if you understand equivalents it can also work on biconditionals (and even exclusive disjunctions, though we will not work with these here). For example:

E18: {[[(P ↔ Q) & (Q → R)] → (~P ∨ R)}
1. (P ↔ Q)
2. (Q → R) ⊢ (~P ∨ R)

3. *[(P → Q) & (Q → P)] 1, ME*
4. *(P → Q) 3, Simp.*
5. *(P → R) 2, 4, CS*
6. *(~P ∨ R) 5, MI*

Here **material equivalence** was employed in 3 to translate the biconditional opening premise into two hypothetical sentences. Since those sentences are conjoined, we can apply simplification in 4 to assert that the first of these hypothetical sentences is true. Putting 2 and 4 together, we derive (P → R) in 5 by means of a chain syllogism. We then use material implication to translate (P → R) into (~P ∨ R) in 6. This is the conclusion of the argument, so we have proved it.

Let's now examine a slightly more complicated argument:

E19: *{[(R → (S ∨ P)) & (P ↔ Q) & (R & ~S)] → (R & Q)}*
1. *(R → (S ∨ P))*
2. *(P ↔ Q)*
3. *(R & ~S) ⊢ (R & Q)*

Simplify premise 3 to get:

4. *(R) 3, Simp.*

This yields:

5. *(S ∨ P) 1, 4, MP*

Next, use communation on premise 3 to get:

6. *(~S & R) 5, Comm.*

Then simplify 6 to:

7. *(~S) 3, Simp.*

Which yields:

8. *(P) 5, 7, DS*

Now apply material equivalence to turn premise 2 into a pair of hypothetical sentences:

9. *[(P → Q) & (Q → P)] 2, ME*

This yields:

10. *(P → Q) 9, Simp.*

Which in turn yields:

11. *(Q) 8, 10, MP*

Which leads to:

12. *(R & Q) 4, 11, Add.*

Well, I think it's fun.

EXERCISE 6.5

I. Write the following arguments out symbolically and then prove their validity using natural deduction.

*1. It is not true that politicians are always wise and have our best interests at heart. But since they do have our best interests at heart they are not always wise.

2. If the polar ice cap is melting and the glaciers are receding then global warming is a fact. Research shows that the polar ice cap is melting; it also shows that glaciers are receding. Global warming is therefore a fact.

*3. If either we study today or study tomorrow or we just don't study at all then we will pass the course. And since we are going to go out both days and not study, we will pass the course.

4. If the Mavericks were going to make the playoffs then the Celtics had to beat the Lakers. The Celtics did not beat the Lakers, so the Mavericks are out of the playoffs.

*5. Either the package arrives today or we put the meeting off until tomorrow, and if we do that then we will have to rework production schedules, so either the package arrives today or we rework production schedules.

6. I can keep working because this therapy helps, and if either it does help or I try something new then I can keep working.

*7. Jones failed but Wong succeeded, and either Wong did not succeed or Mohamed did. Therefore, Mohamed succeeded.

8. Jones succeeded iff Wong did and it is not possible that Wong and D'Souza both succeeded, and D'Souza did succeed so Jones failed.

*9. If you buy that phone you need to buy all its apps and the theft insurance. However, if you buy the theft insurance, you will pay more than 150 dollars a month to use the phone, and since you can't afford that much you can't buy the phone.

10. Only one of these options is possible: either there is an immovable object or there is an irresistible force, and since the latter does not exist there is an immovable object. (This one is a bit different: you're on your own.)

II. Use natural deduction to prove the following.

*1. $\{[(P \leftrightarrow Q) \,\&\, (R \lor \sim P) \,\&\, (R \to S)] \to (Q \to S)\}$

2. $\{[(P \lor Q) \,\&\, (Q \to \sim R) \,\&\, (R \,\&\, S)] \to (P)\}$

*3. $\{[(\sim Q \to P) \,\&\, (\sim Q \lor R) \,\&\, (\sim R)] \to (P)\}$

4. $\{\sim \sim (P \,\&\, Q) \,\&\, (P \to (R \,\&\, S))] \to (S)\}$

*5. {[[(P) & (P → Q) & ((Q ∨ R) → (S & T))] → (T)}

6. {[~ ~(P ∨ Q) & (P → R) & (~R & T)] → (~Q)}

*7. {[(P → (Q ∨ R)) & (~(Q ∨ R) ↔ (S & T)) & (U → S) & (W → T) &~ ~(U & W)] → (~P)}

8. {[(P ↔ Q) & (Q → (R ∨ S)) & (~R) & (P & T)] → (S)}

*9. {[~ ~(P & (Q ∨ R) & (Q → S) & (~R ∨ T)] → (S ∨ T)}

10. {[(P ↔ Q) & (~P ∨ R) & (R ↔ S) & (~T → ~S)] → (Q → T)}

*11. {[~(Q ∨ R) & (~R → (S ∨ T)) & (~T)] → (S)}

12. {[(P → (Q ∨ R)) & (S → (P & Q)) & (~ ~S) & (~R)] → (Q)}

VI. Summary

In this chapter you have been introduced to two methods of *testing* for validity. The first uses the full truth tables while the second, the short method, focuses on a search for invalidity. You have also learned about *natural deduction*, which is a method for *proving* validity.

A solid grasp of validity is essential to critical thought, because an invalid argument fails to demonstrate the truth of its conclusion even if the premises are true. Yet, without training it is very easy to overlook invalid arguments, and people regularly do so. To take a simple case, consider the following example, which I once read in a history text:

E20: *If the Roman Empire had been more cohesive in the fifth century* AD, *then it would have resisted the barbarian invasions. But it wasn't cohesive, so it fell.*

This argument may look convincing, and indeed its conclusion may have a great deal of merit, but I hope you can now see that it is invalid. **E20** commits the formal fallacy of denying the antecedent, which means that the premises do not imply the conclusion. Put differently, even if the premises are accepted as true (notice that the first one is a counterfactual conditional!), the conclusion does not follow necessarily. Perhaps this is just a slip of the pen. Had the author replaced the hypothetical with the biconditional (iff), the argument would have been valid. As it stands, however, the argument proves nothing. Critical thought requires being alert to these kinds of slips or errors, and this in turn requires understanding validity.

APPENDIX:
How to Write Truth Tables

The rule, remember, is this: for a given number of simple sentences, the formula 2^n—where n = the number of simple sentences—will tell you how many different truth distributions there are. The 2 represents the fact that every sentence has one of two values: true or false. So if we were asked to construct a truth table for four sentences, we would know that there will be $2^4 = 16$ sets of truth distributions: four columns of 16 rows each. It would look like this:

P	Q	R	S
T	T	T	T
T	T	T	F
T	T	F	T
T	T	F	F
T	F	T	T
T	F	T	F
T	F	F	T
T	F	F	F
F	T	T	T
F	T	T	F
F	T	F	T
F	T	F	F
F	F	T	T
F	F	T	F
F	F	F	T
F	F	F	F

To get this pattern, use a *doubling* rule. The right-hand column alternates T and F through 16 places; the next column to the left doubles up—TT, FF—and so on until the left-most column, which is top-half T and bottom-half F.

CHAPTER SEVEN

Induction: The Basics

- Definitions of induction
- Probability
- Strong and weak arguments
- Cogent and uncogent arguments
- Generalizing and predictive arguments
- The rules of induction
- Abductive and analogical arguments
- Working hypotheses

This chapter will introduce the method of reasoning known as induction. You will learn how to recognize some different kinds of inductive arguments, how to evaluate them, and how to assess their limitations.

I. What Is Induction?

This section will develop a definition of induction, which, unfortunately, is not as obvious as it may at first sight seem to be.

You have learned that in a valid deductive argument the truth of the conclusion follows necessarily from the truth of the premises. Inductive arguments carry no such guarantee. In an inductive argument, the conclusion is derived from a set of independent premises, each of which is a piece of evidence in its favour. If the premises are true and relevant, the conclusion is *probably* but not necessarily true. We can therefore define induction as follows:

> *Definition: Induction is a process of reasoning that moves from premises derived from experience to a conclusion which, if the premises are true and relevant, is probably true.*

To see how this process works, imagine our extraterrestrial visitor, Ms ET, observing certain beings on Earth. She has been told they are called "humans." She wonders whether these humans are mortal. We don't want to think about the tests she runs (one hopes she just observes us for a very long time), but in the end she might record her observations as follows:

E1:
Observation 1: Bob is mortal
Observation 2: Gina is mortal
Observation 3: Ming Wu is mortal
Observation n: José is mortal
Conclusion: All humans are mortal

In diagram form, **E1** would look like this:

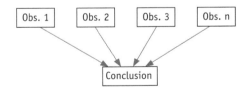

Based on *n* (i.e., an unspecified number) cases of humans, all of whom turned out to be mortal, Ms ET reaches the conclusion that all humans are mortal. Each individual observation is a premise in the argument leading to her conclusion. But unlike a valid deductive argument, this conclusion does not follow necessarily from the premises. Even if all her premises are true, there may nonetheless be immortal humans out there, waiting to be discovered. Since Ms ET cannot observe all humans she has to rely on what she thinks is a sufficient accumulation of evidence—that is, a large enough sample. And yet the fact remains that even with a lot of relevant evidence Ms

ET's conclusion is at best *probably* true. It would be absolutely true only if she could test all humans, but then there would be no argument, only a report about a fact.

Probability, Strength, and Cogency

Since inductive arguments are probabilistic, it is important to be able to assess degrees of probability. To give her conclusion a *high degree of probability*, Ms ET will have to observe a lot of humans, perhaps thousands. If she does so, there is a high degree of probability that, if her observations are relevant (i.e., if those really are humans that she has observed), her conclusion is also true. In that case, her argument is strong. On the other hand, if Ms ET is a bit lazy and makes only four observations, that is not enough evidence to create a high degree of probability. Even if those four observations are relevant, her argument is weak. These are fundamental evaluations of an inductive argument:

> *Definition:* A **strong argument** is an inductive argument where the premises, if true, give the conclusion a high degree of probability.

> *Definition:* A **weak argument** is an inductive argument where the premises, even if true, provide the conclusion with only a low degree of probability.

Note the phrase "if true" in these definitions. To say that an argument is strong is not to say that its premises actually are true, only that they are relevant to the conclusion. After all, Ms ET is an alien and may have gotten humans mixed up with the great apes. But if she has not—if she really has observed thousands of humans—then her strong argument is also cogent.

> *Definition:* A **cogent argument** is a strong inductive argument whose premises are true.

By contrast:

> *Definition:* An **uncogent argument** is either a weak inductive argument or a strong one with false premises.

The relationship among these four terms is shown in Figure 7.1.

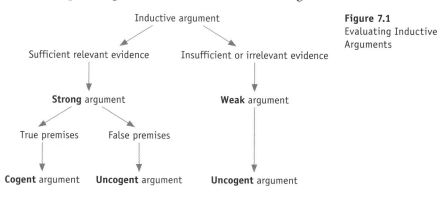

Figure 7.1
Evaluating Inductive Arguments

Let's apply these terms to a common process of induction where the degree of probability can be calculated: a public opinion poll. When a pollster asks 1500 Canadians how they are going to vote in an election, she will indicate in her report that her findings are accurate within plus or minus 3 per cent 19 times out of 20 (i.e., 95 per cent of the time). She has provided two bits of information here: the *range of accuracy* the poll aims at (plus or minus 3 per cent) and the *degree of probability* that the poll will fall within that range (95 per cent). A 95 per cent degree of probability means that, within the specified range of accuracy, the poll is strong.

Nonetheless, the possibility remains that the pollster's data may be wrong or that she may have misinterpreted it. In a recent Canadian election, one pollster said afterwards that he did not take sufficient account of the fact that older citizens, who tended to support the Conservative Party, vote in higher numbers than younger ones, who tended to support other parties. That meant the Conservatives got a higher percentage of the vote on election day than he had predicted on the basis of his polling. What he forgot was that it is not only voter preference that counts, but also voter action. His polls were accurate in terms of tracking *voter preference*, but not in terms of the probability that a respondent would *act on his or her preference*. So, as an argument about voter preference, his polls were strong and probably cogent, but as an argument about how things would go on voting day, they were weak and therefore uncogent. He did not have sufficient data about the probability that the respondents would actually show up at the polls.

There are other problems associated with polls. One is that people sometimes lie to pollsters. In American politics this is known as the *Bradley effect*. When Tom Bradley, a black mayor of Los Angeles, ran for governor of California, polls showed him comfortably in the lead—but he lost. The most common explanation for why the polls were uncogent was that a significant number of white respondents lied about their voting intentions because they did not want to appear to be racist. They said one thing to the pollster but in the privacy of the polling booth they did another. Pollsters do try to account for the fact that people may be lying to them, but they may not always manage to do so successfully.

These difficulties underline the fact that polls, like all inductive arguments, are exercises in probability. Even if a poll is cogent—even if the pollster has, for example, successfully accounted for which respondents are most likely to vote and for the possibility that some people are lying—there is still a 5 per cent chance that the poll may be wrong. No pollster can provide a 100 per cent guarantee that her poll will fall within the range of accuracy she cites. With induction that is simply not possible. Of course, the opposite is also true: a weak poll or a weak argument can turn out to be true. Had Ms ET concluded that humans are mortal after observing only four humans, she would still have been correct. This is called dumb luck and logicians hate dumb luck. That's why they stigmatize such arguments as weak and therefore uncogent even if the conclusion turns out to be true.

In what follows, we shall be more concerned with strength than cogency in inductive arguments, just as in Chapters 5 and 6 we focused on validity rather than truth in deduction. In other words, our principal interest will be the criteria for establishing evidence which, if true, gives the conclusion a high degree of probability. Table 7.1 compares the concepts of strength and cogency in inductive arguments and validity and soundness in deductive arguments.

Table 7.1 A Comparison of Deduction and Induction		
METHOD	CONCEPT	STIPULATION FOR ARGUMENTS
Deduction	Validity	If the premises are true then *necessarily* so is the conclusion.
Induction	Strength	If the premises are true then so *probably* is the conclusion.
Deduction	Soundness	Indicates that the premises of a valid argument are true.
Induction	Cogency	Indicates that the premises of a strong argument are true.

Keeping Induction and Deduction Apart

What follows is a discussion of a rather subtle problem, but one worth considering. To say that the conclusion of an argument is probable is to say that it does not follow necessarily from the premises. But that is also true of invalid deductive arguments. For example:

> **E2:** *Humans are mortal and Socrates is mortal, so Socrates is human.*

This is an invalid deductive argument. The conclusion does not follow necessarily from the premises. Yet, the conclusion *may* be true; it bears *some* degree of probability. After all, "Socrates" is a name some humans have. Does this mean **E2** is really an inductive argument, albeit a weak one? (To strengthen it we would need more evidence, such as "Humans speak" and "Socrates speaks.")

The problem is that if we accept this suggestion we seem to be teetering on the edge of a slippery slope leading to the conclusion that *only* valid arguments are deductive. This would mean that the two formal fallacies introduced in Chapter 5—affirming the consequent and denying the antecedent—are not fallacies at all, but simply examples of weak inductive arguments. We would essentially be replacing the formula "If an argument is deductive then it is either valid or invalid" with "an argument is deductive iff it is valid." Validity tests would therefore actually be tests to determine whether an argument is deductive. This would lead to the following definition of induction:

> **D1:** *An inductive argument is any argument that is invalid.*

Maybe this is the option recommended by the principle of charity, which counsels us to cast an argument in the best light. After all, "inductive argument," even "weak inductive argument," may be a more charitable characterization than "invalid deductive argument" because there is still *something* to be said for it—there is still some chance that, based on the premises, its conclusion is true.

But we need to recall a point made in the subsection on "Validity and Soundness" in Section III of Chapter 4: it is necessary to take into account the reasoner's *intention* in making an argument. If someone intends to put forward an inductive argument he is aiming for strength and cogency, and if he intends to put forward a deductive argument he is aiming for validity and soundness. But sometimes arguments fail—they do not demonstrate what their authors intended them to demonstrate. Sometimes we are right, therefore, to accuse someone of producing an invalid argument because he got the deductive process wrong. However, if **D1** is accepted as a definition for inductive arguments, no one ever makes an invalid deductive argument—no one ever fails in that way. People simply produce an inductive argument instead of a deductive one. They do something different rather than something wrong. In this case, "invalid argument" is simply a synonym for "inductive argument."

A more satisfactory solution is to amend **D1** to bring it into line with the definition of induction on page 208:

> **D2:** *An inductive argument is an argument in which the reasoner intentionally presents his conclusions as probable based on the truth of his premises.*

While intention can be difficult to assess, **D2** is based on the assumption that many arguments are pretty clearly intended to be inductive while others are just as clearly intended to be deductive, even if they are invalid. In fact, sometimes an argument wears its intention on its sleeve. Hypothetical arguments are an example. Consider the following:

> **E3:** *(P1) If there is a divine intelligent being then there are absolute moral values, (P2) and there are absolute moral values, (C) so there is a divine intelligent being.*

E3 is invalid, but it is hard to see how it could be construed as inductive. The whole thrust of the argument is pretty clearly to convince readers that the conclusion follows necessarily from the premises. Moreover, the hypothetical **P1** cannot be tested and probably neither can the more empirical-looking **P2**. What facts would determine its truth value? That means that the argument is indeterminate, which is something inductive arguments cannot be. The only reasonable characterization of **E3** is that it's an invalid deductive argument.

On the other hand, the premises of **E2** make empirical claims whose truth can be tested, so how should it be characterized? This is where judgment comes into play. Despite the fact that it cites evidence, I would suggest that **E2** is pretty clearly deductive in intention. The author seems to be trying to demonstrate that the conclusion follows necessarily from the premises.

But consider this example:

E4: *Everyone with arthritis has the kind of joint pain you describe, so I think you have arthritis.*

Read deductively, **E4** runs as follows:

P1: *If you have arthritis then you have that kind of joint pain;*
P2: *And you do have that kind of joint pain;*
C: *So you have arthritis.*

E4 commits the fallacy of affirming the consequent and therefore, read deductively, is invalid. However, to read it deductively it was necessary to omit the probabilistic phrase, "I think." Are those two words enough to allow one to transfer **E4** to the inductive column, where the premises would consist of a long series of observations of people with "that kind of joint pain"? While I think that, based on the principle of charity, they are, there is room for argument here.

However, accepting that there is room for argument—accepting that sometimes we have to make a judgment—is preferable to the absurdity of restricting deductive arguments to only those that are valid. Moreover, being sensitive to intention (and nuance) makes one a more critical reader and listener. Because we cannot always absolutely establish intention, this is a grey area that cannot be eliminated. So we shall adopt **D2**'s stipulation and say that induction is based on *the intention to construct a probabilistic argument.* That said, in what follows you can set judgment aside; the arguments you will meet in the rest of this chapter are to be treated as inductive.

Two Basic Inductive Arguments: Generalizing and Predicting

We begin with two fundamental kinds of inductive arguments: generalizing and predictive arguments.

*Definition: A **generalizing argument** is one in which a particular characteristic that some members of a class or group possess is assigned to all members of the class or group.*

Generalizing arguments thus usually (but as we shall see below, not always) conclude with the "all" or "no" statements, as in "All kangaroos hop" or "No alligators love cats." In **E1**, Ms ET was generalizing.

Here is another example:

E5: *Every solar system we have investigated that has rocky planets like Earth also has gas giants protecting them, so probably all rocky planets are protected by gas giants.*

Something to Think About

As an addendum to E4 above, I once went to a sports medicine clinic with pain in my right shoulder. The doctor asked me to make a certain movement with my right arm against the pressure of his hand. When it caused me considerable pain, he informed me that I had a torn rotator cuff and prescribed physiotherapy. My shoulder got steadily worse to the point where the physiotherapist sent me back to the doctor, who ordered an x-ray.

It turned out that I did not have a torn rotator cuff but another injury that required different treatment. I complained to the doctor that he had reasoned invalidly by affirming the consequent: "If he has a torn rotator cuff then this motion will cause him pain. It does cause him pain, so he has a torn rotator cuff." He replied that doctors think inductively and that because the probability that the injury was to the rotator cuff was very high he had dispensed with an x-ray. While he had been wrong, he had not been sloppy—merely trying to keep costs down in a non-life-threatening case. It is hard to argue with a doctor who knows logic. (But see the subsection on "Abduction" in Section III below.)

think

The conclusion of **E5** is a generalization about rocky planets. Based on the evidence of some rocky planets, the speaker has concluded that probably a characteristic of all rocky planets is that they are protected by gas giants.

Some arguments with conclusions that fall short of the universal "all" or "no" are still generalizations. For example:

E6: *I have met a number of your friends, and since most of them have been incredibly lazy I have to conclude that most of your friends are incredibly lazy.*

While the speaker has stopped short of concluding that all the person's friends are incredibly lazy—something the evidence will not support—this too is a generalization. Since most of the sample group are lazy, probably most of the whole group are as well. Whether the conclusion is "all" or "most," the generalizing claim is that what is true of the sample is probably true of the class as a whole.

Now we turn to predictive arguments:

*Definition: A **predictive argument** forecasts what will happen in the future based on evidence gathered in the present or the past.*

Since a predictive argument can look like an inductive generalization on occasion, it is important to be clear about the distinction between the two. For example:

E7: *Aisha will never fail a math test. In eleven years of school she has never failed one.*

The conclusion that Aisha will never fail a math test is a prediction, not a generalization. It does not assign a characteristic to a class but rather forecasts future events based on past ones. The "never" in the conclusion of **E7** is general, but predictive arguments can also have very specific conclusions. For instance, we could change the conclusion of **E7** to read as follows:

E8: *Aisha will pass her next math test because in eleven years of school she has never failed one.*

This too is a prediction about a future event based on past events.

So to recap, generalizing arguments assign characteristics to a class whereas predictive ones forecast the future based on available evidence.

EXERCISE 7.1

Exercises marked by an asterisk (*) have answers included in the Answer Key at the end of the text.

I. Indicate whether each of the following is a deductive or inductive argument.

*1. Zoë is pretty clearly going to drop out of college because she hasn't attended any of her classes for a month.

2. Humans are mortal because none of them have ever lived beyond about 120.

*3. If all the research shows—and it does—that Clydesdales are the strongest breed of horse, then we ought to accept that they are.

4. The Conservatives are going to win the election in a landslide, because 50 per cent of the vote would give them a landslide victory and they'll get that easily.

*5. Winters are always hard on me. I have experienced 57 of them, so I should know.

6. Golfers are better athletes than football players because they score higher in all the relevant tests of athleticism except speed and strength.

*7. If you look at all the evidence from every source you will have to conclude that smoking does contribute to cancer and heart disease. And I know you have looked at all the evidence, so you must think smoking contributes to lung cancer.

8. If public opinion polls are accurate 19 times out of 20, and if that degree of accuracy makes something fundamentally trustworthy, then public opinion polls are fundamentally trustworthy.

*9. All the rats injected with the virus died, so it is a safe assumption that the virus is lethal.

10. If reputable tests confirm a connection between a physical condition and a disease then we ought to accept that it exists. Tests do show a connection between cholesterol levels and heart disease, so we ought to assume that there is such a connection.

*11. It doesn't matter that she has no talent because serendipity makes up for a lack of talent, and based on the evidence she certainly is blessed by serendipity.

12. If we look at all the evidence from every source we have to conclude that smoking does contribute to cancer and heart disease.

*13. When events occurred outside the central nervous system of the patients but there was no brain activity, they registered no thoughts. But at other times brain activity indicated thinking

Continued >

even when there was no stimulus from outside the central nervous system. Hence, the crucial step in creating mental events must always be something that goes on inside the brain.

14. Ai-Li has followed the same training pattern as past champions, so it is a good bet that she will do well.

*15. If you are the best ski-racer you always win, and since Roger always wins he is the best ski-racer.

II. *Designate the following inductive arguments as either generalizing or predictive and then as "strong" or "weak."*

1. My son and his wife are both left-handed and are extremely clumsy, so I think that left-handers are probably clumsy.

2. In 87 per cent of presidential elections the taller candidate has won. Smith is taller than Jones, so he will probably win.

*3. I think Tom will be a great college pitcher; I saw him in Little League when he was 11 and he was already great.

4. Vasili has all the requisite skills for academic success. He is literate, disciplined in his work habits, engaged in the material, and mature for his age. He will do well.

*5. I have tried countless times—well, a hundred anyway—to learn how to yodel and I have always failed. I'll never learn.

6. A clear majority of our subscribers preferred this format, so I think it will sell better than the old one.

*7. Canadians love hockey. You know Tom and Ted—they're Canadians and they love hockey.

8. Over the past 10 seasons scarecrows have reduced the number of plants lost to birds by an average of 40 per cent, which is quite substantial. Therefore, most of the time using scarecrows is a good idea.

*9. I have slept through my alarm for two days straight. I am one of those people who always sleep in.

10. Everyone wants him to succeed, and that gives him a lot of motivation, so he probably will.

*11. In the past century, recessions have always followed periods of double-digit inflation, and we're in a recession now so I think if you check the figures you will find that in the previous quarter there was double-digit inflation.

12. Seventy per cent of the students who answered the questionnaire—over a thousand in total, randomly chosen—were in favour of our suggestion, so it's safe to say that most students approve of it.

II. The Three Rules of Induction

This section introduces the three **rules of induction** that govern inductive reasoning. Like the three laws of reason, you cannot ignore them and manage to construct a strong, let alone a cogent, argument.

Rule 1: Don't Be Hasty

Rule 1: The number of observations must be large enough and sufficiently varied to support the conclusion.

This rule governs the quantity and quality of the evidence supporting a conclusion. Let's imagine someone—let's call him Pham—making the following claim:

E9: *All import cars are junk.*

It would be appropriate to ask Pham how many imports he tested before drawing this conclusion. If the reply was "Just the one I own," we would have to reject his conclusion on the ground that the sample size is far too small; his argument is weak. If, however, he had tested a thousand cars, all of which fell under a reasonable definition of "junk" (and, in passing, I hope you noticed that "junk" is one of those vague words that can cause trouble in an argument), then we would have to admit that the sample size was large enough to constitute a strong argument. But if we subsequently discovered that Pham had tested a thousand Siberian Stormriders we would have to reject his argument on the ground that there was no *variation* in the sample. To get a strong argument, he would need to examine a wide variety of imports—ideally every make on the market.

To draw a conclusion without evaluating sufficient, and sufficiently varied, evidence is to commit an informal fallacy of presumption called **hasty generalization**. For example:

E10: *I don't like novels. I read one once and was bored to death.*

A very typical reaction to an experience that is either clearly favourable or clearly unfavourable is to generalize it in the manner of **E10**, but to do so is completely uncritical. Recall the fallacy of misleading vividness from Chapter 3, which consists of drawing a conclusion based on one graphic example. Someone may decide that air travel is unsafe based on one horrific plane crash, but this is to exaggerate its statistical significance and therefore to leap to a hasty conclusion.

Now consider this example:

E11: *Look, people don't think there is too much violence in hockey. Just ask professional hockey players. Almost none of them think there is.*

Even assuming this last claim is true, this is a hasty generalization because professional hockey players probably represent a biased sample, which is to say a sample of people who may well have a vested interest in keeping the game as it is. To get a strong argument it would be necessary to ask all types of people for their opinions.

It is also important to exercise caution with predictive arguments because it's not always self-evident how much evidence is required to produce a strong one. We often need statisticians to tell us how large and how varied samples need to be. For instance, you now know that a public opinion poll of 1500 randomly selected Canadians—randomness assures variation—will be accurate to within plus or minus 3 per cent 95 per cent of the time. The latter figure (95 per cent) is the probability of the poll being accurate within that 3 per cent margin of error. A 95 per cent probability is very high, but as a predictor of which party is going to win an election the poll may not be accurate enough. If the poll shows that the Silly Party is leading the Absurd Party by two percentage points then, given the margin of error, it is possible that the Absurd Party is actually leading the Silly Party. To predict that the Silly Party will win is therefore a risky prediction. It is important to note whether a poll's findings fall within or outside the margin of error because this is an indication of the strength of a given prediction.

What's more, statistics often need to be understood in context. In the case of a public opinion poll, a 95 per cent degree of probability is high and it is reasonable to trust it to be accurate within the margin of error. But if someone told you that the probability of a particular airline's flights reaching their destination safely was 95 per cent you would be foolish to get on one of its planes because 5 per cent of the time it will crash. As airplane flights go, that is a very high number. A 95 per cent probability of landing safely would not constitute a strong argument in support of the conclusion that travelling with that airline is safe. It's an important question: when is the evidence *enough* evidence, and what is it really telling us?

Rule 2: Maintain a Healthy Skepticism

Rule 2: Do not narrow your field of vision too severely. Even when the evidence suggests a particular conclusion, take time to consider whether there is data that might falsify it.

In essence, this rule tells you to act as devil's advocate against all arguments. This is especially important if you are looking for a general conclusion, such as **E9**'s "all import cars are junk." With generalizing arguments that reach a universal "all" or "no" conclusion, a single contradicting instance will falsify the conclusion because then the contradictory statement "some import cars are not junk" will be true. (In logic, the definition of "some" is "at least one.") Even when heading toward a narrower generalization, such as "most import cars are junk," it is essential to look for cases that may weaken the argument. Too often people put blinkers on—which is to say that they fall into the confirmation bias and look only for evidence that supports a certain conclusion.

Consider the social biases presented in Chapter 3, Section IV. They provided examples of conclusions drawn from flawed data—IQ tests were a case of that—but also of conclusions that misinterpreted the data. Let's review one example from that section. For a long time, based on the evidence, many (not all) educators concluded that girls had less aptitude for mathematics than boys, on average. The problem was that this finding did not take into account the social pressures that drove girls away from math. Nor did it take into account the degree to which the belief had become a self-fulfilling prophecy. Tell a group often enough and persuasively enough that they either have or do not have a given characteristic and their behaviour will probably begin to conform to the claim. So, was the fact that girls were, on average, not *performing* as well as boys on mathematics tests proof that they had less *aptitude* for the discipline? Could there be other reasons? A critical thinker of the day should have asked "Do girls have less aptitude for mathematics or are they, for whatever reasons, less interested in developing or displaying their aptitude?"

Finally, remember that even cogent arguments that do not misinterpret the data can turn out to be wrong. Here's a rather famous example:

E12: *All swans are white.*

For centuries the experience of Europeans confirmed this. Then they settled in Australia where there are black swans. Even the most long-standing inductive conclusions may one day be proven false. The great seventeenth-century scientist Isaac Newton treated his laws of nature as provisional, recognizing that future generations might falsify them. And in some cases they did. Great thinkers like Newton are often more *tentative* (i.e., less hasty) in their conclusions than are second-rate thinkers. They understand induction for what it is: a probabilistic, and therefore a fallible, method. This stimulates them to look for evidence that will refute their arguments.

Once again, predictive arguments also need to be subjected to this rule. Section I above contains the example of a pollster whose predictions about a Canadian election were wrong because he did not take full enough account of the fact that older people are more likely to vote than young people. He was, in effect, accusing himself of not looking hard enough for evidence that would contradict his findings.

Rule 3: How Plausible Is the Conclusion?

Rule 3: Consider whether a conclusion is plausible in the context either of your experience or of what you understand to have been reasonably demonstrated by experts.

In the age of the Internet there is a virtual tsunami of alleged data claiming to demonstrate almost anything you can imagine, and therefore you have to take a great deal of care when assessing it. If a conclusion violates your sense of the world or a given part of it (or the sense of relevant experts), be skeptical; withhold agreement until you have examined the matter more closely. Imagine a newspaper headline that read as follows:

E13: *Study proves that men are on average more intelligent than women.*

I would be deeply suspicious of this claim because, in my case, more than 35 years of experience as an educator suggests strongly that this is false. Moreover, I know of almost no reputable researchers who argue that it's true (nor do they argue the opposite is true). So I would want to look *very* closely at the evidence behind this conclusion before accepting it. Even if the argument looked strong, the methods for collecting the data may be biased, inaccurate, or in some way deeply flawed.

And of course data may be fabricated. A famous case concerns the British psychologist Cyril Burt (1883–1971) who conducted studies on human intelligence. He wanted to compare the relative contributions that nature and nurture make to intelligence: is intelligence mainly determined by genetics, or does it depend mainly on upbringing? By 1966, Burt had tested 53 pairs of identical twins who were raised apart. The idea was that if these genetically identical beings tended to have similar IQ's, nature must be the predominant factor in intelligence. If their IQ's varied significantly, nurture (upbringing) was probably more important. All well and good, but think about his data: identical twins are rare; identical twins raised apart are rarer still; identical twins raised apart who know they are one of a pair of twins or who know where the other twin is must be even rarer; and finally, twins who meet these criteria and volunteer to be test subjects must be blindingly rare. How did Burt come up with 53 pairs in Great Britain? The most common, though still disputed, answer is that he did not—the strong suspicion is that he manufactured some of his data. The point to consider here is that the average person's experience (how many sets of identical twins she knows, etc.) should arouse her suspicions, as it aroused those of some of Burt's fellow researchers. The fact that Cyril Burt was a respected scientist helped to hold doubt at bay, especially while he was alive. There is some justification for this. We rely on experts for knowledge we are unable to discover for ourselves, and Burt was an expert. There was, quite reasonably, an element of trust accorded to his findings, but trust should not lead to unquestioning acceptance. Keep an open mind but also a critical mind. Where did all those twins come from?

This raises a related point: when it comes to claims based on studies, it is important to know the source of the study and who funded it. If, for example, the "Society for Promoting Male Superiority" were the source of **E13**'s claim that men are more intelligent than women, you would do well to be suspicious of the result. Political and economic "think tanks" regularly publish studies on all sorts of social issues. Often these studies run true to form. A "conservative" institute will, for example, generally recommend cutting taxes while a "liberal" or "left wing" one will often favour raising them or holding them steady. Conservatives will want to cut funding for public programs whereas those on the left will probably want to increase it, or at least hold it steady. This is not surprising because these are policies each group supports and which are, in many cases, based on careful assessments of the evidence. Therefore, while the studies are not necessarily biased, the fact that you can be pretty certain what their conclusions will be before reading them should make you cautious. The question of plausibility becomes vitally important. Read critically, considering not just the evidence the study presents but whether, returning to the second rule, there is evidence it ignores.

Besides the outright invention of evidence there are other more subtle forms of fabrication. In the leaders' debate in the 2011 Canadian federal election campaign one of the party leaders repeatedly declared that the following:

E14: *Every credible economist supports the tax cuts [my party] is proposing.*

If that were so, there would be good reason to give serious consideration to the man's position. But since anyone who knows anything about academics knows how seldom they manage to achieve unanimity, the claim sounded suspicious. And indeed a little research showed that it wasn't true. *Some* economists favoured tax cuts and *some* did not. The slippery bit lay in the use of "credible," which is one of those troublesome vague words. In the party leader's case, "credible" seemed to mean, Humpty-Dumpty style, "every economist who agrees with me." But if so, then there was really no appeal to the evidence at all. All the politician was saying was "I'm right and therefore economists who agree with me are right, and therefore those economists are credible. Those who disagree with me are wrong and not credible." It was not a question of whether you believed the experts but rather whether you believed the party leader. The implausibility of the original claim should alert the critical listener to the slipperiness of the argument behind it.

Are Rules 2 and 3 Contradictory?

Some readers may think that rules 2 and 3 point in opposite directions. Rule 2 tells us to look for instances that will falsify our conclusions while Rule 3 tells us to hold on to our ideas until good evidence comes along to contradict them. But in fact the

Something to Think About

During the 1936 American presidential election campaign a magazine conducted a poll sampling some 2 million voters to ensure a very high degree of accuracy. The people polled were selected randomly from telephone books around the country. The result of the poll showed the Republican candidate winning by a large margin. In fact, the Democratic candidate—Franklin Delano Roosevelt—won by a large margin. What did the pollsters do wrong? (You may need some information about Republicans and Democrats to answer this) The answer is found in the Answer Key at the end of the book.

rules complement one another insofar as both are reminders not to accept conclusions too easily, either one's own or those of other people. Always be on the lookout for new evidence, and always evaluate it carefully. Both rules encourage a healthy skepticism based on an understanding of what a strong and cogent argument is and on recognizing that even cogent arguments may be wrong. To be skeptical is not to be cynical. It is, at bottom, a reminder to pay close attention to the evidence. And anyway, if you have obeyed rules 1 and 2 you will have good reason to obey rule 3 because your own view will have been carefully tested and should not be abandoned too easily.

EXERCISE 7.2

I. In each of the following, either a rule of induction is being broken or it is being used to criticize someone else's argument. Indicate which rule is at issue and what role it plays in the passage.

*1. Smythe set the experiment out very carefully, meticulously controlling the kind of information to which his subject, Jones, had access. Sure enough, Jones voted as Smythe predicted he would. Smythe had demonstrated that a person's voting habits can be strictly controlled.

2. You say you have discovered a new planet in the solar system because you have found something beyond Pluto that looks big enough to be a planet. Have you verified that it is not a comet?

*3. Yesterday I dreamt I had won a trip to Florida and today I got a letter saying that I had in fact won such a trip. Man, I am psychic!

4. The ball has landed on red on this roulette wheel six times in a row. The wheel is fixed!

*5. So what you're telling me is that you didn't cheat on the test? You simply worked hard and improved from 15 per cent on the previous two tests to 100 per cent on this one?

6. You think I disobeyed you because I wanted to hurt you? Has it ever occurred to you that I simply did what I thought was best?

*7. Sure, he could be innocent. As you say, his body could have been taken over by aliens before he held up the bank, but do you really think that is a reasonable hypothesis?

8. Jane: I prayed that she would get better and she did, so you see, prayer works.

   Matt: Maybe she would have recovered even if you hadn't prayed; after all, she got excellent medical treatment. (Hint: there are two rules here)

*9. Johnson tested 422 male politicians and concluded that they were all egocentric. It was a well-run research program, so I guess politicians are egocentric.

10. My theory must be true. I can show you dozens of confirming instances.

*11. You lied to me! Why should I ever believe you again?

12. I don't care what the scientific evidence says, I believe in ESP.

*13. A polling company contacted 350 people and on that basis predicted which party would win the next American federal election. They predicted the result correctly but were nonetheless fired by the TV network that had hired them. Why?

14. Your research claims that ethnic group A is on average more intelligent than ethnic group B, but the subjects from group A are on average much wealthier than those in group B.

*15. Sure I buy lottery tickets. I once won a relatively large sum of money in a raffle, so I must be lucky.

II. *Based on your experience, do you think the following statements are conclusions of strong or weak arguments? Defend your answers.*

*1. Only women like chick flicks.

2. What can go wrong will go wrong.

*3. Good athletes hate losing more than they like winning.

4. Athletes tend to be well-coordinated.

*5. On average, women are more intelligent than men.

6. On average, men are physically stronger than women.

*7. People always get promoted beyond their level of competence.

8. All successful politicians are ambitious.

*9. Fatigue makes cowards of us all.

10. You get what you deserve.

III. Abduction and Analogy

This section introduces two types of inductive reasoning that are useful in situations of uncertainty: abduction and analogy. They can be very imaginative ways of thinking, but because of this they require caution in their application.

Abduction

So far, all reasoning has been classified as either deductive or inductive. There is, however, an interesting type of contextual argument called abduction that sits halfway between the two. The name was coined by the American philosopher Charles Sanders Peirce (1839–1914).

> *Definition: Abduction* is the process of inference to the best explanation in a context of uncertainty.

In other words, an abductive argument is an attempt to draw the most probable conclusion from evidence *that is not conclusive*. Because these conclusions are at best probably true, abduction is classified as a subset of induction. However, it looks like deduction.

Consider this familiar *modus ponens*, which a deductive reasoner would employ:

E15:
S1: Humans are mortal (i.e., if you are human then you are mortal);
S2: Socrates is human;
S3: Therefore, Socrates is mortal.

An inductive reasoner would rearrange this syllogism as follows:

E16:
S2: Socrates is human;
S3: Socrates is mortal;
S1: Therefore, humans are mortal.

In practice, **E16** would require many more instances of humans being mortal to make a strong argument, but (especially if the author expressed his intention by adding "probably" to the conclusion) it can reasonably be construed as an example of weak inductive reasoning, proceeding from evidence to a probabilistic conclusion.

In contrast to **E15** and **E16**, an abductive reasoner would argue as follows:

E17:
S3: Socrates is mortal;
S1: Humans are mortal (i.e., if you are human then you are mortal);
S2: Therefore, Socrates is human.

As in induction, the abductive reasoner has begun by observing a *particular fact* about the world: (**S3**) Socrates is mortal. But he has then applied a general rule that he thinks is relevant to the observation—(**S1**) humans are mortal—and has concluded that (**S2**) Socrates is human. A close look at the premises will reveal that **E17** can be construed as an invalid deductive syllogism, guilty of affirming the consequent. However, since it begins with an observation it's possible to invoke the principle of charity and argue that the reasoning is inductive and the conclusion is intended to be probable only. But if so, like **E15**, it is a weak inductive argument because "Socrates" could refer to any number of animals, such as pet cats or dogs or even a race horse. So **E17** seems to hover between invalid deduction and weak induction—hardly a strong recommendation for abductive reasoning.

But consider this example:

E18:

S1: The kitchen is really messy;
S2: My son always messes up the kitchen when he is home;
S3: My son is home.

Structurally, **E17** and **E18** are alike. Rewrite **E18:S2** to read "If my son is home then the kitchen is always messy" and once again we have the formal fallacy of affirming the consequent. The difference between the two arguments is that **E18** can be defended on the ground that based on long experience with her son the speaker has applied a rule that generates the most probable explanation for the mess in the kitchen. Lacking more information, there is not as much ground for assuming that the "Socrates" referred to in **E17** is human. Nonetheless, it too can be read as an inference to the best explanation and therefore as an abductive argument. The main difference is that **E18** is stronger than **E17**.

The point is that abduction begins from a conscious recognition of uncertainty—it is *reasoning under uncertainty*. A person is confronted with a fact (or observation) and in the absence of more evidence tries to work out what to make of it. The result is a conclusion that is essentially a working hypothesis.

> *Definition:* A **working hypothesis** *is a conclusion that is weak insofar as it requires further testing, but which is sufficiently probable to be worth testing.*

In **E18**, for example, the working hypothesis is that the woman's son is home, and she will almost certainly try to verify it by calling out to him.

The concept of a working hypothesis returns us to the discussion in Section I of the sometimes blurry distinction between invalid deductive arguments and inductive arguments. The conclusion of that discussion was that we need to be sensitive to a reasoner's intention. The same applies here. Deciding whether an argument is abductive or simply an invalid deduction is a matter of judgment, and that judgment leans heavily on one's assessment of the reasoner's intention, which is revealed by the order of the reasoning—moving from an observation to the application of a rule—and the context of uncertainty in which that reasoning is carried out.

In fact, by taking intention (and therefore order and context) into account, it is possible to argue that even some valid syllogisms are also abductive. To see why, let's turn to the famous fictional detective Sherlock Holmes, who is often described by logicians as reasoning abductively, even though the author of the stories, Arthur Conan Doyle, had Holmes refer to his thought processes as deductive.

As a detective, Holmes begins, as **E18** does, with facts—clues—that are by definition not conclusive—they are uncertain. For example, in one Sherlock Holmes story called "The Golden Pince-Nez," a man has been murdered in his study, stabbed with his own letter opener that was apparently snatched from the man's desk by the murderer. There could be a number of explanations for this, but Holmes assumes that it means that the murderer did not bring a weapon to the house. He then applies the rule that if someone intends to commit murder he does bring a weapon, and concludes that this murder was therefore unpremeditated. This yields the following argument, set out in the order Holmes actually reasoned:

E19:

S1: (fact) The murderer did not bring a weapon;
S2: (rule) If someone intends to commit murder, he brings a weapon;
S3: (conclusion) Therefore, the murder was unpremeditated.

This is a valid syllogism, a *modus tollens* to be precise. Nonetheless, this is also clearly a case of *inference to the best explanation* for two reasons. First, there is the context of uncertainty: the evidence is far from conclusive. Second, there is the order of Holmes's reasoning: he applies a rule based on a prior observation (the murder weapon). Therefore, Holmes's intention—his goal—seems to be to develop a working hypothesis that he can then test. In short, since Holmes has no way of knowing for certain whether **S1** is true—maybe the murderer brought a weapon but didn't have time to use it—and therefore whether **S2** is relevant, his conclusion remains to be proved. However, assuming **S1** to be true and applying **S2** to it provides Holmes with the *most fruitful line of inquiry*—the best inference—*in an uncertain situation.* (Go back to the Something to Think About box on page 214 and you will see that, strictly speaking, the doctor was thinking abductively.)

Let's summarize a little. Abductive reasoning is a subset of inductive reasoning because its conclusions are at best probable. But it takes the form of a deductive syllogism, either valid or invalid. What sets it apart from deduction, then, is not its structure but its context and order, and therefore its intention. With respect to context, the reasoner is aware that she is reasoning in uncertain circumstances. She moves, therefore, from observation of a fact to the application of a rule that she thinks is the most likely to apply. This is the distinctive order of abductive thought. Her intention is to develop a reasonable working hypothesis that can be tested. It's a risky kind of reasoning—by definition that's what reasoning under uncertainty is—but employed responsibly and imaginatively in the right circumstances it can be a useful critical thinking tool.

To underline the element of risk, let's recall Chapter 4, **E2**, where you were presented with an example of the anchoring bias: a case of a juror who decided that the accused was guilty because he would not look directly at the jury. The juror was clinging to one scrap of possibly irrelevant information rather than sorting through all the evidence. Given that he is sitting on a jury, his actual reasoning probably had an abductive structure. He would first observe the accused's failure to look at the jury, then apply the rule that guilty people often will not look people in the eye, and conclude that the accused was guilty. This can be set out as follows:

E20:
S1: The accused did not look the jury in the eye;
S2: If you are guilty then you will not look the jury in the eye;
S3: Therefore, the accused is guilty.

This is an invalid syllogism that affirms the consequent, but were we to flip the antecedent and the consequent in **S2** it would be a (valid) *modus ponens*. While I think **S2** as written is the better reading, it doesn't matter much because the important point is that the jury member almost certainly did not start from the rule. He would first note the accused's behaviour (**S1**) and then decided what rule to apply to it (**S2**). So, **E20** looks like a case of abductive reasoning, where the jury member tries to make sense of the behaviour he has observed by developing an inference to the best explanation.

Unfortunately, the juror has ignored the third rule of induction. His experience in the world should have taught him that there could be many reasons why someone in the accused's situation would look away—shyness, nervousness, a sense of politeness. Given these other possible reasons, the juror should not have placed so much trust in **S2**. So his argument really isn't an inference to the best explanation. Moreover, he could not test his hypothesis, so it really isn't a *working* hypothesis. Therefore, what he settled on as the "best explanation" was in fact a woefully inadequate one with a low degree of probability: hence, a biased bit of reasoning. **E20** is therefore an example of someone who has failed to recognize the uncertainty of the situation—how inconclusive the accused's action is—and the untestable nature of his hypothesis. The result is not good abductive reasoning but rather a disaster for the accused.

The point is that while abduction is useful, even necessary, when you need to generate a working hypothesis, you have to take care not to make unwarranted assumptions. You need to be as certain as possible that the rule you apply is a sufficiently probable one. Make certain, in other words, that induction in the form of a great deal of past experience has already demonstrated the rule's applicability, as is the case in **E18** and **E19** (Holmes is a very experienced detective and the mother knows her son's habits). And keep your mind fixed on the fact that, no matter how much you like your hypothesis, no matter how probable you think it is, you still need to test it.

In closing this section, there is no need to try to make a firm distinction between abduction, induction, and deduction because abductive reasoning is essentially a hybrid of deduction and induction. It is a deductive argument applied to contexts in which the evidence is far from conclusive. The rule you apply stands in, *provisionally,* for the evidence you do not yet have. Abduction is therefore not a substitute for more thorough inductive arguments but rather a preliminary guide to the direction in which those arguments will go.

Analogy

Like abduction, analogical reasoning is a somewhat different, yet common, mode of induction. In fact, it's one people use almost instinctively because it is rooted in our capacity to notice similarity.

> **Definition: Analogical reasoning** moves from the observation that X and Y are similar in one respect to the inference that they are similar in another respect.

For example, consider the following summary of William Paley's eighteenth-century argument for the existence of God:

> **E21:** If we see a watch with all its intricate and interconnected parts, we know that it was designed by an intelligent being. If we look at nature, we see that it is equally intricate and interconnected. So, it too must have been designed by an intelligent being.

Paley's "argument from design" is a famous, and in its time influential, piece of analogical reasoning. He points out the similarity between the structure of a watch and the structure of nature, arguing that since the first is designed, then so must be the second.

In everyday life, we often hear similar arguments. For example:

> **E22:** Quentin Tarantino's movies are really interesting, and since Robert Rodriguez is the same sort of gonzo director, I think his films will be interesting too.

This is simple enough: Rodriguez is like Tarantino; Tarantino's films are interesting; so Rodriguez's probably are too. Essentially, the speaker likes one director's films, so he will probably like those of another who is apparently much like him. That's how we often go about recommending movies, books, video games, and even friends to other people: you like X, and since Y is like X in some way, you will like Y too. This is inductive reasoning because it's probabilistic (and, in the case of **E22**, predictive). None of the conclusions are guaranteed to be true, even if the premises are.

Let's go back to Ms ET's visit to Earth. She too might have reasoned analogically. Imagine she had no concept of humans but noticed that certain earthlings looked much alike. They walked on two legs, spoke languages, possessed low-grade intelligence, and so on. When she noticed that one of them was mortal, she might, by analogy, have assumed that all of them were. Her reasoning would have the following structure:

> **E23:**
> *P1:* X has characteristics a, b, c, . . . n;
> *P2:* Y, Z, etc. have characteristics a, b, c, . . . n;
> *P3:* X is mortal;
> *C:* Therefore, Y, Z, etc. are probably mortal as well.

If she is a critical thinker, Ms ET will wait to see whether persons Y, Z, and so on actually turn out to be mortal. After a few thousand confirming observations, the analogy will look strong: "Since all these life pods that seem to be alike in a variety of ways are mortal, probably all similar life pods are also mortal." And with that generalization in hand, she returns to her planet in the galaxy Andromeda to report her findings. Of course, were she a lazy thinker she might just analogize from a single example and not stick around to gather all that evidence.

As with abduction, one has to be careful with analogical reasoning. An analogy can sometimes be forceful enough to make us forget the second rule of induction and overlook evidence that might point to a different conclusion. Paley's analogy (**E21**) is like that: it's a very graphic image, and in its day it packed a persuasive punch. Yet, several decades after he made it, Charles Darwin marshalled extremely strong evidence for the conclusion that life on Earth was not designed by an intelligent being. But while Darwin's argument is now accepted by virtually the whole of the scientific community, many people are still struck by the elegance of Paley's analogy. Unfortunately, elegance is not necessarily evidence of truth.

Analogies are also risky because in most cases we resort to them for the same reason we resort to abduction: we lack sufficient evidence. In **E22**, the speaker may have seen enough Tarantino films to feel confident in predicting that the next one will be interesting, but it is a riskier thing to transfer, by analogy, this conclusion to the films of a director he has never seen. However, he may be trying to decide how to spend his hard-earned money, and lacking direct evidence about Rodriguez's films analogical thinking is about all he has to go on.

When there is no better way to proceed, analogical reasoning is not an unreasonable method of evaluating a situation, but it will not always produce a strong argument. Therefore, you have to choose your analogies carefully with an awareness of their limitations. For example:

> **E24:** *Andy is a Canadian and he's really boring to talk to. Devi is also Canadian, so I bet she's really boring to talk to as well.*

The speaker connects the fact that Andy is boring to talk to with the probably unrelated fact that he is a Canadian, and then transfers Andy's boring discourse to Devi (and by extension, to all Canadians). It is hard to say here whether a hasty generalization drives the analogy or the analogy drives the hasty generalization, but in either case this is a very weak argument.

So let's amend **E24** as follows:

> **E25:** *Andy is really boring to talk to. He is a middle-aged academic who teaches critical thinking, drives a station wagon, and goes to bed at eight every night. Devi is also a middle-aged academic who teaches critical thinking, drives a station wagon, and goes to bed early. I bet she's boring to talk to as well.*

E25 is much stronger than **E24** because the analogy is based on a variety of similarities between Andy and Devi; ones, moreover, that might actually be relevant. Still, to avoid a hasty generalization it would be preferable to have more than one boring person—Andy—with a certain set of properties before judging that all people with those properties are boring to talk to. That's why the conclusion of an analogical argument is, like an abductive argument, basically a working hypothesis. If Devi and a thousand others like Andy turn out to be equally boring to talk to we may have something, but in the meantime it is best to exercise caution in drawing a conclusion.

Even if there were a lot of points of similarity, a hint of hasty generalization remains. To avoid it, invoke the second rule of induction and look for falsifying evidence. Where analogical reasoning is concerned, this means looking for **disanalogies**—ways in which the things being compared differ. For example, Andy is male, Devi is female; despite being "middle-aged," Devi may be 10 years younger than Andy; she may come from a much different background, live in a different part of the city, have a side career as a stand-up comic (matinees only), skydive, and wrestle alligators in her spare time. These facts suggest that Devi is not as similar to Andy as it first appeared and the analogy begins to break down. In this context, note the disanalogy in Paley's argument in **E21**. A watch is a human artifact and one could argue by analogy that since it is designed so too are other human artifacts. But nature is not a human artifact, a fact that makes the analogy between a watch and nature very uncertain.

Finally beware of an informal fallacy of relevance called **false analogy**. It occurs when you employ an inappropriate or misleading analogy. For example:

> **E26:** *When he insulted my heritage I felt destroyed, like I had been assaulted with a hammer. He should be severely punished for inflicting so much harm.*

The analogy between being verbally insulted and being physically attacked with a hammer is scarcely appropriate. We do not expect an insult to be punished as severely as an assault with a hammer because the two acts are not really comparable.

False analogies often employ idioms (common sayings) inappropriately. For example:

> **E27:** *I don't see the problem with firing 30 per cent of our workforce. We need to restructure and you can't make an omelette without breaking some eggs.*

The omelette comment is a well-known idiom, but in this argument it is essentially irrelevant. Taken literally, the contention of **E27** is that if it is necessary to break eggs to make an omelette, then it is necessary to fire 30 per cent of the workforce to restructure the company. But there is no connection between the two actions. At best, an idiom like this has only a vague application to the situation under consideration: in this case, that it is not possible to restructure the company without some disruption to the employees. But it does not justify any specific action, such as firing 30 per cent of the workforce. The analogy is not part of an argument for doing so, but rather an attempt to avoid making the argument.

Like abductive reasoning, analogical reasoning can be a useful and imaginative way of thinking in situations where there is not yet enough evidence to generate a strong and cogent argument. To that extent, like abduction, analogical arguments produce something closer to a working hypothesis than a highly probable conclusion. This is so even when the analogy looks like an exact fit:

> **E28:** *Motorcyclists ride on public roads, on open two-wheeled vehicles, and they have to wear helmets. Surely bicyclists should have to wear them as well.*

Although I agree with this argument, it is incumbent on me to check the evidence and obey the second rule of induction by looking for disanalogies, such as the fact that bicycles are generally not moving as fast as motorcycles and are more quickly brought under control. While these disanalogies may not carry much weight, they need to be considered along with the relevant comparative statistics about injuries, fatalities, and so on. If we are sloppy about assessing good analogies we may also be sloppy about assessing bad ones. *Be critical*.

EXERCISE 7.3

I. Construct abductive arguments in support of the following conclusions.

   *1. A gerbil did this.

   2. Johan has just broken up with his girlfriend.

   *3. Aliens have abducted Johanna.

   4. I flunked.

   *5. Sarah hates me.

   6. There has just been a terrorist attack.

II. For each of the following, decide whether the reasoner has used abduction responsibly. Articulate your reasons.

   *1. I notice that James is lazy and I know that Canadians are lazy, so James is probably a Canadian.

   2. He's having an affair because he is always out at night.

   *3. Janine has not been herself recently. She's nervous and short-tempered. Something must be bothering her.

Continued >

4. I think he's an alcoholic because I went to his house the other night and he was all alone having a glass of wine.

*5. There have been a lot more bears encroaching on cottages this year. Something must have happened to reduce their normal food sources.

6. The plane has not been heard from in over two hours. Something's wrong.

III. *For each of the following, decide whether the analogy is appropriate or false. "Appropriate" means that the conclusion it implies is worth investigating further. Briefly defend your answer.*

*1. My dad's an old dog, just like my dog, Fido. I can't get Fido to learn anything new, so I doubt I can get my dad to learn anything new.

2. When he was convicted, Bill was given a much stiffer sentence than others who have committed the same offence and, like him, were first offenders. That's not fair.

*3. You shouldn't treat your cat like that. Like us, it's a sentient being, and we don't like to be treated cruelly.

4. Ants are living creatures just like humans. If it is wrong to kill humans it must be wrong to kill ants.

*5. Canada is a big country and so is Russia. Russians like hockey so probably Canadians do as well.

6. When I was in Mississippi I found that people tended to be church-goers. Like Mississippi, Georgia is a southern state, so I imagine Georgians tend to be church-goers too.

VII. Summary

This chapter has introduced you to the basics of *inductive reasoning*. Two principal kinds of induction are *generalizing* and *predictive* arguments. Unlike deduction, where the focus is on producing valid and sound arguments, induction is a method of reasoning about empirical issues, where the conclusion does not follow necessarily from the premises. In other words, induction is a method of reasoning where one gathers evidence in support of conclusions. If the evidence cited in the premises is sufficient and relevant, the result is a *strong* argument. If the premises are also true, the result is a *cogent* argument. To develop cogent arguments you have to obey the *three rules of induction*; violate them and the result will be a *weak* argument. Finally, when there is insufficient evidence but you need a *working hypothesis*, *abduction* and *analogical reasoning* can be creative methods that a critical (and careful) thinker can put to good use.

CHAPTER EIGHT

Induction: Some Applications

- A priori probability
- Relative frequency probability
- Subjective probability
- Causal arguments
- Causality and correlation
- Necessary and sufficient causes
- The methods of induction

This chapter builds on the previous one by introducing some more sophisticated induction tools. These include statistical arguments, causal arguments, and an introduction to the methods of induction, which are ways of developing, testing, and fine-tuning causal arguments.

I. Assessing Probability

This section will introduce some basic concepts of probability, which are used to assess the strength of certain kinds of inductive reasoning. We begin by examining a priori and relative frequency probability, then move on to the concept of subjective probability, and finally to assessments of personal value.

A Priori Probability

It may not surprise you to learn that the study of probability has its roots in gambling. After all, a wise gambler will want to know the odds (or "chances") of a favourable outcome occurring in a given situation. To do so, she will need a grasp of a priori probability.

> **Definition: A priori probability** *refers to situations where the chances of an event occurring are known in advance.*

The simplest example is mentioned in Section V of Chapter 3: the toss of a fair, or perfectly balanced, coin. If a fair coin is flipped you know a priori that it has a 50-50 chance of coming up either heads or tails. If two coins are flipped, the chance of both coming up tails is the chance of tails for the individual coins multiplied by one another. Since each individual toss is 50-50, that equals a 25 per cent probability: $\frac{1}{2} \times \frac{1}{2} = \frac{1}{4} = 25$ per cent.

Let's extend this example one small step. If you flip a coin twice, what are the chances of tails coming up at least once? The solution can be set out like a truth table, showing the four possible distributions of the tosses (Table 8.1).

Table 8.1	
TOSS 1	**TOSS 2**
H	H
H	T
T	H
T	T

A glance reveals that, of the four possible outcomes, only in the first row does tails not come up. So the chances of tails coming up at least once in two flips are three in four, or 75 per cent. The formula here (where Pr = probability and 1 and 2 refer to the tosses of the coin) is:

(Pr1 + Pr2) − (Pr1 × Pr2)

Since the chance of heads or tails in a single toss is 50 per cent (or ½), this yields:

$$(\tfrac{1}{2} + \tfrac{1}{2}) - (\tfrac{1}{2} \times \tfrac{1}{2}) = (1 - \tfrac{1}{4}) = \tfrac{3}{4}$$

This formula works for two options only; add a third and calculations become more complex. Now, if you throw a pair of dice, can you figure out what the chances are that one of the two numbers will be a six?[1]

Some a priori probabilities shed interesting light on the choices we make and on the critical—or not so critical—thinking that goes into them. Consider the lotteries, which millions of people regularly play. It's common knowledge that those who do so are on the short end of very long odds. For example, in Canada the chance of a ticket winning the Lotto 6/49 jackpot is about one in 13.9 million (some lotteries have odds that are only a tenth of that); there are that many possible combinations of six numbers in the range of 1 though 49. To get a sense of how imposing these odds are, suppose a 60-something Canadian male (such as the author of this text), buys a ticket the day before a draw. A statistician (his brother) will tell him that, based on mortality statistics, he has roughly a 2 per cent chance of dying in the next year—news he doesn't really appreciate getting, by the way. That means that he has one chance in 18,250 of dying in the next day ($365 \div 1/50$). These are not bad odds, but the fact remains that he is far more likely to die within the next 24 hours than he is to win the lottery. Even for a 20 year old, the odds are not all that much better.[2]

Relative Frequency Probability

In the preceding discussion, what is known a priori is the chance of a lottery ticket winning the top prize. What is not known a priori is the chance of a 60-something Canadian man surviving for another year. This is an instance of relative frequency probability.

> **Definition: Relative frequency** is an assessment of the probability of an event based on data that have been collected over a period of time.

In this case, the data will tell researchers how often 60-year-old men die before they reach 61. The figures cannot be set in stone, however, because survival rates for any group will change as life expectancy increases or decreases. (A century ago, the chances of a 60-year-old Canadian male dying in the next year were greater than the current 2 per cent.) The knowledge that relative frequency calculations yield is, therefore, a posteriori because we know what the chances of an event occurring are only after we have collected the data. In other words, relative frequency probabilities are open-ended, subject to change. A priori probabilities are, by contrast, closed, not subject to change—a coin has two sides, a die has six sides, and a lottery has a finite set of numbers, so in all these cases we can work out the probabilities of given outcomes in advance.

---

1 $(1/6 + 1/6) - (1/6 \times 1/6) = 11/36$

2 I am told that the best strategy for winning the big prize in a lottery, which offers roughly a one in 14 million chance of success, is to buy a ticket every week for about 3 million years. I'm sure critical thinkers will spot the flaw in this plan.

Despite their variability, relative frequency calculations can be used to make accurate and useful predictions about reference classes.

*Definition: A **reference class** is any group that is being statistically analyzed.*

Medical researchers can, for example, determine the likelihood that members of a given reference class—say, North American women of a certain age and background—will contract a particular disease. Based on that knowledge, preventative measures can be taken and, often, deaths avoided.[3]

Something to Think About

We began this section with a priori probability and the example of flipping a "fair" coin. It is important to think about the slipperiness of this term, because it forces us to confront the fact that "a priori probability" is essentially an oxymoron. Since induction is a process of reasoning from evidence to a conclusion that is probably true, the only way to decide inductively that a coin is "fair" is to toss it a lot of times. If the law of large numbers seems to apply—if the tosses eventually hover around 50-50 heads and tails—you will say that the coin is fair. But since even after a large number of tosses the coin will almost certainly not settle permanently on an exact 50-50 distribution, you cannot say with absolute certainty that it is fair—induction never allows you to say that. Moreover, even if a coin does settle on an exact 50-50 distribution, that does not change the fact that you only know a posteriori—after the coin has been tossed many times—that it is fair. This means that you still only know that it is very probably fair, which of course means that you do not know a priori that it is fair. But this means that all instances of a priori probability are actually cases of very stable relative frequency probability!

The point is that while the concept of a priori probability is a useful tool when it comes to deciding how likely the occurrence of certain events are, in using the concept we have to ignore the fact that all events occur in a world where absolute qualities such as "fairness" in a coin—a guaranteed 50-50 probability of heads or tails—exist only in theory. A coin is never "fair" in advance of the evidence, and after the evidence is in it is only probably fair. The really subtle point is that we seem to be using the term "fair" equivocally. From the perspective of a priori probability, it seems to refer to an intrinsic quality of the coin—one known in advance of the evidence—but from the perspective of relative frequency probability it refers only to the history of how a lot of coin tosses have come out.

Pascal's Wager

Sometimes, however, the chances of an event occurring cannot be worked out either a priori or a posteriori. This occurs when we do not, or cannot, have access to the

---

3 I shall modify this remark somewhat in Chapter 9, Section I, in the subsection "The Rule of the Opposite Hand and the End of Generalization."

relevant information. In the seventeenth century, the French philosopher and scientist Blaise Pascal (1623–1662) addressed this issue in one of the first and most famous of all probabilistic arguments, known as *Pascal's Wager*. Pascal was a child prodigy, a mathematical genius who, by age 16, was doing advanced scientific research. After surviving a horse and buggy accident, he turned his attention to religion. In a collection of remarks and essays entitled *Pensées,* he presented his famous wager about whether one should act as if God exists.

Despite his deep religious beliefs, Pascal begins by conceding that there is no conclusive empirical proof for the existence of God. Nevertheless, he argues, the question of God's existence or non-existence is an extremely important consideration in deciding how we will live our lives. We have to "wager" one way or the other: bet either that God exists or that he does not, and live accordingly. But what are the odds of the wager? Since they cannot be calculated, Pascal applies a version the principle of indifference and treats the chances of God's existence or non-existence as equal.

> *Definition: The* **principle of indifference** *as used here applies to situations where the chances of the possible outcomes are unknown or incalculable. It stipulates that each possibility is then given equal weight.[4]*

If there are n possibilities, assign odds of 1/n for each one. This does not, however, make the wager itself indifferent because it is necessary to consider its expected value.

> *Definition: The* **expected value** *of a wager refers to the balance of what can be won or lost in making it.*

In other words, it is necessary to consider the stakes of the bet—what can be won and what can be lost. Though the figures in it are mine, Table 8.2 reproduces Pascal's opening version of the outcomes of the wager.[5]

Table 8.2 Pascal's Wager

	CHOICE	TRUTH VALUE	OUTCOME	WIN/LOSS
1.	Believe	True	Eternal bliss	+1,000,000
2.	Believe	False	Loss of 70 years	−1
3.	Not believe	True	Gain of 70 years	+1
4.	Not believe	False	Eternal damnation	−1,000,000

---

4 The principle of indifference is commonly applied to a priori probabilities where, like the flip of a coin, each outcome has an equal probability. I am restricting its use, however, to situations where the odds are unknown.

5 I am indebted to Graham Priest's discussion in his book *Logic: A Very Short Introduction* (Oxford: Oxford University Press, 2000), Chapter 13.

Seventy years is an arbitrary figure representing an average lifespan. Pascal argues that when that period of time is measured against the possible rewards and punishments, it becomes obvious that a person who believes there is a God, and who lives accordingly, risks very little to gain a lot, because 70 years is almost nothing compared to eternity. (Actually, since eternity is outside time, there is no basis for comparison . . . but never mind.) Compare choices 1 and 2 and you will see that the believer's wager is like a lottery where he puts down a dollar to win a million at 50-50 odds. If he is right, the prize is eternal bliss; if he is wrong, all he has lost is a mere 70 years of worshiping a non-existent god. (One could argue that since, in this case, there is no afterlife he has lost everything, but we shall also let that slide.)

On the other hand, Pascal's reckoning shows that the non-believer has very little to gain and much to lose. A glance at choices 3 and 4 shows that it's like putting down a million dollars for a chance of winning an extra dollar, something no reasonable person would do. If the non-believer is right, she gets to do what she wants with her life instead of having to worship a non-existent god, but if she is wrong she faces eternal damnation. To repeat, Pascal's claim is that, compared to our short lives, eternal bliss and eternal damnation are very big deals with very high values attached to them. They should actually be infinite values, but to make calculation possible, eternal bliss has been arbitrarily assigned a value of 1,000,000 and damnation −1,000,000. To work out the expected value of each person's wager, subtract the potential loss from the potential gain. This produces the following results:

EV for the believer: 1,000,000 − 1 = 999,999
EV for the non-believer: 1 − 1,000,000 = −999,999

Based on this, it's not even close: a reasonable person will bet on the existence of God every time.

The concept of expected value can also be applied to lotteries. As we've already established, since there are approximately 13.9 million possible combinations of six numbers, to assure yourself of winning the big prize you would have to bet on each combination. You would, therefore, have to buy 13.9 million tickets. At two dollars a ticket that would cost you $27.8 million. Unfortunately, the most common payout is about $4 million. So to guarantee a win, the expected value of your "wager" would be $4 million − $27.8 million = −$23.8 million. That's a real sucker's bet. Add in all the lesser prizes, however, and the expected value rises because the lottery corporation actually pays out 45 cents on the dollar to ticket buyers. This means that the expected value of a $2 ticket is $0.90 − $2.00 = −$1.10. You are still in the hole, just not as far in the hole.

To return to Pascal's wager, everything depends on whether you accept his application of the principle of indifference. Some people argue that the theory of evolution and the theory of the big bang that governs the origins of the universe strongly suggest that the chances of there being a god are vanishingly small—so small, in fact, that we can be *morally certain* there is no god. **Moral certainty**[6] means that, according to one's calculations, the chance of a particular outcome is so high that it is rational to act on it. Unfortunately, there is an element of subjectivity in such calculations, and someone with deep religious beliefs may argue that, based on evidence, he is morally certain there is a God. In either case, someone who decides that one or the other outcome is a moral certainty will reject the principle of indifference, and this will greatly alter the expected value of her wager.

Pascal understands that a non-believer in particular might reject his use of the principle of indifference. That's why he emphasizes the expected value of the wager. His point is that even for someone who thinks the probability of there being a God is very low, an eternity in hell is a lot to risk. Better, therefore, to follow the ways of the church. Well and good, but what about people who believe there is a God but do not believe in hell and damnation? For them, the negative value attached to unbelief disappears and ironically, despite their belief, the expected value of the wager tilts toward non-belief.

Subjective Probability

Pascal's Wager shows us that there is often a subjective aspect to our choices. It is not always simply a matter of calculating odds, but also of working out what one hopes to gain (or fears losing) and how great that hope or fear is. What the bettor *objectively* knows has to be weighed against these *subjective* considerations. For someone who believes in the existence of God or who wishes for salvation Pascal's argument may be very persuasive. For one who does not, it will likely be much less so. This brings us to a third type of probability known as subjective probability.

> *Definition: Subjective probability refers to an individual's personal, non-statistical evaluation of the chances of an event occurring.*

In the case of believing or not believing in God, the odds a person assigns to either possibility may depend in part on how much he wants the claim "God exists" to be true. Subjective considerations may induce him to ignore the principle of indifference, in which case a critical thinker will simply warn him that he may be allowing what he wants to be true to override what he can actually know.

While this temptation may be understandable (if not advisable) in situations where the principle of indifference applies, subjective considerations should never intrude on cases of a priori or relative frequency probability. For example:

> **E1:** *Someone has to win the lottery. I think I have a good chance; I feel lucky.*

---

6 This is not a term statisticians use, but for our purposes it's a useful concept.

Feelings aside, this person's chance of winning are objectively the same as anyone else's, but her desire has imposed a higher (and incorrect) subjective probability on the wager.

There are, however, situations where subjective considerations are unavoidable. For example:

> **E2:** *I think there's a good chance that there will be a surprise quiz tomorrow because the professor usually only does a summary of a lecture when she's going to give one, and she gave a summary today.*

Once again we have an imprecise phrase, "a good chance," but in this case it makes sense. Based on past experience, the speaker clearly feels that there is a better than 50-50 chance that there will be a quiz, even though he has no precise idea what the actual figure is. So **E2** is something like a subjective estimate of relative frequency probability in a situation where precise odds cannot be calculated but where experience suggests going beyond the principle of indifference.

This is an important point: sometimes people have to estimate probability without being able to put an exact figure on it. I once sat on a jury where the judge informed us that to convict we had to be "morally certain" the accused was guilty. She then defined this as being 99.9 per cent certain. This was useful advice insofar as the judge was pointing out the very high standard a finding of guilt had to meet, but how could any of us sitting on the jury ever really put an accurate number on our certainty? What the 99.9 per cent figure represented was a sense that, given the evidence, no reasonable person could believe the accused was innocent. Each jury member had to anchor his or her judgment in his or her experience of the world to arrive at a "reasonable" assessment of what a "reasonable person" would believe. But since everyone's experience is limited, whether one was morally certain that the accused was guilty inevitably had a subjective element.

Precisely this problem arose in the famous 1994 trial of the football star O.J. Simpson. The question was whether the Los Angeles police had planted evidence (a bloody glove) at his home to make him look guilty. Given that the Los Angeles police department had a history of troubled relations with the black community, it is not surprising that black Americans thought this a more probable occurrence than did white Americans. In both cases, estimates of what it was reasonable to believe were governed in part by a subjective sense of how trustworthy the police were.

There is one more way in which subjectivity may be factored into one's choices. Even when outcomes are matters of a priori or relative frequency calculations of probability, it remains important to consider their personal value:

> **Definition: Personal value** *is a measurement of the value of a bet (or choice) in relation to both a person's objectively measurable resources and subjective preferences.*

A lottery ticket is inexpensive, and most people can afford one. Therefore, the personal value of the bet—a shot at the big prize compared to a $2 loss plus an opportunity to dream about what you would do with all that money—is probably sufficient to justify the expenditure. However, someone who spends hundreds of dollars a week on the lottery had better be reasonably well off because, if not, she is making a fool's bet with money she can ill afford to lose. As the number of tickets purchased increases, the personal value—the reward to risk ratio—decreases. The dreams don't get bigger, but the losses do.

Personal value enters into many day-to-day choices. Imagine someone reporting the following:

> **E3:** *Man, I lined up for six hours to buy the latest iPad. Long time, but I just had to have one.*

The speaker has invested a lot of time to have what he wants now rather than wait, say, six months when there will be no line-up. Unless he really needs a new iPad, then insofar as it can be calculated the expected value of the purchase is not very high, because he has wasted a lot of time. But the expected value of the decision may be outweighed by considerations of personal value. (The phrase "I just had to have one" almost certainly expresses "want" rather than "need"—subjectivity rather than objectivity.) However, if he has skipped work to stand in line and is subsequently fired from a job he needs, it would be hard to argue that the personal value of the choice was anything but low.

The Puzzle of the Three Doors

The concept of personal value tells us that even when odds are known a priori, subjective elements other than assessments of subjective probability may influence one's decision, and in some cases properly so. Here's an interesting puzzle that illustrates this idea:

> **E4:** *You are on a game show, where you are confronted with three doors. The host tells you that behind one of the doors there is a million dollars, whereas behind the others there is nothing. You choose Door 1, but before the host opens it, she tells you that she is going to show you an empty door. She opens Door 3 and sure enough, it is empty. She then tells you that you have a choice: you can stick with Door 1 or switch to Door 2. What do you do?*

Most people elect to stay with the door they originally chose, figuring that there is no advantage in switching. But in fact you are much better off to switch doors. To see why, consult Table 8.3, which sets out the three possible distributions of the money.

	DOOR 1		
DISTRIBUTION	(YOUR CHOICE)	DOOR 2	DOOR 3
1	$	—	—
2	—	$	—
3	—	—	$

Table 8.3 The Three Doors

A priori probability dictates that you had one chance in three of choosing the correct door. You chose Door 1, and in Distribution 1 that's where the money is. So, in that case, the host had a choice—she could have shown you either Door 2 or Door 3 because both are empty. But in Distributions 2 and 3 you chose an empty door. In those cases, the host had no choice. Because you had taken one of the empty doors (1) out of circulation, there was only one empty door left for her to show you. In Distribution 2 it is Door 3, and in Distribution 3 it is Door 2. What this means is that, two times out of three, the host shows you the door she does because she has no choice—the money is behind the other "unchosen" door. Put differently, two times out of three you have chosen the wrong door and will win if you switch doors. So you are twice as well off to accept the host's offer to switch doors. Objectively, your chances of winning go from the original one in three to two in three: they double.

Unfortunately, there are subjective considerations. Is changing worth the psychological risk? If you move away from the correct door, will the pain of losing be much greater than the joy of winning? Will you be kicking yourself for as long as you live? If so, perhaps the personal value of staying where you are and accepting the one in three odds outweighs the expected value of changing and risking total heartbreak if you have moved off the winning door. Even more unfortunately, once you understand the odds, recognizing that they double if you change doors, you will also kick yourself forever if you lose because you did not switch. Sometimes ignorance really is bliss and knowledge is painful. At any rate, in this case, even when you understand the probabilities, it is hard to say what the "rational" choice is because it is bound up with relevant subjective considerations.

The Prisoners' Dilemma

Another perhaps more important way in which non-statistical factors are relevant to our decisions arises when moral considerations are involved. To illustrate, let's consider a famous conundrum called the *Prisoners' Dilemma.*[7] Two people suspected of a crime are arrested. Neither person knows who the other is. They are taken to separate rooms where each is told the following, and is also informed that the other is being told it as well:

E5: *You can confess or not confess. If one of you confesses and the other does not, the confessor will go free and the non-confessor will get four years. If neither of you confesses you will each get a year anyway, because we have "evidence." If you both confess, you will each get three years.*

What should the prisoners do? (Ignore the question of whether they are guilty or innocent. Assume they have amnesia and don't know and, moreover, that neither is keen on going to jail.) The possible outcomes are shown in Table 8.4.

Table 8.4 The Prisoners' Options				
	PRISONER A	PRISONER B	A'S PENALTY	B'S PENALTY
1	Confess	Not confess	0 years	4 years
2	Not confess	Confess	4 years	0 years
3	Confess	Confess	3 years	3 years
4	Not confess	Not confess	1 year	1 year

Without bringing any other considerations into play, confessing is statistically the better option. Since a confessor (prisoner A in Rows 1 and 3 and prisoner B in rows 2 and 3) either goes free or gets three years in jail, his total exposure to risk is three years. By comparison, the non-confessor (prisoner A in rows 2 and 4 and prisoner B in rows 1 and 4) balances one year against four years for a total exposure to risk of five years. Over the decades I have done this exercise in class, matching students up randomly, the confessors have always come out ahead, spending on average less time in jail (in roughly the ratio of 3:5) than the non-confessors. So, if staying out of jail is the goal, confessing is the better—objectively, the more rational—option, because it has a higher expected value.

However, if both prisoners reason this way, they will end up serving three years each. Therefore, why not co-operate, refuse to confess, and accept a year each? As a pair with a mutual interest in staying out of jail, that is surely the more rational option. If they were together in a room and could discuss the matter, they would almost

---

7 The concept of the Prisoners' Dilemma was originally developed by the economist John Nash (portrayed by Russell Crowe in the movie *A Beautiful Mind*).

certainly choose it. Moreover, since this choice shows concern for the welfare of the other person, and since it involves co-operating rather than competing, it is arguably the morally superior option as well. Perhaps a moral person alone in his cell, unable to confer with the other prisoner, should choose it. Still, if he does he is, on average, going to end up doing more time than if he confesses.

The dilemma is that each prisoner has to decide whether he should try to co-operate with a stranger without knowing whether the stranger will co-operate with him. What assumptions should he make, not only about the rationality of the other prisoner but also about his moral duty to treat a stranger as an important person in her own right? Someone who has trust in human rationality or who thinks he has a duty to the other prisoner may, somewhat subjectively, be drawn toward the "non-confess" option, whereas someone who is an exponent of "rational self-interest" will probably confess, opting for the objectively higher expected value.

And even if the caring non-confessor ignores the odds and ends up going to prison for four years, he may feel that fulfilling what he views as a moral obligation gives his choice not to confess a higher personal value than the choice to confess. (The issue of your moral connection to the unknown person in the other room is interesting because it can be expanded to include your sense of moral obligation to unknown people on the other side of the world. For example, as a consumer of the planet's resources, is it more morally correct to pursue your immediate self-interest or to take those strangers into account in your choices, even though they may well not take yours into account?)

While statistics can allow you to compare the prisoner's choices as jail-avoiding strategies, they can't tell you how to evaluate the morality, or in the end even the rationality, of the choices. Nor can they tell you how to evaluate the other person's thought processes. This is, therefore, a case where subjective *but not irrational* considerations are relevant. Mere numbers cannot tell you what the better (the more moral or even the more rational) choice really is.

A Brief Summary

This section has introduced three kinds of probability:

1. *A priori probability* refers to cases where the chances of an event occurring are known in advance, as in the toss of a fair coin. These chances are *objective*.

2. *Relative frequency probability* refers to cases where the probability assigned to the occurrence of an event comes from knowledge about the *reference class* to which the events in question pertain. Here, the odds cannot be fixed in advance of examining the data. They are, therefore, known a posteriori and can vary over time, but within those limits they too are *objective*.

3. *Subjective probability* refers to cases where the odds assigned to an event depend at least in part on personal, and necessarily imprecise, judgments about what is likely

to happen or even what you want to happen. This can skew a person's judgment away from objectively rational choices, but not always.

Sometimes even when you know what the odds are, and therefore what the *expected value* of a choice is, *subjective considerations* may enter into the calculation as an assessment of *personal value.* The whole spectrum of human emotions—desire, fear, desperation, hope, love of risk, aversion to risk, psychological and moral considerations—can and will insert themselves into our reasoning. Finally, the *principle of indifference* applies to situations where the odds cannot be calculated. Every possibility is assigned an equal probability.

Something to Think About

Back to the toss of a fair coin: use your knowledge of truth tables to work out what the chances are that a fair coin flipped 10 times will come up heads at least once. The answer is in the Answer Key at the end of the book.

EXERCISE 8.1

Exercises marked by an asterisk (*) have answers included in the Answer Key at the end of the text.

I. For each of the following, decide which of the three types of probability—a priori, relative frequency, or subjective—apply.

*1. Based on what we know about the weather patterns in this part of the country, I think it is very likely that a storm is coming.

2. Records show that, in this part of the country, 90 per cent of the time a warmer-than-average spring follows a colder-than-average winter. Since this winter has been colder than average, there is a 90 per cent chance that the spring will be warmer than average.

*3. Don't speak to her like that; if you do, almost certainly all hell will break loose.

4. Almost every time I actually study for a test I pass it. I studied for this one, so I'd estimate there's a 95 per cent chance I passed it.

*5. The chance of being dealt a royal flush—10 through ace of the same suit—in poker.

6. The chance of being selected for jury duty in a given jurisdiction.

*7. We know that 76 per cent of respondents from small towns—no matter their socioeconomic status—favoured ending the gun registry. Since Sam is from a small town, there's a good chance he's opposed to the gun registry.

8. As Canadians always say, hosers like beer, and boy is he a hoser, so offer him a beer.

Continued >

*9. People respond better to politeness than to rudeness.

10. If someone flips a fair coin five times there is a really good chance it will come up heads at least twice.

*11. The chance of drawing a red or black card from a deck of cards.

12. The likelihood that someone you know may be lying to you in a given situation.

*13. The chance of being struck by lightning.

14. The chance that a fair coin that has come up tails 19 times in a row will come up heads the twentieth time.

II. *What considerations might affect the expected value of the following choices?*

*1. Whether to go into debt to get an education.

2. Whether to put off a holiday to help a friend move.

*3. Whether to work overtime for no extra pay.

4. Whether to get the "luxury package" on your new car.

*5. Whether to go on a holiday or continue to work.

III. *How might the expected value of the following be modified by considerations of personal value?*

*1. Buying a ticket in a charity raffle.

2. Betting thousands of dollars on the flip of a coin.

*3. Cheating on an exam in a situation where you are very unlikely to be caught.

4. Lending money to good friend who probably cannot pay you back.

IV. *The following is an exercise in a priori probability.*

*1. There are 10 balls in a box. Each has a different number on it between 1 and 10. You are asked to pick a number between 1 and 10, then two numbers are drawn from the box. What are the chances that one of the numbers will be the one you picked?

II. Causal Arguments

This section deals with *causal arguments*. We begin by examining the difference between *causality* and *correlation* and then move on to the distinction between *necessary* and *sufficient* causes.

How Causal Arguments Work

Many inductive arguments are causal:

> **Definition:** A **causal argument** is an attempt to work out why something (an effect) happened by assigning a **cause** or causes to it.

As this definition suggests, causal arguments often work backwards, beginning with an effect and attempting to demonstrate why it occurred. For example, consider the following assertion:

> **E6:** *A recent study of colds has shown that lack of sleep makes people more susceptible to them.*

Stated formally as a hypothetical sentence, **E6** reads:

> **HS:** *If (cause) you are sleep deprived, then (effect) you are more susceptible to colds.*

The study would, of course, cite evidence to demonstrate that this is so. In this formulation, the cause precedes the effect because, temporally speaking, causes always do. However, so far as research into causes of colds is concerned, the effect preceded the cause. Researchers began not by observing sleepless people, but rather by observing people with colds and trying to work out what sorts of things cause them. This sense of working back from an effect to a cause is a hallmark of a causal argument. Of course, once a cause has been assigned to an effect the argument will look predictive. A doctor who accepts the findings of the study cited in **E6** will tell her patients that sleep deprivation will make them susceptible to colds. But this is still a causal argument, not a predictive one.

Consider the following:

> **E7:** *(P) Jagat has always done well in job interviews, (C) so I think he will do well if he is interviewed for that job he wants.*

This argument is predictive. No causal relationship exists between the premise and the conclusion. **E7** simply proceeds from the fact that Jagat has always done well in job interviews to the prediction that he will do well in future job interviews. It could, however, be turned into a generalized causal argument as follows:

> **E8:** *Research shows that having done well in interviews in the past is a cause of doing well in future ones.*

Here, researchers have begun with an effect—doing well in interviews—and have assigned a cause to it: prior success in interviews.

Causality and Correlation

One difficulty with causal arguments is that causes and effects are not always obvious. Researchers are often confronted with correlations:

> **Definition:** *Events are **correlated** if they regularly appear either simultaneously or sequentially.*

When two events appear simultaneously the relation between them is not causal. Barring coincidence, they will both be effects of the same cause: for instance, heat and smoke are correlated effects of fire. When two events appear sequentially, the relation between them may or may not be causal.

Deciding that correlated events have a causal relationship calls for a great deal of caution. It may be difficult to determine whether two correlated events are sequential, and if they are in which order they appeared. For example, political scientists may notice a correlation between nationalist movements and political instability in the regions in which these movements occur, but it may not be clear which, if either, of these conditions came first. Researchers who are studying nationalism may argue that political instability causes nationalism, while ones who are studying political instability may argue that nationalism causes political instability. One or the other (or both—the former in some cases, the latter in others) may be true, or it may be that nationalism and instability are correlated effects of some other cause or set of causes, such as poverty, recent conquest, or linguistic, ethnic, and religious differences. Figure 8.1 shows a diagram of these possibilities.

Figure 8.1
Correlation and
Causation

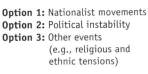

Option 1: Nationalist movements
Option 2: Political instability
Option 3: Other events
  (e.g., religious and
  ethnic tensions)

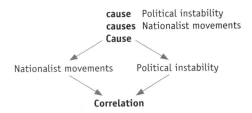

cause Political instability
causes Nationalist movements

Even when the sequence of two correlated events is clear you have to make certain that the prior one really is the cause of the latter one. It is important to avoid the informal fallacy of **post hoc ergo propter hoc**, a Latin phrase meaning "after this, therefore because of this." This fallacy of presumption consists in assuming, without the support of evidence, that because event A occurred before event B, A must be the cause of B. For example:

> **E9:** *Politician: Inflation has declined by 50 per cent since my party took office, so how can you say that our economic policies haven't been effective?*

The politician may be correct, but one would need to see evidence that she is. The fact that inflation fell after her party took office is not automatically proof that her party's policies are the cause of it or even *a* cause of it.

In **E9**, it is at least possible that the politician's policies caused the drop in inflation, but sometimes the post hoc fallacy amounts to a virtual non sequitur because there seems to be no connection between the alleged cause and effect. For example:

> **E10:** *The reason for all the natural disasters lately is the legalization of same-sex marriage.*

Most people with an understanding of inductive arguments (and the third rule of induction) will agree that there is no evidence of a causal relation between these events; it's a connection that cannot be demonstrated. But consider this case:

> **E11:** *I feel so guilty! You know how I really dislike my home room teacher? Well he gave me a detention yesterday and I said to myself, "I wish he'd just drop dead." And this morning he did. But I didn't really mean it!*

While this is not a non sequitur, experience strongly suggests that it is highly improbable that a causal relation exists between these events. The intensity of the student's dislike for the teacher and the immediacy with which the teacher's death followed the expression of that dislike has made him feel that he caused the death, but the two events are almost certainly coincidental.

As **E10** and **E11** demonstrate, the post hoc fallacy is a species of false cause argument in which there is no demonstrable causal relation between two events, no matter how spatially or temporally proximate they may be. However, as **E10** and **E11** also demonstrate, these are often matters of judgment that have to be made against the background of one's experience and knowledge. For example, a student might say:

> **E12:** *Of course I failed; my teacher hates women.*

While this could be true, experience suggests that it is rarely the cause of failure. The student's reasoning sounds suspiciously like a self-serving attempt to excuse her poor performance in a course. Bear in mind, however, that since we are invoking the third rule of induction by measuring the student's argument against what experience suggests is probable, it would help if that experience included some knowledge of the teacher in question. The difference between **E10** and **E11** on the one hand and **E12** on the other is that in **E10** and **E11** the alleged causes are actual events. They are, however, ones that seem to have no bearing on the effect. By contrast, in **E12** there is no assurance that the *alleged* cause—the teacher's hatred of women—even exists. But if it can be demonstrated that it does exist it needs to be considered carefully as a possible cause of the student's failure.

Necessary and Sufficient Causes

When a cause has been isolated, the next step is to determine what kind of cause it is. First let's consider necessary causes:

> **Definition:** *A **necessary cause** is one that must be present for a given effect to occur but that on its own is not sufficient to guarantee its occurrence.*

For example, consider the following:

> **E13:** *(Effect: **E**) For national currencies to collapse so suddenly, (Cause: **C1**) banks have to have been irresponsible in their lending practices and (Cause: **C2**) unemployment has to have been above 10 per cent for at least a year.*

In this example, **C1** and **C2** are put forward as causes of **E**. Each is pretty clearly being proposed as a necessary cause of **E** because the strong implication is that while each has to exist for **E** to exist, neither one is a sufficient cause of **E** on its own.

> *Definition: A **sufficient cause** is any cause or set of causes that will guarantee the appearance of an effect.*

In **E13**, the sufficient cause of **E** is the combination of **C1** and **C2**—only when they appear together will **E** occur. So a necessary cause is essentially *negative*: take it away and you will not get the effect. If either of **C1** or **C2** is absent, so is **E**. A sufficient cause is essentially *positive*: its presence guarantees the effect. Together **C1** and **C2** guarantee **E**. It is important to understand, however, that a sufficient cause may not be a necessary one. Watering a lawn is a sufficient cause of it getting wet but so too is a rainy day. Consequently, neither is a necessary cause of wet lawns.

Sometimes, however, a single cause may be both necessary and sufficient. For example:

> **E14:** *My experience has shown that the only thing that (**C**) makes her angry is (**E**) other people's tardiness.*

Here, "other people's tardiness" is presented as a necessary and a sufficient cause of the woman's anger; that and *only* that will make her angry. In summary, with respect to individual causes, there are three possibilities, which are summarized in Table 8.5.

Table 8.5 Necessary and Sufficient Causes	
CAUSE	EXAMPLE
Necessary but not sufficient	It is necessary to write an exam to pass it.
Sufficient but not necessary	Going for a run is a sufficient cause of getting sweaty, but there are other ways to do so.
Necessary and sufficient	Answering all questions correctly to get 100 per cent on a multiple-choice test.

Can there be causes that are neither necessary nor sufficient? Yes, there can. Consider this example:

> **E15:** *If you get regular exercise, eight hours of sleep per night, and follow the prescribed diet you will feel better. However, if you are not in a position to follow the prescribed diet take this medication instead.*

It would seem that regular exercise, eight hours of sleep, and a prescribed diet are, collectively, a sufficient cause of feeling better. But so are exercise, eight hours of sleep, and taking the medication. That means that exercise and sleep are, individually, *necessary* causes of feeling better, but the prescribed diet and the medication are not because either one can take the place of the other. One of these two causes must be present to get the desired effect, but neither is either necessary or sufficient.

A Note on Terminology

In the previous subsection the term "cause" has been used exclusively, even though "condition" may sometimes seem to be the more natural reading. The problem is that "condition" can bear a couple of meanings. On the one hand, it can be a cause that has not yet been actualized, such as the conditions for passing a course set out at the beginning of a term. In such cases, a condition is something that precedes an effect and can be substituted for "cause" without much confusion. On the other hand, unlike "cause," "condition" can refer to an event that does not precede an effect but occurs simultaneously with it. For example:

> **E16:** *A basketball game begins with a jump ball.*

We can reasonably describe the jump ball as a necessary and sufficient condition for starting a basketball game but, strictly speaking, they are one and the same event. If we want to describe the one as a condition of the other, then the condition and the effect occur simultaneously. Similarly, we can say that being human is a sufficient condition for being a mammal, but "being human" isn't prior to "being a mammal." To avoid this confusion, only the term "cause" has been employed here. We are, after all, considering causal arguments.

EXERCISE 8.2

I. Decide whether each of the connections in the following arguments (or claims) are causal, have a correlative connection, or neither. With respect to the "neither" option, look for instances of the post hoc fallacy and ones where the argument relies on mere coincidence.

*1. Mengyuan: Look, there's Bonnie.

   Jonas: Anita will be right behind her. She always appears right after Bonnie does.

2. Our research shows that two teaspoons of Miracle-Cure every morning will significantly reduce susceptibility to colds.

*3. Never lie. I told a lie the other day and after that I broke my leg.

4. The increased carbon footprint of the Western world has contributed to global warming.

Continued >

*5. The easy availability of divorce since the 1970s has caused the decline in moral standards that began in the 1980s.

6. Global warming has led to the melting of the polar ice caps.

*7. He's illiterate because he's poor.

8. I wore my blue sweat socks again yesterday and, sure enough, we won again. That's three times in a row.

*9. Of course I acted like that; I'm a Leo.

10. Abraham Lincoln and Charles Darwin were born on exactly the same day; I think that's because they were destined for greatness.

*11. My fever has given me a headache.

12. The dinosaurs became extinct probably because of a huge asteroid striking Earth, perhaps somewhere in what is now Mexico.

II. *In the following, identify causes as necessary (N), sufficient (S), or necessary and sufficient (NS). There is room for debate in some cases.*

*1. **C**: practising playing violin diligently; **E**: being very good at playing the violin

2. **C**: drinking alcohol; **E**: getting drunk

*3. **C**: understanding the material; **E**: passing the test

4. **C**: lack of exercise; **E**: lack of physical fitness

*5. **C**: being attracted to someone; **E**: loving him or her

6. **C**: arthritis; **E**: joint pain

*7. **C**: an obsessive-compulsive disorder; **E**: obsessive-compulsive behaviour

8. **C**: the desire to run a marathon; **E**: running a marathon

*9. **C**: Hitler's aggression toward neighbouring countries; **E**: World War II

10. **C**: being mortal; **E**: eventual death

III. Methods of Induction

To posit a causal connection between events is to impose order on the world. However, you have to take care not to impose a false order, as in the post hoc fallacy. In the nineteenth century, the English philosopher John Stuart Mill (1806–73) enumerated some ways of avoiding this mistake, that is, of ensuring that research is properly conducted and saves the phenomena. They are called the methods of induction.

*Definition: The **methods of induction** are methods for developing cogent causal arguments.*

Method 1: Agreement and Difference

These are really two methods, but they are often found in combination because they are the basic methods of most empirical research. Let's take each one in turn.

*Definition: The **method of agreement** is the process of looking for common factors that always precede a particular effect.*

Suppose I suffer from migraines and want to know what triggers them. I keep a diary in which I list as many factors as I can observe: what I ate and drank on a given day, how much sleep I had, how much exercise, what the weather was like, and so on. I then examine the days immediately preceding a migraine (which we shall call effect E). For simplicity's sake, we will restrict this to three migraines, although in reality that is far too small a sample. On day one (i.e., the day before my first migraine), I discover that (a) I ate red meat, (b) I had a beer, (c) I got very little sleep, (d) I exercised, and (e) the barometric pressure changed rapidly. Designating each of these by its parenthetical letter, we get, for day one:

(a, b, c, d, e) → E

Suppose that the other days throw up more possible causes, f and g, such that the chart for the three days looks like Table 8.6. The table reveals that a and e—"ate red meat" and "rapid barometric change"—are the only two factors common to all three days. A reasonable preliminary inference is that they are, individually, *necessary causes* of my migraines and together the *sufficient cause* for them.

Table 8.6 The Method of Agreement: Possible Causes of Getting a Migraine	
Day 1	(**a**.b.c.d.**e**) → E
Day 2	(**a**.c.d.**e**.f) → E
Day 3	(**a**.b.**e**.f.g) → E

However, even if this pattern holds for several more pre-migraine days, the evidence is not yet strong enough to warrant this conclusion. Perhaps a or e alone is the necessary and sufficient cause, while the presence of the other is merely coincidental. To test this possibility, I turn to the method of difference:

*Definition: The **method of difference** is the process of attempting to break the connection between an alleged cause and effect.*

First, I look to see if I ever ate red meat on a day when the barometer was stable; second, I abstain from eating red meat when the barometer is changing rapidly. With **a** representing "ate red meat" and **e** representing "rapid barometric change," my findings may look like Table 8.7. What this shows is that when either a or e is absent, so is effect E (the migraine). E occurs only on Days 1, 2, and 3, when both a and e are present. There are now much better grounds for the claim that, individually, a and e are necessary causes of E and, collectively, a sufficient cause of it.

Table 8.7 The Method of Difference: An Expanded Correlation Chart for Migraines	
Days 1, 2, 3	(a, e) → E
Days 4, 5, 6	(a, ~e) → ~E
Days 7, 8, 9	(~a, e) → ~E

But remember, a sufficient cause may be a single cause only. In Table 8.7, if only a showed up before every migraine, this would be grounds for concluding that it was the necessary and sufficient cause of E. If, on the other hand, on some occasions a preceded E while on others e did, then the most probable conclusion would be that a and e were both sufficient but not necessary causes of E.

Taken as a pair, the methods of agreement and difference constitute the principal thrust of causal arguments. "Agreement" is the process of establishing a probable cause for an effect, while "difference" is the process of testing that probable cause by looking to see whether there are circumstances under which the relation between it and the effect can be broken. The method of difference can also determine whether a cause is necessary or sufficient or both.

Method 2: Concomitant Variations

*Definition: The **method of concomitant variations** is the process of quantifying a relation between cause and effect by investigating the way in which variations in an effect are related to variations in a cause.*

While "agreement" and "difference" are the fundamental methods of induction, whereby researchers establish a possible cause and then test it by trying (in the spirit of the second rule of induction) to break the connection between it and the effect, something more is often needed. Sometimes causes have to be *quantified*, registered on some kind of scale.

Going back to my migraine example, imagine there were days when the barometer changed rapidly (e) but I did not get a migraine. Instead of discarding barometric change as a cause, I might take a closer look at it and discover that, while the barometer changed rapidly on those days, it did not change *as much* or *as quickly* as it did on the days when I got a migraine. By comparing different days, I might manage to quantify the barometric cause (e), working out *how much* the barometer had to change and *how quickly* that change had to take place for it to cause a migraine.

In the previous paragraph, only the cause of the migraines was quantified, but often both cause and effect are. I might, for example, have discovered that the faster the barometer changed the more painful or longer-lasting my migraine was. In other words, *variations in the cause may lead to variations in the effect.* These variations can be direct or inverse. For example, compare the following two statements:

> **E17:** *The more I talk the more agitated she gets.*
> **E18:** *The less I say the happier she is.*

E17 is an example of direct variation:

> *Definition: **Direct variation** occurs when cause and effect vary in the same direction.*

E18 is an example of inverse variation:

> *Definition: **Inverse variation** occurs when cause and effect vary in opposite directions.*

Many causal relations have to be quantified. For example, we know that in general smoking increases the risk of lung cancer, but researchers investigate how this risk is affected by the number of cigarettes a person smokes and the length of time he has smoked. Roughly, the more one smokes the greater the risk, so the variation is direct.

Concomitant variations may also reveal both kinds of variation in the same relationship. For example:

> **E19:** *When I drink one cup of coffee in the morning I concentrate better than if I don't have any, and with two cups I concentrate even better, but if I drink three cups my concentration level starts to go down again.*

In this case, there is a direct variation of cause and effect for the first two cups of coffee: more coffee, better concentration. But by the third cup, inverse variation takes over: more coffee, worse concentration. So far as the speaker's concentration goes, two cups would seem to be optimal.

Method 3: Residues

> *Definition: The **method of residues** is the process of searching for residual, or undiscovered, causes for an effect.*

A residue is what is left over. If researchers have accounted for all possible causes and have still not accounted for—or not *fully* accounted for—the effect, then they have to resort to this method. In the 1840s, astronomers noted that Uranus had unexplained deviations in its orbit. Since the cause of these deviations had to be gravitational pull, and since neither the gravitational force of the sun nor of the other known planets could, based on the law of gravity, fully account for them, astronomers concluded that there had to be another body large enough and near enough to exert an extra gravitational pull on Uranus. As a result, they were led to look for another planet to explain Uranus's erratic behaviour. In other words, they were forced to look for a residual cause, which turned out to be Neptune.

Now consider this example. Suppose that, in an effort to lose weight, you go on a diet. Your doctor tells you the following:

E20: *Given your age, weight and metabolic rate, you should lose six kilograms in three months.*

Ninety days later you have lost nine kilograms. You assure your doctor that you have followed the diet to the letter and he responds by asking whether you have started exercising—which indeed you have. The likelihood is that the loss of the other three kilos was due to exercise.

Two Views of Causes and Effects

If you compare **E20** with the migraine example set out in the discussion of the methods of agreement and difference, you may notice that they contain different views of how causes and effects are related.

View 1: There may be more than one cause for an effect.

This is in keeping with the migraine example, where eating red meat and barometric change were the twin causes of the headaches. It grows out of the fact that the method of agreement may turn up multiple causes. But there is also another view:

View 2: Every cause has just one effect.

This is in keeping with **E20**, where diet is responsible for the loss of six kilos and exercise for the loss of three kilos. (These, by the way, are sufficient but not necessary causes because there are other ways to lose weight, such as illness and stress.) View 2 demonstrates the method of residues, because it entails apportioning relative values to distinct effects. In the Neptune example, Neptune is not the cause of all of Uranus's behaviour, only of certain deviations in its orbit. Depending on the situation, one view or the other may seem more appropriate.

EXERCISE 8.3

For each of the following, indicate (a) the effect to be explained, (b) the suggested causes, (c) the method or methods of induction that were used, and (d) the outcome (confirmation or falsification). Note that while the methods of agreement and difference may occur separately in these examples, they may also be present together.

*1. If rats were the cause of the plague then it would not exist where there are no rats. But research shows that it does, so they must be at least a necessary cause of it.

2. Let's think about this carefully. Every time I get angry it's when she's talking to me, so I guess she just makes me angry. But there's a problem: the relation is not biconditional. I don't get angry every time she talks to me. If she just says a few words I'm fine, but if she goes on for more than a minute, off I go.

*3. You say that raising corporate tax rates discourages technological innovation. But if that is so, then this country would have seen few instances of such innovation in the five years since the government raised corporate tax rates. But in fact technological innovation has continued at the same pace as in the five years before the tax increase.

4. The medicine wasn't working until we increased the dosage, and then he started to respond. However, when the dosage got too high, his condition worsened again.

*5. When we changed the patient's diet her pain lessened but did not go away entirely. So we looked for a virus and sure enough she had one. When we treated it, the pain went away entirely.

6. Oh sure, he loves you for your money, but he loves you so much he must also love you for yourself.

*7. Everyone at the picnic who ate the oysters got sick, so the oysters are to blame.

8. I don't play well when I don't get enough time to practise, but it's not easy to figure out the relation here. Three, two-hour practice sessions a week or four, one-and-a-half hour sessions work well, but if I have three sessions of, say, an hour, I don't play as well. Strangely, if I have five or six sessions of an hour and a half to two hours a week, my playing also seems to decline. So six hours of practice seems to be just about right.

*9. We didn't know why she was failing the course so we tried to isolate a lot of factors. It seemed that she was getting very little sleep—only about four hours—on the nights before classes, so it looked like she was unable to pay attention in class. So she made sure she got at least eight hours before classes for a whole month and, sure enough, she did much better on the test.

Continued >

10. I know that one of the reasons I'm so poor is an absolute lack of ambition. I'm unbelievably lazy. But even that wouldn't account for the depths of my penury. I think I'm also unlucky.

*11. The test subjects were divided into three weight categories: normal for height and age; overweight; and obese. Test results showed that the normal category had the fewest health issues while the obese category had the most.

12. Studies show that men tend to have certain mechanical and spatial abilities that *may* give them an advantage over women in professions such as engineering. But it could only account for something in the order of a two-to-one ratio of men to women in the profession. Yet the ratio is more like three or four to one, even higher in some specialties. So we investigated social factors and discovered that, for a variety of reasons, women tend to find engineering less appealing than men do.

*13. Joan ate one tuna sandwich and was really sick; Bob ate three and threw up just once; Janelle ate five and was fine.

14. Researchers divided the test subjects into two groups. Both were exposed to cold germs, but one group was given the proposed cold remedy in advance. The group that got the remedy contracted 65 per cent fewer colds and the colds this group did contract were on average 50 per cent shorter in duration.

*15. I noticed that every time I mentioned the importance of a particular game the team goalie got very nervous. So I stopped mentioning it, and sure enough she played with more confidence.

IV. Summary

In Section I you were introduced to some statistical concepts that are an important part of inductive reasoning, in particular, *a priori* and *relative frequency* calculations. You also learned about the *principle of indifference,* which is applied to cases where the odds of a particular outcome are unknown; you saw how Pascal's Wager made use of this principle. The wager also introduced the concept of *expected value*, as well as highlighting the importance of *subjective* considerations, in particular the concept of *personal value.* The *Prisoners' Dilemma* demonstrated how objective and subjective (or personal) considerations can overlap in our reasoning.

In Section II we turned to *causal arguments*, first distinguishing *causation* from *correlation,* and then *necessary* and *sufficient* causes. In Section III, you saw how John Stuart Mill's *methods of induction* help one develop causal arguments by generating possible causes and then testing and, where necessary, quantifying them.

CHAPTER NINE

The Scientific Method

- The scientific revolution
- The scientific method
- Attributes of good scientific theories
- Experimental controls
- Pseudo-science
- The scientific method revised

This chapter will begin with some background on the rise of modern science and then introduce a combination of inductive and deductive reasoning known as the scientific method. It will also examine experimental controls before moving on to the topic of pseudo-sciences—practices that claim to be scientific but that do not meet the standards of science. The chapter will end with some revisionary comments on the scientific method.

I. An Overview of the Issues

This section contains some historical background on the scientific revolution and its relation to inductive reasoning. It also explains how this revolution has affected our concept of proof and thereby changed the way we think about the world.

The Rise of Science

Induction, which is essentially the experimental method of testing the world by drawing conclusions based on evidence, is an integral part of modern science. Any claim not based on empirical evidence, not encased in a cogent or at least a strong inductive argument, will not meet the standards of contemporary scientific research. This view can be traced to the English scientist Isaac Newton (1642–1727), whose work profoundly shaped modern science. Newton argued that any assertion not based on experiment had no claim to be called knowledge. Moreover, what experiment showed to be true—Newton's law of gravity, for instance—had to be accepted, even if no one fully understood why it was true. And before Newton, here is how the sharp-tongued Italian scientist Galileo Galilei (1564–1642) responded to requests by the Catholic Church to recant on his claim that Copernicus's heliocentric astronomy was correct: "It vexes me that they would constrain science by the authority of the Scriptures and yet do not consider themselves bound to answer reason and experiment."

Newton and Galileo were giant figures in the **scientific revolution** that ran from the sixteenth to the eighteenth century in Europe. This revolution, which marks the birth of modern science, transformed our conception of knowledge in large part because it transformed our conception of proof—of how we justify claims about the world. What people of any era call knowledge is closely linked to their idea of what proof is, and that idea is not exactly the same in every age. Medieval thinkers often displayed little respect for experimental proof (and therefore paid little attention to induction), which they sometimes treated as "mere" demonstrations for those who were unable to reason properly—that is, to reason deductively by starting from certain a priori "truths" (often Biblical truths) that they took to be absolute. By the seventeenth century, a rapid development in technology began to undercut this attitude. The telescope and microscope, which are products of this era, extended and sharpened the human senses, allowing scientists to discover and closely examine many things that had hitherto been imperceptible. With a telescope, Galileo discovered Jupiter's moons and made observations of their movements that demonstrated that Copernicus's heliocentric theory was correct. With a microscope, the English scientist William Harvey (1578–1657) observed how blood circulates in bodies. In short, technological advances allowed scientists to begin to replace a priori assumptions, rough estimates, or even outright guesswork with more precise observations of the world around them.

If technology was one principal support of modern science, mathematics was the other. The development of calculus, invented more or less simultaneously by Newton and the German philosopher and mathematician Gottfried Leibniz (1646–1716), allowed scientists to make sophisticated calculations based on their observations. Gradually, science was transformed into a domain of mathematical laws. The subsequent discoveries of such luminaries as Albert Einstein (1879–1955), Niels Bohr (1885–1962), and Stephen Hawking (b. 1942) would have been next to impossible without these mathematical techniques. In addition, in the nineteenth and twentieth centuries the invention of advanced research equipment as well as the telegraph, telephone, radio, television, and finally the computer greatly enhanced our ability to collect, store, disseminate, and compare data. It is not surprising that empirical evidence—measurable facts made mathematically precise—is now an essential element of proof for a scientific hypothesis. Without it there is, quite simply, no scientific knowledge.

These remarks return us to the first rule of induction. What scientists want is not just evidence, but a lot of very good evidence. Charles Darwin's immensely influential book *On the Origin of Species* is essentially a mountain of evidence in support of a relatively small number of conclusions. Although the book is over 400 pages long, Darwin referred to it as an "abstract," an abridged version of what he had intended to write, because so much of his data had to be left out to keep the work to a manageable length. But it was all that data that made his book one long and strong inductive argument.

The Structure of Proof

In summary, after the scientific revolution deductive reasoning alone could not produce scientific knowledge. Scientific arguments now needed the empirical support that induction offers. Recall the argument trees from Chapter 2. Those with an essentially deductive structure of codependent premises still need the support of independent, inductively derived premises to supply the evidence that the codependent premises are (probably) true. They are required to demonstrate that the argument is sound as well as valid.

For example, let's go back and look at William Paley's argument about the design of nature set out in Chapter 7:

E1: *(P1) If we see a watch with all its intricate and connected working parts, we know that it was designed by an intelligent being. (P2) If we look at nature, we see that it is equally intricate and interconnected. (C) Hence, it too must have been designed by an intelligent being.*

This is an analogical argument. Insofar as analogical arguments are inductive, the premises are independent bits of evidence for the conclusion. Diagrammed, Paley's argument looks like this:

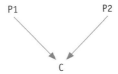

But this doesn't seem right. A problem with analogical arguments is that the premises seem to need to be connected in a codependent manner. Since it's an analogy, **P1** must somehow be connected to **P2**. If you don't see the connection between the premises, you don't see the analogy and, therefore, you don't see the point of the argument. But to connect **P1** and **P2** requires an implicit premise:

> *IP: What is true of the watch is true of all things that are intricate and interconnected.*

The argument can now be restated deductively, with **P1** and **IP** combined to produce **P1a**:

> *P1a: Anything that is as intricate and interconnected as a watch has been designed by an intelligent being;*
> *P2: Nature is as intricate and interconnected as a watch;*
> *C: Therefore, nature has been designed by an intelligent being.*

Now the argument has a deductive structure with codependent premises:

Restate **P1a** conditionally as "If something is as intricate and interconnected as a watch then it has been designed by an intelligent being" and the result is a *modus ponens*.

While this approach may solve the problem of how to connect the premises of an analogy, it raises another issue. Scientists will still want to know *why* the premises are true—why the argument should be accepted as sound as well as valid. What empirical evidence supports them? This means that each premise has to be a sub-conclusion of an inductive argument. Paley could offer lots of evidence in support of **P2**—living beings have intricate and interconnected parts, as does the environment they live in—but what could he offer in support of **P1a**? If he simply assumes, a priori, that it is true, his argument looks something like this:

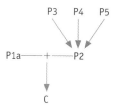

P3, **P4**, and **P5** represent evidence in support of **P2**, but **P1a** remains unsupported, and so the argument is at best indeterminate. We don't know whether it's sound, which means of course that we don't know whether the conclusion is true. If, on the other hand, Paley offers as evidence all the human artifacts that are "designed," and based on this evidence induces **P1a** as a sub-conclusion, he can claim that **P1a** is very probably true. But as is the case with all inductive generalizations, he also has to accept that if anyone can show that there is at least one orderly and interconnected thing that is not designed, **P1a** is false and his argument collapses. The whole thrust of Darwin's theory was to do just that—to show that evolution falsifies **P1a** because the evidence points emphatically to the conclusion that nature is not designed. So the analogy from human artifacts to nature cannot be defended.

The point made in Chapter 7 was that people are sometimes too easily persuaded by analogies, often because they confirm what they want to believe or do believe. In the eighteenth century, when the belief that God had designed the world was still widespread, Paley's analogy looked like basic commonsense that did not require testing. To a certain degree, the *modus ponens* simply told people what they already knew. But in a world where supporting evidence for claims is required and where the second rule of induction is always applied, analogies come under close scrutiny. Scientists will look for cases where they don't hold true. Even commonsense is put under a microscope.

In summary, the scientific revolution gave birth to a world in which we can claim to know only what we can prove, and what we can prove is based on empirical evidence and, therefore, on inductive reasoning. (This means, by the way, that most of what we call "knowledge" is probably true, not absolutely true.)

While most of us are now quite used to the idea of presenting evidence for what we think is true, it can subvert some deeply held beliefs. For example:

> **E2:** *My uncle was really sick in the hospital. We all prayed for him and he got better. So obviously prayer works.*

Unfortunately, things are not that straightforward. First, this is a hasty generalization based on one instance. There is not nearly enough evidence here to suggest a causal relation between prayer and recovery. After all, patients for whom no one prays also recover. In fact, quite a few studies have been conducted on the relation between prayer and recovery, and the evidence is, at best, inconclusive. One study divided preoperative patients into three groups:

Group A: *Patients who were told they were being prayed for*
Group B: *Patients who were not told they were being prayed for*
Group C: *Patients who were not prayed for*

The study turned up no noticeable difference between Group B and Group C, but a surprisingly high number of Group A patients developed postoperative complications, as if prayer was somehow harmful. No one could say why, and indeed we have to be cautious about drawing any conclusion because this is just one study. But what it does show is that, under the microscope of scientific attention, many beliefs turn out to be hard to demonstrate. That is the difference between "belief" and "knowledge" in today's world. Belief can exist without proof, but knowledge requires the support of cogent inductive arguments.

The Rule of the Opposite Hand and the End of Generalization

The need for empirical evidence, and therefore inductive arguments, can produce an unlikely effect. As our ability to collect data grows, general laws or rules may in some cases become not broader and stronger but, strangely, narrower and weaker (once again, the data may undermine commonsense). It is possible to collect so much evidence that everything becomes an exception to the rule. Paradoxically, generalizing arguments may become victims of our ability to collect evidence.

Let's consider baseball, a sport that has always made use of statistics to predict success rates. However, the data one could gather, store, and manage was once much less in volume than it is now that personal computers have appeared on the scene. This has affected some of the inductive rules that have been generated over the years. For instance, consider the fate of what I call the *rule of the opposite hand*. This is one of those rough generalizations, or **rules of thumb**, we often rely on, and it goes like this: in baseball, it is better for a left-handed batter to face a right-handed pitcher, and vice versa. In compliance with this rule, managers of batting teams have often sought "opposite" matchups in important situations, while the opposing managers have tried to avoid them.

But imagine today's manager with his laptop whirring away in the dugout. In the late innings, his team is facing a right-handed pitcher, Dunlop. He looks down his bench and sees that Libedinsky, a left-handed batter, is available to bat for the right-handed Sanchez. Before he makes his move, however, he consults his trusty laptop. First, he discovers that Libedinsky does indeed have a higher batting average (success rate) than Sanchez against right-handed pitchers, which seems to confirm the wisdom of sending him in to pinch hit. But the next bit of data tells him that there is no appreciable difference between either batter's success rate against Dunlop. Moreover, in the past year Sanchez has actually had more success than Libedinsky against Dunlop. That's because, while Libedinsky has hit Dunlop a little better in night games, Sanchez has hit him a lot better in day games—and this current game is a day game. The figures don't lie: the manager allows Sanchez to face Dunlop.

Unfortunately, Sanchez strikes out and the manager is fired for ignoring a long-standing rule. Still, his reasoning seems strong. With all the information at his finger-tips, the rule of the opposite hand was revealed for what it is: a rough generalization that in this instance didn't seem to hold. The data the manager gathered from the computer led him to replace the *generalization* of the rule of thumb with the inductive *prediction* that Sanchez would do better than Libedinsky in this specific situation. In the pre-computer age, the manager would simply have applied the rule of thumb and substituted Libedinsky for Sanchez but, increasingly, rules are made to be broken. In fact, with enough information they are not made at all. We no longer *generalize*, we *predict* individual cases.[1]

There is an important caveat here, one that is rooted in the first rule of induction. The manager's laptop will produce reliable information only if he has entered enough data and if he has the ability to judge whether the information is relevant and reliable. For example, the players have to have faced the pitcher often enough to allow him to make a strong prediction. If Sanchez has batted against Dunlop only six times and Libedinsky nine, any conclusion the manager draws will be a hasty one. In that case, he might do better by sticking with the rule of thumb because he knows that for more than a century it has been (roughly) borne out. So he needs a fair bit of data about these individual players to go against the rule, but once he has enough he can ignore it.

An example more serious than baseball concerns class action lawsuits. These are lawsuits brought against a company or an institution or a government by a large group of people who claim to have been harmed by something the company, institution, or government has done or not done. Imagine, for instance, a group of cancer patients suing a hospital for damages related to excessive wait times for surgery. The sensible rule of thumb is the longer the wait the greater the threat, and therefore the harm, to the patient. However, when the data is crunched this may not turn out to be true. Some patients may be harmed by a delay of three months, but others may not.

---

1 The manager's problem is that all batters have a low success rate. A very good one will get a hit only about 30 per cent of the time, a bad one about 22 or 23 per cent of the time. Although Sanchez had a better chance than Libedinsky of getting a hit, neither had a *good* chance.

There are a whole host of things specific to each individual patient that need to be considered: different cancers, the different stages at which the cancer was detected, differences of age and lifestyle, differences in the kinds of treatment the patients may have already received, and so on. It may be possible to demonstrate physical harm in some cases, but not in all of them.

But now we seem to be working backwards. The class of people who are eligible to sue the hospital is composed of all the individuals who have been harmed. In other words, harm has to be demonstrated *in advance*, case by case, patient by patient, to develop a class. The class cannot be assumed at the outset; it can't simply be composed of everyone who had to wait for treatment. So, in this case, the rule of thumb that delay equals physical harm (mental anguish has been left out of this account) is of no use when it comes to designating a class. And without the rule a class of people decomposes into a bunch of individuals.

Increasingly, and to good effect, insurance companies use this kind of case-by-case procedure to replace the practice of sorting people into classes for purposes of pricing insurance policies. Classes are based on distinctions. Fifty year olds will not be considered alongside 20 year olds; 50-year-old men will be in a different class than 50-year-old women; 50-year-old men who smoke will be in a different class than those who do not, and so on. But with enough data, a company can simply *personalize* risk. That is, it can determine it on an individual basis rather than by membership in a class of people. As in the baseball example, a *prediction* about an individual replaces a *generalization* about a class of people.

EXERCISE 9.1

Exercises marked by an asterisk (*) have answers included in the Answer Key at the end of the text.

I. Use your critical faculties—and concepts from Chapter 8—to decide whether each of the following meets the standard of a scientific argument. Defend your answer.

*1. I think it is obvious that there are other planets in the universe with intelligent life on them. After all, there are probably billions of planets out there and it stands to reason that some of them, if only a very small fraction, will have intelligent beings.

2. Girls tend to demonstrate more facility with language than boys in the first decade or so of life. We can, therefore, expect that girls will do better than boys in the primary grades of school.

*3. When geologists first came across fossils, scientists had to consider the possibility that they were the remains of living but as yet undiscovered animals. However, it was extremely unlikely that large creatures such as dinosaurs were still living and undiscovered—no searches ever turned them up. Moreover, when geologists compared older strata of rock with newer ones, they discovered that certain fossils disappeared from the record while others entered it at later times. This suggested that many species had become extinct and no longer walked on Earth or swam in its waters. By contrast, others had come into being at a later date.

4. Not every person who has contracted AIDS has been tested to see if they are HIV positive, but of the thousands and thousands of AIDS sufferers who have been tested, virtually all have been definitively proven to be HIV positive. This strongly suggests that HIV is causally connected to AIDS.

*5. The bubonic plague is caused by *Yersinia pestis* bacteria, which are typically spread through the bite of a flea most commonly carried by rats. It is likely, therefore, that the rats that infested medieval cities in Europe were the cause of the bubonic plague in the fourteenth century. After all, those rats often arrived on ships that had come from places where the plague already existed.

6. After sifting through voting data, the political party's advisers concluded that male voters seem to prefer policies that left money in their pockets over ones that taxed them but provided services. Focus groups tended to confirm this, so the party advocated giving money for childcare directly to families as opposed to providing that service from tax revenue. Sure enough, polling showed that a higher percentage than usual of married men with young children voted for the party in the next election.

*7. The sun, Earth, and Milky Way will align at the galactic equator on December 21, 2012, which is the winter solstice, the shortest day of the year, and the end of the Mayan calendar. This only happens every 25,800 years! For the first time in recorded history, our entire solar system will move *below* the Milky Way Galaxy. These combined cosmic events will be the end of the world as we know it. About 6 billion people will perish in just a few short years if this cosmic catastrophe occurs.[2]

II. *Which of the following are rules of thumb? Could they be replaced by more specific data? If so, what kind of data would make the rule redundant?*

*1. Girls learn to read more quickly than boys.

2. Any appliance that does several things does none of them as well as one that does only one thing.

---

2 From www.212warning.com.

Continued >

*3. Geminis are more romantic than people of other signs.

4. If a coin that is being tossed comes up heads six times in a row it is not a fair coin.

*5. If there are 60 people in a room, two of them will probably share a birthday.

6. What can go wrong will go wrong.

*7. If you walk into a bar full of guys in baseball caps, there will be mainly country music on the jukebox.

8. If you can't talk easily while jogging your heartbeat is too high.

*9. When buying an engagement ring you should spend about two month's salary.

10. A baby will double its weight in six months.

*11. If you toss a single die you will, on average, get a four 16.7 per cent of the time.

II. The Scientific Method

A Basic Outline

Although induction is essential to scientific research, it is not the sole component of what is known as the scientific method.

> **Definition:** The **scientific method** is a synthesis of inductive and deductive reasoning used to develop and test hypotheses.

Sometimes this method is also called the *hypothetical-deductive method*.[3] Figure 9.1 shows what it looks like in diagram form.

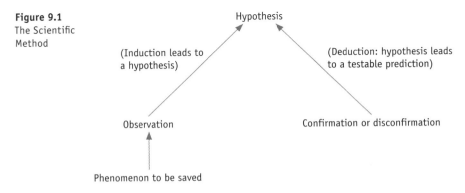

Figure 9.1
The Scientific Method

Hypothesis

(Induction leads to a hypothesis)

(Deduction: hypothesis leads to a testable prediction)

Observation

Confirmation or disconfirmation

Phenomenon to be saved

---

3 Much of this discussion of the scientific method is based on the work of the German philosopher Carl Hempel (1905–97), and his deductive-nomological model of scientific inquiry.

The idea is that in the pursuit of knowledge we observe the world and notice conditions, events, and so on for which we have no immediate explanation. These are the phenomena to be saved. To do so, we gather evidence and inductively build a hypothesis.

> **Definition:** A **hypothesis** is provisional conclusion suggested by evidence but that requires further testing.

(A hypothesis differs slightly from a working hypothesis—see Chapter 7, Section III—insofar as it already has strong evidence supporting it.) The hypothesis is then tested by applying it to an appropriate case from which a certain result is expected to follow. If the expected result does follow (time after time), the hypothesis is accepted as confirmed and will be used to predict or explain similar occurrences in the future.

Let's look at an example:

> **E3:** *Researchers suspected that the cause of an epidemic was a new virus, because people seemed to fall ill and often die within a couple of days of being in direct contact with someone who was already ill. Eventually they isolated a virus, which they then injected into lab mice, all of which showed the expected symptoms and died within 48 hours of injection.*

Here, there is:

1. The *phenomenon* to be saved: an epidemic that is killing people
2. The relevant *observations:* illness seems to spread through contact with those who are already ill

This leads to:

3. The *hypothesis* that the illness is viral

And:

4. A *test:* a virus, once isolated, is injected into mice

At this point, one of two things will happen:

1. The mice die
2. The mice survive

If **1** occurs, as it did in **E3**, this is taken as **confirmation** that the hypothesis is correct. If **2** occurs (no mice or only a few die), the hypothesis is **disconfirmed**, or falsified. Essentially, the testing process applies the inductive methods of agreement and difference, either establishing a causal connection between a hypothetical cause and an effect or demonstrating that there is none. In **E3**, researchers have established a connection and are therefore well on their way to demonstrating that the virus is a sufficient and probably necessary cause of the mice dying.

This scientific method also works at an everyday level. For example:

E4: *I wondered why Johnny was a little unfriendly. Then one day I noticed that I was the only person who still called him "Johnny." Everyone else called him "John," and he was always friendly with other people. So I started calling him "John" and he became much friendlier. He was too polite to say anything, but he doesn't like being called "Johnny."*

Here too there is:

1. A *problem* (phenomenon) to be solved (saved): the reason for moderate unfriendliness
2. *Observations:* no one else calls him "Johnny"
3. A *hypothesis* to be tested: he wants to be called "John"
4. A *test:* calling him "John"
5. And a *confirming result:* he's now friendly

From these examples it should be apparent that in Figure 9.1 the upward side of the scientific method is inductive: observations lead to a hypothesis with a fairly high degree of probability. By contrast, the downward side of the diagram is expressed as a *deductive* syllogism whose opening premise posits a connection between the hypothesis and the expected result of the forthcoming tests. It is a hypothetical sentence in which the antecedent is the hypothesis and the consequent is the expected result. Its general form is as follows:

> *Hypothetical premise:* If my hypothesis is correct then the expected result will follow.

The second premise then records whether the expected result has occurred. At this point, the difference between a confirming and a disconfirming test emerges:

E5: Confirming:
P1: If (hypothesis) the virus is deadly then (expected result) the mice will die;
P2: (actual result) the mice died;
C: The virus is deadly.

Disconfirming:
P1: If (hypothesis) the virus is deadly then (expected result) the mice will die;
P2: (actual result) the mice did not die (or only a few did);
C: The virus is not deadly.

Note that the confirming test is expressed as an invalid syllogism that affirms the consequent. By contrast, the disconfirming test is a valid *modus tollens*. This underscores something important: while we can be absolutely certain that some hypotheses are false, we can never be absolutely certain that any of them are true. In the disconfirming case, the certainty that the hypothesis is false stems from the fact that the negative conclusion follows necessarily from the premises. But the positive conclusion of the confirming test does not follow necessarily, so even if the premises are true the conclusion may not be. What the confirming test tells us is not that *necessarily* the hypothesis is *true,* but that it is *not necessarily false.* If you run enough tests and never get a disconfirming result, the probability that the hypothesis is true rises toward a moral certainty. A whole lot of "not necessarily falses" eventually add up to "very probably true." Remember, the thrust of the scientific method is inductive: the search for cogent arguments.

Experimental Controls

The fact that the scientific method confirms a hypothesis by failing to falsify it tells us once again that the scientific method must always respect the second rule of induction. (It also suggests that there is really no such thing as absolute truth, but we won't get into that.) Look for falsifying instances and assume the hypothesis is confirmed only if, after extensive testing, you do not find them. The Austrian philosopher of science Sir Karl Popper (1902–94), insisted that a hallmark of a scientific theory is that it is *falsifiable.*

I have just introduced a new term, *scientific theory,* which needs to be defined.

> **Definition:** A **scientific theory** is a collection of related observations and laws (confirmed hypotheses, in essence) that explains a broad range of phenomena.

For example, Darwin's theory of evolution explains how all life developed on Earth; Einstein's theory of relativity explains the structure of space and time; and quantum physics explains how atoms work (and possibly how the universe began). Sometimes people denigrate a set of scientific ideas as "just a theory," but this is wrong. A respectable scientific theory is, like those just mentioned, one whose hypotheses have been borne out by repeated tests that could potentially have falsified it. In essence, an idea is "just a hypothesis" until it has been tested and verified, at which point it can be incorporated into a theory as a fact or a law. Like living things, because aspects of theories go on being tested the theories develop and change over time. Parts or even all of a theory may later be falsified, but nonetheless theories are never mere educated guesses because they have stood up to rigorous testing.

When it comes to hypotheses, scientists must avoid the confirmation bias—the tendency to look only for confirming evidence and to ignore disconfirming evidence. This is why researchers often conduct controlled experiments using a control group. These concepts were applied in the discussion of **E2** above, but it is time to introduce them explicitly.

> **Definition:** A **controlled experiment** is one that uses a **control group**, which is a group of test subjects not exposed to whatever is being tested.

Control groups are especially important when researchers are looking for a specific cause, such as whether a particular pill prevents colds. Randomly selected test subjects are given the pill and then exposed to the cold virus. The control group—randomly selected from the same cross-section of people as the test subjects—is also exposed to the cold virus after being given a placebo, which is a pill without any medicinal qualities. If the control group's rate of catching colds does not differ significantly from that of the test subjects, this is evidence of the pill's ineffectiveness. If the control group catches significantly more colds, this is evidence of the pill's effectiveness. In some experiments, the control group will not be given a placebo. Instead they will be subjected to the standard method of treatment that will then be compared to the method of treatment being tested.

A control group helps researchers obey the second rule of induction because it's a way of actively looking for disconfirming evidence by using the methods of agreement and difference. However, for the control group to work, the test must be blind:

> *Definition:* In a **blind test** *the volunteers do not know whether they are part of the test group or the control group.*

Often experiments are double blind:

> *Definition:* In a **double-blind test** *neither the test subjects nor the researchers know which group is the control group.*

Medical researchers will, for example, distribute pills to both groups, but they will not know which one is the drug they are testing and which is the placebo. In other cases, they will not know which group is receiving the standard treatment and which the new treatment.

A control group is essential if you want to test a null hypothesis:

> *Definition: A* **null hypothesis** *is the hypothesis that there is no relation between an effect and its reputed cause.*

Imagine researchers suspect that a particular pill on the market has no medicinal value. By using a control group, they can confirm or disconfirm that hypothesis. In scientific experiments, a null hypothesis is always possible; otherwise the alternative, positive hypothesis would not be falsifiable. Since a test without a null hypothesis would be necessarily true (and so not in need of testing) it would violate a fundamental fact of induction, which is that no hypothesis is necessarily true.

A Note on the Ethics of Scientific Tests

Testing living beings—animals or humans—inevitably raises ethical concerns.

> *Definition:* **Ethics** *is, in general, the study of proper, moral ways of conducting our lives, including conducting scientific research.*

A control group may present no insurmountable problems when a cold remedy is being tested, but issues do arise when cures for lethal diseases are at issue. No one can be given something that is potentially harmful—that must be ruled out in advance—but if people with a certain kind of cancer are the test subjects, and if the new treatment being tested gets confirming results, then the control group has arguably been deprived of a treatment that could save their lives. Therefore, the following ground rules apply:

1. Participation in such tests must be voluntary.
2. The subjects have to be fully informed about the nature of the tests and any risks inherent in them.
3. The tests must be carefully conducted and subjects closely monitored.

It is possible, however, that the need to conduct thorough tests may conflict with an individual's right to the most effective treatment. It is an important issue, and perhaps one that cannot be resolved to everyone's satisfaction.

Attributes of a Scientific Theory

Beside the fact that its claims must be empirically testable and hence falsifiable, there are other attributes that a scientific theory must have.

1. To be incorporated into a theory, the tests that confirm or disconfirm a hypothesis must, as far as possible, be repeatable by any competent researcher in the field.

It is necessary to give other researchers the opportunity to confirm or disconfirm the original researcher's work. This is one of the problems with astrology, a practice that will receive more attention in Section III of this chapter. Independent researchers have had next to no success in duplicating the reported findings of astrologers with respect to the influence of the stars and planets on our lives. Moreover, the conclusions astrologers reach about a given issue vary widely. The inability to develop standard, repeatable tests that reach uniform conclusions undermines the claims of astrologers to be practitioners of a science.

2. A theory should have strong predictive or explanatory powers.

A surprising prediction that emerged from Einstein's general theory of relativity (1915) was the following:

E6: *Time should appear to pass more slowly near massive bodies (such as the Earth) than it does farther away from them.*[4]

What's more, his theory predicted what the time difference would be as one moved away from the surface of Earth. In 1962, extremely accurate atomic clocks

---

4 In this explanation, I am indebted to Stephen Hawking's *A Brief History of Time* (New York: Bantam Books, 1988), 32–3.

were mounted at the top and bottom of a water tower. The one at the bottom ran slower than the one at the top by exactly the amount predicted by Einstein's theory. Since then, Einstein's prediction has been consistently confirmed. Navigation systems like GPS, which rely on satellite signals, need this knowledge to work accurately. Without it, the locations they pinpoint would be off by as much as several kilometres.

E6 also introduces another attribute of a good scientific theory:

3. A theory should be fruitful.

*Definition: A **fruitful theory** will explain (or save) a whole range of phenomena, including ones its original developers had not considered.*

For example, as a sports fan I used to wonder why (as I had been informed) the following was true:

E7: *World-class sprinters decelerate after 60 or 70 metres of a 100 metre race, even though they are not yet tired.*

It seems a curious phenomenon, but it becomes less so if we consult Isaac Newton's three laws of motion, laws which are an integral part of his theory of physics.

*Definition: A **scientific law** is a generalization of a set of observations about how some part of nature works.*

Laws begin as hypotheses, are repeatedly tested, confirmed, and then integrated into a theory.

With respect to a sprinter, Newton's first law of motion tells us that if there are no external forces acting on a body, it will remain as it is, either "at rest" or moving uniformly. This is the law of inertia, and what it means for a sprinter is obvious: if he does not exert force against the starting blocks, he will never get going in the first place.

Newton's second law of motion then tells us that acceleration is proportional to the force acting upon a body in the same direction. This is rendered as "force equals mass times acceleration," or F = ma. In other words, once the sprinter is underway he has to push against the ground very hard with his feet and legs causing the ground, which is the external force, to push back—that is, to exert force on the sprinter, pushing him forward. This allows him to accelerate toward the finish line.

Our sprinter is now well out of the blocks, accelerating like mad until, at about 60 metres, he is racing along at close to 45 kilometres an hour, fast enough to get him a speeding ticket in school zones. He is now depending on Newton's third law of motion, which tells us that for every action there is an equal and opposite reaction. This specifies the second law. As the sprinter pushes against the track, he goes in one direction and the piece of the track he was exerting force against goes, relative to him, in the other direction. The force of the track on the sprinter is equal to the force he exerts on the track.

But now there's a problem. A common saying in sports is that (metaphorically) speed kills (one's opponents). However, it also kills itself. If you look closely at a runner at full sprint, you will see that his feet are often off the ground. Running is, in effect, a series of forward leaps and falls. The faster he runs, the more time the sprinter spends in the air and the less time on the ground. But he can obey Newton's laws only when his feet are on the ground, and the faster he goes the less time his feet are in contact with the track. (In a 10-second race, a world-class male sprinter's feet spend only about three seconds on the ground.) Eventually they aren't on the ground long enough to exert the force necessary to continue to accelerate. The dilemma is how to exert more and more force in less and less time. Ultimately, he cannot do so, which means that he cannot go faster and so, because of the effects of friction, which he can no longer counteract quite so efficiently, he will begin to decelerate slightly. The best he can hope for is to maintain his speed more efficiently than his competitors.

So there you have it: the 100 metres according to Newton, where the winner of the race is the one who decelerates more slowly than his competitors. It's a safe bet that Newton never thought much about sprinters, but since his laws are fruitful they can explain all sorts of things he never thought about. This tells us that his theory of physics, to which these laws belong, was and still is a very good one.

E6 and **E7** are examples of how a fruitful theory will save all sorts of phenomena. However, Occam's razor is also important because it reminds us to look for direct causes and to be suspicious of theories or hypotheses that are overly complex. Therefore:

4. A scientific theory or a scientific hypothesis should be as simple as it can be and still save the phenomena.

One has to take care here because some things that look very simple are in fact not simple at all. For example consider the following hypothesis:

E8: *I am pretty certain that his illness is a form of possession by demons.*

The third rule of induction suggests that this is a fairly implausible hypothesis, at odds with the whole of modern science. Should researchers nonetheless decide to treat it seriously, they would have to identify what they mean by demons and then devise a test to try to prove or disprove their existence. Should they manage that, they would then have to develop experiments that would test whether demons can "possess" someone. This would entail showing how supernatural causation works, and prior to that, that it even exists. By comparison, the hypothesis that the illness is caused by a virus is immediate, direct, and empirically testable: it is much simpler. On the virus hypothesis there is only nature, whereas on the demon hypothesis there is nature and super-nature. Two levels of existence are more complicated than one, especially when you have to show how they interact. **E8** may look simple, but in fact it's extremely complicated.

Even if empirical tests do not isolate a virus, a scientist will be reluctant to hypothesize a cause that takes her beyond nature. She will not want to add that second, untestable, supernatural level to her theory of how the world works. The simpler hypothesis is not always the better one, but a critical thinker will be suspicious of ones that seem needlessly complex, and in the case of **E8** untestable.

In closing, Figure 9.2 is a simple diagram that shows how the concepts of "hypothesis," "law," and "theory" are related.

Figure 9.2
The Development
of a Theory

1. Hypothesis: provisional conclusion based on observation

2. Law: a generalization based on a confirmed hypothesis

3. Theory: a collection of laws, observations, and concepts that explains how some part of nature works

EXERCISE 9.2

I. For each of the following, indicate (a) what the event in question is, (b) what the observations, if any, are, (c) what the hypothesis is, (d) what tests, if any, are carried out, and (e) whether those tests confirm or disconfirm the hypothesis. If there is no test, try to work out what one might be.

*1. Meteorologists have noted that in arid climates any significant loss of vegetation seems to be followed by a further reduction in precipitation. One view is that the loss of vegetation causes that reduction because less sunlight is now absorbed by plants, which leads to greater heat loss from the ground. This heat loss leads to clearer skies and hence less rainfall.

2. In the nineteenth century, a standard explanation for the fermentation process was that it was the result of micro-organisms that generated spontaneously in nutrient broths. Louis Pasteur exposed freshly boiled broths to air in vessels that contained a filter to prevent all particles from passing through to the growth medium as well as vessels with no filter at all, with air being admitted via a long tortuous tube that would not allow dust particles to pass. Nothing grew in the broths; therefore, the living organisms that grew in such broths came from outside, as spores on dust, rather than being spontaneously generated within the broth. Thus, Pasteur dealt the death blow to the theory of spontaneous generation and supported germ theory.[5]

*3. Based on other experiments with light, Isaac Newton wondered whether our perception of colour was affected by pressure on the eye. To investigate, he "took a bodkin (knitting

---

5 From WordIQ.com, www.wordiq.com/definition/Louis_Pasteur.

needle) and put it betwixt my eye and the bone as near to the backside of the eye as I could: and pressing my eye with the end of it there appeared several dark, white and coloured circles. [These] circles were plainest when I continued to rub my eye with the point of the bodkin, but if I held my eye and the bodkin still . . . the circles would grow faint and disappear."[6]

4. Albert Michelson and Edward Morley used a device called an interferometer to split a beam of light such that one part was sent off parallel to the motion of the Earth's orbit around the sun and the other perpendicular to it. The beams were then reflected back to a common source. If the beams arrived at different times, this would be evidence that they were moving through a so-far undetectable "ether" because the perpendicular beam, moving against the ether, would have been slowed by its resistance, whereas the parallel one, moving with the ether, would not have been. But there was no meaningful difference between the beams. They both seemed to have travelled at the same speed.

*5. Ivan Pavlov wondered whether animals could learn by associating one stimulus to another stimulus. He tested this on dogs, which naturally salivate when presented with food. Just before giving them food, Pavlov emitted sounds from such things as whistles and tuning forks. After a while the dogs began to salivate at the sounds. This suggested that the unconditional reflex of salivating at food could be transformed into the conditional reflex of salivating at a sound associated with food.

6. Solomon Asch performed a series of experiments to test whether group pressure could enforce conformity. In each experiment, someone was asked to participate in a "vision test." That person was ushered into a room full of people and told that they were also test subjects but these people were collaborators with the experimenter. The test subject and the fake subjects were asked to look at a series of lines and pass judgment on their relative lengths. The fake subjects all gave incorrect answers. Most of the real test subjects eventually changed their correct responses to agree with the erroneous answers of the fake subjects. A control group, with no exposure to fake peer pressure, always got the answers right.

*7. The eighteenth-century English doctor Edward Jenner wondered if the local folk tales about the relatively mild cowpox being an effective way of preventing the much more virulent smallpox were true. He inoculated a young boy with the cowpox virus, who fell ill but soon recovered. When he was then injected with the smallpox virus, he turned out to be immune. This experiment was repeated on other subjects with the same result.

---

6 J.E. McGuire and Martin Tamny, *Certain Philosophical Questions: Newton's Trinity Notebooks* (CUP, 2002), 482.

Continued >

8. In his general theory of relativity (1915), Einstein argued that space could be bent or distorted by the gravitational effect of very large objects. If that were so, then light passing through that space would also be bent, travelling in a curved path. Arthur Eddington realized that the theory could be tested during an eclipse of the sun because, for the few minutes when the sun's light is obscured, it is possible to see the light from distant stars that appear close to the sun in our sky. If Einstein's theory was correct, the sun's gravity would shift the apparent position of these stars away from their actual position observed at times of the year when they appeared further from the sun. When measurements were taken during an eclipse, the apparent position of the stars had indeed noticeably shifted.

*9. Smith noticed that her cat kept showing up in different parts of the house. It always looked the same, but was it, she wondered, *really* the same cat? Maybe it was a new cat each time. Maybe objects were temporally non-continuous. So she followed the cat everywhere it went for a week, even going so far as to place video recorders in every room of the house. What she noticed was that the cat never once disappeared and reappeared. It existed continuously throughout the whole of the week. Smith was very pleased.

10. Dodgson wondered whether gerbils were as serendipitous as they seemed to be, so he took 3342 of them and let them loose in the world. Not only did they all survive, they all found good homes and three of them won Nobel prizes. The rest won lotteries and lived happily ever after.

II. *Explain why each of the following fails to meet either the standards of the scientific method or one of the ethical restraints placed on it.*

*1. In the experiment, Group A were informed that they were going to receive the new drug and group B was informed that they were going to receive the standard medication now on the market.

2. I know there are possible side effects, but if we advertise them no one will volunteer as test subjects.

*3. Look, everybody who took this course improved their reading skills, so it must work.

4. I think our idea will work. It just stands to reason that it will.

*5. I have to admit that I am not absolutely certain what the effect of this treatment will be. There may well be harmful side effects, but since it can potentially save lives we need to start testing it right away.

6. I think there is reasonable doubt about the guilt of the accused. It is possible that his body was taken over by aliens who then committed the robbery.

*7. Investing in property has to be safer than investing in the stock market because property can't just disappear.

8. A: How can you say my theory is wrong? Look at my test results.

   B: But you are the only one who has been able to get those results.

*9. I think the world is only five minutes old because the creator who was supposed to make it forgot to do so until just now. But he has made us believe it is much older by implanting false memories in us and by making everything look much older than it is.

10. I am pretty sure this investment strategy will work, but to be sure let's divide our investors into two groups and use the new strategy on one and the old strategy on the other.

*11. Student: I know I'll get an extension from my professor if I approach him this way; it worked the last time I tried it on a professor.

III. *For each of the following observations develop a hypothesis that will explain the observations and an experiment to test it. Use your imagination.*

*1. People who live near the mountains seem, on average, to have higher IQs than those who live in valleys.

2. Certain groups of people are dying of strange diseases that are usually not fatal.

*3. Voters in a particular riding have never elected a candidate from the same party twice in a row. This has gone on for more than a century.

4. Students are not paying attention in a particular class.

*5. There is a sudden and statistically unusual rise in violent crime in a particular neighbourhood.

6. There is a sudden increase of bear attacks in a particular area.

*7. Someone you are romantically interested in but who has never paid any attention to you suddenly starts to pay more attention to you.

III. Beware of Pseudo-Science

Evolution and Creationism

From Sections I and II, it follows that a hypothesis that is impervious to empirical testing, and that is consequently unfalsifiable, is unscientific. This is what distinguishes science from **pseudo-science**. To get a sense of the difference, let's compare the theory of evolution with creationism. Some fundamentalist Christians—in particular "dominionists," who believe that the Bible is the only reliable source of truth—insist that creationism (or "intelligent design") should be taught in science classes as an alternative to the theory of evolution. To see what's at stake, consider the basic comparison of evolution and creationism shown in Table 9.1.

Table 9.1 Evolution versus Creationism		
	EVOLUTION	CREATIONISM
Hypothesis 1:	Species originate and become extinct at various times	God created all life at the same time
Evidence:	The fossil record	The Bible
Hypothesis 2:	Species mutate	God created all living beings in their finished state
Evidence:	Observation of flora and fauna; comparison of current species with fossils of ancestors; genetics and molecular biology	The Bible

As Table 9.1 shows, the theory of evolution comes furnished with empirical data and tests that can support or disprove its claims. Over the years, most of its claims have been verified, a few have been falsified, and others are still matters of dispute, either because scientists are not sure how to test them or because they have not yet found sufficiently strong evidence for them. In other words, the theory of evolution has undergone a fairly continuous process of testing and development in the century and a half since Darwin published *On the Origin of Species*. For example, Darwin knew nothing of genetics and very little about molecular biology (compared to what we know today, that is), yet these disciplines are integral to current theories of evolution. Evolution is a strong, well-confirmed scientific theory.

Creationism, by contrast, is based primarily on the authority of the Bible. There is, therefore, no real scope for testing, updating, and developing its claims. As a result, strict creationists such as dominionists pay little attention to the second rule of induction. For example, some of their numbers argue that fossils are the remains of animals drowned in the great flood, from which only those aboard Noah's Ark escaped. The problem is that, by the standards of science, this claim is demonstrably false. The fossils can be reliably dated to a time period long before humans walked on Earth. Anyone who accepts as holy writ that Earth is only 6000 years old and that all life forms were created at the same time has to ignore this scientific evidence and these disconfirming tests. So while evolution is a fruitful, ever-expanding scientific theory, strict creationism is not a scientific theory at all. It is, more accurately, a belief system that stands opposed to contemporary science.

These remarks are not meant to disparage the biblical story of creation or the religion that gave rise to it, only to emphasize that creationism is not a scientific theory. Creationists assert what they take to be the truth, but they do not subject it to scientific analysis. In fact, by making their assertions a matter of faith they reject the very possibility of testing it. Not surprisingly, many creationists spend more time trying to disprove evolution than they do trying to prove creationism. What is objectionable in all this is not the demand that creationism should be taught in schools but that it should be taught as science. Perhaps this demand says a lot about the power the idea of science has over all of us, because even creationists seem to feel the need to ask for its blessing. But that means that their views must meet the standards of science, which is precisely what creationists generally refuse to accept.

The Case against Astrology

Given the mind boggling array of pseudo-sciences floating through cyberspace, the protection that the rules of induction provide against uncritical thinking is extremely important. Perhaps the oldest of the pseudo-sciences, one which was in fact long considered a science, is astrology. Its fundamental premise is that the alignment of the sun, planets, and stars at birth determines one's destiny. It's a familiar concept—most of us know our astrological signs, and newspapers and websites regularly publish horoscopes that are often taken seriously by readers. Apparently many people believe that our personalities and our destinies are determined by our astrological signs. The problem is that no amount of research has ever managed to uncover convincing confirming evidence for these claims.

Much of the time evidence is replaced by anecdotes, as in this example:

E9: *My cousin is a Virgo and she's insightful and discriminating, just like the astrology books say. I'm a Gemini and I'm romantic, like Geminis are supposed to be. I tell you, astrology is true.*

Two or three stories do not add up to a science, especially when vague terms such as "insightful," "discriminating," and "romantic" are in play. To investigate **E9**'s claim, researchers would have to agree on definitions of these terms, find some precise way of quantifying them, and then study hundreds or even thousands of individuals born under all signs. (To see a sample of these studies, conduct an Internet search for "studies testing astrology.") In violation of the first rule of induction, the speaker in **E9** has put forward only a couple of anecdotes in support of her view. Since that view is largely inconsistent with our knowledge of physics, she has also violated the third rule of induction, and since she has not looked for disconfirming evidence she has violated the second rule as well—a trifecta of shoddy reasoning.

Like most pseudo-sciences, astrology can be extremely vague in its claims. Perusing the Internet for information about my sign—Cancer—reveals that my strengths are that I am adaptable, loyal, attached to family, and empathetic, qualities almost any adult of a certain age will think he or she has. My weaknesses are, apparently, small sins. I can be moody, overly sensitive, emotional, and indecisive at times. There are very few people in the world, born under any sign, who cannot be described by these very general human characteristics.

As I write this, I have just glanced at my horoscope from today's newspaper, which, admittedly, has to be very general. It reads:

E10: *How sure of someone are you? To what extent can you rely on a situation always being the way it is now? These are questions you need to ask, yet you must also recognize that there may never be fully satisfactory answers.*[7]

You could map these vague questions onto virtually anyone you know or apply them to any situation and make them fit. Take the first one: How sure of someone are you? This is vague (what precisely does "sure" mean?), but I suppose I could say that I'm very sure of my wife but the guy who just moved in across the street looks a little suspicious. The question, which is almost certainly meant to incite suspicion that someone I know is about to betray me in some way, is of the open "can't lose" variety. If someone does betray me, the believer in astrology can say, "See? That's exactly what was predicted." On the other hand, if no one betrays me the believer can say, "Well, I guess you were sure of your friends and colleagues. Good for you." There's no way to test, and therefore potentially to falsify, the question's implication because it simultaneously implies one thing and its opposite. To give him credit, in the end the author of the horoscope is right: there are no satisfactory answers to the questions (this is a common caveat that also renders failure impossible). But that is because these are unsatisfactory questions.

Some astrologers argue that astral twins provide proof of astrology's claims. Astral twins are people who are born at the same time and place and who therefore have virtually identical horoscopes. Astral twins would include real twins, but depending how strict one is about the definition of time and place (to repeat, vagueness is always a problem with pseudo-sciences) there are also many sets of astral twins who do not know one another. In fact, we all could have many such twins. If we construe "same time" as "same day," most hospital obstetric wards are going to contain astral twins. Consider the following not untypical bit of information about astral twins from the website of an astrology believer:

E11: *Studies show that similar events occur at similar ages all through the lives of Astral Twins.*

---

7 *Toronto Star*, 9 October, 2010.

> *In one instance, the lives of Astral Twins (born of different parents) went to the same school, graduated school the same year. Then both of them got married in the same year and on the same day. They, in fact, married each other!*
>
> *What is even more interesting is that if Astral Twins are born almost the same minute in time, then they would also have the same Ascendant or Rising Sign, which influences physical appearance. As a result, there is a good likelihood that many Astral Twins resemble each other in physical characteristics.*[8]

Questions abound: in the first place, what studies? An Internet search will turn up a number of reputable scientific research projects dedicated to twins (not necessarily astral twins) and astrological signs, but none of them cite confirming evidence for the sort of claim this writer is making. So, once again, in place of a study the writer offers an anecdote about two astral twins who married. No names are provided, but never mind. Finally, the third rule of induction should incite skepticism about the claim that astral twins born at almost the same moment in time will tend to resemble one another. This is an unimaginably vague claim. How is resemblance judged if the twins are male and female or of different races? How many astral twins have been studied? Could we see photos? Even though the writer asserts only that there is "a good likelihood" that astral twins will physically resemble one another—another instance of shielding oneself from falsifying evidence—the claim defies belief. There is no reliable evidence to support it, and certainly no report of scientifically rigorous tests that confirm it. Yet the claim is offered not as a hypothesis but as a fact.

The Claims of ESP

Another controversial claimant of scientific status is extrasensory perception, or ESP. ESP takes a variety of forms. One is *telepathy,* the ability to access other people's thoughts and transmit one's own thoughts to others in a direct mind-to-mind fashion. Another is *precognition*, the ability to foretell another person's thoughts or actions or to predict future events. As always, a good reason for being suspicious of these claims comes from the third rule of induction. Besides contradicting everything science tells us about the laws of nature, including human neurology, the idea that the future is predetermined runs counter to what experience suggests.

This is not to say that no one can make successful predictions. For example:

E12: *If you don't study harder, you will fail the exam.*

If the person in question fails this is a successful prediction, but it is hardly an example of precognition. Since the person in question was not destined to fail, the speaker could not

---

8 Martin Schulman, "Astral Twins: The Proof of Astrology." www.articledashboard.com/Article/Astral-Twins-the-Proof-of-Astrology/112141.

absolutely know that she would. Based on past experience—on subjective probability—the speaker might well have good grounds for concluding that the most probable outcome of her not studying is failure. Predictive arguments are a common form of inductive reasoning but, like all inductive arguments, their conclusions are never necessarily true. Therefore, **E12** does not represent a priori knowledge of a predetermined future.

By contrast, precognition allegedly involves predictions that are fated to happen. They are, therefore, not really predictions at all but, as the term "precognition" implies, instances of a priori knowledge. Consider this claim I once heard an astrologer make on the radio:

E13: _____ *(a fellow astrologer) predicted the exact moment of the Soviet Union's fall.*

Let's start, as always, with the vague language. Is there is an "exact moment" when the Soviet Union "fell"? "Fell" is, after all, a metaphor, because empires don't literally fall. In this case, republics gradually seceded from the Soviet Union until only Russia was left. It was a gradual disintegration rather than an abrupt fall. So when, exactly, was the process of disintegration finished? Was it the moment when the Soviet Union formally changed its name back to Russia?

Invoking the principle of charity, the speaker was probably referring to the fall of the Berlin Wall in 1989, which is a symbolic moment associated with the metaphorical "fall" of communism, but also a moment when a real wall fell. So let's assume that the astrologer predicted the date (9 November 1989) on which people began to tear down the Berlin Wall. It would be interesting to know how often he managed to make such successful "predictions," but alas the man on the radio did not reveal his colleague's track record. However, since someone who makes a lot of predictions will probably be right once in a while, the ability to be right on a regular basis is an important facet of one's claim to have the gift of precognition, and so the track record is important. Another question is, "How far in advance of the wall coming down did he make the prediction?" A few days in advance would not be terribly impressive, because the events that led to it were beginning to unfold, but 10 years in advance would be impressive. Again, the speaker left his audience in the dark.

To have any claim to scientific respectability, a claim to possess precognitive powers has to be tested under strict conditions. Researchers need to determine whether the claimant is able to predict certain kinds of events with a degree of accuracy noticeably beyond the normal range that could be explained by probability. These tests—for example, testing someone's ability to predict the order in which cards from a deck will be turned over—have to be designed, carried out, and vetted by competent researchers using control groups. But when claims about precognition are tested in this way they have a very, very poor track record.

In closing, let's return to the question of fate. People began to tear down the Berlin Wall on 9 November 1989, but was that fated to happen? If it was, as most people believe, a contingent event dependent on a whole host of circumstances, might it not have happened on another date, or not at all? Stated in general terms, is the future predetermined? If someone could make accurate and specific "predictions" about the future that might be evidence that it is, because they would seem to be demonstrating a priori knowledge of it. However, since this is knowledge that, under close examination, no one seems to possess, the opposite conclusion is far more probable: we cannot know the future precisely because the future is not predetermined.

It is not surprising, therefore, that, like astrology, the evidence cited in support of precognition and of ESP in general is often anecdotal:

> **E14:** *I won a rather large prize in the lottery this week, but what is so amazing is that last week my aunt told me it was going to happen.*

Anecdotes record those occasions when this sort of prediction is borne out. They are examples of the fallacy of misleading vividness. They strike people forcefully and seduce them into exaggerating their value as proof of precognition. This force probably owes much to the fact that, in everyday experience, they seem so unusual and the unusualness is taken uncritically as grounds for acceptance rather than caution. But something that happens rarely is more likely a fluke than evidence of a paranormal ability.

Sometimes, however, supporters of ESP make a type of residues argument, claiming that ESP must be true because there are some ESP-like events that science cannot explain. Fair enough, but that is at best a hypothesis, and no hypothesis can be accepted without testing. It's important not to fall victim to the **ad ignorantiam** fallacy. This is an informal fallacy of presumption that entails arguing that something must be true because no one has been able to prove that it is false. For example:

> **E15:** *Ghosts must exist. No one has ever been able to prove conclusively that they don't.*

There are two problems here. In the first place, the fact that one cannot prove that X is false does not warrant the claim that it is true. That's the *ad ignorantiam* fallacy. In the second place, there is an equivocation on "conclusively." No one can prove that the Loch Ness monster doesn't exist unless, perhaps, we empty a whole lake in the Scottish highlands, and even then some people would simply say that it has moved elsewhere. If "conclusively" means, as it seems to mean in **E15**, that there is no *absolute* proof for the non-existence of the monster, then that claim simply ignores the fact that empirical research never yields that kind of certainty (maybe aliens abducted poor Nessie). But if "conclusively" means that the evidence from years of fruitless searching is so strong that any reasonable person will be convinced by it, then there is conclusive evidence that the Loch Ness monster does not exist.

Research on ghosts, ESP, and astrology has been similarly fruitless. Just as the failure to falsify a hypothesis eventually leads to the conclusion that it is very probably true, the constant failure—under proper research conditions—to find confirming evidence provides strong grounds for concluding that a hypothesis is very probably false. Confronted with high degrees of probability, you can always reply that it is still *possible* that the opposite is true—that there are ghosts or that there are monsters in deep Scottish lakes—but at some point it is unreasonable to entertain the possibility. It is possible that you could win millions of dollars in a lottery, but no reasonable person will adopt that possibility as his basic plan for achieving financial security.

Something to Think About

In 1973, late night talk-show host Johnny Carson had Uri Geller, a self-described "paranormalist," as a guest on his Tonight Show. Geller claimed to be able to bend spoons by means of ESP. Carson, who began his career as a magician and who was therefore well aware of magicians' tricks, was skeptical. Geller brought his own spoons to bend but Carson, in a perfect example of a proper experimental control, substituted another set, which Geller was unable to bend. Geller's career never quite recovered from this debacle. One failure does not mean that Geller could not do what he claimed, but repeated failures would have strongly suggested that conclusion. Geller never submitted to such controlled tests, so he never risked failure.

EXERCISE 9.3

Do some research and decide which of the following meet the standard of a scientific theory and which do not. Think about how to defend your position.

*1. The time cube

2. Cold fusion

*3. Psychoanalysis

4. Intelligent design

*5. The general theory of relativity

6. Genetics

*7. Numerology

8. Handwriting analysis as a predictor of one's personality

*9. Homeopathy

10. Acupuncture

IV. The Scientific Method Revised

Section III promoted the virtues of critical thought over credulity and blind belief in matters of scientific knowledge, but it has to be noted that in science, as in most practices, there are standard ways of going about things, and these ways may sometimes blunt the critical attitude. The late philosopher of science T.S. Kuhn coined the term "normal science"[9] to refer to the set of standards and practices that scientists in a given field share. For example, physicists accept that Newtonian theory explains perfectly well how physical objects moving at speeds well below that of light behave. So they use that theory as a framework for their research about such objects, allowing it to tell them in advance what their observations should be. This serves as a reminder that scientists seldom engage in research "from scratch"; they seldom begin with pure observation. Rather, they begin with well-established theories that they use to make sense of the world. Even when a new phenomenon comes to their attention, they will tend to think abductively, selecting an established theory that best explains it. So, of course, do students, who are taught by teachers whose job it is to explain scientific theories, often by introducing experiments designed to demonstrate how they work. This seems to involve thinking backwards: starting from accepted truths rather than inductively arriving at them.

William of Occam provides one good justification for this procedure. It would be an enormous waste of time to let every student rediscover every scientific theory for himself. What's more, in most cases he would fail to do so. It's unreasonable to assume that a student will move from observations of bodies falling or the moon orbiting Earth to the "proper" Newtonian hypothesis about the law of gravity and then develop experiments to test it. Students learn in a context, which textbooks and teachers provide by bringing them up to date on a particular discipline, explaining what the theories are and why they work. Someone who is really interested may progress from there into the uncharted waters of original scientific research. But the fact remains that however justified this procedure is it does make science at least a little self-confirming. The message to a student (and even a scientist) is, "Here is what you will observe, so you had better observe it."

In light of this, consider the revision of the scientific method shown in Figure 9.3. Note that in the figure "theory" has replaced "hypothesis" from Figure 9.1. This takes into account the fact that teaching and research generally begin with scientific theories already in place. As a result, it is possible to enter the circle at either "observation" or "theory."

---

9 T.S. Kuhn, *The Structure of Scientific Revolutions*, 2nd ed. (Chicago: University of Chicago Press, 1970), Ch. II.

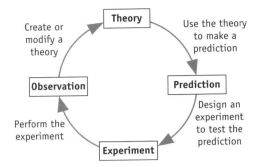

Figure 9.3
The Scientific Method Revised

To begin with observations is theoretically to start "from scratch," as we might do when we are presented with an absolutely new phenomenon. A curious person who observed falling bodies but knew nothing about the law of gravity would have to begin by thinking inductively. In accordance with Figure 9.1, she would have to build (or abduct) a hypothesis that she could then test. But that's a big problem for a novice student, who might, for example, reason as follows:

Observation 1: A stone falls rapidly to the ground;
Observation 2: A feather falls slowly to the ground;
Observation 3: A toy airplane falls faster than a feather but slower than a stone;
Hypothesis: Therefore, everything falls at its own rate of speed.

Our student has not managed to arrive at Newton's law and its accompanying principle of equivalence, which states that all bodies near the ground will fall—move toward Earth's centre—at the same rate if they are not affected by air resistance. In short, in a vacuum a stone, a feather, and a toy plane will all fall at the same rate.

If, on the other hand, the student is first taught Newton's theory of gravity and then carries out an experiment explained in her textbook, she will think deductively (in a *modus ponens*) as follows:

P1: If Newton's theory is true then my observations must agree with what the text tells me;
P2: And Newton's theory is true;
C: Therefore, my observations must agree with what the text tells me

Here, the student accepts in advance that the stone, feather, and toy plane will fall at different rates because of each object's varying susceptibility to the air's resistance. In this case, her observations do not indicate that her original hypothesis—everything falls at its own rate of speed—is probably correct; instead they show her how air pressure affects objects as they fall. Somewhat contradictorily, the theory tells her, in advance of her observations, how objects will behave under the influence of gravity and the resistance of air pressure. The student has to interpret the evidence in the way the theory dictates, and if she does not she is simply wrong. There is no room for her to develop a new hypothesis or to think that she has found evidence that falsifies Newton's theory.

To take another example, if a chemistry teacher wants students to understand etho-thermic reactions—ones where energy is released as light, heat, or sound—she may have them do the "barking dog" experiment, where nitrous oxide is mixed with carbon disulphide and ignited. The result is a bright blue flash accompanied by a sound reminiscent of a dog's "woof." Should a student fail to get these reactions he is not congratulated for disproving a chemical law, he is told he did the experiment incorrectly.

What is true for the student is also true for established scientists—their research tends to respect existing laws. A scientist will begin with a theory, which is to say she will start with what she assumes is already known. For example, when scientists were trying to work out how to send a spaceship to the moon, they accepted Newton's law of gravity and applied it. As reasonable as this procedure is, there is a risk that the circle in Figure 9.3 can become a kind a self-perpetuating trap from which it is difficult to escape, even for experienced scientists. The problem is that apparently disconfirming observations may be adjusted to fit the theory, and even if that can't be done they may simply be discounted. If the theory in question is well tested that makes good sense, but sometimes it takes a genius to depart from good sense. Albert Einstein recognized that Newtonian physics, which assumed that space (or in Einstein's theory, space-time) was flat, led to some inaccurate predictions about how planets moved through their orbits. As a result, in his theory of general relativity Einstein argued that space-time was not flat but curved by the gravitational effect of energy and massive bodies such as planets and stars (more precisely, he postulated that gravity just was the curvature of space). Light travelling through curved space-time would therefore bend rather than travel in a straight line. This assumption (or hypothesis) had to be confirmed by experiments, which it was. This capacity to see things in a new light, to rethink old truths, is a rare and valuable commodity in the pursuit of knowledge, in part because scientists, like everyone else, may have trouble breaking out of the enclosure of accepted truths, even when those truths no longer seem to be true. It's what we commonly call the inability to think outside the box.

EXERCISE 9.4

Let's finish with an abductive exercise. What theories might explain the following? You may need to do some research.

*1. Near-death experiences

2. Seeing ghosts

*3. The sense of déjà vu

Continued >

4. Succeeding at something after you have prayed for success

*5. Girls outperforming boys in school

6. Winning five hands of poker in a row when wearing your lucky sweater

*7. A dream that accurately predicts a future event

V. Summary

In this chapter, induction and deduction have been combined to make the *scientific method*. Since science is based on empirical evidence, the first leg of the method is inductive, leading to a *hypothesis*. Therefore, the methods and rules of induction set out in Chapters 7 and 8 are fundamental to scientific research. Once a hypothesis has been developed, it has to be tested by experiments that are relevant, empirical, and *repeatable* by other researchers in the field. These experiments can be expressed as mixed hypothetical syllogisms. A *confirming* result will be expressed as an invalid syllogism that affirms the consequent. What it shows is that the test has not falsified the hypothesis. Eventually, a lot of "not false" results add up to "very probably true." A *disconfirming* result will be expressed as a *modus tollens*, showing that the hypothesis is definitely false.

The result of a series of confirming tests or experiments should be a *fruitful law* encased in a *theory* with strong predictive and explanatory powers. But since researchers do not live outside science they generally begin their work equipped with well-established theories that can become self-confirming. This may, in some circumstances, prevent them from considering the world in a new light. Imagination is, therefore, an important attribute for a scientist—indeed, for any critical thinker.

Finally, the scientific method can be applied to everyday life because it is a model for critical thinking. Pay attention to the world around you, and when you run into new phenomena do not ignore them. Try to work out what a good explanation for them might be; try to develop a reasonable and testable hypothesis. Be careful about accepting explanations without supporting evidence or ones that are contrary to well-established theories. This means, of course, that you ought to be scientifically and socially literate. Put differently, you ought to know what a good explanation or argument looks like and be able to distinguish *science* from *pseudo-science*. When you are uncertain, do some research and avoid hasty conclusions. When I was young, there was a popular song called, *Do You Believe in Magic?* For a critical thinker, the answer has to be, "not without an awful lot of supporting evidence." Reason is not everything in our lives, but it is an important, in fact essential, attribute of our humanity. We ignore it at our peril.

Something to Think About

Let me leave you with something completely different: the Zen Buddhist's option of not-discussing, of offering profoundly illogical answers that force the questioner to set reason aside. They are called "koans." For example, a Buddhist monk asks the master, "What is Buddha?" and the master answers, "Three pounds of flax." This may seem to go beyond puzzling into nonsense, but we need to exercise caution in our judgment. For one thing, koans have a functional connection to the guides to good reasoning introduced in Chapter 4 because they are intended to help the student concentrate his mind.

Unlike the guides, however, the point of the koans is not to focus people on thinking logically, but rather to protect them from the urge to do so. For the Zen master, the box to get outside of is critical thought itself. Zen masters know that logic can be a mechanical way of pursuing knowledge, full of rules and methods. Sometimes, they suggest, it is better to sit quietly awaiting knowledge's arrival. Sometimes it is better to empty the mind than to fill it with facts, ideas, and the like.

I'm not recommending that this practice should always, or even often, replace the use of critical thinking skills, but it is an interesting reminder that—sometimes—there can be value in emptying your mind and allowing things to come. Leave room for imagination and inspiration. Scientists often speak of solutions to a problem arriving in a flash of inspiration, at moments when they were not consciously thinking about the problem. Before tests, I always tell my students to take a deep breath and empty their minds. Thinking can be hard work requiring intense concentration, and perhaps it sometimes needs to be balanced by a Zen-like openness, a kind of creative unthinking. Put differently, sometimes we need to impose order on the world and sometimes we need simply to be receptive to the world. Maybe this is the yin and yang of rational beings.

Answer Key

Chapter 1

Exercise 1.1

I

1.

P: **Because** your profits depend on unsound environmental practices;

P: And **since** that actually hurts the economy;

C: **Therefore**, your company must change its ways.

3.

P: **Since** the ban on electronic devices has reduced car accidents;

P: And **because** many pedestrians who are killed have been distracted by using electronic devices while walking;

C: We should **therefore** extend the ban on using electronic devices to include pedestrians.

5.

P: **Because** it is only when criticism is randomly distributed across the political spectrum that there is no reason to suspect bias;

P: And **because** in your blog all criticism is directed at the Conservatives;

C: **Therefore** your blog is biased.

7.

P: **Because** people will always break promises when it suits them;

C: **Therefore**, the moral rule that tells us we ought to keep our promises is unnatural.

9.

P: **Because** three different studies have concluded that undergraduates do worse than normal on open-book exams;

P: And **given that** our mandate is to help students succeed;

C: **Therefore** I think it's reasonable to ban open-book exams.

11.

P: **Because** I've seen dozens of sci-fi movies;

P: **Because** they always bore me;

P: **Because** only nerds enjoy them;

P: **Because** nerds only like boring things;

C: **It follows that** sci-fi movies are boring.

13.

P: **Because** Tony does everything his girlfriend tells him to without exception;

P: And **given that** anyone who does this is a drowning man;

C: **It follows that** Tony is a drowning man.

15.

> **P: Because** governments should not be in the business of executing their citizens;
>
> **C: It follows that** capital punishment is wrong.

17.

> **P: Because** you never re-tweet when you take our stuff;
>
> **C: Therefore** no one should have respect for you.

19.

> **P: Assuming that** this news network only broadcasts propaganda;
>
> **P: And assuming that** it lies to viewers;
>
> **C: There is therefore** no reason to watch it.

II

1. The premise is irrelevant, because if the clock is broken you won't know when it is accurate. As well, being accurate for two moments in a day is scarcely an argument in favour of a clock.

3. It's hard to say whether this is a relevant reason for not voting for a given party. Since it can be perfectly reasonable to change one's voting pattern, this premise would require more support to make it persuasive.

5. Taken literally, the premise says that staying in school is the best available option and to that extent it is relevant.

7. Having a boil lanced is not, generally speaking, dangerous at all. So this premise is false and does not support the conclusion.

Exercise 1.2

1. Explanation

Em: Natural selection entails an interface between genes and the environment;

Es: Genetic mutations are random (i.e., they occur in the organism);

Es: The environment determines whether that mutation is beneficial, harmful, or neutral in terms of the organism's chances of survival.

3. Argument

P: Since if you gave Crosby better wingers he'd be leading the scoring race by 20 points;

C: Ovechkin is **therefore** not a better player than Crosby.

5. Argument (I assume this is not something the person being spoken to will see as uncontroversial)

P: Because you constantly do stupid things;

P: And because only idiots do stupid things;

C: Therefore you're an idiot.

7. Explanation

Em: U'll 4give him;

Es: b/c u're divine.

9. Argument (even though the speaker seems unaware of this)

P: Since the Green Party is the only political party that shows genuine concern for the state of the environment;

P: And since that is the single most important issue facing the world today;

C: Therefore you should vote for the Green Party.

11. Argument (not everyone would agree with this opinion)

P: Because everyone has different views on what's right and what's wrong;

P: And because they always will;

C: Therefore there are no absolute moral values.

13. Explanation

Em: The value of mortgage funds tends to go up when interest rates go down;

Es: Because the mortgages in the fund are now yielding a higher rate of interest than new mortgages are.

15. Explanation

Em: In the past population growth has led to the collapse of some civilizations;

Es: Because it forced people to expand farming from the prime lands first chosen onto more marginal land to feed the growing number of hungry mouths;

Es: Because it also forced them to adopt unsustainable practices that led to environmental damage, resulting in agriculturally marginal lands having to be abandoned again;

Es: Because this resulted in food shortages, starvation, wars . . . and overthrows of governing elites by disillusioned masses.

Exercise 1.3

1. Argument

P: Since if reputable tests confirm a connection between a physical condition and a disease then we ought to accept that such a connection exists;

P: And since tests do show a connection between cholesterol levels and heart disease;

C: We ought **therefore** to assume that heart disease is related to cholesterol levels.

3. Report on an argument

P: Since *cause* is simply an idea we impose on the world to make sense of what we observe;

C: Therefore, the world does not contain causes.

5. Report on an argument and a counterargument

Report on an argument:

P: Because of the rapid growth of social media;

C: There is, **as a result**, a growth in the worldwide demand for democratic institutions.

Counterargument:

P: Because technology can't create democratic movements unless other social conditions, such as a sufficient level of education, are already in place;

C: Therefore, social media alone cannot be the cause of the growing demand for democratic institutions.

The premise of the counterargument is relevant.

7. Argument and counterargument

Argument:

P: Because there has been a serious build-up of snow in the last two weeks and the roof is in danger of collapse;

C: Therefore, we have to shovel the snow off the cottage roof this weekend.

Counterargument:

P: But the forecast is for mild weather this week;

C: So we might as well let Mother Nature do the work for us.

The premise of the counterargument is relevant.

9. Report on an argument

P: Smith's cat keeps showing up, without warning, in different parts of the house;

P: For a week it kept disappearing and reappearing somewhere else some time later;

C: Smith's cat is (according to Smith) temporally non-continuous.

11. Report on an argument (Li's)

P: Because the result of not treating people with respect increases tension in our own lives, which can lead to health problems;

P: And because a number of reputable studies confirm this;

C: We should **therefore** treat other people with respect.

13. Argument and counterargument.

Argument:

P: Because I can't swim and will probably drown;

C: Therefore, I shouldn't jump.

Counterargument:

P: Because the fall alone will probably kill you;

C: Therefore, you should jump.

The premise of the counterargument is irrelevant since the issue at hand is not how the Sundance Kid will die but whether he will die.

15. Report on an argument

P: Because Janine thinks thugs can be rehabilitated if we treat them with kid gloves;

C: She **therefore** thinks we should be soft on crime.

Red flag: It is doubtful that Janine used the word "thugs" or the phrases "kid gloves" and "soft on crime".

Exercise 1.4

Bolded passages are relevant.

1. Argument

Systems of education, which are cumbersome beasts at the best of times, rarely work in the best interests of students if this government report is to be believed, and since given the sagacity of this particular government *I am sure it ought to be, I think we can conclude that systems of education* are indeed cumbersome beasts that *rarely work in the best interests of students.*

P: Since if this government report is to be believed systems of education rarely work in the best interests of students;

P: And **since** this report should be believed;

C: We can **therefore** conclude that systems of education rarely work in the best interests of students.

3. Counterargument to the assertion that there are extraterrestrials on the moon waiting to invade Earth:

I have no idea how you can say that. You must be nuts, because when someone claims—as you just have—that there are extraterrestrials on the moon waiting to invade Earth, they are really and truly nuts.

P: Because when someone claims that there are extraterrestrials on the moon waiting to invade Earth they are nuts (and should not be listened to);

P: And **because** you have made that claim;

C: Therefore, you are nuts (and should not be listened to).

5. Argument

*You really must listen closely: **there is no way**—no way at all—**that Smythe could be the murderer.** In the first place he is possibly the least violent person I have ever met—and I have met a lot of people. But there's more, much more: **there is no physical evidence linking Smythe to the crime scene** nor is there any motive that I can think of.* If you really need something more, I can add that **Jones is a much more likely suspect for reasons of motive and opportunity.** *So please spare me your insane theories about Smythe.*

P: Because Smythe is possibly the least violent person I have ever met;

P: Because there is no physical evidence linking Smythe to the crime;

P: Because Jones had a greater motive to commit the murder;

P: Because Jones had more opportunity to commit the murder;

C: Therefore, there is no way that Smythe could be the murderer.

7. Counterargument to the assertion that absolute justification for the values of a culture is possible.

Despite what my colleague has said, there is no absolute justification for the values of any culture. Certainly, I have never seen an irrefutable argument that there is. Because of this we are caught between the Scylla of relativism and the Charybdis of ethnocentrism. So, when it comes to cultural values, you have to be either a relativist or an ethnocentrist.

P: Because there is no absolute justification for the values of any culture;

P: And **because** this means that we are caught between the Scylla of relativism and the Charybdis of ethnocentrism;

C: Therefore, when it comes to cultural values, you have to be either a relativist or an ethnocentrist.

9. Argument

The government's unwillingness to fund abortions to improve the health of mothers in poor countries indicates contempt for the women it says it wants to help. When will the government do the right thing for women instead of playing politics with their lives?

It's not for us to decide whether a woman should choose to have an abortion. That decision belongs to her. Our role should be to ensure that she has reproductive rights and access to real options for her health and that of her children. We have the means and opportunity to make a difference; unfortunately, we have neither the will nor the leadership.

P: Because the government's role is not to decide whether a woman can choose to have an abortion;

P: And because the government's role is to ensure that women have access to real options for her health and that of her children;

C: Therefore, the government's unwillingness to fund abortions to improve the health of mothers in poor countries indicates contempt for the women it says it to want to help.

11. Argument

Every time I see people celebrating the Olympics I want to cry. I am very upset about where this country is headed. How can so many people enjoy something that has devoured billions of dollars that could otherwise have been spent on helping the poor in Vancouver?

A nation is judged by the way it treats its most vulnerable citizens, and it is a disheartening statement about our priorities when the speed of a luger going down a hill generates greater public reaction than human suffering does.

P: Because the evolution of society is measured by how well it treats its most vulnerable citizens;

P: And because we prefer spending money on the Olympics to spending to help those who are vulnerable;

C: It follows that we are not a very evolved society.

Exercise 1.5

1. IP: The more athletic a game is, the better it is.

3. IC: Hard work alone won't make you a professional athlete.

5. IP: And civil rights legislation bans corporal punishment.

7. IP: Atheists and agnostics are open to the aesthetic and emotional qualities of art.

9. IP: The individualistic account of knowledge presupposes the existence of an isolated rational individual who has no biases or preconceptions.

11. IC: Hence, if existing scientific theories bind the scientist too tightly, science will not continue to develop.

Exercise 1.6

1. At most, this is the conclusion of an argument. The principle of charity might prompt us to insert a premise stating that "concussions are serious risks in contact sports" and perhaps a second premise stating that "concussions are on the increase." The problem is that we really are putting words in the author's mouth.

3. Insert the premise "and since cellphones distract drivers."

5. Since "nobody goes there anymore" is nonsense in this context, you could rephrase it as "No one interesting (or no one who counts) goes there anymore."

7. "Shot" is certainly a gross exaggeration; substitute "severely punished."

9. Obviously a feeble attempt at a joke; how about inserting the premise "And since godliness is well beyond our reach"?

11. "It is the twenty-first century, after all" is almost certainly a slightly cryptic way of saying "In modern times, monarchy is outdated."

Something to Think About
Answer: Page 39

My Interpretative Effort
I had to resort to four arguments, not that they work very well. Some "arguments" can't really be saved, no matter how charitable you are.

Argument 1:

P: Because the geometric point in the centre of a sphere is nature's symbol of uniqueness;

IP: And because the symbol of uniqueness is itself unique;

C: Therefore, a centre is always unique.

Argument 2:

P: Because being is unique;

IP: And because what is unique is real;

IC: It follows that being is real.

Argument 3:

P: Because uniqueness is being;

P: And because being is real; (this is the conclusion of A2)

C: Therefore, uniqueness is real.

Argument 4:

P: Because uniqueness is real;

P: And because a centre is unique;

C: Therefore, a centre is real.

So we have "proved" that being, uniqueness, and centres are all real. Essence and truth had to be ignored; they were unsalvageable.

Chapter 2

Exercise 2.1

1. (P1) If the murder was premeditated the murderer would have brought a weapon. (P2) But he did not bring a weapon, (C) so the murder was not premeditated.

3. (C) She should leave you (P1) because you're always working, (P2) you're self-absorbed, and (P3) you're having an affair with someone else.

5. (P1) On average, women live several years longer than men, (C) so women should expect to be widowed (P2) because they tend to marry men who are older than they are.

7. (C) The senator should not have to resign (P1) because the money she took from Mega-Corp was not for work that was related to any of her governmental duties. Besides, (P2) she gave most of the money to charity, (P3) has otherwise led an exemplary life, and (P4) has served her country honourably for many years.

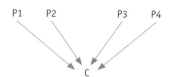

9. (C) Democracy is the only viable system of government (P1) because the only alternatives are either dictatorship or anarchy. (P2) Both of these are terrible systems of government, and (P3) terrible systems are not viable.

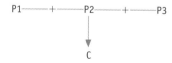

11. (P1) If you have talent it's easier to be motivated, (P2) and if you are motivated you are more likely to succeed, (P3) and that means you will likely have more control over your life, (P4) which in turn means that you will be happier. (C) So talent does contribute to happiness.

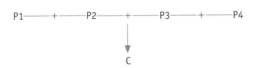

Exercise 2.2

I

1. (C) Money can't necessarily buy happiness (P1) because some things that make people happy—(P2) such as a child's smile—can't be bought.

This can be restated as: (P2) Because a child's smile can't be bought and (P2) because a child's smile makes people happy, (C) therefore money can't necessarily buy happiness.

3. (P1) Judged sports should be excluded from the Olympics (P2) because there is too much subjectivity in them, and (P3) subjectivity undermines the appearance of fairness. (P4) It is crucial that Olympic sports be seen as fair. So (P5) because boxing is a judged sport (C) it should be excluded from the Olympics.

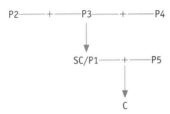

5. (P1) Because space travel over huge distances will not be possible for a very long time, if ever, (P2) and because you and I will not live that long, (P3) we will never get to other solar systems. (P4) Nor are we likely to receive messages from outer space. (C) So it is likely that we'll never know for certain whether there is other intelligent life out there.

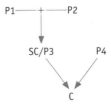

7. (P1) Since if we adopt your standards we'd never wear any makeup, (P2) and since we like wearing makeup, (P3) and since we also like doing what we like, (C) we shouldn't listen to people like you. (P4) And anyway, you're never in favour of anything that's any fun.

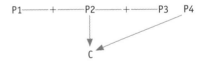

9. (P1) Since the cost of holding the Olympics is prohibitive—(P2) just look at what the last Games cost—(P3) and since they pose real security risks, (C) we should not bid on them. (P4) We also have more urgent priorities that the bid money could be spent on.

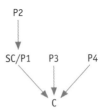

11. (P1) The Olympics are well worth the cost of holding them. (P2) Cities that host them benefit from increased tourism, (P3) athletes get to compete at the highest level, (P4) and for two weeks the world comes together. (C) And if something is worth it, we should go for it.

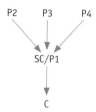

II

3. Example: (P1) Philosophy is not a useful discipline because (P2) it is not directed to practical matters, (P3) as all useful disciplines are. (P4) Add to that the fact that university subjects should be useful and (C) we have to concede that philosophy shouldn't be taught in universities.

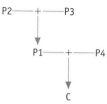

6. Example: (P1) There is lots of credible scientific evidence to support the claim that global warming is taking place. (P2) We can thus expect this warming to lead to more droughts in the west; (P3) we can also expect it to melt the polar ice cap and do irreparable damage to our Arctic territories; further, (P4) we can expect it to cost taxpayers untold billions of dollars. (C) We need to take the threat of global warming seriously.

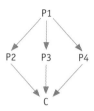

Exercise 2.3

1. (C) Rocks do not make good pets (P1) because they have no emotional lives, (P2) they're heavy to carry, (P3) and they can hurt you if you drop them on your foot. (P4) Besides, a pet should have a heartbeat.

IP: Rocks don't have a heartbeat

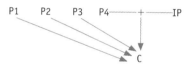

3. (P1) According to quantum physics, a subatomic particle can take two different paths at the same time. (P2) Since we can't really comprehend that sort of idea, (C) there is no point in even thinking about quantum physics.

IP: There is no point in thinking about what we can't understand.

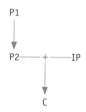

5. (P1) Physics is difficult; (P2) chemistry is difficult; (P3) biology is difficult; (P4) physiology is difficult.

IC: Science is difficult.

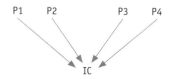

7. (C) Studying philosophy, literature, and art are important aspects of higher education. (P1) Such disciplines make us more rounded people by opening us up to ideas and experiences we would otherwise know nothing about.

IP: Making us more rounded people by opening us up to new ideas and experiences is an important aspect of higher education.

9. (C) People who don't like baseball are barbarians. (P1) Unlike football, which is a warlike game played by gladiators in stadiums, baseball is a peaceful game played in parks. (P2) What's more, baseball is a relaxed game where no clock is ticking; (P3) it just goes on until it's over.

IP: People who don't like peaceful and relaxed games are barbarians.

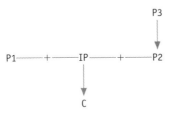

11. (P1) If you go to a professional basketball game you will pay several hundred dollars for a decent ticket for the privilege of being bombarded by extremely loud music even when the play is on. (C) It's not worth going.

IP: It is not worth paying several hundred dollars to be bombarded by extremely loud music.

13. (P1) She has texted me every day, (P2) she has asked me for help with her essay, (P3) she has offered me rides home, (P4) and she has asked me out for coffee.

IC: She likes me? She is interested in me? There seems to be an implicit conclusion, but be careful not to read too much into this argument.

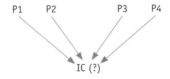

Exercise 2.4

1. (P1) All the studies done on this topic clearly state that there is absolutely no evidence that prayer has any observable effect. (P2) Maybe prayer has an effect on God but (P3) in that case God doesn't seem inclined to do anything about it. (C) So, the war in Libya is not going to be changed in any way by appeals to God.

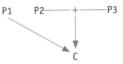

3. (C) Far from helping the economy, the stimulus package may actually undermine it (P1) because a stimulus package makes people believe that they are always entitled to government aid, (P2) and this will sap their initiative. (P3) In addition, because those who were most responsible for the recession are the most likely to be rewarded by bank bailouts and forgiveness of bad mortgages, (P4) bad habits will be encouraged, (P5) which will further undermine the economy. (P6) Finally, the government will have to run a deficit, (P7) because there is no way it can meet these obligations and balance its budget.

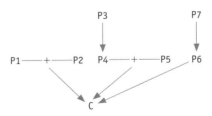

5. (P1) The skeptic can doubt everything except that he doubts, (P2) because to doubt he doubts is also to doubt. (P3) And since to doubt is to think, (P4) neither can the skeptic doubt that he thinks. (C) This means that the skeptic cannot doubt that he exists.

IP: And since to think is to exist . . .

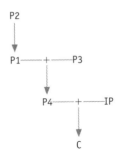

7. (P1) People say that if evolution is true then our lives have no meaning, but that's not so (P2) because all evolution suggests is that there is no preordained purpose to our lives, and (P3) a lack of preordained purpose does not indicate a lack of meaning (P4) because, even without preordained meaning, we can decide what makes our lives meaningful. (C) So people should stop going on about how evolution destroys meaning.

P1 can be rewritten as "It's not true that evolution robs our lives of meaning."

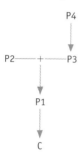

You could add an IP to go with P1: "People should stop saying what is not true," though it hardly seems necessary.

9. (P1) If there really are magical powers then our trust in the laws of nature is misplaced, and (P2) since experience shows us that misplaced trust is foolhardy, (P3) if there are magical powers our trust in science is foolhardy. (P4) But since there are no magical powers—(P5) because every claim that someone possesses them has been discredited by reputable tests—(C) there is no reason to mistrust science.

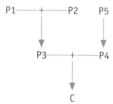

11. (C) Evolution is not a theory in crisis. (P1) It is not teetering on the verge of collapse. (P2) It has not failed as a scientific theory. (P3) There is evidence for evolution, gobs and gobs of it. (P4) It is not

just speculation or a faith choice or an assumption or a religion. (P5) It is a productive framework for lots of biological research, and (P6) it has amazing explanatory power. (P7) There is no conspiracy to hide the truth about the failure of evolution.

Note: Because of the absence of premise indicators, there may be more than one defensible diagram of this argument.

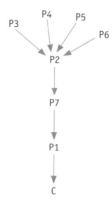

***13.** The philosopher of science T.S. Kuhn argued as follows: (C) when there are competing scientific theories the question of which is the better theory cannot be settled by reference to the standards of either theory, (P1) since it is precisely those standards that are being questioned. (P2) Hence any argument that does refer to one of these sets of standards will necessarily be circular, (P3) because it will amount to claiming that the theory is true because it is true.

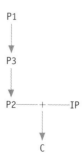

It may help to restate this argument as follows:

(P1) Since when comparing two theories it is the standards of the theories that are being questioned,

(P3) justifying a theory by its own standards will amount to saying it's true because it's true. (P2) Hence, any argument that does so will be circular and (**IP**) since circular arguments are bad arguments, (C) therefore the question of which is the better theory cannot be settled by reference to the standards of either theory.

15. (C) My English teacher argues that going to see Shakespeare performed on the stage is a far better use of my time than playing video games, but she's wrong. (P1) After all, pleasure is a legitimate pursuit, (P2) and since I get much more pleasure out of video games than I do out of Shakespeare, (P3) I should go with the games. (P4) Moreover, times change and standards change with it. (P5) Since I'm a child of my times and the teacher is a child of her times (P6) her standards are different than mine, (P7) but I don't think they are necessarily better.

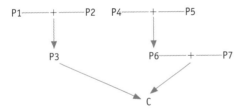

Exercise 2.5

1. There's a lot of repetition here. All the argument amounts to it this:

P1: Because when people want something they will try to get it;

C: Therefore, when they don't try to get something they don't really want it, even if they say they do.

3.

IP: Because the legislation that protects Canadian music industry reduces competition;

P1: And because more competition would increase choice;

P2: And because as a comparison of prices in New York and Toronto shows;

P3: Under the legislation Canadians pay more than Americans for music by Canadian artists;

C: Rebecca is therefore wrong to defend the legislation.

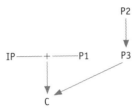

5.

P1: Because hockey is played on skates;

P2: It is faster than soccer;

P3: And because hockey has more body contact;

P4: It is more physical than soccer;

P5: It follows that hockey is more of a challenge and a greater test of a player's courage than soccer is;

IP: And because these qualities make a sport more interesting;

C: Hockey is more interesting than soccer.

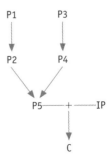

7. Restate: (C) After a lifetime of listening to the big government/small government "debate," it may be time to redefine the issue. (P1) As much as anything, that is because neither party produces a smaller government. (P2) Even though one side supports a stronger national safety net and the other supports a bigger military, (P3) the results in terms of budget size and government employees remain about the same. (P4) Moreover, both sides want reductions in the other side's agenda. (P5) And both sides are reluctant to tell voters they have to pay for what they want.

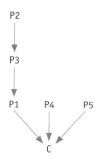

9. Restate: (P1) The United States is so large that no matter what you do, it's often going to feel like it's a meaningless drop in the ocean. (P2) The legislative process is so slow that people become disconnected from it. (P3) So people feel they cannot make a difference. (C) But individuals, and especially small groups of people, really can make a difference. (P4) This battle over health care reform is one time when they did. (P5) [W]hole bunches of small groups of people, in states and Congressional districts across the nation, turned a handful of Senate races and a dozen or two House races around and, (P6) 16 or so months later, their work is . . . most likely going to change the country.

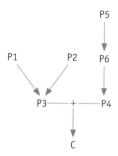

11. Restate: (SC) Universities have an obligation to protect the free exchange of ideas on campus, no matter how offended some people may be by the expression of these ideas. (P1) Yesterday, it was Ann Coulter who was silenced, and it will be someone else tomorrow. (P2) Even though unpopular ideas will necessarily offend many people, the free exchange of ideas is essential to the democratic process.

Note the order of the premises below, with more restatement:

P2: Because the free exchange of ideas, even unpopular ones, is essential to the process of democracy;

IP: And because universities have an obligation to respect the democratic process;

SC: Therefore, universities have an obligation to protect the free exchange of ideas on campus no matter how offended some people are by their expression.

P1: And because to silence one person threatens the democratic process;

IC: Ann Coulter should have been allowed to speak.

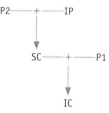

13. Restate: (IC) The NCAA basketball tournament is fine as it is. (P1) Everyone can dream, whether they are universities with undergraduate enrolments of 60,000 or private colleges with enrolments of 1500. (P2) The tournament is the ultimate meritocracy. (P3) The best players play, and the best teams advance. (P4) Success is earned.

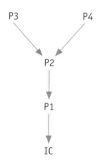

Note that the comment about expanding the tournament to 128 teams has been omitted. It is, strictly speaking, irrelevant to the argument.

Chapter 3

Exercise 3.1

1. *Tu quoque*

3. Poisoning the well

5. Appeal to ridicule

7. No fallacy: this may be perfectly true

9. Red herring

11. *Ad hominem*

13. Appeal to pity

15. Appeal to flattery

17. No fallacy

Exercise 3.2

1. Appeal to novelty and bandwagon

3. No fallacy

5. Appeal to tradition

7. Appeal to novelty

9. Appeal to popularity and tradition

11. Bandwagon

13. Misleading vividness

15. No fallacy

Exercise 3.3

I

1. "Tribal" is a loaded word often used to denigrate the disputes in question as local and unimportant.

3. This may simply be a blunt but accurate description.

5. In the context of this sentence, "not the most willing accomplice" sounds like a euphemism for "innocent," or at least "not as guilty as others." The speaker seems to have used it because he wants her punished. In short, he has softened what is for him the harsh truth—that she is not really to blame.

7. The descriptions of Chelsea players have negative connotations whereas those of Manchester United players have positive connotations. The language is loaded.

9. "Shortfall" is a term in general use, but it is also a euphemism for deficit. It makes the situation seem less serious.

11. "Downturn" may be a euphemism for recession; it may minimize what is happening.

13. The Internet is not literally "organic," but the term generally connotes something positive—natural.

15. In many fan magazines, "exploit" operates as a code word for "has done something bad or embarrassing." It is a loaded word.

II

1. As this is a lawyer defending a client, "immature" would have the more appropriate connotation. An immature person cannot help himself. It's a negative connotation, but that is probably what the lawyer needs here.

3. "Ambled" fits nicely with "calm," but if you were trying to describe someone who is in charge of things "walk" would be better since "ambled" carries the negative connotation of looseness, almost idleness.

5. "Woman of faith" has a generally positive connotation of someone with deep religious beliefs; "Baptist" simply denotes a religious sect, though like most words someone could use it as a coded word, perhaps for strict and unbending.

7. If the aggrieved child is complaining, and she seems to be, to make her point, she should say "miser." If she is merely reporting a fact "frugal people" would be the better choice.

9. Since the speaker seems to be trying to minimize his action, he should say that he "spoke forcefully." It is in this case a euphemism for "shouted."

11. "Undersized" is a euphemism that avoids the bluntness of "short," and the speaker is obviously trying to persuade her audience of this player's usefulness.

III

1. My opponent tends to lie.

3. Innocent people were killed.

5. She's not very bright.

7. People are losing their jobs.

9. We killed the terrorist.

11. Some people are poor.

Exercise 3.4

1. Cultural bias: the queen seemed unaware that people might have nothing to eat.

3. Stereotype

5. In-group bias

7. No bias: dyslexic children commonly do experience trouble learning to read.

9. This depends on who is speaking; if it is someone from a "first-tier" university it could be an in-group bias.

11. Stereotype

13. In-group bias: us against the world

15. Cultural bias

Exercise 3.5

1. Anchoring bias

3. This could be true, but it looks like a self-serving bias.

5. Misleading vividness fallacy

7. Bandwagon fallacy and anchoring bias

9. Most of the time if the team tries to score a touchdown from this position they will succeed, so this is an example of the loss aversion bias. However, coaches may understand this and argue that in this case it is rational.

11. No bias: it's a colourful exaggerated metaphor, but that is *potentially* what cigarettes are.

13. Anchoring bias: the rise in the bear population is not the only consideration to be taken into account. Other concerns include what the bears' food supply is like, whether they are coming into contact with humans more often, and so on.

15. No bias: the polls are probably correct.

17. Gambler's fallacy

Something to Think About Answers

Page 95

1. Antonin Dvorak was a Czech composer; the other three are/were Czech writers, although technically Kafka's nationality was Austro-Hungarian.

2. All are nineteenth-century English novelists, but (Charles) Dickens is the only male. (Note that *George* Eliot was a woman, whose real name was Mary Anne Evans.)

3. Lady Gaga is the only one who is not a hip-hop artist. She is also the only woman, but you get less credit for that answer.

4. Pelé was a Brazilian footballer; the others are Argentineans. However, Messi is the only active player, so take your choice.

5. These are all films. Martin Scorsese directed all of them but *Psycho*, which was directed by Alfred Hitchcock.

Page 103

Since the answer is 40,320, the estimates are wildly off. The problem is that people do not have time to multiply the whole list, so they multiply two or three numbers—whatever they can do in five seconds—and then estimate based on that figure. If you begin at the left the number you get after multiplying two or three numbers will be lower than if you begin at the right. So the estimates are much lower in the first case than in the second, but in neither case do the average estimates approach the correct answer.

Chapter 4

Exercise 4.1

1. This may or may not be a violation of Occam's razor. If someone is on foot, it is obviously simpler to walk one block north and one block east. But perhaps these are instructions to someone driving through a system of one-way streets, in which case it may be the most direct path. Remember, simplicity is contextual.

3. This seems to raise the issue of failing to save the phenomena. However, if the scientists have no choice but to leave out some data then they are saving as much of it as possible. Like simplicity, thoroughness is contextual.

5. Occam's razor: Adding might be the simplest way to add up a few numbers, but for a long sequence of numbers the formula

$$\frac{N^2 + N}{2}$$

will yield the answer more quickly. How quickly could you add up 150 numbers or enter them into a calculator?

7. Save the phenomena: This argument contends that, with respect to complex organs like the eye, evolution cannot save the phenomena because it cannot explain how such organs could develop piecemeal over time. Scientists do not take this argument seriously, but they have had to develop an explanation for why they do not. In other words, they have to show how the theory of evolution saves the phenomena with respect to complex organs like the eye.

9. The author is accusing Pinker of failing to save the phenomena. Her point is that the concepts he rejects so quickly are the products of longstanding, serious philosophic traditions. He has failed to give them sufficient (i.e., thorough) consideration.

11. Occam's razor: The fact that the person making this argument does not like pension plans is irrelevant. It is an unnecessary addition to the argument and therefore a needless complication of it. Irrelevant reasons are a kind of excess. The rest of the argument does not violate either guide.

Exercise 4.2

I

1. Law of the excluded middle: This is the fallacy of false dichotomy. The writer presents the matter as if there were only two options: eradicate starvation or do nothing at all. The third, or middle, option is to try to do something about solving the problem even if you cannot do everything.

3. Law of non-contradiction: This is a version of the Liar's Paradox. If sentence i is true then sentence ii is true, which means that sentence i is false. But if sentence i is false then sentence ii is false, which means that sentence i is true. Of course, these are empty sentences so it's hard to see how they can be true or false.

5. No law has been broken. If the statement is true then all Canadians tell the truth; if it is false then some Canadians lie, including the author of this statement.

7. Law of identity: While the conclusion could be true, there is an equivocation on "nothing." In its first appearance it means "not so great," but in its second usage it means "absolutely the best."

9. Law of non-contradiction: We have a theory of ethics that leads to the conclusion that there can be no theories of ethics. The argument is a *reductio ad absurdum*.

11. Law of non-contradiction: But it's a great line that reminds us that language is sometimes the better for ignoring logic. However, without a grasp of the law of non-contradiction you won't see the joke. See Chapter 1, exercise 1.6, question 5.

13. Law of identity: This statement equivocates on "energy." Its first usage refers to energy as the correlate of matter; the second usage refers to fuel.

15. Law of the excluded middle: This is a false dichotomy because on the first day of class there may be students who will drop the course and therefore will neither pass nor fail.

17. Law of identity and law of excluded middle: Since some apples are a mixture of red and green we need to be more precise: all apples either have at least *some* red or they do not.

II

1. A posteriori

3. A priori

5. This one can generate arguments, but I would contend that you only know a posteriori that these terms are equivalent. For example, does $(26 \times 52) = (1356 - 8)$? You probably have to work it out.

7. A posteriori, although the chance that there will be is more than 99 per cent.

9. This is the Goldbach conjecture, and if it can be known at all it will be known a priori. Since there is an infinite number of numbers they cannot all be checked, so there can be no a posteriori proof, which means that any proof would have to be a priori. (There is much disagreement about this.)

11. A priori: Given the definition of sons you know a priori that if I have sons this is false.

13. It's an a priori assumption of Einstein's science, but who knows? After the big bang the universe apparently expanded faster than the speed of light.

15. A posteriori: This is not a tautology. She could be exactly my age.

Exercise 4.3

I

1. Invalid

3. Valid

5. Invalid

7. Invalid

9. Valid

II

1. Sound, although if we were really strict we could say 'indeterminate' because humans keep being born, so the evidence is incomplete.

3. Unsound: This is not how the American electoral system works; Gore got more votes than Bush and still lost the election.

5. Indeterminate: The implicit premise is that "the sun will continue to do what it has done in the past" and this is, strictly speaking, indeterminate since there is no way to test the truth of a claim about an indefinite future.

7. Sound

9. Indeterminate: The implicit premise is something like "because humans will always live on Earth and not become extinct" and that would make the argument valid. However, there is no way to know whether the premises are true.

Something to Think About Answers

Page 130

1. Employ the law of the excluded middle and divide the 10,000 slips of paper in half, reminding yourself of the apparently trivial tautological truth that the highest sum is either in the first 5000 or the second 5000 slips. The same is true of the second highest sum. This tells you that there are four possible distributions of their locations. The following chart—where "1" stands for the highest sum and "2" for the second highest—shows what they are:

DISTRIBUTION	FIRST 5000 SLIPS	SECOND 5000 SLIPS
Distribution 1	1	2
Distribution 2	2	1
Distribution 3	1,2	
Distribution 4		1,2

Since each of these distributions is equally probable, each has a 25 per cent probability. Bet on distribution 2. Turn over all of the first 5000 slips of paper and take note of the highest sum of money you find there. Then go through the second 5000 slips of paper until you get a higher sum. This gives you a 25 per cent chance of finding the highest sum of money. Of course, if either the first or third distribution is the actual one, you will lose. However, if the fourth distribution is the actual one, you still have a chance because the highest sum is in the second 5000 numbers. Here, it gets complicated, but to begin with, there is a 50-50 chance that the third highest number is among the first 5000. If it is, you will, with this method, consider it the second highest sum and select the first higher sum you run across in the second 5000. That will be either the highest or second highest sum, whichever comes first. You need it to be the highest sum, and there is a 50-50 chance that it will be.

So do the math: there is a 25 per cent probability of the fourth distribution, a 50 per cent chance within it that the third highest sum is among the first 5000 numbers and a 50 per cent chance that the highest sum will show up before the second highest sum in the second 5000 sums. This gives us a $\frac{1}{4} \times \frac{1}{2} \times \frac{1}{2} = 1/16$ (or 6.25 per cent) chance. Add this to 25 per cent and you arrive at 31.25 per cent. But this is not the end: if the third highest sum is in the second 5000 and the fourth highest sum in the first 5000, there is still a chance of winning, and so on with the fifth, sixth, etc. numbers. These small sums keep adding up so the fourth distribution approaches, but never quite arrives at, a 1/8 or 12.5 per cent extra chance of getting the highest sum. Add 12.5 per cent to 25 per cent and that's your answer. If you employ the strategy of assuming the second distribution your chances of winning edge up to (but never quite arrive at) 3/8, or 37.5 per cent, much higher than an intuitive guess of 1/10,000.

2. This is a law of identity issue. The question is, "How do we define knowledge?" If we define it to mean that which we are absolutely certain of, then the only person who can know he has a headache is Timothy, since no one else can be absolutely certain he is not lying. But if we assume that knowledge comes from experience, then coming to know something entails trying to overcome

doubt as much as you can. To do so, you conduct experiments, run tests, collect evidence and, if the results strongly suggest a certain conclusion, you treat that conclusion as knowledge.

Now with respect to Timothy's headache, he has no doubt about having it. (Will he say, "I think I have a headache"?) So if we define knowledge according to the experiential model of overcoming doubt, Timothy cannot claim to *know* he has a headache because his so-called "knowledge" is immune to doubt. But because Tina can doubt his claim, she needs to consult the evidence—dilated pupils, sensitivity to light and sound, and so on—to decide whether she is at least reasonably certain Timothy is telling the truth. She has to go through the process of *acquiring* knowledge by overcoming doubt. Having done so, she can claim to know Timothy has a headache (or is faking), whereas a similar claim by him is redundant—completely unnecessary. He doesn't say, "I know I have a headache"; he just says "I have a headache." He doesn't make a knowledge claim. "Knowledge" is an abstract word, and you need to make certain what you mean by it—law of identity and all that—before employing it in an argument. So does Timothy know he has a headache or does Tina, or do they both know? You decide.

Page 136
It depends on what premises you accept as true. If you accept as true the premise that humans are mortal, then you have to conclude that this person is not human. If, on the other hand, you accept as true the premise that this person is human, then you have to conclude that not all humans are mortal.

Chapter 5

Exercise 5.1

I

1. RC: Someone who utters this sentence probably does not intend it to be understood empirically but poetically. Still, given a clear enough definition of "hurt" it would be an ES and therefore S.

3. S, NS

5. S, ES: You could test it.

7. S, ES

9. U: It's paradoxical. If the rule is true there is no exception to it, but if there is an exception it is false.

11. U: This is nonsense, courtesy of Lewis Carroll's poem "Jabberwocky." Yet it wonderfully appears to be saying something empirical. One feels that all we need are some definitions.

13. S, NS: To be empirical it would have to read, "It is against the law to exceed the speed limit."

15. S, E

II

1. I: Strictly speaking, it is impossible to say whether all humans make mistakes even though all the evidence suggests that they do.

3. U: Okapis can't fly.

5. I: The premises are normative statements.

7. S

9. U: Canada doesn't practise capital punishment.

11. S

Exercise 5.2

1. P = it is too cold to play golf; Q = it is too expensive to play golf

    (P ∨ Q)

3. P = it is Monday; ~P = it is not Monday. This is a tautology: the law of the excluded middle.

    (P ∨ ~P)

5. P = it rains tomorrow; Q = I will go shopping; R = I will get some work done at home

    (P → (~Q & R))

7. P = I can go home; I can stay away = I can not go home = ~P

    ~(P & ~P) (This is the law of non-contradiction.)

9. P = I am going home right now; Q = I return within the hour; R = I will text you

    (P & (~Q → R)) (Note that Q is negated and the order of precedence has been set aside.)

11. P = this procedure will work; Q = we begin right away; R = we don't stop until it is absolutely finished = we go on until it is absolutely finished.

    (P ↔ Q) & R)

13. P = you read this story; Q = you will be moved by this story

    ~(P → Q)

15. P = I am sympathetic to your cause; Q = I am emotionally distant from all your concerns

    ~(~P & Q)

17. P = It's Thursday; Q = I get paid; R = I will go to the movies

    You have to try to choose the most natural reading here. I suggest:

    P → (Q → R)

Exercise 5.3

I

1. P = unemployment rates decline; Q = we will enter a recession

    {[(P ∨ Q) & (~P)] → (Q)}
    DS

3. P = I get paid; Q = I am going out to celebrate; R = it is Thursday

    {[(P → Q) & (R → P)] → (R → Q)}
    CS

5. P = I had passed this exam; Q = I would have graduated

    {[(P → Q) & (~P)] → (~Q)}
    DA (Invalid)

***7.** P = we want to revise the manuscript; Q = we wait until Monday

    {[(Q → ~P) & (P)] → (~Q)}
    MT

9. P = something is difficult; Q = something (math) is abstract

{[[(Q → P) & (P)] → (Q)}
AC (Invalid)

Note: The hypothetical premise reads "If something is difficult then it is abstract," but you can apply this as "If math is abstract then it is difficult" and work with only two variables.

11. P = someone is arrogant; Q = someone is self-absorbed; R = someone tends to megalomania; S = someone is psychotic

{[(P → Q) & (Q → R) & (R → S)] → (P → S)}

Note: The phrase, "which is a kind of psychosis" constitutes a third premise that, rendered formally, would read "If someone tends to megalomania then they are psychotic." The conclusion would then read "If someone is arrogant then they are psychotic."

13. P = wishes came true; Q = I'd be rich

{[[(P → Q) & (Q)] → (P)}
AC (Invalid)

15. P = I stay home and work tomorrow; Q = I get way behind.

{[[(P ∨ Q) & (~Q)] → (P)}
DS

Note that "I can't go out tomorrow" in the conclusion is equivalent to "I have to stay home and work tomorrow."

17. P = something (jazz) is free form; Q = something (jazz) is hard to understand

{[[P → Q & (P)] → (Q)}
MP

II

1. MP

3. DA

5. AC

7. MT

III

1. P = we cancel the game; Q = we play in these conditions

{[[(P ∨ Q) & (~Q)] → (P)}

3. P = people go on tweeting obsessively; Q = civilization will come to an end; R = all is well with the world

{[~(P → Q) & (~Q → R)] → (P → R)}

5. P = Jamal will present that material; Q = Ai Li will present that material; R = Jamal will chair the meeting

{[[(P ∨ Q) & (P → ~R)] → (Q ∨ ~R)}

7. P = James is happy; Q = Anna is happy; R = Sonia is happy

{[[(~P & Q) & ~(R & ~P)] → (R → ~Q)}

9. P = I will pass this course; Q = hell freezes over; R = global warming slows down

{[[(P ↔ Q) & (Q ↔ R)] → ~(~R & P)}

Exercise 5.4

I

1. If (P) we can move then (Q) there is another apartment in the neighbourhood, (Q) but (~P) right now there is not an apartment available in the neighbourhood so (~P) we can't consider moving.

{[[(P → Q) & (~Q)] → (~P)}
MT

3. If (P) I can really enjoy life then (Q) I'm healthy, and since (~Q) I'm not healthy, *therefore* (~P) I can't enjoy life.

{[[(P → Q) & (~Q)] → (~P)}
MT

5. If (P) students forget a lot of what they have learned from one semester to the next *then* (Q) the breaks between semesters are too long, and (P) students do forget a lot of what they have learned from one semester to the next, so (Q) the breaks between semesters are too long.

{[[(P → Q) & (P)] → (Q)}
MP

7. If (~P) we don't have the right tools then (~Q) we can't fix the flux capacitor and if (R) we can get back to the future then (Q) we can fix the flux capacitor. So, only if (P) we have the right tools (R) can we get back to the future.

{[(~P → ~Q) & (R → Q)] → (R → P)}
But: (~P → ~Q) is the transposition of (Q → P)
So: {[(Q → P) & (R → Q)] → (R → P)}
CS

9. If (P) love is a good thing then (Q) love hurts, and (P) love is a good thing, (Q) so love hurts.

{[(P → Q) & (P)] → (Q)}
MP

11. If (~P) cyclists in the Tour de France don't take drugs then (~Q) they can't win the race and (Q) they all want to win the race, therefore (P) they should take drugs.

{[(~P → ~Q) & (Q)] → (P)}
MT

13. If (P) people are treated disrespectfully then (Q) people become angry and (~P) she has not been treated disrespectfully, therefore (~Q) she's not angry.

{[(P → Q) & (~P)] → (~Q)}
DA

II

1. If we do not have a picnic then it is too hot.

3. (P → Q)

5. If we did not come second then we won this game.

7. If we make the playoffs then we won this game.

Exercise 5.5

1. (Q) I knew I'd be late *if* (P) I did*n't* hurry, *but* I did hurry *so* I wasn't late.

{[(~P → Q) & (P)] → (~Q)}
DA

3. *If* (P) the time it takes Mercury to rotate around its axis is the same as the time it takes to revolve around the sun, (Q) it will always present the same side to the sun. *If* that is so,

then that will be the only side we can see. Thus, *if* Mercury's period of rotation equals its period of revolution, we will only ever see one side of it.

{[(P → Q) & (Q → R)] → (P → R)}
CS

5. (P) Current will *not* flow *unless* the circuit is broken, *and* as this circuit is broken the current is flowing. Therefore, P = current will flow; Q = the circuit is broken

Not . . . unless = iff
{[(P ↔ Q) & (Q)] → (P)}
The first premise is clearly false, but the argument is valid.
N

7. *Either* (P) I am going to have the life I wanted *or* (Q) I am going to be horribly disappointed *because either* (R) I will succeed as a dancer *or* I will not. *If* I succeed I'll have the life I want, *and if* I don't succeed, I will be horribly disappointed

{[(R ∨ ~R) & (R → P) & (~R → Q)] → (P ∨ Q)}
N

9. *One cannot both* (P) engage in market specula-tion *and* (Q) pursue a full-time job *because if* (P) you engage in market speculation *then* (R) that re-quires enormous attention to detail *and if* (Q) you have a full-time job *then* (R) you cannot pay such attention.

{[(P → R) & (Q → ~R)] → ~(P & Q)}
N

11. *If* (P) my theory is correct *then* (Q) Wilson's theory is wrong *and* (R) so is Petrocelli's, which means that (S) Wong's conjecture has serious flaws. *But since* I'm certain that Wong's conjecture is faultless, my theory is false.

{[(P → (Q & R)) & ((Q & R) → S) & (~S)] → (~P)}
N

13. *Either* (P) we work overtime tonight *or* (Q) we work tomorrow, *and since* we don't want to work tomorrow we need to work overtime tonight.

[(P ∨ Q) & (~Q)] → (P)}
DS

15. *Only if* (P) we negotiate secretly (Q) will the treaty be signed, *because if* (~P) we negotiate openly (R) the media will report every detail, *and if* they do that (S) protesters will take to the streets, and if that happens we will never get a signed treaty.

$$\{[(\sim P \rightarrow R) \,\&\, (R \rightarrow S) \,\&\, (S \rightarrow \sim Q] \rightarrow (Q \rightarrow P)\}$$
N

Something to Think About Answers

Page 146

The problem is that this is a paradox and, as you know, paradoxes won't stand still. By the law of the excluded middle, the barber—a male citizen of Seville—either shaves himself or he does not. If he *does not* shave himself then, by rule, he *does* shave himself (because he shaves all the men who do not shave themselves). But if he *does* shave himself then, by rule, he *does not* shave himself. So if he does, he doesn't and if he doesn't, he does. Clearly, no such man can exist who fits this description. Because the barber is the standard used to divide self-shavers from non-self-shavers (i.e., you are either shaved by the barber or you are not, and if you are not you shave yourself), he cannot be part of either group. He may be a man of Seville, but if we are to avoid a paradox he cannot be subject to the rule. If he is, the paradox holds and the poor barber disappears in a puff of logic.

Page 163

Let A = humans, B = mortal, and C = prone to error. The syllogism would then read "All humans are mortal and all mortals are prone to error, so all humans are prone to error." This could be translated into sentential logic as "If (P) you are human then (Q) you are mortal, and if you are mortal then (R) you are prone to error. So, (P) if you are human then (R) you are prone to error." Symbolized: $\{[(P \rightarrow Q) \,\&\, (Q \rightarrow R)] \rightarrow (P \rightarrow R)\}$. It's a **CS**.

Page 174

S1 ("In a valid argument, if the premises are true then necessarily so is the conclusion") indicates the relation that constitutes validity. It means that if the premises are true then the truth of the conclusion follows necessarily. **S2** ("If the premises are true then the conclusion is necessarily true as well") makes a very different claim, this time about truth. It claims that the conclusion could not, under any circumstances, be false.

But validity is not proof of truth! In fact, the only sentences that are necessarily true are tautologies. All the other sentences we use in arguments have two possible truth values, which is to say that they could be true or false irrespective of the validity of the argument. They are *contingently* true or false, which means that you need evidence to determine which they are. For example, the sentence "Mammals are warm-blooded" is contingently true, but "Mammals are either warm-blooded or they are not" is necessarily true. Think of Ms. ET as your litmus test: if she accepts a statement as true without asking for evidence, then it is necessarily true; if she asks for evidence then it is contingently true. Since she knows nothing about the world, she will treat all empirical claims and normative statements as only contingently true. She will only accept tautologies as necessarily true and contradictory claims like "There is an object that is simultaneously movable and immovable" as necessarily false.

Chapter 6

Exercise 6.1

I

1. T	**9.** T	**17.** T
3. F	**11.** T	**19.** T
5. T	**13.** T	**21.** F
7. T	**15.** F	

II

You don't know if any of them are true. Questions 1, 2, 3, 6, and 7 are counterfactual conditionals, so we can't really assess their truth or falsity. Questions 4, 5, 8, and 9 are material implications, but you don't know the truth values of the individual statements.

Exercise 6.2

I

1. Not equivalent

3. Not equivalent

5. Not equivalent

7. Not equivalent

9. Equivalent

11. Equivalent

13. Equivalent: the antecedents—(~(P & Q) and (~P ∨ ~Q))—are equivalent by De Morgan's Rule.

15. Not equivalent

17. Equivalent by the principle of commutation, (~ ~Q ∨ ~P) = (~P ∨ ~ ~Q). Remove the double negation on Q and you have material implication.

19. Not equivalent

21. Equivalent: material implication

II

1. {[(~P ∨ Q) & (P)] → (Q)}: **MI** = {[(P → Q) & (P)] → (Q)} = **MP**

3. {[~(P & Q) & (Q)]} → (~P)}: **DM** = {[(~P ∨ ~Q) & (Q)] → (~P)} = **DS**

5. {[~(P & Q) & (~R ∨ Q)] → ~(R & P)}

First premise: By **DM** ~(P & Q) = (~P ∨ ~Q); by **MI** (~P ∨ ~Q) = (P → ~Q); by **transposition** (P → ~Q) = (Q → ~P)

Second premise: By **MI** (~R ∨ Q) = (R → Q)

Conclusion: Like first premise: (R → ~P)

{(R → Q) & (Q → ~P)] → (R → ~P)} = **CS**

7. {[(~(P & Q) & ~(~P & ~Q)) & (P)] → (Q)}
(~(P & Q) & ~(~P & ~Q)) = (P ⊻ Q)
{[(P ⊻ Q) & (P)] → (Q)} is invalid.

Exercise 6.3

1. P = We fix the flux capacitor; Q = We retain the integrity of the vehicle; R = We are forever marooned in the past.

P	Q	R	{[~(P & Q) & (~P → R)] → (Q → R)}
T	T	T	T
T	T	F	F F T T F
T	F	T	T
T	F	F	T
F	T	T	T
F	T	F	T F F T F
F	F	T	T
F	F	F	T

The conclusion is a hypothetical, which can be false iff Q = T and R = F. Since the argument can be invalid only if it has a false conclusion (and true premises), you need only check the two cases where Q = T and R = F. In both cases, one of the premises is false, which means that the argument is valid.

3. P = We should invest in this stock; Q = This stock goes up by Wednesday; R = We know the takeover will happen.

P	Q	R	{[(Q → R) & (R ∨ ~P)] → (Q → P)}
T	T	T	T
T	T	F	T
T	F	T	T
T	F	F	T
F	T	T	T T T F F
F	T	F	F F T T F
F	F	T	T
F	F	F	T

Invalid

5. P = Emily is intelligent; Q = Emily is articulate.

P	Q	(P → Q)	&	(Q)	→	(P)
T	T				T	
T	F				T	
F	T	T	T	T	F	F
F	F	T	F	F	T	T

Invalid (fallacy of affirming the consequent)

7. P = Your grades bother you; Q = You will work harder; R = You spend all your time playing video games.

P	Q	R	(P → Q)	&	(R → ~Q)	&	(R)	→	(~P)
T	T	T	T	F	F	T	T	T	F
T	T	F	T	T	T	F	F	T	F
T	F	T	F	F	F	T	T	T	F
T	F	F	F	F	T	F	F	T	F
F	T	T						T	
F	T	F						T	
F	F	T						T	
F	F	F						T	

Valid

9. P = Things have improved; Q = The war was a mistake; R = We will bring the troops home.

P	Q	R	(P ∨ Q)	&	(Q → R)	→	(~R → P)
T	T	T				T	
T	T	F				T	
T	F	T				T	
T	F	F				T	
F	T	T				T	
F	T	F	T	F	F	T	F
F	F	T				T	
F	F	F	F	F	T	T	F

Valid

11. P = You can trust someone; Q = She knows logic.

P	Q	(P ↔ Q)	&	(~Q)	→	(~P)
T	T	T	F	F	T	F
T	F	F	F	T	T	F
F	T				T	
F	T				T	

Valid

13. P = Loss is difficult to deal with; Q = Loss tears at the fabric of the human spirit.

P	Q	(Q → P)	&	(Q)	→	(P)
T	T				T	
T	F				T	
F	T	F	F	T	T	F
F	F	T	F	F	T	F

Valid (**MP**)

15. P = We can succeed; Q = We try; R = We ask too little of ourselves.

P	Q	R	(~Q → ~P)	&	(~Q → R)	→	(P ∨ R)
T	T	T				T	
T	T	F				T	
T	F	T				T	
T	F	F				T	
F	T	T				T	
F	T	F	T	T	T	F	F
F	F	T				T	
F	F	F	T	F	F	T	F

Invalid

17. P = I am dreaming.

P	(P ⊻ ~P)	&	(~P)	→	(~ ~P)
T	T	F	F	T	T
F	T	T	T	F	F

Invalid

Exercise 6.4

1. {[(~P → ~Q) & (Q)] → (P)}

    T [T]   T   F   [F]   [T]   F

Valid: MT

3. {[(~P ∨ Q) & (R → ~Q)] → ~(P & R)}

  F [T] T   F   T   [F]   F   [T]   T F T

Valid

5. {[(P ↔ (Q ∨ R)) & (~R)] → (P → Q)}

  T [T]   F (T) T   F   [F]   [T]   T [F] F

Valid

7. {[(R → (S ∨ P)) & (P ↔ Q) & (~S)] → ~(R & ~Q)}

  T [T] T T F   T   F [T] F   F   [F]   [T]   T F T

Valid

9. {[(~P ∨ Q) & (~Q ↔ R) & (R ∨ S) & (~S)] → (P ∨ ~R)}

  F [T] T T F   [T] F T F [T] T F   [F]   [T] T [F] T

  T [T] F T T   [T] T T T [T] F T   [T]   [F] F [F] F

Invalid

11.

{[(P ↔ Q) & (Q ∨ R) & (~R ∨ S) & (T → ~S) & (T & U)] → (P → ~U)}

T [T] T T T T [T] F T T T [T] F T T [T] T T T [T] T [F] T F F

Invalid: in this example, after you have entered the values for P and U in the premises, it is best to work backwards from U; that way you will not go wrong in assigning R a truth value.

13. {[(P & Q) & (P & R)] → (Q & R)}

  T [T] T   F   T [F] F   [T] T [F] F

  T [F] F   F   T [T] T   [T] F [F] T

  T [F] F   F   T [F] F   [T] F [F] F

Valid

15.

{[(P → Q) & (Q → P) & (P ↔ R)] → (Q ↔ R)}

T [T] T   T   T [T] T   F   T [F] F   [T]   T [F] F

F [T] F   T   F T F   T   T [T] T   [F]   F [F] T

Invalid

Note that the first two premises amount to (P ↔ P). Q essentially disappears so it can't appear in the conclusion. Note also that in the first line I have begun with the middle premise, where 'P' has to have a 'T' value. In the second line, I have begun with the first premise, where 'P' has to have an 'F' value.

Exercise 6.5

I

1. P = Politicians are always wise; Q = Politicians have our best interests at heart

    1. ~(P & Q)
    2. (Q)   ⊢ ~P
    3. (~P ∨ ~Q) 1, DM
    4. ~P 2, 3 DS

3. P = We study today; Q = We study tomorrow; R = We just don't study at all; S = We will pass the course

    1. ((P ∨ Q) ∨ (R)) → (S)
    2. (R)   ⊢ S
    3. ((P ∨ Q) ∨ (R)) 2, Add.
    4. S 1, 3, MP

5. P = The package arrives today; Q = We put the meeting off until tomorrow; R = We have to rework production schedules

    1. (P ∨ Q)
    2. (Q → R)   ⊢ (P ∨ R)
    3. (~P → Q) 1, MI: If (~P ∨ Q) = (P → Q), then (P ∨ Q) = (~P → Q)
    4. (~P → R) 2, 3, CS
    5. (P ∨ R) 4, MI

7. P = Jones failed; Q = Wong succeeded; R = Mohamed succeeded

    1. (P & Q)
    2. (~Q ∨ R)   ⊢ R
    3. (Q & P) 1, Comm.
    4. Q 3, Simp.
    5. R 2, 4, DS

9. P = You buy that phone; Q = You need to buy all its apps; R = You need to buy the theft insurance; S = You will pay more than $150 a month to use the phone

1. ((P → (Q & R))
2. (R → S)
3. ~S   ⊢ ~P
4. (P → (R & Q)) 1, Comm.
5. (P → R) 4, Simp.
6. (P → S) 2, 5, CS
7. (~P) 3, 6, MT

II

1.

1. (P ↔ Q)
2. (R ∨ ~P)
3. (R → S)   ⊢ (Q → S)
4. (P → Q) & (Q → P) 1, ME
5. (~P ∨ R) 2, Comm.
6. (P → R) 5, MI
7. (Q → P) & (P → Q) 4, Comm.
8. (Q → P) 7, Simp.
9. (Q → R) 6, 8, CS
10. (Q → S) 3, 9, CS

3.

1. (~Q → P)
2. (~Q ∨ R)
3. (~R)   ⊢ (P)
4. (~P → Q) 1, Trans.
5. (Q → R) 2, MI
6. (~P → R) 4,5 CS
7. (P) 3,6, MT

5.

1. (P)
2. (P → Q)
3. ((Q ∨ R) → (S & T))   ⊢ (T)
4. Q 1,2, MP
5. (Q ∨ R) 4, Add.
6. (S & T) 3,5, MP
7. (T & S) Comm.
8. (T) 6, Simp.

7.

1. (P → (Q ∨ R))
2. (~(Q ∨ R) ↔ (S & T))
3. (U → S)
4. (W → T)
5. ~ ~ (U & W)   ⊢ (~P)

6. ~(Q ∨ R) → (S & T) & (S & T) → ~(Q ∨ R) 2, ME
7. (S & T) → ~(Q ∨ R) & ~(Q ∨ R) → (S & T) Comm.
8. (S & T) → ~ (Q ∨ R) 7, Simp.
9. (U & W) 5, DN
10. (U) 9, Simp.
11. (S) 3,10, MP
12. (W & U) 9, Comm.
13. (W) 12, Simp.
14. (T) 4,13 MP
15. (S & T) 11, 14, Conj.
16. ~(Q ∨ R) 8, 15, MP
17. (~P) 1,16, MT

9.

1. ~ ~ (P & (Q ∨ R))
2. (Q → S)
3. (~R ∨ T)   ⊢ (S ∨ T)
4. (P & (Q ∨ R)) 1, DN
5. ((Q ∨ R) & P) 4, Comm.
6. (Q ∨ R) 5, Simp.
7. (~Q → R) 6, MI
8. (R → T) 3, MI
9. (~Q → T) 7, 8, CS
10. (~T → Q) 9. Trans.
11. (~T → S) 2, 10 CS
12. (T ∨ S) 11, MI
13. (S ∨ T) 12, Comm.

11.

1. ~(Q ∨ R)
2. (~R → (S ∨ T))
3. (~T)   ⊢ (S)
4. (~Q & ~R) 1, DM
5. (~R & ~Q) 4, Comm.
6. (~R) 5, Simp.
7. (S ∨ T) 2, 6, MP
8. (S) 3, 7, DS

Something to Think About Answers

Page 187

To write everything with negations and con-junctions would take too long and be too hard to follow. It would be more complicated rather than less so. That's why we don't speak that way. For example, (P $\underline{\vee}$ Q) is the equivalent of (~(P & Q) & ~(~P & ~Q)). Try saying this: "It is not the case that P and Q are both true and it is not the case that P and Q are both false." That's bad enough, but substitute real sentences for the variables and this becomes unmanageably complicated. It is much easier to say "Either P or Q but not both" or "Exactly one of these options is true." So far as language and symbolic logic go, it is more natural, more efficient, and therefore simpler to employ the whole range of logical constants.

But here's another idea that underlines the basic nature of negation. If everything were written as conjunction and negation, you could actually drop the conjunction since, for example, (P Q) would by definition mean (P & Q). All sentences would simply be a combination of negated and unnegated variables. For instance, (P → Q) would be ~(P ~Q) and (P $\underline{\vee}$ Q) would be ~(P Q) ~(~P ~Q). At the deepest level, bivalent (two-valued T, F) logic is like any binary system—like computer language, for example. There are two options: yes and no, or 0 and 1, or T and F, or negation and non-negation. But unlike computers, humans find a little more variety easier to deal with.

Page 317

Let's start with the disagreement. C has called B a liar. If C is telling the truth, he is a knight and B is a knave. If C is lying, he is a knave and B is a knight. So of B and C, one is a knight and the other a knave. But which is which?

Start with B's statement—it is, exclusively, either true or false (T $\underline{\vee}$ F). Imagine it is true. If so, then B is a knight and C is a knave and, as B claimed, A really said "There is only one knight among us." Let's call this statement X. Of course, if A said X, then X is either true or false. Assume X is true (it is always good to think the best of people). If so, then there is only one knight among them. But we are assuming B is a knight, and if A told the truth, he too is a knight—that is two knights. So if X is true there are two knights, which makes X

false! Symbolically, it could look like this (I stands for knight):

$$\{[(X^T \rightarrow (A^I \& B^I)) \& ((A^I \& B^I) \rightarrow X^F)] \rightarrow (X^T \rightarrow X^F)\}$$

This is a chain syllogism proving that if X is true, X is false. Assume X is false and you will discover, by another chain syllogism, that if X is false, X is true ($X^F \rightarrow X^T$). By the principle of material equivalence (($X^T \rightarrow X^F$) & ($X^F \rightarrow X^T$)) = ($X^T \leftrightarrow X^F$). This is a paradox, and in a land where everyone either tells the truth or lies, paradoxical statements—ones that have no settled truth value—are impossible. So A could not have uttered sentence X. Therefore, B lied (he is a knave) and C told the truth (he is a knight).

Here's how it looks as a modified truth table, where I and A stand for knight and knave and A, B, C represent the three men:

	A	B	C	(STATEMENT X)
1.	I	I	I	F
2.	I	I	A	F
3.	I	A	I	F
4.	I	A	A	T
5.	A	I	I	F
6.	A	I	A	T
7.	A	A	I	T
8.	A	A	A	F

The boxed distributions are the three cases where statement X would be true—that is, where there is exactly one knight. But it is A who supposedly said X, and in the latter two of these distributions A is a knave. So these would be cases of a knave telling the truth, which is impossible in the land of knights and knaves. But what about the first of these three distributions (4), where A is a knight and correctly says that there is only one knight among them? The problem here is that B and C are both knaves in this distribution, and that is impossible because, as we have seen, they cannot have the same identity. So there are no possible distributions under which A could have uttered X. While we therefore know C is a knight and

B a knave, we cannot know what A is. Either the third row or the seventh row is the correct distribution, but there is no way to tell which of the two it is.

Chapter 7

Exercise 7.1

I

1. Inductive

3. Inductive

5. Inductive

7. Deductive

9. Inductive

11. Deductive

13. Inductive

15. Deductive

II

1. Generalizing: weak because two examples do not constitute sufficient evidence for the conclusion.

3. Predictive: weak because the evidence is out of date; a lot can change for a child between 11 and 18 or 19.

5. Predictive: strong

7. Generalizing: weak, not enough evidence

9. Generalizing: weak because there is not enough evidence to allow the speaker to assign himself to the class of people who sleep in.

11. Predictive: strong

Exercise 7.2

I

1. Violates rule 1: Smythe tested only one person, so there is not enough evidence to support his conclusion.

3. Violates rule 1 (not enough evidence to draw the conclusion) and rule 3 insofar as psychic powers run counter to most of our experience and we should therefore be suspicious of any claim to possess them.

5. The speaker is employing rule 3 to dispute the test result by arguing that experience shows that students do not improve that much without cheating.

7. The speaker is using rule 3, arguing that experience rules out the other person's hypothesis.

9. Violates rule 1: the evidence is not varied enough because he did not test female politicians.

11. Violates rule 1: is one lie enough to go on? It also violates rule 2: has the person ever told the speaker the truth?

13. They were fired because of rule 1: polling 350 people will not sufficiently support accurate predictions, so they were simply lucky.

15. Violates rule 1: it's a hasty generalization. Also rule 2: how often has the speaker failed to win?

II

1. It is probably weak unless one takes the term "chick flick" to refer, by definition, to movies only women like. Then it is true by definition, but probably there are no movies that will fall under that definition.

3. Anecdotally (i.e., listening to good athletes) I have always suspected this is largely true, but stated as a generalization (as it is here) it is probably a weak and therefore uncogent argument because it is unlikely to apply to all good athletes.

5. "More intelligent" needs to be defined here. Once it is, one would have to see the research before evaluating the argument's strength. However, based on rule 3 I would be very suspicious of it, just as I would be very suspicious of the claim that on average men are more intelligent than women.

7. This is known as the *Peter Principle* and those of us who envy success may want to believe it, but in keeping with the second rule of induction I know of falsifying instances.

9. This is an old adage, and like most (although not all) adages that last for a long time, there is probably some truth to it. But I suspect that it is a weak argument, in part because "coward" is a vague term. Fatigue makes us less capable, but that is another matter.

Exercise 7.3

I

1. Example: There is a real mess in this room; this is just the sort of mess gerbils make; a gerbil did this.

3. Example: I just saw a spaceship take off from Johanna's yard; aliens only come to Earth to abduct people; aliens have abducted Johanna.

5. Example: Sarah just called me an idiot; people only do that when they hate you; Sarah hates me.

II

1. No, because the generalization that (all) Canadians are lazy is a weak one and, moreover, it is highly unlikely that only Canadians are lazy.

3. Yes, because it's an appropriate application of a rule to arrive at a reasonable, if vague, conclusion.

5. Yes, since the encroachment of bears into populated areas usually means that they are searching for food not available in their normal habitat.

III

1. False: the father is only metaphorically an "old dog."

3. Appropriate: sentient beings can suffer whether they are cats or humans.

5. False: the size of the countries is not a good basis for this prediction; that they are northern countries with long winters would be a much better analogy.

Something to Think About Answer

Page 221
In 1936, home telephones were relatively rare and expensive, which meant that the poll was skewed toward the wealthier portion of society, which tended to vote Republican in higher numbers than the rest of the population (who were largely without phones). The pollsters thought they were polling American citizens when in fact they were polling well-to-do American citizens.

Chapter 8

Exercise 8.1

I

1. Relative frequency

3. Subjective: the speaker has probably not carried out statistical research.

5. A priori

7. Relative frequency

9. Subjective, unless there is a study to quote.

11. A priori: 50-50

13. Relative frequency

II

1. One thing that might affect this decision is the likelihood of getting a secure and well-paid job upon graduation.

3. Perhaps doing so will lead to other rewards like a promotion.

5. How badly do you *need* a holiday? How long have you been planning this one? Is it worth the financial sacrifice?

III

1. You may have only a small chance of winning, so your expected value is low, but the fact that you are contributing to charity may give the action a high personal value.

3. While you may be unlikely to be caught and will therefore get a good grade, you may find cheating morally repugnant and so be unwilling to do it.

IV

The formula (Pr1 + Pr2) − (Pr1 − Pr2) = (1/10 + 1/10) − (1/10 × 1/10) = 20/100 − 1/100 = 19/100

Exercise 8.2

I

1. Correlation

3. Coincidence

5. This could be an example of the post hoc fallacy, but even for it to be one, you would have to demonstrate that moral standards have declined.

7. There may well be a causal connection here.

9. This expresses a causal connection. However, it is almost certainly a false cause.

11. Probably these are correlative effects of, for example, a virus.

II

1. Necessary but not sufficient: some of us simply do not have the basic talent.

3. Assuming one can communicate what one understands, it is sufficient. It is not necessary because we cannot discount luck (or cheating).

5. Necessary probably, but not sufficient.

7. Necessary and sufficient.

9. Sufficient, since it did result in war, but since other causes might have triggered the war we do not know whether it was necessary.

Exercise 8.3

1. Effect: plague; Cause: rats; Method: difference; Result: disconfirmed

3. Effect: decline in technological innovation; Cause: increased corporate taxes; Method: difference; Result: disconfirmed

5. Effect: Patient's pain; Cause: diet, but only partly diet; Method; residues: new cause (virus); Result: confirmed

7. Effect: illness; Cause: oysters; Method: agreement; Result: confirmed

9. Effect: failing in school; Cause: too little sleep; Method: agreement and difference; Result: confirmed

11. Effect: good health; Cause: normal weight for height; Method: concomitant variation; Result: confirmed

13. Effect: not throwing up; Cause: tuna sandwiches; Method: concomitant variation (the more sandwiches one ate the less one threw up); Result: confirmed

15. Effect: nervous goalie; Cause: mentioning how important the game was; Method: agreement and difference; Result: confirmed

Something to Think About Answer

Page 236

With 10 tosses, each of which will be either heads or tails, there are $2^{10} = 1024$ possible distributions of heads and tails. However, only one of these will be all tails (assuming that the top row of a truth table will be all heads, this distribution will be the bottom row). Therefore, the chances of getting heads at least once are 1023/1024, or 99.1 per cent.

Chapter 9

Exercise 9.1

I

1. While the argument is probabilistic, it is, as you have seen, indeterminate: there is really no reliable way of deciding how probable the conclusion is. So the claim that "it stands to reason" that there are some planets with intelligent life is essentially a statement of subjective probability. This is not the best basis for a scientific argument. However, more data could be introduced to make this argument stronger. Scientists are beginning to discuss estimates of how many potentially life-sustaining planets there are in the universe.

3. This is scientifically respectable. The argument might be set out as follows: **P1**: there are fossils of dinosaurs; **P2**: there are no reports of dinosaurs today; **P3**: the fossil record includes lots of species that cannot be found on Earth today; **P4**: species enter the fossil record at different times; **C**: species evolve and sometimes suffer extinction.

It is an inductive argument, composed of independent premises:

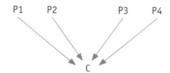

5. This is a scientifically respectable inductive argument insofar as it cites reasonably strong evidence to suggest that there is a connection between rats and the plague. At minimum it is a good working hypothesis.

7. This is not scientifically respectable. There is a huge leap in reasoning from a fact about the Mayan calendar and the location of the solar system at a certain moment in time to a prediction about the end of the world. No evidence is put forward in support of the connection. It's almost certainly an example of "false cause." Since you are reading this after December 21, 2012, you know the prediction was wrong.

II

1. This is a rule of thumb suggested by research, but there are so many variables involved—schools, home circumstances, and so on—that it almost certainly will not apply in many cases. Like all rules of thumb, it has to be treated with a great deal of caution.

3. This is not a rule of thumb insofar as there is little evidence to suggest that astrological signs have any effect on personality (see Section III of this chapter).

5. This is not a rule of thumb: the odds are over 99 per cent that there will be a shared birthday (day and month). This is a case of very high a priori probability.

7. This is a rule of thumb, tying musical tastes to mode of dress. It often works quite well as an abductive working hypothesis, but it is hardly infallible.

9. This was a slogan used to advertise diamond rings. It was explicitly presented as a rule of thumb but it's actually a case of the merchant trying to impose a standard on the buyer. What evidence could demonstrate it?

11. This is not a rule of thumb; it's a case of a priori probability.

Exercise 9.2

I

1. (a) aridity; (b) correlation between loss of vegetation and aridity; (c) loss of vegetation causes aridity; (d) no tests are reported, but replanting an arid region to see if that resulted in increased rainfall might be possible

3. (a) perception of colour; (b) no specific evidence cited, only "other experiments"; (c) perception of colour is caused by pressure on the eye; (d) prodding the back of the eye with a knitting needle; (e) hypothesis confirmed

5. (a) how animals learn; (b) dogs have unconditional responses, like salivating when presented with food; (c) unconditional reflexes could be transformed into conditional (learned) ones; (d) testing to see whether dogs salivate at sounds that regularly preceded food; (e) hypothesis confirmed

7. (a) immunity to smallpox; (b) reports of a folk remedy involving exposing people to cowpox; (c) inoculation with cowpox is a safe way of preventing smallpox; (d) a child and then others are inoculated (e) hypothesis confirmed

9. (a) the temporally continuous or non-continuous nature of Smith's cat; (b) cat shows up suddenly in various parts of the house; (c) it is a different cat every time (and so is temporally non-continuous); (d) Smith follows and videos the cat for a week; (e) hypothesis disconfirmed

II

1. If the groups are informed of which drug they are receiving, the test is not blind.

3. There is no mention of a control group. If so, the null hypothesis has not been tested.

5. This raises ethical issues: can one go ahead with tests without a more precise understanding of what the potential dangers are?

7. There is no reference to evidence. Like stocks, property can disappear in the sense of becoming worthless, so one would need evidence to show that investing in real estate is less risky than investing in the stock market. It would also be necessary to establish time frames for the tests. For example, one may be riskier than the other in the short term but not in the long term.

9. First, Occam's razor suggests that this is a very complicated theory involving a supernatural but forgetful creator. There is also no way to test it.

11. Since every professor is probably a bit different, it's risky to predict the outcome of this strategy based on one previous deployment of it. As stated, it's not even a rule of thumb.

III

1. Take two randomly selected groups of test subjects, one mountain people whom you then move to a valley and the other valley people whom you move to mountains. Give them IQ tests before and after the move. You will also need two control groups, ones that do not move from their original locations.

3. One hypothesis might be that there are an unusually large number of swing voters in the riding (people who have no particular party allegiance). Or perhaps economic conditions are so unstable in the riding that voter dissatisfaction is always high. Polling could test these hypotheses. Despite the long time frame, one would be well advised to consider a kind of null hypothesis: maybe there is no specific reason and this is essentially a series of coincidences.

5. Perhaps the neighbourhood has been hit particularly hard by recent economic problems like unemployment, or perhaps social services have been cut. Isolate a few potential causes and compare this area with other similar neighbourhoods that have faced a similar problem. What changes preceded increases in violence in them? Once you develop a hypothesis, you would need to be able to enact measures that you think will reduce the violence. Subsequent events will either confirm or disconfirm your hypothesis.

7. One hypothesis is that she really likes your best friend. Start showing up without him and see what happens.

Exercise 9.3

1. If you have mastered Gene Ray's concepts of time points and time squares, you may wonder what the evidence for their existence is. A theory has to be tested. Are there experiments available to test this theory, ones that will meet the scientific method?

3. This one really is up for debate. Psychoanalysis has been around for well over a century now. In that time, its merits have been debated and its methods have been developed in a number of directions. The question is whether it is a "hard science" like physics or chemistry. Are there laws of psychoanalysis in the way that there are laws of physics? Or is psychoanalysis as much an art as a science? Let's take a central idea of its originator, Sigmund Freud: can we really verify that there is an "unconscious mind"? What is the evidence? Is this an example of science, pseudo-science, or a "soft science" that is only incompletely testable?

5. We have already mentioned that Einstein's general theory predicted that light was bent by the gravitational effect of massive objects in space, something we'll explore in more detail in Section IV. This was confirmed by experiments carried out during an eclipse of the sun in 1921. Scientists were able to determine that light passing close to the sun was indeed bent. It has since been confirmed many times and used to make accurate predictions.

7. Numerology is roughly the belief that numbers have a magical or occult significance. During the murder trial of the football star O.J. Simpson, many people claimed that the fact that the numbers from the date of the murder—12 June 1994, or 1,2,6,1,9,9,4—added up to 32, which was the number of Simpson's football jersey, proved that he was guilty. Need I say more?

9. Homeopathy has detractors and defenders. It looks like a testable theory, and tests do not seem to provide strong support for its effectiveness. This is not surprising as it seems to depart from standard scientific ideas.

Exercise 9.4

1. When a person is dying, her brain is shutting down. All sorts of chemical processes are at work, and they can certainly produce all sorts of strange effects. This is an explanation for near-death experiences—looking down on the room from above, seeing lights, tunnels, and so on—that does not resort to the supernatural.

3. The fact that a person has an eerie feeling of having already experienced what she is now experiencing is not conclusive evidence that this is so. It is unlikely that we will experience exactly the same event twice. Events separated by time may, of course, be very much alike, but not identical.

It is more likely that the brain has somehow constructed a false sense of identity either by linking roughly similar events or by giving the impression that something is being remembered when it is not. People who experience the feeling of déjà vu are often vague about just what they have supposedly re-experienced. The feeling is strong, but the content of the memory is unspecific.

5. In North America, there is evidence to suggest that girls are outperforming boys in school. There are many possible reasons for this. Girls develop verbal skills earlier; they are better suited to paying attention in class; they find school more fulfilling. Research does not suggest, however, that they are simply, on average, more intelligent than boys.

7. Like déjà vu, the claim that a dream has accurately predicted the future is hard to verify unless one can accurately assess the content of the dream. This is difficult if not impossible to do. Our recall of dreams is notoriously vague. Moreover, dreams themselves are vague: they seldom depict the world in a straightforward manner. Hence, when we recall dreams we have a tendency to do a lot of editing to make them make sense. Finally, to believe this claim you have to accept that the future is predetermined, and very few scientists will accept this. So, like déjà vu, prophetic dreams should be treated with a great deal of suspicion.

Glossary of Fallacies

Informal Fallacies

Fallacies of Relevance

***Ad Hominem* (to the person):** Attacking the person making the argument rather than the argument itself.

> *Example: That is just the kind of argument I would expect from a lunkhead like you.*

***Ad Ignorantiam* (to ignorance):** Arguing that a claim must be true because it has not been (or cannot be) proved false.

> *Example: I am positive there is life elsewhere in the universe; no one can show me that I'm wrong.*

Appeal to Flattery: Flattering the audience (and so appealing to their emotions) rather than making a reasoned argument.

> *Example: As people who care deeply about the future of this country, I think you will understand the need to support this legislation.*

Appeal to Novelty: Arguing in favour of something because it is new.

> *Example: This new computer is just out, the very latest thing; we really need to get one.*

Appeal to Pity: Replacing a reasoned argument with an appeal to the audience's emotions (I deserve pity).

> *Example: You shouldn't punish me for what I did because I had a really hard day.*

Appeal to Popularity: Appealing to the audience's emotions by arguing that something should be accepted because many people like it.

> *Example: Of course American Idol is a great show; look at the ratings it gets.*

Appeal to Ridicule: Appealing to the audience's emotions by trying to get people to laugh either at the argument or at the person who has made it.

> *Example: That's the same weak-kneed argument you always make about going easy on criminals.*

Appeal to Tradition: Claiming that an idea is true because it has been believed for a long time.

> *Example: Women don't deserve the same pay has men. Men have always been paid more.*

Bandwagon: Claiming that an idea is a good one because it is becoming increasingly popular. This fallacy is closely related to an appeal to popularity.

> *Example: What's wrong with really baggy uniforms? More and more players are going to that style.*

Misleading Vividness: Allowing one incident (or a very few) to outweigh evidence that points to the opposite conclusion.

> *Example: I am definitely going to buy a bungalow. My neighbour, Ellen, fell downstairs last night and broke her leg in three places.*

Poisoning the Well: Attacking, or otherwise undermining, the person who is about to make the argument before she makes it.

> *Example: Are you about to give me that sissy argument that there are too many hits to the head in football? Come on, it's a man's game.*

Red Herring: Raising a tangential or irrelevant issue that has nothing to do with the argument and then claiming that it is relevant.

> *Example: I know he was speeding but he's a busy man who has a lot of claims on his time.*

***Tu Quoque* (you too):** Turning a criticism back on the person who has made it as a way of justifying one's actions. This fallacy is closely related to the maxim that two wrongs do not make a right.

> *Example: You accuse us of terrorism but we have done nothing that groups from your country have not already done.*

Informal Fallacies of Ambiguity

Equivocation: Applying different but unstated definitions in the course of an argument to make an invalid argument look valid.

> *Example: A ham sandwich is better than nothing, and nothing is better than a day at the beach, so a ham sandwich is better than a day at the beach.*

Informal Fallacies of Presumption

False Analogy: Using a weak or inappropriate analogy to prove a point.

> *Example: Like businesses, universities are big organizations and so, like businesses, they need to think mainly about the bottom line.*

False Dichotomy: Presenting a situation as if there are only two options when in fact there are more.

> *Example: Either we take up arms against injustice or we submit passively to it.*

Gambler's Fallacy: The failure to understand that fixed (a priori) probabilities never change.

> *Example: I have been buying lottery tickets every week for years now. Surely I'm due for a big win.*

Hasty Generalization: Drawing a conclusion based on insufficient evidence or biased samples.

> *Example: Insufficient evidence: Don't fly that airline; they're never on time. I used them once and they were really late.*

> *Example: Biased sample: People don't attend church often enough. The Council of Bishops confirms that this is so.*

Post Hoc Ergo Propter Hoc (after this therefore because of this): Assuming that because event A was followed by event B, that A caused B.

> *Example: I was thinking about Aunt Mary and a few minutes later she phoned me. I think she did so because I unconsciously willed it.*

Formal Fallacies

Affirming the Consequent: To affirm the consequent of a hypothetical premise in the second premise of a mixed hypothetical syllogism.

> *Example: If pigs can fly then tomorrow is a holiday, and indeed tomorrow is a holiday, so pigs can fly.*

Denying the Antecedent: To deny the antecedent of a hypothetical premise in the second premise of a mixed hypothetical syllogism.

> *Example: If pigs can fly then tomorrow is a holiday, but pigs can't fly, so tomorrow is not a holiday.*

Glossary of Terms

Abduction: Inference to the best explanation. It is a subset of inductive reasoning, but one that has the appearance of deductive reasoning.

Addition: If any simple sentence is true, then any inclusive disjunction it appears in will also be true: $P \rightarrow (P \vee Q)$.

Affirmation: Maintaining negation or lack of negation from one occurrence of a variable to the next.

Analogical reasoning: A form of induction in which the inference is that because two entities are similar in some ways they will be similar in others.

Anchoring bias: The tendency to tie one's thinking to one bit of information and therefore to be misled by it.

Antecedent: The first (if) part of a hypothetical sentence. It establishes a condition: $(\mathbf{P} \rightarrow Q)$.

A posteriori knowledge: Knowledge that requires evidence and is not self-evident. For example, "light travels at more than 300 kilometres a second."

A priori knowledge: Knowledge you have without evidence or experience; it is self-evident. For example, an aunt has at least one sibling.

A priori probability: Where the chances that an event will occur are known in advance.

Argument: In critical thinking, an argument consists of one or more premises in support of a conclusion.

Bias: The tendency to adopt a point of view to the exclusion of other points of view.

Biconditional: A logical constant $(P \leftrightarrow Q)$ that stands for "P iff Q."

Blind test: A test in which the participants do not know whether they are part of the test group or the control group.

Causal argument: An argument that attempts to demonstrate why something (an effect) happened by assigning a cause or causes to it.

Cause: What made a given effect occur.

Chain syllogism (CS): A pure hypothetical syllogism in which the consequent of one premise is the antecedent of the other. The remaining antecedent and consequent form the conclusion.

Example: $\{[(P \rightarrow Q) \& (Q \rightarrow R)] \rightarrow (P \rightarrow R)\}$.

Code words: Words that seem innocuous but connote a perhaps sinister idea that only some people understand.

Codependent premises: A set of two or more premises that jointly give support to a conclusion.

Cogent argument: A strong inductive argument whose premises are true.

Cognitive bias: Faulty judgment caused by a failure to evaluate evidence properly.

Compound sentence: Two or more simple sentences joined by a logical constant.

Conclusion: A claim supported by premises.

Confirmation: A hypothesis turns out to be true.

Confirmation bias: The tendency to look only for confirming evidence and to ignore disconfirming evidence.

Conjunction: A logical constant (&) that stands for "and" or "but." In natural deduction, conjunction stipulates that if two simple sentences are true, then a compound sentence in which they are conjoined will also be true: P & Q → (P & Q)

Connotation: An idea or image associated with a term; the associative rather than the literal meaning.

Consequent: The second (then) part of a hypothetical sentence. It is what follows from an antecedent: (P → **Q**)

Control group: A group identical to the test subjects that is not exposed to whatever is being tested.

Controlled experiment: A test that uses a control group.

Correlation: A regular relationship between two events, where one always accompanies the other either simultaneously or sequentially.

Counterargument: A response to a previous argument drawing the opposite conclusion.

Counterfactual conditional: A hypothetical sentence in which the antecedent refers to what would have happened *if* a particular event had occurred.

Cultural bias: Treating views or knowledge specific to a culture or group as universal.

Deduction: The process of reasoning from premises to a conclusion which, if the argument is valid, follows necessarily from them.

De Morgan's rules: A pair of logically equivalent statements named after the mathematician Augustus De Morgan (1806–71). These statements are:

$$\sim(P\ \&\ Q) = (\sim P \lor \sim Q)\ and \sim(P \lor Q) = (\sim P\ \&\ \sim Q).$$

Denial: An affirmative and a negative version of the same sentence are denials of one another. Hence, denial entails not maintaining negation or lack of negation from one occurrence of a variable to the next: P and ~P.

Denotation: The literal meaning of a term.

Dialogical situations: Situations where two people present arguments and counterarguments.

Differentiae: Phrases that distinguish between objects in the same class. For example, a bungalow is a type of house with only one storey. "With only one storey" is a differentia that distinguishes bungalows from other types of houses.

Direct variation: The quantity of cause and effect vary in the same direction.

Disanalogy: A way in which two things being compared analogously differ. It also indicates a failed analogy.

Disconfirmation: A hypothesis turns out to be false after testing.

Disjunction: A logical constant meaning "either . . . or." There are two types: inclusive (P ∨ Q) where *at least one* of the alternatives is true, and exclusive (P ⊻ Q) where *exactly one* of the alternatives is true.

Disjunction rule: Unless it entails a contradiction, identify all disjunctions as inclusive.

Disjunctive syllogism (DS): A mixed syllogism with a disjunctive premise: a simple premise that denies one of the disjuncts and a conclusion that affirms the other.

Double blind test: Neither participants nor researchers know which group is the control group.

Empirical claim: A factual claim that can be verified by sensory experience.

Entailment: When the truth of one sentence establishes the truth of another.

Equivalents: Compound sentences that assert the same thing in different ways; that is, by employing different logical constants. See De Morgan's rules.

Ethics: The study of proper, moral ways of conducting our lives, including conducting scientific research.

Euphemism: A term used to soften blunt hard truths or harsh views.

Exclusive disjunction: A logical constant meaning "either . . . or" where *exactly one* of the alternatives is true: (P ⊻ Q).

Expected value: The balance of what one expects to gain or lose from a wager.

Explanandum (Em): The fact that is being explained. It is analogous to the conclusion of an argument.

Explanans (Es): The statements that explain a fact. They are analogous to the premises of an argument.

Explanation: The process of setting out the conditions that show why an idea that is uncontroversially accepted as true *is* true.

Factual claim: An assertion that a certain fact exists. If you assert that Toronto is farther north than New York you have made a factual claim.

Fallacies of relevance: A group of informal fallacies where the premises of the argument have nothing to do with the conclusion.

Fallacy: Errors in reasoning where the premises do not support the conclusion of an argument. See formal and informal fallacies.

Fallacy of ambiguity: Violating the law of identity by not making the meaning of a term clear.

Fallacy of presumption: Assuming something you have no grounds for assuming.

Fixed probabilities: Where the odds of an action having a given result (e.g., flipping a fair coin) remain the same no matter how often the action is carried out.

Formal fallacy: A fallacy in which the problem lies in the structure of the argument, with the result that the premises do not support the conclusion. It renders a deductive argument invalid.

Formal method of reasoning: A method of reasoning where there are precise rules for determining an outcome. Deduction is a formal method because there are rules for determining validity.

Fruitful theory: A theory that explains many different things, including phenomena that its developer was not trying to explain or had not considered.

Generalizing argument: An inductive argument that draws a general conclusion from particular bits of empirical (experiential) evidence.

Hypothesis: A provisional conclusion that appears to be true based on the available evidence but that needs to be tested.

Hypothetical: A logical constant $(P \to Q)$ that stands for "If P then Q."

Implicit assumption: A premise or conclusion that has been left unstated but that is necessary if the argument is to be stated in its most complete form.

Implicit premises: Unstated premises that are always codependent with a premise that is already stated explicitly.

Inclusive disjunction: A logical constant meaning "either . . . or" where *at least one* of the alternatives is true: $(P \lor Q)$.

Independent premise: A premise that does not rely on any other premise for its contribution to the argument.

Indeterminate argument: A valid deductive argument where it is impossible to decide between soundness and unsoundness.

Induction: The method of reasoning from independent premises derived from experience to a conclusion that is probably true.

Informal fallacy: A fallacy in which the content of the premises does nothing to support the conclusion.

In-group bias: The tendency to give preferential treatment to members of one's own group.

Invalid argument: A deductive argument in which the conclusion does not follow necessarily from the premises.

Inverse variation: When the quantity of cause and effect vary in opposite directions.

Law of identity: Everything that exists has a specific nature that allows us to distinguish it from all other things.

Law of large numbers: Repeat a random process often enough and the actual value will tend to match the expected value. For example, flip a fair coin often enough and the number of heads and tails will hover around 50-50.

Law of non-contradiction:

> *Version 1: Contradictory states cannot simultaneously exist.*
> *Version 2: Contradictory claims cannot both be true.*

Law of the excluded middle: For all X, everything either is X or it is not X; there is no third or "middle" option.

Loaded words: Words where the associative meaning involves deception.

Logical constants: Words or symbols that link simple sentences together to make compound sentences. (e.g., &, ∨)

Logical paradox: A statement or argument that leads to contradictory conclusions, such as making the sentence simultaneously true and false.

Logical tautology: An either-or statement that is necessarily true. For example, "Jane is either at home or she is not at home." It obeys the law of the excluded middle.

Loss aversion bias: The preference for avoiding losses over seeking gains that involve only a moderate risk.

Material equivalence: Another term for "biconditional." It stipulates that a biconditional $(P \leftrightarrow Q)$ is equivalent to two conjoined hypotheticals $[(P \rightarrow Q) \& (Q \rightarrow P)]$.

Material implication: A term that asserts the following equivalence: $(P \rightarrow Q) = (\sim P \vee Q)$. This tells us that either a false antecedent or a true consequent is sufficient to make a hypothetical true.

Method of agreement: An inductive method whereby one looks for common factors that precede an effect.

Method of concomitant variations: The process of quantifying the relationship between cause and effect by investigating the way in which variations in an effect are related to variations in a cause.

Method of difference: Testing a possible cause by trying to break the connection between it and the effect.

Method of residues: The process of searching for residual or undiscovered causes for an effect.

Methods of induction: Methods of carrying out empirical research in the search for causes; they are intended to produce cogent arguments. They include the method of agreement, method of concomitant variations, method of difference, and method of residues.

Mixed hypothetical syllogism: A mixed syllogism in which the compound premise is a hypothetical sentence.

Mixed syllogism: A two-premise argument in which one premise is a compound sentence, and the other premise and the conclusion are simple sentences.

Modus ponens: A mixed hypothetical syllogism with a simple premise that affirms the antecedent of the hypothetical premise. The conclusion affirms the consequent of the hypothetical premise. It is always valid.

Modus tollens: A mixed hypothetical syllogism with a simple premise that denies the consequent of the hypothetical premise. The conclusion denies the antecedent. It is always valid.

Moral certainty: When the probability of something occurring or not occurring is so high that you can take it as a given.

Natural deduction: A method of proving validity from a basic set of valid inferences.

Necessary cause (or condition): A cause that must be present for the effect to occur but that on its own is not sufficient to produce the effect.

Negation: A symbol (~) that stands for "not" and therefore negates a sentence. Negation is not the same thing as falsehood—a negative sentence can be true. For example, "It is not raining."

Non-ostensive definition: Assigning a term to a class and then distinguishing it from other members of that class.

Normative statement: A "value" statement that sets a standard that is intended to guide thought or action.

Null hypothesis: The hypothesis that there is no relation between an effect and its reputed cause.

Occam's razor: The principle of economy that stipulates that an argument or explanation should be only as complicated as is necessary to explain the phenomena in question.

Open variable: A variable that can be assigned either a T or an F value without falsifying the compound sentence in which it occurs.

Order of precedence: The order that stipulates how sentences with more than one logical constant are to be read. The sentence is named after the variable with precedence.

Ostensive definition: Defining a term by pointing out an example of it.

Personal value: A measurement of the value of a bet or choice in relation to both a person's objectively measurable resources and subjective preferences.

Predictive argument: An argument that forecasts what will happen in the future based on available evidence.

Premise: A statement that is intended to support the conclusion of an argument.

Principle of charity: Try to cast someone else's argument in its strongest form.

Principle of indifference: When the odds of an event are unknown, treat all options as equally probable: $1/n$. In Chapter 8 it was distinguished from cases of a priori probability, but this is a distinction not everyone makes.

Pseudo-science: Disciplines that claim to be scientific but that fail to meet the standards of science.

Pure syllogism: A syllogism in which all the premises and the conclusion are compound.

***Reductio ad absurdum*:** Disproving a claim by showing that it leads to a contradictory conclusion or proving one by showing that its denial would lead to a contradictory conclusion.

Reference class: A group that is being statistically analyzed.

Relative frequency: Calculation of probability based on reliable data.

Report on an argument: A second-hand account of someone else's argument.

Rhetoric: The art of speaking persuasively, of being able to convince or emotionally move an audience.

Rhetorical question: A question not calling for an answer because it is obvious what the answer is.

Rule of commutation: Except for hypothetical sentences, the order of the variables in compound sentences can be reversed without changing the meaning of the compound. For example, $(P \& Q) = (Q \& P)$.

Rule of validity: In a valid deductive argument it is not possible for the premises to be true and the conclusion false.

Rules of induction: The three basic rules that govern inductive reasoning:

> *Rule 1:* In an inductive argument, the number of observations is large enough and varied enough to support the conclusion.
> *Rule 2:* In an inductive argument, look for evidence that will falsify your conclusion.
> *Rule 3:* Carefully assess the conclusions of inductive arguments in light of your experience or the experience of appropriate experts.

Rules of inference: Rules that determine how to test arguments for validity using natural deduction.

Rule of thumb: A rough rule based on experience that seems to work most of the time.

Save the phenomena: A guide for reasoning that stipulates that an argument or explanation should be as thorough as possible.

Scientific law: A generalization of a set of observations about how some part of nature works.

Scientific method: A method of developing and testing scientific hypotheses. It is sometimes called the hypothetical-deductive method.

Scientific revolution: The rapid development of science in sixteenth- and seventeenth-century Europe.

Scientific theory: A collection of related observations and laws that explains of a broad range of phenomena.

Self-serving bias: The tendency to attribute success to one's own efforts and failure to external, uncontrollable factors.

Sentence rule: Any normative or empirical sentence that is not paradoxical can be used in an argument.

Sentential logic: A form of deductive reasoning in which the basic units are sentences.

Simple sentence: A non-contradictory sentence with one subject and one predicate.

Simplification: If a conjunctive sentence is true, then each of its parts is individually true: $(P \& Q) \rightarrow P$.

Social bias: Preconceived ideas that, without good reason, favour one group over others.

Sound argument: A valid argument with true premises.

Standard definition: The common definition of a term; one you would find in a dictionary.

Stereotype: An oversimplified view of a group that attributes certain characteristics to all members of the group.

Strong argument: An inductive argument in which the evidence, if true, gives the conclusion a high degree of probability.

Sub-conclusion: The conclusion of an argument within a larger argument in which it has the role of a premise.

Subjective probability: An individual's personal, non-statistical evaluation of the chances of an event occurring.

Sufficient cause: A cause or set of causes that guarantees an effect.

Syllogism: A deductive argument with two premises and a conclusion.

Symbolize: To replace sentences with variables (P, Q, R, etc.) and connective words with logical constants (&, ∨, etc.)

Three laws of reason: The laws that govern whether an argument makes sense. They are identity, excluded middle, and non-contradiction.

Transposition: An equivalent way of stating hypothetical sentences by reversing the antecedent and consequent and denying them. For example, $(P \rightarrow Q) = (\sim Q \rightarrow \sim P)$.

Truth condition: The conditions under which a sentence is true or false.

Truth tables: Tables that establish the truth conditions for compound sentences.

Truth value: In two-valued logic, all sentences have one of two truth values: true or false.

Two-valued logic: Logic in which all sentences are either true or false.

Uncogent argument: An inductive argument that is either weak or that has false premises.

Unsound argument: An invalid argument or a valid one with at least one false premise.

Valid argument: A deductive argument in which the conclusion follows necessarily from the premises.

Variable: A letter (P, Q, etc.) that stands for a simple sentence in an argument.

Weak argument: An inductive argument whose premises, even if true, give the conclusion only a low degree of probability.

Working hypothesis: A conclusion that requires further testing but that is sufficiently probable to be worth testing.

Index